INDIA

INDIA

SIR JOHN STRACHEY, G.C.S.I.

GYAN

Published by

Gyan Publishing House
5, Ansari Road
Daryaganj, New Delhi-110002
Phone: 011-47034999, 9811692060
E-mail: books@gyanbooks.com

Distribution Network
gyanbooks.com
India, USA, Canada, UK, Australia, France

ISBN : 978-81-212-9578-9 (PB)
First Published, 1888

2nd Impression 2023

Printed at: Gyan Press, Delhi.

INDIA
Author: SIR JOHN STRACHEY

INDIA

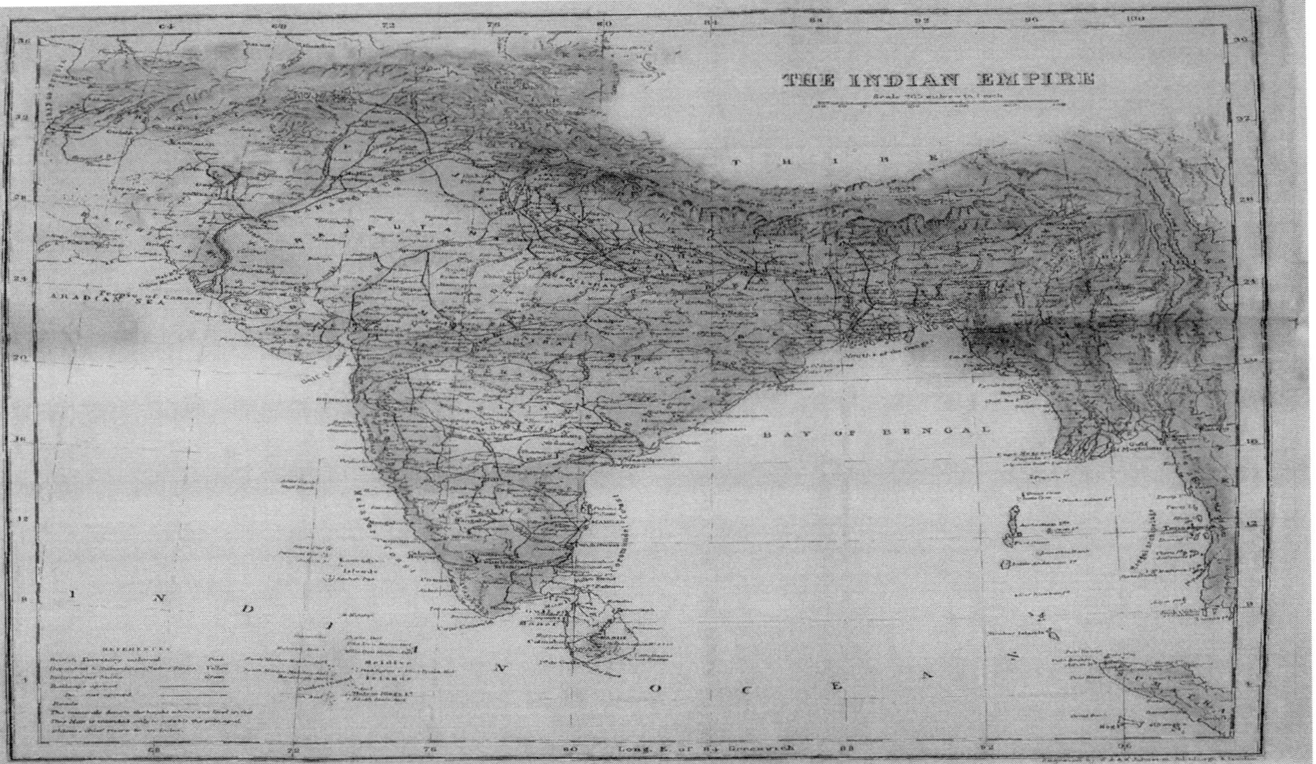
THE INDIAN EMPIRE
THIBET
ARABIAN SEA
BAY OF BENGAL
INDIAN OCEAN
Long. E. of Greenwich

INDIA

BY

SIR JOHN STRACHEY, G.C.S.I.

1888

TO

SIR JAMES FITZJAMES STEPHEN, K.C.S.I.
&c. &c. &c.

My dear Stephen,

Fifteen years ago you dedicated one of your books to me, and in now offering to you this less worthy gift, the fittest words that I can find are almost those which you addressed to me. I dedicate this book to you as an expression of strong personal regard and of gratitude for great kindness, and in recollection of that time in India when we served together and which neither of us can forget.

I am, my dear Stephen,

Your sincere friend and late colleague,

JOHN STRACHEY.

October 1888.

PREFACE.

In 1884, on the invitation of the Historical Board, I gave a course of lectures on India before the University of Cambridge. They formed the basis of the present work, but they have been much altered and amplified.

I have to thank Sir WILLIAM HUNTER for allowing me to use for this book the map prepared for his 'Imperial Gazetteer of India.'

JOHN STRACHEY.

October 1888.

PREFACE

CONTENTS.

LECTURE I.

INTRODUCTORY.

LECTURE II.

THE CONSTITUTION OF THE GOVERNMENT IN INDIA AND AT HOME.

LECTURE VII.

EDUCATION IN INDIA.

LECTURE VIII.

AN INDIAN PROVINCE.

LECTURE IX.

AN INDIAN PROVINCE (*continued*).

PAGE

LECTURE X.

AN INDIAN PROVINCE (*continued*).

LECTURE XI.

NATIVE STATES.

INDIA.

LECTURE I.

INTRODUCTORY.

ENGLISH IGNORANCE REGARDING INDIA—INDIA NOT A COUNTRY BUT A CONTINENT—THE NAME HINDUSTAN—THE GREAT DIFFERENCES BETWEEN THE COUNTRIES OF INDIA—BENGAL AND NORTHERN INDIA—NO COUNTRIES OR NATIONS OF THE EUROPEAN TYPE—SIR ALFRED LYALL'S 'ASIATIC STUDIES'—NO UNITY IN INDIA, PHYSICAL, POLITICAL, SOCIAL, OR RELIGIOUS—PROFESSOR SEELEY ON THE CONQUEST OF INDIA—THE ENGLISH NOT FOREIGNERS—THE BRITISH GOVERNMENT—THE GROWTH OF A SINGLE INDIAN NATIONALITY IMPOSSIBLE—DANGER OF GENERALISATIONS—THE MAIN FEATURES OF INDIAN GEOGRAPHY—THE INDO-GANGETIC PLAIN—THE COUNTRIES INCLUDED IN IT—PRESIDENCIES AND PROVINCES—THE TABLE-LAND OF CENTRAL AND SOUTHERN INDIA—AREA AND POPULATION OF BRITISH PROVINCES AND NATIVE STATES—PHYSICAL CAUSES OF THE GREAT DIFFERENCES BETWEEN THE COUNTRIES OF INDIA—SINDH AND BENGAL—METEOROLOGY—THE MONSOONS—THE PERIODICAL RAINS AND THEIR DISTRIBUTION—MR. BLANFORD ON THE CONTRASTS BETWEEN INDIAN CLIMATES—THE HIMÁLAYA—ITS INFLUENCE ON INDIA—ITS GEOGRAPHY—THE GREAT RIVERS OF INDIA—THE GANGES AND GOGRA—BRITISH AND NATIVE HIMÁLAYAN DISTRICTS—THE KUMÁON HIMÁLAYA—SCENERY OF THE HIMÁLAYA.

SIR HENRY MAINE, referring to the ignorance regarding India which prevails even among educated men in England, has declared his conviction that for one who desires to unveil the stores of interest which India contains, the first necessity is that he should not shrink from speaking on matters which appear to him too elementary to deserve discussion, that he should sympathise with an ignorance which few felicitous efforts have yet been made to dispel, and that he should remember that the language of administration and government in India has become so highly specialised and technical that it forms an imperfect medium for the communication of ideas to Englishmen. Believing this, I make no apology for beginning these lectures with some very elementary matters, and I ask at starting this elementary question, What is India? What does this name India really signify? The answer that has more than once been given sounds paradoxical, but it is true. There is no such country, and this is the first and most essential fact about India that can be learned.

✓India is a name which we give to a great region including a multitude of different countries. There is no general Indian term that corresponds to it. The name Hindustan is never applied in India, as we apply it, to the whole of the Indian continent; it signifies the country north of the Narbada River, and especially the northern portion of the basins of the Ganges and Jumna.

✓ I have been told by intelligent Natives of India who have visited Europe that they could see little difference between the European countries through which they had travelled; the languages being equally unintelligible offered to them no marks of distinction; the cities, the costumes, the habits of life, the manners and customs of the people, so far as a passing oriental traveller could judge, seemed much the same in England, in France, and in Italy. The differences between the countries of India, between, for instance, Bengal and the Punjab, or between Madras and Rájputána, seemed to them, on the other hand, immense, and beyond comparison greater than those existing between the countries of Europe. Englishmen have often similar impressions in visiting India; they cannot see the great diversities that exist. As to persons who know nothing of geology or botany or agriculture, rocks and trees and crops present comparatively few distinctive features, so it is with those who look with uninformed minds on conditions of life and society to which they have not been accustomed.

The differences between the countries of Europe are undoubtedly smaller than those between the countries of India. Scotland is more like Spain than Bengal is like the Punjab. European civilisation has grown up under conditions which have produced a larger measure of uniformity than has been reached in the countries of the Indian continent, often separated from each other by greater distances, by greater obstacles to communication, and by greater differences of climate. The diversities of language, religion, and race are as wide in India as in Europe, and political catastrophes have been as frequent and as violent. There are no countries in civilised Europe in which the people differ so much as the Bengáli differs from the Sikh, and the language of Bengal is as unintelligible in Lahore as it would be in London. An educated Mohammedan gentleman of Northern India has more in common with Englishmen than with the Bengáli graduates of the University of Calcutta. Such facts often explain much that is unintelligible to Englishmen.

Again, people complain that Indian authorities differ so greatly among themselves that you can never be sure that you have learned the truth. These apparent contradictions have frequently no real existence, but arise from false generalisations.

To one, for instance, who has gained his knowledge

of India in Lower Bengal, India is a country of almost constant heat and damp, luxuriant vegetation, rivers, tanks, rice-fields and cocoanuts, with few cities and no monuments of art, densely inhabited by a mild and timid population. To such an India as this, a vivid imagination could hardly conceive a completer contrast than the India of Agra or Lahore. Instead of one of the dampest and greenest countries of the earth, you find in the early summer one of the brownest and most arid, a country scorched with winds like the blast of a furnace, but in the winter it has the climate of an Italian spring, cold, frosty, and invigorating. In the latter season, instead of the tropical vegetation of Bengal, you find thousands of square miles covered with wheat and barley and the products of the temperate zone. It is a country with famous cities and splendid monuments, and its population is not inferior to that of many parts of Europe in manliness and vigour.

I have spoken of the different countries of India, but they are not countries in the ordinary European sense. A European country is usually a separate entity, occupied by a nation more or less socially and politically distinct. But in India, as Sir Alfred Lyall has explained in his 'Asiatic Studies,' a work that is a mine of knowledge and wisdom on Indian matters, there are no nations of the modern European type. The same fact has been clearly brought out by Professor Seeley in his admirable lectures on the 'Expansion of England.'

'Geographical boundaries,' says Sir Alfred Lyall, 'have no correspondence at all with distinctive institutions or groupings of the people, and have comparatively little political significance. Little is gained toward knowing who and what a man is by ascertaining the State he obeys, or the territory he dwells in; these being things which of themselves denote no difference of race, institutions, or manners. Even from the point of political allegiance, the Government under which a man may be living is an accidental arrangement, which the British Viceroy or some other inevitable power decided upon yesterday and may alter to-morrow. Nor would such a change be grievous unless it divorced from him a ruler of his own tribe or his own faith. . . The European observer—accustomed to the massing of people in great territorial groups, and to the ideas (now immemorial in the West) contained in such expressions as fatherland, mother-country, patriotism, domicile, and the like—has here to realise the novelty of finding himself in a strange part of the world, where political citizenship is as yet quite unknown, and territorial sovereignty or even feudalism only just appearing. For a parallel in the history of Western Europe we must go back as far as the Merovingian period, when chiefs of barbaric tribes or bands were converting themselves into kings or counts; or, perhaps, he should carry his retrospect much further, and conceive himself to be looking at some country of Asia Minor lying within the influence of Rome at its zenith, but just outside its jurisdiction. He gradually discovers the population of Central India to be distributed, not into great governments, or nationalities, or religious denominations, not even into widespread races, such as those which are still contending for political supremacy in Eastern Europe, but into various and manifold denominations of tribes, clans, septs, castes, and sub-castes, religious orders, and devotional brotherhoods.'[1]

I must not continue my quotation, but I invite those who wish to understand what India really is, to study Sir Alfred Lyall's most interesting book.

This is the first and most essential thing to learn about India—that there is not, and never was an India, or even any country of India, possessing, according to European ideas, any sort of unity, physical, political, social, or religious; no Indian nation, no 'people of India,' of which we hear so much.

[1] *Asiatic Studies*, p. 152. Sir Alfred Lyall was specially referring to Central India in this passage, but it is equally true of India generally.

Until we rightly appreciate the significance of such facts we shall, among other things, never understand how our Indian Empire has come into existence, and how this vast dominion is maintained by a handful of Englishmen. There was never, as Professor Seeley has shown, any conquest of India by the English, according to the ordinary sense of the word 'conquest.' The conquest was rather, to borrow his expression, 'in the nature of an internal revolution,' directed by Englishmen but carried out for the most part through the Natives of India themselves. No superiority of the Englishman would have enabled England to conquer by her own military power the continent of India, with its 250 millions of people, nor could she hold it in subjection, if it had been occupied by distinct nations. In the words of Professor Seeley, 'the fundamental fact is that India had no jealousy of the foreigner, because there was no India, and therefore, properly speaking, no foreigner.'[1]

It is a consequence of all this, that in every great Indian province the political sympathies of large sections of the population towards men who, geographically speaking, are their own countrymen, are often as imperfect as they are towards their English masters. We have never destroyed in India a national government, no national sentiment has been wounded, no national pride has been humiliated; and this not through any design or merit of our own, but because no Indian nationalities have existed. They no more exist in the so-called Native States than in our own territories, and the most important of those States are ruled by princes who are almost as much foreigners to their subjects as we are ourselves.

[1] *The Expansion of England*, p. 206.

The diversities between the countries of India and the people inhabiting them extend, more or less, to their administration by the British Government. The ordinary English notion is that the Secretary of State for India and the Viceroy and his Council carry on, somehow or other, the government of India. Few Englishmen understand how comparatively little these high authorities have to do with the actual administration, or appreciate the fact that the seven or eight chief provinces of British India, which may be compared, in area and population, to the chief countries of Europe, have all their separate and, in a great measure, their independent governments. Under circumstances of such extreme diversity as those which exist in India, no single system of administration could be appropriate. Instead of introducing unsuitable novelties from other countries, Indian or European, we have taken, in each province, with some unfortunate exceptions, the old local institutions as the basis of our own arrangements. Good or bad administration in India depends to a far greater extent on the Government of the province than on the distant authorities in Calcutta or London. The vast majority of the population is hardly conscious of the existence of the Viceroy and his Government. From time to time a glimpse is caught of the great Lord Sáhib. He passes perhaps along the streets of some famous city with a train of elephants recalling the traditions of Aurangzeb, or at some immense gathering, more picturesque and magnificent than any of the ceremonial shows of Europe, he receives in Darbár the homage of princes and chiefs. From the splendour of his surroundings people derive some vague notions of an authority above the powers by which they know that they are governed.

Although in the management of the greater portion of the public business immediately affecting the everyday interests of the 200 millions of people inhabiting British India the part of the so-called Government of India is comparatively small, this central power, administered by the Governor General in Council, under the supreme authority of the British Government at home, has, of course, from another point of view the highest importance. It regulates and harmonises the Governments of the British provinces, controls the Native States and our relations with foreign powers, provides for military defence, makes war and peace, and manages those branches of the administration which directly concern the general interests of the empire.

It must not be supposed that such bonds of union can in any way lead towards the growth of a single Indian nationality. However long may be the duration of our dominion, however powerful may be the centralising attraction of our Government, or the influence of the common interests which grow up, no such issue can follow. It is conceivable that national sympathies may arise in particular Indian countries; but that they should ever extend to India generally, that men of the Punjab, Bengal, the North-Western Provinces, and Madras, should ever feel that they belong to one great Indian nation, is impossible. You might with as much reason and probability look forward to a time when a single nation will have taken the place of the various nations of Europe.

I wish at the outset of these lectures to insist on the fact that you can never hope to arrive at any accurate knowledge of India until you properly appreciate the immense diversities of the countries included under that name, and understand that there is no part of the world in regard to which it is more easy to be misled by generalisations.

India has an area of nearly 1,600,000 square miles, and contains about 258 millions of people. Excluding Burma, it may be roughly divided into two regions.

The first of these is a vast alluvial plain, lying immediately below the Himálaya, and stretching with an unbroken surface for some 1,700 miles across Northern India. Its eastern and central portions are watered by the Ganges and Bráhmaputra and their tributaries, the northern and western portions by the river-system of the Indus. At its highest point, on the watershed between the feeders of the Indus and Ganges, it is not more than 1,000 feet above the sea. At its eastern end, it extends over the delta of the Ganges and Bráhmaputra, and includes the greater part of the province of Bengal. At its northern and western extremities, it spreads down the Indus to the Arabian Sea, over the Punjab, Rájputána, and Sindh. The central portion of the plain comprises the North-Western Provinces and Oudh. The alluvial deposits of which this vast tract is composed are, as General Strachey says, 'so finely comminuted that it is no exaggeration to say that it is possible to go from the Bay of Bengal up the Ganges, through the Punjab, and down the Indus again to the sea, over a distance of 2,000 miles and more, without finding a pebble, however small.'[1] The Indo-Gangetic plain comprises the richest, the most fertile, the most populous, and historically the most famous countries of India. It covers more than 500,000 square miles, an area as large as France, the German and Austrian empires, and Italy, and it contains 150 millions of people.

A glance at the map will show that the political

[1] *Encyclopædia Britannica*, Art. 'Asia.'

limits of the provinces that I have named—and the same may be said of India generally—have little connection with any physical characteristics. They have been fixed from time to time, as the British power advanced, or as the necessities of the moment required.

The greater part of the northern plain, excluding the countries on the extreme west, was formerly included, for certain purposes, in the so-called Presidency of Bengal. I shall have to explain how the name Bengal has had, at different periods, different meanings, and how the term 'Presidency,' although still used in official papers, has almost ceased to have any special signification. British India is now divided not into the three presidencies of Bengal, Madras, and Bombay, but into provinces, eight of which are extensive countries under separate Governments.

The second region of India lies to the south of the Indo-Gangetic plain, and includes the great triangular peninsula which projects into the Indian Ocean. It has an area of about 1,000,000 square miles, with a population of about 100 millions.

The greater part of this tract consists of a hilly table-land,[1] having an average elevation above the sea of about 1,500 feet, but rising in the south, in Mysore, to 3,000 feet. On the western and eastern sides of the peninsula, the table-land terminates in the ranges known as the Western and Eastern Gháts. Roughly speaking, they run parallel to the coast on the two sides of Southern India, leaving between them and the sea a more or less broad strip of low-lying land. The

[1] I take the following note from Colonel Yule: 'A friend objects to this application of "table-land" to so rugged a region of inequalities. But it is a technical expression in geography, applicable to a considerable area, of which the lowest levels are at a considerable height above the sea.'—*Hobson Jobson*, Art. 'Tibet.'

Eastern Ghāts are an ill-defined range of no great height. The Western Gháts rise steeply from the sea to about 4,000 feet, and near their southern extremity reach more than 8,000 feet in the Nilgiri mountains. Further north, nearly in the same line with the Western Gháts, the Aravali range, in which Mount Abu rises to 5,600 feet, forms the western border of the table-land. The northern border cannot be sharply defined; it is broken up into hills which pass more or less gradually into the plains of the North-Western Provinces.

The Vindhia and Satpura ranges, the highest points of which have an elevation of more than 4,000 feet, run from west to east across the northern parts of the table-land of Central India. 'Now pierced by road and railway (says Sir William Hunter), they stood as a barrier of mountain and jungle between Northern and Southern India, and formed one of the main difficulties in welding the whole into an empire. They consist of vast masses of forests, ridges, and peaks, broken by alternated valleys and broad high-lying plains.'[1]

Through two deep and almost parallel depressions in this tract, the waters of the Narbada and Tapti flow westward to the Arabian Sea. With these exceptions, all the chief rivers of the central plateau, the Són, the Máhánadi, the Godáveri, and the Kistna, flow eastward, and excepting the Són, which joins the Ganges, they all fall into the Bay of Bengal. The high ranges of the Gháts, on the western edge of the plateau, throw off nearly the whole of its drainage to the eastward.

This table-land, with the low-lying tracts on its borders, comprises the British provinces of Madras and Bombay, the Central Provinces, and many of the chief Native States in India. Among the latter are the

[1] *Imperial Gazetteer of India*, Art. 'India.'

Maráthà States of Sindhia and Holkar, and those of the Nizam and Mysore.

Besides the countries that I have named, there remains the great province of Burma, the latest addition to our empire. Although a dependency of the Government of India, it is completely cut off and differs essentially from every part of India. Before the late conquests, the province known as British Burma had an area of nearly 90,000 square miles and a population of nearly 4 millions. The territories of Upper Burma, now united to it, cover nearly 200,000 square miles, and the population has been estimated at from 3 to 4 millions.

The provinces of British India cover more than 1,000,000 square miles, and contain more than 200 millions of people. The Native States cover 510,000 square miles, with a population of 55 millions. The Indian Empire has altogether an area of nearly 1,600,000 square miles, and a population of 258 millions. Excluding Russia, Europe is about equal in extent to India, but falls short of it in population.

If the main natural features of India are as simple as I have stated them to be, if India below the Himálaya can in general terms be said to consist of two well-defined regions, the most important of which is one vast unbroken plain, how does it happen that there are such remarkable differences between the climates and many of the physical conditions of its various countries, differences which I have declared to be greater than any to be found in Europe? The explanation is not difficult.

Excepting in temperature, and in a rainfall the amount of which varies within no very wide limits, the general climatic conditions of the countries of Europe, excluding those in the extreme north, are not very different. On the other hand, it is hardly possible to imagine greater contrasts than those which often exist between the climates of various parts of India.

Take, for example, the two extremities of the great northern plain, Sindh on the western, and Lower Bengal on the eastern side of India. These countries are almost in the same latitude; each of them is an unbroken alluvial plain, slightly elevated above the sea. In Sindh, so little rain falls that the country may be said to be rainless. It is the Egypt of India, and without artificial irrigation would be an uninhabitable desert. Bengal, on the other hand, is a country of abundant rain and luxuriant vegetation. The rainfall on the mountains along its eastern borders is heavier than any that has been observed in any other part of the world. At Cherra Punji, on the Khasiya hills, on the frontiers of Eastern Bengal, 600 inches is not an unusual fall for the year; sometimes it is much more. The average annual rainfall of London is about 25 inches, a quantity less than that which sometimes falls in twenty-four hours in Eastern Bengal.

It is not difficult to imagine from this illustration, taken from two Indian provinces, how great must be the differences in physical conditions between countries presenting such extraordinary contrasts of climate.

The one characteristic, common at certain seasons to the whole of India, except at great elevations, is excessive heat. The southern half of India, including the greater part of the Madras and Bombay Presidencies, lies within the tropic. The northern half, including nearly the whole of the Indo-Gangetic plain, lies outside the tropic. Although in the southern or tropical region the mean temperature of the year is higher, the variations of temperature between summer and winter are comparatively small; and it is in the second region, in the plains north of the tropic, where the days are longer and the power of the sun more continuous, that Indian heat reaches in the summer months its greatest intensity. In parts of the Punjab and of the North-Western Provinces, and in the desert on the borders of Sindh, the temperature in May and June is probably exceeded in no part of the world; but this extreme heat brings by its own action the relief without which all life would perish.

'The dominant feature of Indian meteorology (I am quoting from Mr. Blanford, the head of the Meteorological Department in India) is the alternation of the monsoons, the annual reversal of the prevailing wind-currents. This alternation is consequent on the fact that, in the early summer, the broad plains and table-lands of India are heated to a far higher temperature than the seas which bathe their shores; whereas, in the winter, the seas retain much of their warmth, while the land radiates away and throws off into stellar space much more heat than it receives from the oblique rays of the sun during the shorter winter days, and, especially as regards Northern India, speedily cools down to a temperature much below that of the surrounding seas.'[1] Observations of these phenomena and their consequences, especially in regard to the winds and the rainfall, show us, as Mr. Blanford says, 'how each season in succession affects in diverse modes the different portions of the country; why one province may sometimes be devastated by flood while another is parched with drought, and why, with special adaptation to the peculiarities of its own seasons and resources, each of

[1] *Statistical Atlas of India*, chap. iii.

them has its own agricultural system, its own staples, its own rotation of crops.'

After March the heat in Northern India rapidly increases. As the air above the heated earth becomes hotter, the pressure becomes less. At the same time an increase of pressure is going on over the ocean south of the equator, which has then its winter. Thus, a current of air laden with moisture is gradually established towards the continent of India from the sea. This is the so-called south-west monsoon, which brings the periodical rains every year to India, when the heat of the summer has reached its greatest intensity. Towards the end of May the monsoon has usually become established in the south-western extremity of India, and before the end of June it has extended to the greater part of the northern provinces.

The quantity of rain that falls in any part of India depends mainly on the configuration of the surface of the land, and on its situation with reference to the vapour-bearing winds. As the amount of watery vapour which air can hold in suspension varies with the temperature of the air, and increases with the temperature, any cause which cools the current from the sea leads to condensation of the vapour and to the fall of rain.

One of the chief of such causes is the existence of mountains which stand in the path of the winds, and force the vapour-bearing currents to rise over them. Thus, the range of the Western Gháts, which form an almost continuous barrier along the western coasts of Southern India, meet first the whole force of the monsoon as it comes saturated with moisture from the sea. A great condensation of rain is the immediate result of the fall in the temperature of the hot moist air as it is forced to rise in passing across the mountains. On the face of the Ghâts, not far from Bombay, the annual rainfall in some places exceeds 250 inches; but a very large part of the moisture which the current of air contains is drained away by the excessive precipitation near the coast, and, as the current flows on over the land, the quantity of rain is greatly reduced. At Poona, only sixty miles from the sea, the annual rainfall is not more than 26 inches.

Similar phenomena are observed in a still more remarkable form on the Himálaya. The line of maximum elevation is not far from the southern edge of the great mountain mass. When the monsoon winds strike the outer ranges of the Himálaya, a large amount of rain immediately results; the quantity diminishes as the wind passes over the mountains, and when it reaches the regions of perpetual snow, about 100 miles from the plains of India, almost the whole of its remaining moisture is condensed. Thus, the periodical rains are completely stopped by the ranges of the southern face of the Himálaya; they can find no entrance to the mountains beyond, or to the tableland of Tibet, one of the driest and most arid regions of the world.

Similar causes shut off the rain-bearing south-westerly winds from the Madras provinces, on the south-eastern coast of India. These winds cannot carry much moisture over the obstacle to their course formed by the Western Ghâts, and little rain falls in the eastern districts of Madras during the summer months. But, as I shall presently notice, the remedy for this deficiency is not wanting.

Where, on the other hand, the configuration of the land is such that no obstacles are offered to the passage of the monsoon current from the sea, there may be no condensation of its moisture. Thus, when the wind strikes upon the coast of Sindh, very slightly elevated above the sea, it finds a hotter and not a cooler surface than that which it has left, and it passes on with all its watery vapour for 1,000 miles across the rainless plains to the Punjab, where at last the Himálaya converts the vapour into rain. If, as General Strachey has observed, there had been a range of mountains connecting the high land of the Indian peninsula with that of Baluchistán, hardly a drop of rain would have reached the Punjab and the North of India.

It would be easy to multiply illustrations of the manner in which geographical position and configuration determine the fall of rain in the various provinces of India, and even local conditions of a kind which might have seemed of little importance produce remarkable results. Thus, for instance, a deep depression in a range of mountains may afford an opening for the entrance of the vapour-bearing streams, and give an ample supply of rain to a tract of country which would have been almost rainless if the mountains had been continuous. In this manner, the valleys of the Tapti and Narbada rivers, which enter the sea north of Bombay, are gates through which the monsoon finds access to the provinces of Central India, and makes them fertile and prosperous.

As the sun travels southward after midsummer, the south-west monsoon passes gradually away, and towards the latter part of September it ceases to blow over Northern India. Causes acting in the converse direction, but similar to those which brought it with its rain-bearing currents, lead to its cessation. The temperature falls as the sun goes south, and the vast dry tracts of the Asiatic continent become rapidly colder; the barometric pressure over the land increases, and winds begin to blow from the north towards the south. These winds are the north-east monsoon.

This monsoon, although far less important than its predecessor to the greater part of India, is essentially necessary to Madras and the south-eastern provinces of the peninsula, which, as already explained, are cut off by their geographical position from the benefits of the monsoon from the south-west. When the wind from the north-east is established, these are the only parts of India which it reaches after passing across the sea, and, while everywhere else it is dry, it takes up in its passage across the Bay of Bengal a supply of moisture. Under the operation of the same laws which give their rainy season in the summer to the other provinces, the moisture brought by the north-east monsoon from the sea is precipitated in rain on the eastern districts of Madras and Southern India from October to December.

Thus, at one season or another, in the summer or in the winter, the Indian continent receives the rain which it requires.

This slight sketch of some of the main facts of Indian meteorology may serve to illustrate the causes which render the physical conditions of various parts of India so extremely different. As Mr. Blanford has observed, we may speak of the climates, but not of the climate of India. 'The world itself (he says) affords no greater contrast than is to be met with, at one and the same time, within its limits.' When these facts are understood, it will no longer seem surprising that India and its inhabitants, its natural productions, and all the conditions of life, should present such contrasts and diversities.

I have spoken of the two regions into which India

is divided; but there is a third region on and outside its borders, the influence of which over a great part of the Indian continent is so important that some knowledge of it is essential to a proper comprehension of Indian geography. I refer to the Himálaya. Without these mountains some of the richest tracts of India would be deserts; they give to India her principal rivers, and, through the effect that they produce on the monsoons and the rainfall, they affect all the conditions of life in the plains above which they rise. This is a subject in which I have always taken a special interest; it is one on which books on India have usually not much to say, and I shall devote to it the rest of this lecture.

It is unfortunate that we are taught to call these mountains the Himălāya, instead of giving them their more euphonious old Sanskrit name Himālăya, 'the abode of snow.' You will find an excellent general account of the Himálaya in the last edition of the 'Encyclopædia Britannica.' In it General Strachey shows that the Himálaya is not a mountain chain in the ordinary acceptation of the term. There stretches across a large part of Asia, immediately to the north of India, 'a great protuberance above the general level of the earth's surface.' We usually call the whole of its southern border by the name Himálaya, and its northern border, in a much less definite way, Kuenlun. The table-land of Tibet, with an average elevation above the sea of 15,000 feet or more, forms the summit of the mountain mass. Neither the Himálaya, nor Kuenlun, nor the Tibetan table-land, have any special or separate existence. The whole constitutes one huge agglomeration of mountains known to science under the general name of Himálaya.

A range of mountains like those to which we are accustomed in Europe gives no notion of the Himálaya. It extends from east to west for some 2,000 miles, and from its southern to its northern edge the average distance exceeds 500 miles. The Himálaya would stretch from England to the Caspian, and it covers 1,000,000 square miles, an area as large as that of Great Britain, the German and Austrian Empires, France and Spain, and European Turkey all together. Mountains like those of Europe have never been obstacles very difficult to pass; but except for a comparatively short distance on the north-western frontiers of India, where the mountains of Afghánistán and Baluchistán run southwards from the ranges of perpetual snow, the Himálaya and its offshoots form a barrier between India and the rest of Asia, which for all practical purposes may be called impassable. Except in the quarter that I have named, the Himálaya has in all ages given protection to India along a frontier 2,000 miles in length. But the exception has been a serious one. From this vulnerable side, in the course of the last eight hundred years, a swarm of invaders has five times come down upon India, sometimes to conquer, sometimes only to destroy. Who shall say that she has seen the last of these invasions?

As might be supposed from its vast extent, the Himálaya comprises many countries, differing from each other in almost everything except in this, that they consist entirely of mountains. You will find in them every possible variety of climate, of vegetation, and of all natural products, and they are peopled by tribes of various origin in most different stages of civilisation. The Himálaya offers a good illustration of the misleading generalisations which are common in regard to almost everything Indian. Some authorities tell you that the mountains between the plains of India and the regions of perpetual snow are bleak and bare and arid, and that their scenery, in spite of its stupendous scale, is uninteresting; others tell you that they are covered with forest and rich vegetation, and present, in the higher regions, scenes more beautiful and sublime than anything to be found in Europe. Both stories are true; but considering, as I have just said, that these mountains would stretch from England to the Caspian, you might as reasonably expect to find the same conditions in the Grampians, the Alps, and the Caucasus, as to find them in the Himálaya.

It is only with that portion of the Himálaya which rises immediately above the plains of Northern India that I am now concerned. The highest peaks hitherto measured in the Himálaya or in the world are, for the most part, found on the southern side of the watershed between India and Tibet, at a distance of about 100 miles from the Indian plains. Mount Everest reaches 29,000 feet; many of the peaks exceed 25,000, and still higher points may possibly remain to be discovered. The elevation of the passes from India into Tibet is seldom less than 16,000 feet, and the average elevation of the watershed probably exceeds 18,000 feet. The table-land of Tibet is usually 15,000 or 16,000 feet above the sea.

I have already referred to the manner in which the Himálaya forms an impassable obstacle to the south-west monsoon, which brings the periodical rains to India from the sea. The moisture-bearing currents cannot pass its icy barrier, and all their vapour is condensed on the southern or Indian side of the chain. It is now well known that this furnishes the simple explanation of the fact formerly discussed by Humboldt and others, and long misunderstood, that the line of perpetual snow is lower on the southern than on the northern slopes of the Himálaya. Although on the north of the Indian watershed, in Tibet, the winter cold is almost arctic in its intensity, there is very little snow below 18,000 or 20,000 feet, because the air is so dry that snow can hardly form, while on the southern slopes of the chain the snow-line is found at an elevation of 15,000 or 16,000 feet.

The greatest rivers of India all come from the Himálaya. It is remarkable that, although their courses through India to the sea are so widely divergent, their chief sources are not far apart from each other, and they all lie beyond the Indian watershed. They are in the high Tibetan plateau, near the lake of Mánasarowar and the peak of Kailás, names among the most sacred of Hindu mythology. This is strictly true of the Indus, the Sutlej, and the Bráhmaputra, and, although the Ganges seems to be an exception, it can hardly be said to be one.

The true story of the sources of the Ganges is curious. We all know how, in the last century, Bruce was supposed to have discovered the sources of the Nile, and how it afterwards appeared that he had been to the head, not of the great river, but of one of its tributaries. Something of the same sort may be said of the Ganges.

Almost every work on the geography of India still tells us that the Ganges has its origin in the glacier, or, as it is oftener and inaccurately called, the snow-bed of Gangotri, where it issues from the ice-cave, the 'cow's mouth' of the sacred books of the Hindus. The truth is that, apart from mythology and religion and common belief, and judging as we judge less holy streams, Gangotri has no claim to be called the source of the Ganges. The river which comes from Gangotri is the Bhágirathi, one of the numerous Himálayan feeders of the true Ganges, into which it falls about forty miles above Hardwár, where the Ganges enters the plains of India. The main stream is that of the Alaknanda, which has a much longer course and a much larger body of water than the Bhágirathi; its most distant sources are on the southern side of the watershed, near the Niti and Mána passes into Tibet, and it collects the drainage of the peaks and glaciers of the Kumáon and Garhwál Himálaya, from Nanda Devi to the sacred shrines of Badrináth and Kedárnáth. But the Ganges, like the Indus, the Sutlej, and the Bráhmaputra, has also its trans-Himálayan sources. The Gogra, or more correctly the Ghágra, which joins the Ganges above Patna, about 500 miles from the sea, is hardly known to European fame, but in the upper portion of its course it is a much larger river than the Ganges. It rises on the north of the Indian Himálaya, not far from the sources of the other great rivers, near the lake of Mánasarowar, finds its way through the mountains of Nepál, under the name of Kauriáli, and flows on through Oudh until it joins the Ganges. The Kauriáli, near the borders of Nepál, after it has entered the plains, is said to have a minimum discharge of 11,000 cubic feet per second, whereas that of the Ganges at Hardwár is only 6,300 feet. Whether at the junction between the Ganges and the Gogra, the former, after its longer course through the plains of India, has become the larger stream, is a question to which no certain answer has hitherto been given; but it is curious that it should still be possible to doubt whether the Gogra can properly be called an affluent of the Ganges, and whether it ought not rather to be held that the Ganges, in its passage from the mountains to the sea, falls into a river greater than itself, the very name of which is hardly known in Europe.

Between Assam, the British province on the extreme north-east of India, to the western frontiers of Kashmir, a distance of 1,500 miles, the countries of the Indian Himálaya are mostly under Native rule, and among them the most important is Nepál, the one State in India, or on its borders, which has remained entirely independent of our power. In 1815 and 1816 the Nepalese measured their strength against ours, and lost in consequence Kumáon and Garhwál, their richest districts. Since that time they have preserved an unvarying policy of absolute but friendly isolation. The British representative at Kátmándu, their capital, is treated almost as a highly honoured prisoner, and Central Africa is more accessible to European travellers than the greater part of Nepál. However unenlightened from our point of view this policy, which the geographical position and configuration of the country alone rendered possible, may have been, it has had the result of shutting out all causes and opportunities of dispute, and of preserving the independence of Nepál. The other Native Hill States are all under British control.

In the Western Himálaya, in the Punjab Lieutenant-Governorship, several districts, of which Kángra is the most important, are under British administration, and in one of them, a small patch surrounded by Native States, is Simla, the summer head-quarters of the Government of India. But the most considerable tract of British territory in the Himálaya, except Assam, is the province of Kumáon and Garhwál, bordering on the plains of Rohilkhand, in the North-Western Provinces.

It would be foreign to my purpose to speak to you at length regarding this or any other portion of the chain, and, as I have just said, in treating of so vast a subject as the Himálaya it is easy to be misled by generalisations. I will, however, say something about Kumáon, because in its main features it affords instructive illustrations of many of the chief and most widely prevailing characteristics of these mountains, and because it is a country with which I have had unusual opportunities of making myself acquainted.

The province of Kumáon has an area of more than 12,000 square miles. Its whole surface is covered by mountains. They rise like a wall with strange suddenness from the plains of India. You pass almost in a moment into the mountains, and when you have once entered them, you will hardly find level ground again until you have gone 400 or 500 miles across the Himálaya, Tibet, and the Kuenlun. The Gágar range, described with enthusiastic admiration by Bishop Heber, rises immediately above the plains to more than 8,000 feet, and in one of its valleys lie the little lake and station of Naini Tál, the summer head-quarters of the Lieutenant-Governor of the North-Western Provinces.

After travelling through Kumáon for more than 100 miles, through a constant succession of high ranges and deep gorges, you pass the great peaks of the Indian Himálaya, and cross over into Tibet, but, looking northward from the watershed, you see again fresh snowy ranges and mountains that look as endless and as vast as those that you have left behind.

In the earlier part of my Indian life I had the good fortune to be employed for about ten years in various offices in Kumáon and Garhwál, and I spent many summers in the higher regions of the Himálaya, sometimes among the almost countless glaciers at the sources of the Ganges and its tributaries, or visiting the passes into Tibet, one of them more than 18,000 feet above the sea, or on the forest-covered ranges immediately under the snowy peaks. I have seen much of European mountains, but in stupendous sublimity, combined with a magnificent and luxuriant beauty, I have seen nothing that can be compared with the Himálaya.

Although none of the Kumáon summits reach an elevation equal to that attained by a few of the peaks in other parts of the chain, for only two of them exceed 25,000 feet, it is probable that the average elevation of the snowy range of Kumáon is nowhere surpassed. For a continuous distance of some 200 miles the peaks constantly reach a height of from 22,000 to more than 25,000 feet.

The Alpine vegetation of the Kumáon Himálaya, while far more luxuriant, closely resembles in its generic forms that of the Alpine regions of Europe; but after you have left the plains for 100 miles and have almost reached the foot of the great peaks, the valleys are still, in many cases, only 2,000 or 3,000 feet above the sea, conveying, as General Strachey says, 'the heat and vegetation of the tropics among ranges covered with perpetual snow.' Thus, he adds, the traveller may obtain at a glance a range of vision extending from 2,000 to 25,000 feet, 'and see spread before him a compendium of the entire vegetation of the globe from the tropics to the poles.' Something similar may be said of the animal world. Tigers, for instance, are common in the valleys; and it is not very unusual to see their footprints in the snow among oaks and pines and rhododendrons 8,000 or 10,000 feet above the sea.

If I wished to give to anyone some notion of the

scenery of the Kumáon Himálaya, at elevations of about 6,000 to 10,000 feet, I should advise him to travel in the Italian valleys of the Alps, to which, on a far greater scale, the gorges of the Himálaya have often a strong resemblance. The Val Anzasca, as you go up towards Macugnaga through the chestnut woods, with Monte Rosa always before you, is not unlike in miniature a valley in the Himálaya, and I hardly like to say that it is less beautiful. But the Indian mountains are grander, their forests are nobler, their whole vegetation is more rich and varied, and nowhere in Europe will you find the splendour of the atmospheric effects and colouring of the Himálaya.

Still less is comparison possible in the higher regions of the mountains. To the traveller who remembers the wild magnificence of the peaks and glaciers of the Himálaya, and the general sublimity of its aspect, Zermatt and Chamouny seem insignificant. The mere fact that the ranges of the Himálaya are often twice as high as those of the Alps gives no idea of their relative magnitude. The whole of the Bernese Alps might, it has been said, be cast into a single Himálayan valley. You might almost as reasonably, when the Scotch or Welsh hills are white with snow, compare them with Mont Blanc and Monte Rosa, as compare anything in the Alps with Nanda Devi and Trisul. If, preserving the form of its great obelisk, you could pile the Matterhorn on the Jungfrau, you would not reach the highest summits of the Himálaya, and would have a mountain less wonderful than the astonishing peak of Dunagiri.

Among earthly spectacles, I cannot conceive it possible that any can surpass the Himálaya, as I have often seen it at sunset on an evening in October from the ranges thirty or forty miles from the great peaks.

One such view in particular, that from Binsar in Kumáon, stands out vividly in my remembrance. This mountain is 8,000 feet high, covered with oak and rhododendron. Towards the north you look down over pineclad slopes into a deep valley, where, 6,000 feet below, the Sarju runs through a tropical forest. Beyond the river it seems to the eye as if the peaks of perpetual snow rose straight up and almost close to you into the sky. From the bottom of the valley to the top of Nanda Devi you see at a glance almost 24,000 feet of mountain. The stupendous golden or rose-coloured masses and pinnacles of the snowy range extend before you in unbroken succession for more than 250 miles, filling up a third part of the visible horizon, while on all other sides, as far as the eye can reach, stretch away the red and purple ranges of the lower mountains. 'In a hundred ages of the gods,' writes one of the old Sanskrit poets, 'I could not tell you of the glories of Himáchal.'

I must add that few of those who spend the summer in the hill stations of Northern India have the opportunity of witnessing such scenes as these. If they suppose, at a place like Simla, that they have seen the Himálaya, they greatly deceive themselves. In my own opinion, you may see more magnificent mountains among the Alps.

LECTURE II.

THE CONSTITUTION OF THE GOVERNMENT IN INDIA AND AT HOME.

PRESIDENCIES AND PROVINCES—THE PRESIDENCY OF BENGAL—FIRST CONSTITUTION OF THE GOVERNMENT—THE REGULATING ACT OF GEORGE III.—HASTINGS AND HIS COUNCIL—CHANGES BETWEEN 1773 AND 1833—RENEWAL OF THE EAST INDIA COMPANY'S CHARTER IN 1833—THE GOVERNOR-GENERAL OF INDIA IN COUNCIL—SEPARATION OF THE NORTH-WESTERN PROVINCES FROM BENGAL—RENEWAL OF THE CHARTER IN 1853—A LIEUTENANT-GOVERNOR APPOINTED FOR BENGAL—THE MUTINY OF THE NATIVE ARMY—TRANSFER OF THE GOVERNMENT TO THE CROWN—THE INDIAN COUNCILS ACT OF 1861—THE EXISTING CONSTITUTION OF THE SUPREME AND PROVINCIAL GOVERNMENTS—THE GOVERNOR-GENERAL IN COUNCIL—THE INDIAN LEGISLATURES—THEIR POWERS—THE GOVERNMENTS OF MADRAS AND BOMBAY—THE LIEUTENANT-GOVERNORS OF BENGAL, THE NORTH-WESTERN PROVINCES, AND PUNJAB—THE CHIEF COMMISSIONERS OF BURMA, THE CENTRAL PROVINCES, AND ASSAM—FORMER CUMBROUS MODE OF TRANSACTING BUSINESS—OPINION OF MR. J. S. MILL—OBSERVATIONS OF SIR HENRY MAINE—CHANGES MADE BY LORD CANNING AND BY THE INDIAN COUNCILS ACT—REFORMS COMPLETED BY LORD LAWRENCE—THE COUNCIL CONVERTED INTO A CABINET—THE MANNER OF TRANSACTING BUSINESS—POWER OF GOVERNOR-GENERAL TO OVERRULE THE COUNCIL—EXERCISE OF THIS POWER BY LORD LYTTON—MIGRATION OF THE GOVERNMENT TO SIMLA—RELATIONS BETWEEN SUPREME AND PROVINCIAL GOVERNMENTS—MR. BRIGHT ON THE GOVERNMENT OF INDIA—DECENTRALISATION—THE VARIOUS DEPARTMENTS AND SECRETARIATS—THE HOME GOVERNMENT—THE SECRETARY OF STATE AND COUNCIL OF INDIA—MODE OF TRANSACTING BUSINESS—NATURE OF CONTROL EXERCISED OVER THE GOVERNMENT OF INDIA.

In the earlier times of the East India Company, the affairs of the three principal settlements in Bengal, Madras, and Bombay, were, in each case, administered by a President and a Council composed of servants of the Company, and the term 'Presidency' was applied to the whole tract over which their authority extended. The term has lasted to the present day, and is still used in official papers, but it has almost ceased to have any special meaning. British India is not divided into presidencies, but into provinces, eight of which are extensive countries under separate Governments. The presidencies of Madras and Bombay are now the provinces of the same names.

The term 'Presidency of Bengal' requires some explanation.

The name Bengal has had, at different periods since the country came into our possession, very different meanings. It was originally applied, as it still is by the Natives of India, to the tract sometimes called Lower Bengal, including the deltas of the Ganges and Bráhmaputra, and inhabited by the people who speak Bengáli. The earliest factories and settlements on that side of India were established in Bengal, and, as British authority went on extending, the name Bengal was applied to all the territories administered from Fort William, the official head-quarters in Calcutta. Thus, the Presidency of Bengal, or, according to its proper official designation, Fort William in Bengal, came to include not only Bengal and the neighbouring provinces of Behár and Orissa, but the whole of the British conquests in Northern India. Some remnants of the old system still survive. There is a single army for the three provinces of Bengal, the North-Western Provinces and Oudh, and the Punjab, and this, although, as I shall have again to notice, it has not a single native of Bengal in its ranks, is still called the Bengal Army. Another survival from old times is seen in the Bengal Civil Service. The members of the Indian Civil Service, recruited under the system of open competition, are appointed, before they leave England, to the provinces to which under ordinary circumstances they remain permanently attached. The Civil Services of the North-Western Provinces and the Punjab are, for all administrative purposes, as distinct from that of Bengal as from those of Madras and Bombay; but, in regard to some matters connected with annuities to widows and children, they are still treated as a single body and included in the so-called Bengal Civil Service.

The first Act of Parliament which prescribed a definite system of government for the affairs of India was that of 1773.[1] It provided for the appointment of a Governor-General and a Council of four members for the Presidency of Bengal. The administration was to be carried on in accordance with the votes of the majority of the Council, and the Governor-General had no power to set aside their decisions. Certain powers of control, vaguely defined, were given to the Government of Bengal over the presidencies of Madras and Bombay. Warren Hastings was the first Governor-General of Bengal. The scandalous dissensions in his Council, under the malignant influence of Francis, have become a well known matter of history. They showed that government by the constantly shifting majority of a Council was impossible; but although similar facts repeatedly occurred to illustrate the folly of such a system, it was not until 1786 that a partial remedy was applied, after Lord Cornwallis had made it a condition of his acceptance of the office of Governor-General that the power of overruling his Council should be given to him. On the renewal of the Company's Charter in 1793,[2] the powers of the Governor-General were further extended; authority to overrule their Councils

[1] Regulating Act, 13 Geo. III. c. 63. [2] 33 Geo. III. c. 52.

was given to the Governors of Madras and Bombay; the power of the Governments of those presidencies to make laws and regulations for their own territories was recognised; and the supreme authority of the Governor-General in Council over the whole of India was distinctly declared. No very important changes in the constitution of the Government were made after this until the renewal of the Charter in 1833,[1] when the trading powers of the Company ceased. The Governor-General in Council of Bengal then became the Governor-General of India in Council. Bengal was to be divided into two presidencies, Fort William in Bengal and Agra. The Governor-General was to be Governor of the former, and a Governor was to be appointed for the latter. The Agra presidency was not constituted, but by an amending Act passed in 1835[2] the territories which were to have been included in it were placed, under the name of the North-Western Provinces, under a Lieutenant-Governor without a Council. Madras and Bombay retained their Councils, but no Council was appointed for Bengal.

In 1853 the Charter of the Company was again renewed,[3] and an important change in the Government was made. It had long been obvious that it was impossible for a single person to discharge the double duty of Governor-General of India and Governor of Bengal, and the administration of Bengal had notoriously become less efficient than that of any other province in India. The Governor-General was relieved from this charge, and a Lieutenant-Governor, without a Council, was appointed.

In 1857 came the mutiny of the Bengal Native army. In the following year, by the 'Act for the better

[1] 3 and 4 Will. IV. c. 85. [2] 5 and 6 Will. IV. c. 52.
[3] 16 and 17 Vic. c. 95.

government of India,'[1] the Government was transferred from the East India Company to the Crown, and it was provided that all the powers of the Company and of the Board of Control should be exercised by a Secretary of State, in concert, in certain cases, with a Council. This Act, of which I shall again have to speak, applied almost solely to the Government in England, and the Government in India was carried on as before.

In 1861 important changes were made in the constitution both of the Supreme and Provincial Governments in India. The 'Indian Councils Act'[2] then passed still regulates, for the most part, the Governments in India. I shall describe its principal provisions.

The Governor-General and the members of his Council are appointed by the Crown. No limit of time is specified for their tenure of office, but custom, not often disregarded, has fixed it at five years. The term 'Viceroy' has been commonly applied to the Governor-General since the transfer of the Government to the Crown, but it is not recognised by law. There are five ordinary members of Council, and, by an Act passed in 1874,[3] a sixth member may, at the discretion of the Crown, be appointed for public works. Three of the members must have served in India for at least ten years; two of them are members of the Covenanted Civil Service, and the third is a military officer; but this distribution is a matter of custom, not of law. One of the two remaining members must be a Barrister, or a member of the Faculty of Advocates in Scotland, of not less than five years' standing; he has charge of the legislative department. The fifth member has charge of the finances. The Commander-in-Chief in

[1] 21 and 22 Vic. c. 106.
[2] 24 and 25 Vic. c. 67.
[3] 37 and 38 Vic. c. 91.

India may also be, and in practice always is, an extraordinary member of the Council. The Governors of Madras and Bombay become extraordinary members if the Council meets within their presidencies. Whenever it is declared by the Governor-General in Council to be expedient that the Governor-General should visit any part of India without his Council, he may nominate one of the members of his Council to be President of the Council. The President, during the absence of the Governor-General, exercises the powers which the Governor-General may exercise at meetings of the Council, except that of assenting to or withholding assent to laws; and the Governor-General, when so absent, may himself exercise all or any of the powers which he might exercise as Governor-General in Council, except the power of making laws. The Council may assemble at any place in India which the Governor-General in Council appoints.

For the purposes of legislation, additional members are nominated to the Council. The Legislative Council is often spoken of as if it had a separate existence, but this is a mistake; only one Council is known to the law. Not less than six nor more than twelve additional members are nominated by the Governor-General, and they join the Council when it meets for legislative purposes. Not less than one-half of the number must be persons not holding offices under the Government; some of them are always Natives of India. The Lieutenant-Governor of any province in which the Council may meet acts as an additional member.

The official element in the Council is so strong that the Government can always command a majority. The Act was designedly passed in such a form that the Council, when it meets for legislative purposes, has no power to interfere with any of the functions of the executive Government. It can occupy itself with no matters except those directly connected with the special legislative business transacted by it.

Certain Acts of Parliament under which the Government of India is constituted cannot be touched, and no law can be made affecting the authority of Parliament or allegiance to the Crown, but with these exceptions there are no restrictions on the legislative powers of the Governor-General in Council. Measures affecting the public debt or revenues of India, the religion of any of her Majesty's subjects, the discipline or maintenance of the military or naval forces, and the relations of the Government with Foreign States, cannot be introduced by any member without the previous sanction of the Governor-General. Every Act requires the Governor-General's assent. The assent of the Crown is not necessary to the validity of an Act, but the Crown can disallow any Act that has been passed.

Apart from these ordinary legislative powers, the Governor-General in Council was authorised in 1870[1] to make, without calling in the additional members, 'Regulations' having the force of law for the less advanced parts of the country, where a system of administration simpler than that in force elsewhere is desirable. The effect of this was to put on a legal basis the administration of the so-called 'Non-Regulation Provinces.'

Further, in cases of urgent necessity, the Governor-General can, on his own authority and without reference to his Council, make ordinances which have the force of law for six months. This power was given by the Act of 1861 for the first time. It has seldom been exercised, and only for reasons of temporary convenience.

[1] 33 Vic. c. 3, sec. 1.

The constitution of the Executive Governments in Madras and Bombay was not altered by the Act of 1861, and they still retain some signs of their former dignity and partial independence. In certain matters they correspond directly with the Secretary of State, a privilege not possessed by other provincial Governments. The Governor and the members of Council are appointed by the Crown. The Governor is usually an English statesman sent from England. The local Commander-in-Chief and two members of the Civil Service constitute the Council. The power of legislation, which had been taken away in Madras and Bombay by the Act of 1833, was restored in 1861. Much of the description which I have given of the manner in which legislative business is carried on by the Council of the Governor-General is equally applicable to the Councils of the provincial Governments. The Governor nominates not less than four, nor more than eight additional members, who join the Council when it meets for legislative purposes, and at least half of them must be non-official persons. No law is valid until sanctioned by the Governor-General. The powers of the Governor-General in Council to legislate for all matters throughout India are not affected by the establishment of the local legislatures, but, as a general rule, the latter are left to deal with subjects of local and provincial interest. They cannot repeal or amend any Act of Parliament, or any law passed in India before the time when the Indian Councils Act of 1861 came into operation, nor, except with the previous sanction of the Governor-General, can they take into consideration any measure affecting the public debt, customs, imperial taxation, currency, the post office and telegraph, the penal code, religion, the military and naval forces, patents, copyright, or relations with Foreign States.

In the other great provinces of India the Governments are differently constituted. Bengal, the North-Western Provinces, and the Punjab, are administered by Lieutenant-Governors; they must be chosen from officers in the service of the Crown who have served in India for at least ten years; they are appointed by the Governor-General with the approval of the Crown; and, with one exception, they have always been members of the Covenanted Civil Service.[1] The Lieutenant-Governors have no Councils for executive business, but the Governor-General in Council may establish in each province a Council for legislative purposes only. This power has been exercised in Bengal and in the North-Western Provinces; their Legislative Councils are precisely similar to those in Madras and Bombay, the Lieutenant-Governor taking the place of the Governor. The Governments of Burma, the Central Provinces, and Assam, are administered by Chief Commissioners. Excepting in name and dignity and in amount of salary and patronage, there is little difference between them and Lieutenant-Governors.

I must now speak of the manner in which the executive business of the Governor-General in Council is transacted. The system is very different from that in force under the Government of the East India Company. Although after the Act of 1793 the power of the Governor-General to overrule his Council was not open to question, the fundamental idea, on which previous legislation had been based, still remained, that the Government was to be carried on by the Governor-General in concert with the whole Council. All public business of every kind, however trivial, was supposed to come before all the members of the Government. Questions

[1] 5 and 6 Will. IV. c. 52, sec. 2, and 16 and 17 Vic. c. 95, sec. 16.

were ordinarily decided by the majority, the Governor-General having a casting vote if the votes were equal. If the Governor-General determined to overrule the majority, it was provided that he and the members of Council should 'mutually exchange with and communicate in writing to each other the grounds and reasons of their respective opinions.' They were then to meet a second time, and if both parties retained their first opinions, their minutes were to be entered on the consultations, and the orders of the Governor-General were to be carried out.

In his 'Essay on Representative Government,' published in 1861, when the procedure which I have described was still legally in force, Mr. J. S. Mill described the manner in which he considered that Ministers in charge of the great departments of an Executive Government ought to be assisted by Councils.

'The Councils should be consultative merely, in this sense, that the ultimate decision should rest undividedly with the Minister himself; but neither ought they to be looked upon, or to look upon themselves as ciphers, or as capable of being reduced to such at his pleasure. The advisers attached to a powerful and perhaps self-willed man ought to be placed under conditions which make it impossible for them, without discredit, not to express an opinion, and impossible for him not to listen to and consider their recommendations, whether he adopts them or not. The relation which ought to exist between a chief and this description of advisers is very accurately hit by the constitution of the Governor-General and those of the different presidencies in India. These Councils are composed of persons who have professional knowledge of Indian affairs, which the Governor-General and Governors usually lack, and which it would not be desirable to require of them. As a rule, every member of Council is expected to give an opinion, which is, of course, very often a simple acquiescence; but if there is a difference of sentiment, it is at the option of every member, and is the invariable practice, to record the reasons of his opinion; the Governor-General or Governor doing the same. In ordinary cases the decision is according to the sense of the majority; the Council, therefore, has a substantial part in the Government, but if the Governor-General or Governor thinks fit, he may set aside even their unanimous opinion, recording his reasons. The result is that the chief is, individually and effectively, responsible for every act of the Government. The members of Council have only the responsibility of advisers; but it is always known, from documents capable of being produced, and which, if called for by Parliament or public opinion, always are produced, what each has advised, and what reasons he gave for his advice; while from their dignified position and ostensible participation in all acts of government, they have nearly as strong motives to apply themselves to the public business, and to form and express a well-considered opinion on every part of it, as if the whole responsibility rested with themselves.'

I must continue my quotation, for Mr. Mill's commentary on the system thus described is remarkable:—

'This mode of conducting the highest class of administrative business is one of the most successful instances of the adaptation of means to ends which political history, not hitherto very prolific in works of skill and contrivance, has yet to show. It is one of the acquisitions with which the art of politics has been enriched by the experience of the East India Company's rule; and like most of the other wise contrivances by which India has been preserved to this country, and an amount of good government produced which is truly wonderful considering the circumstances and the materials, it is probably destined to perish in the general holocaust which the traditions of Indian government seem fated to undergo, since they have been placed at the mercy of public ignorance and the presumptuous vanity of political men.'

Mr. Mill's anticipations have been to some extent verified. The manner of transacting business which existed under the East India Company has perished, but, I venture to say, not for the reasons which he predicted, but because it was not the wise contrivance which he supposed. The principle which he laid down was undoubtedly true, that while a man in the position of Governor-General of India ought to possess, in the last resort, power to act upon his own judgment, he ought also to be obliged to hear the opinions of experienced councillors, and that those councillors should have the right of making their opinions known, whether they were followed or not. This principle has not been infringed. If Mr. Mill had himself seen in operation the system which he described, he would, I am sure, have given it a different character. The truth is that a more cumbrous, I might say a more impossible, system of administration for a great empire could hardly have been invented than that which prevailed under the government of the East India Company, when every case was supposed to be laid before the Governor-General and the whole Council, and to be decided by them collectively. The only reason that enabled such a system to last so long was that in matters requiring prompt and vigorous action it was not really acted upon.

In the latter years of the East India Company, and for a few years after the transfer of the government to the Crown, the Governor-General was frequently separated from his Council. His presence was often required in Northern India by reasons of political necessity. He was authorised to exercise, while absent from the Council, all the powers of the Governor-General in Council, except the power of legislation. The Council remained in Calcutta under the presidency of the senior member, who exercised, during the Governor-General's absence, all the powers of the Governor-General in Council, except the power of giving assent to laws. There was a double Government, with a division of authority and responsibility fatal to good administration. Sir Henry Maine has described, from his own observation as a member of Council, the manner in which the system actually worked :—

'A division of business was made between the Governor-General in the Upper provinces and the President in Council at Calcutta. Everything which was of importance was referred directly to the Governor-General, and there was either a rule or an understanding that if any matter which came before the President in Council assumed, contrary to expectation, the least importance, it should be sent on to the Governor-General. . . Except in regard to matters belonging to the Foreign department, of which it was usual for the Governor-General himself to undertake the primary management, the severance of the Governor-General from the Council dislocated the whole machinery of Government. I was myself in Calcutta, as a member of Council during the absence of Lord Elgin in the Upper provinces, in the summer of 1863. I believe it to be impossible for any human arrangement to have worked more perversely. Lord Elgin was distinguished by remarkable caution—though I doubt whether his caution was practically greater than that which any man comparatively fresh from England would display under similarly vast responsibilities—and all or most important matters were transferred by him over a distance of 1,500 miles for the opinions of his Council. The result was that a great deal of work was done twice over, and a great deal not done at all.'[1]

In earlier times, when there were no railways or telegraphs, and hardly any roads, the duties of the Government were very different from what they are now. Kingdoms were annexed and conquered, and stirring events were constantly going on, but the ordinary business of the Central Government was comparatively small. But in the years immediately preceding the mutinies of 1857 rapid changes had begun

[1] Memorandum on the Administration of Bengal, December, 2, 1867.

in all branches of the administration, and when the great reign of Lord Dalhousie was over he declared it to be morally and physically impossible that the Governor-General should efficiently discharge all the duties imposed upon him.

The events of 1857 made the burden still heavier. The insertion by Parliament of a few words in the Indian Councils Act of 1861 gave to Lord Canning and his successors the means of reforming a system of government which had become intolerable. It empowered the Governor-General to make from time to time rules and orders for the more convenient transaction of business in his Council, and provided that any order made or act done in accordance with such rules and orders should be deemed to be the order or act of the Governor-General in Council. These provisions made it possible to bring legally to an end the system under which the whole Council was supposed to take part collectively in the disposal of all the business of the Government.

Rules were made by Lord Canning, assigning to each member of the Council the charge of a separate department of the administration, and the Council was virtually converted into a Cabinet, of which the Governor-General was the head. When this change was made it became obvious that the separation, for long periods of time, of the Governor-General from his Council was incompatible with efficient administration. The reform of procedure was completed by Lord Lawrence. Since his time the old plan of double government, under which the Governor-General was frequently absent from the Council, with a President in Council in Calcutta, has been abandoned. It is now never adopted except as an occasional measure of merely temporary convenience.

Although the separation of departments in India is less complete than in England, and the authority of a member of Council much less extensive and exclusive than that of an English Secretary of State, the members of Council are now virtually Cabinet ministers, each of whom has charge of one or more of the great departments of the Government. Their ordinary duties are rather those of administrators than of councillors. The Governor-General regulates the manner in which the public business shall be distributed among them. He usually keeps the Foreign department in his own hands; the other departments are—Home, Revenue and Agriculture, Finance and Commerce, Military, Public Works, and Legislative. While the member of Council takes the place of the English Secretary of State, there is in each department a Secretary holding a position analogous to that of a permanent Under-secretary in England. It is the duty of this secretary to place every case before the Governor-General or member in charge of his department, in a form in which it is ready for decision. He submits with it a statement of his own opinion. In minor cases the member of Council passes orders which are final. If the matter be one of greater importance, he sends on the papers, with his own orders, to the Governor-General for his approval. If the Governor-General concurs, and thinks further discussion unnecessary, the orders are issued. If he does not concur, he directs that the case shall be brought before the Council, as in England an important case might come before the Cabinet. The duty rests upon the secretary, apart from his responsibility towards the member of Council in charge of the department, of bringing personally to the knowledge of the Governor-General every matter of special importance. All orders of the Government are issued in the name of the Governor-General in Council.

Although, when a question comes before the whole Council, it is usually decided in accordance with the opinions of the majority, power is reserved by law to the Governor-General to act on his own opinion alone, whenever the safety, tranquillity, or interests of the British possessions in India may, in his judgment, be essentially affected.[1] Recourse to this power is very seldom necessary. The only occasion in recent times on which it has been exercised in a matter of importance occurred in March 1879, when Lord Lytton, in opposition to the opinion of a majority of his Council, partially abolished the Indian import duty on English cotton goods. The occasion will be remembered in the economic history of India, because this measure rendered inevitable the speedy application to India of the policy of the freedom of trade.

Another consequence has followed from the changes that I have described. The abandonment by Lord Lawrence of the system of double government, and the establishment of the departmental responsibility of the members of Council, rendered it necessary that when the Governor-General left Calcutta for Northern India he should be accompanied by the Council. Lord Lawrence made Simla the ordinary summer head-quarters of the Government. There has been much criticism of these annual migrations, but no one who has had personal knowledge of the Government of India doubts the increased efficiency of its administration since it has passed a portion of every year in a climate less enervating than that to which it was exposed in the tropical heat of Calcutta, and in which Englishmen can work as

[1] 33 Vic. c. 3, sec. 5.

vigorously as at home. The Government does not go to Simla for a holiday, but for the hardest and most continuous portion of its work. The evil influence of the climate is not the only reason why the Government of India should not remain permanently in Bengal. It has no local duties. Its business is one of general control, and the countries of Northern and Western India will always be those which demand the largest share of its attention and anxiety. There is no province less suitable for the permanent head-quarters of the central Government than Bengal, because there is no province so unlike everything else in India, and none where the character and opinions of the educated classes of the Natives are so much at variance with those that prevail elsewhere. The influence of Bengal on the policy of the Government is, therefore, very likely to be misleading.

I shall give in another lecture some account of the manner in which the administration of a great British province is carried on. The last twenty years have seen a great and beneficial change in the relations between the supreme and provincial Governments.

In the speeches on India made by Mr. Bright, about the time when the Government of India was transferred to the Crown, one of the principles on which he insisted was the necessity of decentralising the Government. There is much in those speeches with which I am unable to agree, and much that was once true has ceased to be applicable, but I wish to read to you some passages which seem to me to indicate the principles on which government in India can alone be successfully conducted. Mr. Bright's speeches are accessible to everyone, and I need not be accused of misrepresenting his views if I quote only those passages with which I myself agree, and which serve my present purpose:—

'The point which I wish to bring before the Committee and the Government is this, because it is on this that I rely mainly —I think I may say, almost entirely—for any improvement in the future of India. I believe a great improvement may be made, and by a gradual process that will dislocate nothing. What you want is to decentralise your Government. . . You will not make a single step towards the improvement of India unless you change your whole system of government—unless you give to each presidency a Government with more independent powers than are now possessed. What would be thought if the whole of Europe were under one Governor who knew only the language of the Feejee Islands, and that his subordinates were like himself, only more intelligent than the inhabitants of the Feejee Islands are supposed to be? . . . How long does England propose to govern India? Nobody answers that question, and nobody can answer it. Be it 50, or 100, or 500 years, does any man with the smallest glimmering of common-sense believe that so great a country, with its twenty different nations and its twenty languages, can ever be bound up and consolidated into one compact and enduring empire? I believe such a thing to be utterly impossible. We must fail in the attempt if ever we make it, and we are bound to look into the future with reference to that point.'

Mr. Bright, seeing that the union of the various countries of India into a single state was impossible, went on to propose that each of the five great provinces should have a separate and almost independent Government of its own, directly subject to the British Crown, but that the central Government of India under the Governor-General in Council should be abolished. It is with no want of respect for Mr. Bright that I say that the latter suggestion was not feasible. There is nothing more essential to the maintenance of our empire than a strong central authority; but Mr. Bright's belief was undoubtedly true that there can be no successful government in India unless each great province be administered by its own separate Government with a minimum of interference from outside.

There was a time when the tendency in India was towards greater centralisation; but since the Viceroyalty of Lord Mayo the current has happily turned in the other direction, and the provincial Governments are now more independent than they were twenty years ago. This change has been mainly the result of the measures of financial decentralisation initiated in 1870, which have been pronounced by Sir Henry Maine to be 'much the most successful administrative reform which has taken place in India in his time.'[1] I shall speak of this in another lecture.

The Government of India now interferes very little with the details of provincial administration, and it invariably happens that the wisest and strongest Viceroys are those who interfere the least. They recognise the fact that the provincial Governments necessarily possess far more knowledge of local requirements and conditions than any to which the distant authorities of the central Government can pretend.

Although the Governor-General in Council exercises only a general supervision over the internal administration of the empire, there are some branches of the public business which concern the whole of India, and which obviously can be efficiently managed by the central authority alone. The military defence of India, and the conduct of our relations with Foreign powers and with the Native States of India, rest with the supreme Government. Although the duty of administering the laws rests with the provincial Governments,

[1] *The Reign of Queen Victoria*—'*India*,' vol. i. p. 516.

and with the local courts and authorities, the Government of India is in a great measure responsible for the excellence or imperfection of the laws themselves. Subject to the control of the Secretary of State, it makes provision for the construction of the railways and canals, without which there can be no proper development of the public wealth, or protection against drought and famine. It administers the post office and telegraph. It is mainly responsible for the management of the finances, and it lays down the principles by which the fiscal policy of the empire is to be guided. It depends on its decisions whether commerce shall be free, or fettered by unwise restrictions, whether salt and clothing shall be cheap, or made dear by taxation.

I must now refer to the Act of 1858, by which the Government of India was transferred to the Crown. It provided that all the powers of the East India Company and Board of Control should be exercised by a Secretary of State, in concert, in certain cases, with a Council, and, although various changes have been made in it by subsequent legislation, it remains in essential respects still in force.[1]

The Council, styled the Council of India, consists of fifteen members appointed by the Secretary of State. Twelve of them hold office for ten years, and this term may, for special reasons of public advantage, which must be laid before Parliament, be extended for five years more. Three of the members 'having professional or other peculiar qualifications' may be appointed for life. The majority of the Council must be persons who have served or resided in India for at least ten years,

[1] The principal Acts referring to this subject are the following:—Act 21 and 22 Vic. c. 106; Act 22 and 23 Vic. c. 41; Act 23 and 24 Vic. c. 100; Act 32 and 33 Vic. c. 97; Act 39 Vic. c. 7.

and who have not left India more than ten years before their appointment. Most of the members are always men who have held high office in India. If you look at the present list of the Council, you will see that five of them belonged to the Indian Civil service, and have been either lieutenant-governors of provinces or members of the Viceroy's Council, four of them are soldiers, two are engineers, one is a banker, and three are men of diplomatic, official, or mercantile experience. The object aimed at by the law is to give to the Secretary of State, who must ordinarily have little personal knowledge of the details of Indian administration, the help of a body of experts. The position of the Council differs essentially from that formerly held by the Court of Directors of the East India Company, for, unlike that body, which possessed and exercised large independent powers, it has no initiative authority. Questions of the greatest importance, notorious to all the world, may be pending, but the Council can give no opinion on them until they are laid before it by the Secretary of State.

Every order proposed to be made by the Secretary of State must, before it is issued, either be submitted to a meeting of the Council or be placed in the Council-room for seven days for the perusal of the members, unless the Secretary of State considers the matter urgent, in which case, recording his reasons, he may make the order. There is one limitation on the powers thus given to him. He cannot order expenditure without the consent of a majority of the Council. The Act of 1858 provides that 'the expenditure of the revenues of India, both in India and elsewhere, shall be subject to the control of the Secretary of State in Council, and no grant or appropriation of any part of such revenues, or of any other property coming into the possession of the Secretary of State in Council by virtue of this Act, shall be made without the concurrence of a majority of votes at a meeting of the Council.'

The powers thus given to the Council in controlling expenditure are, however, far from being as great as at first sight they seem to be, for they can only be exercised in regard to the ordinary business of the administration. Orders involving large expenditure may be given by the Secretary of State without either the consent or the knowledge of the Council. In dealing with questions affecting the relations of the Government with Foreign powers, making war or peace, prescribing the policy to be followed towards Native States, and generally in matters in which secrecy is necessary, the Secretary of State acts on his own authority alone. Before the transfer of the Government to the Crown, the Board of Control was empowered to send to India any orders on these subjects through the Secret Committee, which consisted of not more than three members of the Court of Directors, and those powers were transferred to the Secretary of State. Despatches from India on similar matters may be marked 'Secret' in India, and they are not communicated to the members of the Council unless the Secretary of State shall so direct. Such questions as an Afghan war, the negotiations with Russia and the Ameer of Kábul regarding the boundaries of Afghánistán, or the annexation of Burma, do not come before the Council. Its members have not only no power of interference, but they have no recognised means of obtaining information in regard to such subjects other than those of the general public.

Apart from questions of this character, most of the ordinary business passes through the Council, and, consisting as it does of men possessing special experience of Indian affairs, its advice is naturally, in the great majority of cases, followed by the Secretary of State.

The business is distributed among the various departments, each of which is in charge of a permanent secretary, and the Secretary of State appoints, for consideration of the questions coming before each department, a committee consisting of three or four members of the Council. They are chosen according to their presumed knowledge of the subjects likely to be referred to them. The recommendations of the committees are laid before the Secretary of State, and, if he so directs, before the Council.

It has often been said that one result of the transfer of the Government of India to the Crown has been to increase very greatly the interference of the Home Government, and to weaken the authority of the Government in India itself. There is no foundation for such statements. Having myself been a member of the Government of India for nearly nine years, under five Viceroys, from Lord Lawrence to Lord Ripon, and afterwards a member of the Council of the Secretary of State, the point is one on which I feel that I have authority to speak. The increased facilities of communication, the establishment of telegraphs, the greater interest in India taken by the English public and by Parliament, the growth of the business of the Home Government in consequence of the large investments of British capital in India, and other causes, have made the relations between the two countries far more intimate than was formerly the case, but it is an error to suppose that the Secretary of State is constantly interfering in the ordinary work of Indian administration.

The description of the Home Government given by Mr. J. S. Mill in the time of the East India Company is as applicable now as when he wrote:—

> 'It is not,' he said, 'so much an executive as a deliberative body. The Executive Government of India is, and must be, seated in India itself. The principal function of the Home Government is not to direct the details of administration, but to scrutinise and revise the past acts of the Indian Governments; to lay down principles and issue general instructions for their future guidance, and to give or refuse sanction to great political measures which are referred home for approval.'

The action of the Secretary of State is mainly confined to answering references made to him by the Governments in India, and, apart from great financial questions, the number and nature of those references mainly depend on the character and wishes of the Governor-General for the time being. Some men in that position like to minimise personal responsibilities, and to ask for the orders of the Home Government before taking action. Others prefer to act on their own judgment and on that of their councillors. The Secretary of State initiates almost nothing.

So long as the Government of India is content to carry on the administration without largely increasing the cost of existing establishments, and without incurring new and heavy charges, it is practically almost independent, so far as its action in India is concerned. Even in matters connected with the public expenditure, in regard to which, as I have said, special responsibilities which cannot be avoided have been placed by Parliament on the Secretary of State in Council, the financial powers of the Governor-General in Council and of the local Governments in India have been largely extended since the transfer of the government to the Crown.

Although by far the greater part of the administrative improvement of the last thirty years has been due to the Governments in India, credit for some of it must be given to the Government at home. A body constituted like the Home Government of India is slow to move and sometimes obstructive, and its general policy has been conservative and cautious. The more ardent among Indian reformers have sometimes chafed under the restrictions placed upon them, but in their anxiety for improvement they are sometimes more aggressive than is politically prudent. The most important part of our administration in India has the inestimable advantage of being carried on by comparatively young men, but youth and prudence do not always go together. One of the weakest points in our government is the incessant process of change in the *personnel* of the administration, and the constant waste of mature experience. Neither the Viceroy nor any member of his Council, nor any Governor or Lieutenant-Governor, holds his office for more than five years, nor is there much greater permanency in the tenure of other offices held by Englishmen. The climate, and the peculiar conditions under which the government has to be carried on in a foreign country by a small body of men, make these constant changes unavoidable. This renders it difficult to maintain at all times a wise continuity of policy, and in this respect the India Office often exercises an important influence. The advisers of the Secretary of State, although their knowledge is apt to get rusty, often know more about India than most of the officers of the Government in India itself; they preserve the traditions of administration and the lessons of experience.

LECTURE III.

THE ARMY IN INDIA—THE FINANCES AND THE PUBLIC REVENUES.

THE ADVANCE OF RUSSIA TOWARDS THE FRONTIERS OF INDIA—CONSEQUENT CHANGES IN OUR POSITION—THE ARMIES OF INDIA BEFORE THE MUTINIES—THE MUTINIES OF 1857—THE REORGANISATION OF THE ARMY—ITS PRESENT CONSTITUTION—THE STAFF CORPS—INCREASE TO THE ARMY CAUSED BY THE ADVANCE OF RUSSIA—ITS PRESENT STRENGTH—THE DEPARTMENT OF FINANCE AND COMMERCE—REFORMS INSTITUTED BY MR. JAMES WILSON—FINANCIAL DECENTRALISATION—THE EXISTING SYSTEM OF FINANCIAL ADMINISTRATION—GROWTH OF THE PUBLIC REVENUES SINCE 1840—THEIR PRESENT AMOUNT—SMALL PROPORTION OF THE REVENUES DERIVED FROM TAXATION—THE SOURCES OF THE PUBLIC INCOME—THE LAND REVENUE—ITS NATURE DESCRIBED BY MR. FAWCETT AND MR. J. S. MILL—ITS INCIDENCE UNDER NATIVE AND BRITISH GOVERNMENTS—MODERATION OF ASSESSMENT—AURANGZEB'S REVENUES—RATES ON LAND—THE OPIUM REVENUE—THE MANNER OF RAISING IT—THE CONSUMPTION OF OPIUM IN CHINA—MISTAKEN IDEAS ON THE SUBJECT—CHINA NOT DEPENDENT ON INDIA FOR THE SUPPLY OF OPIUM—THE CHEFOO CONVENTION—CONSUMPTION OF OPIUM IN INDIA—FORESTS—TRIBUTES FROM NATIVE STATES—POST OFFICE—TELEGRAPHS.

In speaking, as I now propose to do, of the work that falls on the Government of India, I can only select some matters of special interest. There are others of the utmost gravity which I do not wish to discuss. Among these stand out prominently the great questions connected with the advance of Russia towards the frontiers of India, and our relations with Afghánistán. If I say nothing on these subjects, it must not be supposed that I fail to recognise their importance. The proximity of a great European power has profoundly altered our position in India, nor is it only our military position that has been affected. The change is felt throughout India both in our own dominions and in the Native states. It has thrown into the minds of men uncertainties and hopes and fears regarding the future; it has seriously disturbed the finances, it has retarded the progress of works essential to the prosperity of the country, and has checked improvement in the administration. No Englishman need doubt that it is in our power to render India invulnerable to attack, but statesmen and soldiers will do well never to forget that nothing can save us, sooner or later, from a struggle for the maintenance of our empire except the certainty on the part of those who might desire to assail us that every hostile attempt upon India must end in disastrous failure.

I shall begin this lecture with an account of the manner in which the army in India is constituted. When you remember the great military revolt of 1857, the most serious event in the history of British India, and recognise the fact that the ultimate basis of our dominion is our military power, you will understand that this is a part of my subject which cannot be passed over in silence.

In the earlier times of the East India Company, when the formation of the British Empire was beginning in Bengal, Madras, and Bombay, a military force grew up in each of the three presidencies. Three distinct armies came into existence, and they remain at the present day.

The principal extensions of territory having occurred, since the beginning of this century, in the presidency of Bengal, the army of Bengal became the most important of the three; in 1856, the year before the mutinies, it was more numerous than the other two armies together. In that year the British forces in India consisted of 39,000 Europeans and 215,000 Natives, besides several contingents, as they were called, maintained for the protection of Native States, and at their expense.

The Native army of Bengal, consisting in 1856 of 74 regiments of infantry, with 10 regiments of regular and 18 of irregular cavalry, was mainly recruited, especially for the infantry, from the Brahmans and Rájputs of Oudh, and in a lesser degree from the North-Western Provinces. A part of the Bombay army and of the contingents was supplied from the same classes. The army of Madras was recruited from its own presidency. Besides the Regular army, and various local corps, there was a strong force of so-called Irregular cavalry and infantry, the most important part of which was raised in the Punjab from Sikhs, Patháns, and other warlike races. This guarded the northern frontier, and was under the orders of the Provincial Government. The greater part of the artillery was manned by Native soldiers.

About one-third of the European infantry, and all the European artillery were local troops, raised by the East India Company for permanent service in India. They numbered about 14,000 men.

In 1857 almost the whole of the Bengal Native army, a part of that of Bombay, and the contingents in Northern India, mutinied. The Madras army remained faithful. The Punjab Irregular force was not only faithful, but rendered admirable service in the suppression of the revolt.

Before peace was restored the old Bengal army had ceased to exist. The Government was transferred to the Crown, and the whole military organisation was altered. The local European army was abolished. The artillery, which had been chiefly Native, became wholly British. The place of the local European infantry was supplied by British regiments of the line. The total strength of European troops was largely increased, while that of the Native army was largely diminished. Three distinct armies—those of Bengal, Madras, and Bombay—were still maintained. After the new arrangements had been completed, the army in India consisted of about 62,000 British, and 135,000 Native troops.

I quote from the Report of the Indian Army Commission of 1879 the following summary of the changes made after the mutinies; but, as I shall show, it became necessary in 1885, in consequence of the advance of Russia towards the north-western frontier, to increase the numbers both of British and Native troops:—

'On the reorganisation of the army, after the mutiny was quelled, it was decided that the proportion of Native and European troops in India should never greatly exceed two to one, and that the field and other artillery should be exclusively, or almost exclusively manned by Europeans. . . . All the fortresses in the country are now served by British artillery. All the heavy batteries and all the batteries of field artillery are manned by Europeans. The lessons taught by the mutiny have thus led to the maintenance of the two great principles of retaining in the country an irresistible force of British troops, and of keeping the artillery in the hands of Europeans.

'Our position in the country has very materially changed, and a force of 62,000 European soldiers represents a power far in excess of that which it represented in 1857. In those days the British troops were scattered in small forces throughout the country, and it was a matter of great difficulty, delay, and expense to concentrate even a small British force on any one spot in India. When the mutiny broke out we had hardly 400 miles of railway complete in the country, while at the present moment we have 8,312 miles of railway open.[1]

'All our great cantonments, all our fortresses and arsenals, save one, are now connected with each other, and with the seaboard, by railway. The strength of our European troops for action at any point, within or without the borders of British India, has thus been enormously increased. For example, whereas in 1857 a regiment took three or four months to march from the seaboard to Lahore, it can now move from Calcutta to Lahore in a week. Reinforcements from England, which then occupied three months on a voyage round the Cape, now land in Bombay within thirty days of leaving England. Again, the power of British troops has been indefinitely increased by their armament with breech-loading rifles, and by the substitution of rifled field-pieces of higher power for the smooth-bore six-pounder, nine-pounder, and mountain guns of the mutiny era. In any contest within the borders, or on the frontiers of India, these improved armaments would tell heavily; for the troops of Afghánistán, Burma, Nepál, Gwalior, Hyderabad, and the Cis-Sutlej States, are for the most part still armed with smooth-bore muzzle-loading weapons.'

The efficiency of the British troops has been greatly increased by another cause. Among all the changes that have occurred in India since the transfer of the Government to the Crown, there is not one over which we have better reason to rejoice than the improvement in the health of our soldiers. The Royal Commission which inquired in 1859 into the sanitary condition of the army, reported that the average death-rate among the British troops in India, for the forty years ending with 1856, had been 69 per 1,000. This was six times as high as the rate among Englishmen of the same ages at home. The Commission expressed the hope that the death-rate might be reduced by measures of sani-

[1] In the beginning of 1888, 14,383 miles of railway were open and 2,487 miles were under construction or sanctioned.

tary improvement to 20 per 1,000, or even lower. This hope has been more than fulfilled. In the ten years ending with 1879 the death-rate was 19 per 1,000. In 1883 it was less than 11 per 1,000, and in the worst of the four following years it hardly exceeded 15 per 1,000. No efforts have been spared to improve in every way the position of the British soldiers in India. They now live in barracks which, in comfort and in all sanitary conditions, excepting those conditions of climate over which we have no control, surpass any that can be found in any other country. Cantonments for more than 20 per cent. of the whole force have been provided at stations in the Himálaya or in other mountains. Since 1858 more than 30,000,000*l.* has been spent on military works in India.

Supreme authority over the army throughout India is vested by law[1] in the Governor-General in Council. The military member of Council has charge of the Military department, which corresponds to the War Office in this country. Subject to the administrative control of the Governor-General in Council, the chief executive officer of the army is the Commander-in-Chief in India. He has special command of the troops in the Bengal presidency, and he exercises a general control over the armies of Madras and Bombay, each of which has its local Commander-in-Chief. The Governments of the minor presidencies possess certain administrative powers, but the ultimate military authority rests with the Governor-General in Council.

The British officers of the Native army are taken from the Indian Staff Corps. A Staff Corps for each of the three armies of Bengal, Madras, and Bombay, was established in 1861, when the Native army was re-

[1] 3 and 4 Will. IV. c. 85.

organised. The officers of the Staff Corps were, in the first instance, transferred from the East India Company's army, but they are now drawn from British regiments of the line or artillery. Officers are admitted to the Staff Corps under certain conditions, and after passing examinations in the native languages and in professional subjects. The three Staff Corps include more than 2,000 officers. They are employed not only in the Native army and in military appointments on the staff, but also in a large number of civil posts. They hold the majority of appointments in the political department, and many administrative and judicial offices in non-regulation provinces.

Before the mutinies of 1857 duties were often performed by the Native army which were really duties of police, and the great reduction, amounting to more than 90,000 men, made in the numbers of the army was followed by a complete reorganisation of the police throughout India. The number of men available for military duty was, therefore, not diminished to the extent that the figures seem to show. Exclusive of the village police, of whom there are some 700,000, the regular police force in India consists of about 150,000 men, of whom about 55,000 have firearms, and are more or less drilled.[1] There is no part of British India in which the people habitually carry arms, or commonly possess them, and the occasions are rare, not, on an average, more than two or three in each year, on which, usually in consequence of religious disputes between Hindus and Mohammedans, or between other sects, it is neces-

[1] This is exclusive of the military police in Upper Burma, nearly 20,000 strong. The disturbed condition of that province after annexation rendered it necessary to maintain a larger police force than will ultimately be required.

sary to call out troops to assist the civil power in maintaining order. Considering that the population of British India exceeds that of the five great powers of Europe together, this furnishes a good illustration of the quiet character of the people.

The so-called Bengal army is by far the most important of the three armies of India, not only because it is more numerous than the two others together, but because, being chiefly recruited from the more vigorous races of the northern provinces, it is, as a fighting machine, incomparably more efficient. The term 'Bengal army' has long been a misnomer, since, as I shall again have to explain, there is not a single native of Bengal Proper in its ranks, and only a small part of it is ever stationed in Bengal. The Bengal army garrisons the whole country from the Bay of Bengal to the frontiers of Afghánistán, and occupies the Punjab, the North-Western Provinces, and Oudh. In Bengal Proper a few thousand men are stationed at places on the railway to the northern provinces and the frontier towards Nepál and the other Hill States, and there are usually between 4,000 and 5,000 men in Calcutta and its neighbourhood. In the rest of the lieutenant-governorship of Bengal, with its population of 69,000,000, there are no troops. Sir William Hunter is well within the mark when he says that 'probably 40,000,000 people go through life without once seeing the gleam of a bayonet or the face of a soldier.'

The defence of the north-western frontier is mainly entrusted to the Punjab Frontier force, a body more than 12,000 strong. It formed until lately a virtually distinct army, under the Government of the Punjab; but this arrangement has ceased, and, although it preserves its separate organisation, it has been brought, like the rest of the army, under the orders of the Commander-in-Chief. This admirable force is almost entirely recruited from the warlike races of the Punjab and of the north-western frontier.

The organisation of the Native army has been completely changed since the mutinies of 1857. Up to that time the infantry of the Bengal army was, as I have already said, mainly recruited from the Brahmans and Rájputs of Oudh and the North-Western Provinces. Although men of fine physique, they were not remarkable for fighting efficiency, and the former reputation of the Native army of Bengal was certainly exaggerated. Most of its triumphs were largely due to the British troops who were associated with it. The ruinous consequences of drawing the larger proportion of our soldiers from a single class, under the influence of the same feelings and interests, and holding more than any other people in India the strictest prejudices of caste, were shown by the events of 1857. The old system no longer exists; I quote from the Report of the Indian Army Commission a description of that which has taken its place :—

'The systems of recruiting for the several armies are diverse. Regiments of the Madras and Bombay armies draw their recruits from many tribes and castes over the several recruiting grounds of those presidencies, and the Bombay regiments have an admixture of Sikhs and Hindustanis from Northern India in their ranks. These armies are thus composed of what are called 'mixed recruits'—that is to say, of corps in which men of different races, several religions, and many provinces are thrown together into the same company or troop. In the Bengal and Punjab armies the majority of corps are what are called 'class-company regiments'—that is to say, the regiments draw recruits from three or more different races and recruiting grounds, but the men of each class or race are kept apart in separate companies. Thus, an infantry regiment may have two companies of Sikhs, two companies of Hindustani Brahmans and Rajputs, two companies of Punjabi Mohammedans, one company of Trans-Indus Patháns, and one company of Dogras from the Kángra or Jamu hills; such a regiment would be a class-company regiment; the native officers of each company would ordinarily belong to the race, tribe, or sect from which the company was recruited. In the Northern army are a limited number of 'class regiments,' which are composed of men belonging to one caste or tribe. Such for instance, are the Goorkha corps, recruited entirely from the hardy short-statured highlanders of the Nepál hills, the Pioneer regiments, which consist exclusively of men of the Muzbi tribe, who in the early days of Sikh rule were despised outcasts, whose noblest calling was thieving, but who are now among the flower of the Northern army.'

Thus, what has been called 'the policy of water-tight compartments' has been applied throughout the Indian army. The object aimed at has been to prevent the growth of any dangerous identity of feeling from community of race, religion, caste, or local sympathies. In 1885, taking the total strength of the Bengal and Punjab army at about 59,000 men, nearly 37,000 were recruited from the Punjab and the districts on the north-western frontier, 15,000 from the North-Western Provinces, Oudh, and other countries, and 7,000 from Nepál and other districts of the Himálaya. The Mohammedans numbered more than 18,000, the great majority of them coming from the Punjab, the frontier districts, and the Delhi territory. Nearly one-half of the cavalry was Mohammedan. There were nearly 20,000 Sikhs or men belonging to other warlike classes of the Punjab and the frontier districts. About 3,000 Brahmans, 5,000 Rajputs, and 5,000 Hindus of other castes, came from Oudh and the North-Western Provinces, and belonged to the classes from which the

Bengal Sepoy army before the mutinies was mainly recruited. The remaining 7,000 men were chiefly Gúrkhas from Nepál, for fighting qualities one of the most valuable parts of the Native army, and hardly to be surpassed by any troops in the world. A large addition has lately been made to this important section of our army.

The figures that I have given show approximately the strength of the army in the years immediately preceding 1885. The altered position of Russia on the frontier of Afghanistan, and the apprehension of war, then rendered it necessary to reconsider the whole question of our military position. The result was a determination to increase both the European and Native army. The British force received an addition, in cavalry, artillery, and infantry, of about 11,000 officers and men, while the number of the Native troops was increased by 19,000. Five new battalions of Gúrkhas formed part of the addition to the infantry. Altogether, the army in India was increased by nearly 30,000 men. The total strength in 1887 was about 230,000 men of all arms, of whom about 73,000 were British. This is exclusive of the active reserve now in process of formation for the first time in India; it consists of men who have served with the colours in the Native army from five to twelve years, and it may ultimately attain large proportions.

Considering the great variety of the sources from which the Native army is recruited, there is much variety in its military qualities. But it would be difficult to find in any country finer fighting material than that furnished by Gúrkhas, Sikhs, and Patháns, and there is hardly any practical limit to the number of excellent troops that, in case of necessity, we could at short notice raise from the martial races of Northern India. At the present time there are probably not less than 50,000 or 60,000 men in the Native army equal to the troops of any European State, and fit to take their places in battle by the side of our 70,000 British soldiers.

In speaking of the additions to our military strength, I must not omit to mention the formation of Volunteer corps. There are already in India 23,000 Volunteers, nearly all British, effective and well-armed. The defensive value of this force can hardly be over-stated. If it had existed in 1857, many of the catastrophes of that time would have been prevented.

I must also notice the works undertaken for the defence of the north-western frontier. All points at which attack seems possible will soon be guarded by fortified positions, and connected with the railway system of India.

Regarding the armies of the Native States, I shall speak in another lecture.

I must now come to other subjects, and the first to which I shall refer is that of the financial administration.

I have explained that the final responsibility for the control of the finances of India has been placed by Parliament on the Secretary of State in Council. Although he cannot divest himself of this duty, the administration could not be carried on unless the authorities in India itself were invested with ample financial discretion. The Secretary of State has therefore delegated to the Government of India large but strictly defined powers, under which it can sanction fresh expenditure and create new offices of minor importance. This is for ordinary times, but in cases of emergency, when reference to England would cause delay injurious to the public interests, there is practically no limit to the financial powers which the Government of India exercises.

In the time of the East India Company a properly organised system of financial administration hardly existed. After the mutinies of 1857 an immense increase of expenditure took place; their suppression and the restoration of order involved an addition of more than 42,000,000*l.* to the public debt; there was hardly a branch of the administration which was not more or less reorganised, and demands arose for every sort of improvement. The revenues were insufficient, and the financial difficulties of the Government were serious. No reforms were more urgent than the establishment of an efficient system of public accounts and of strict financial control throughout India. This work was begun most efficiently in 1860 by Mr. James Wilson, the first financial member of the Governor-General's Council under the Crown, and it was afterwards actively continued and completed.

In carrying out these reforms it was perhaps inevitable at the outset that the central Government should retain in its own hands a larger measure of financial control than it would ultimately be expedient that it should exercise. In its anxiety to prevent extravagance it imposed rules of such stringency that no financial authority remained except its own. The whole of the revenues from all the provinces of British India were treated as belonging to a single fund, expenditure from which could be authorised by the Governor-General in Council alone. The provincial Governments were allowed no discretion in sanctioning fresh charges. They could order, without the approval of the Supreme Government, and without its knowledge, the adoption of measures vitally affecting the interests of millions of people, they could make changes in the system of administration that might involve serious consequences to the State, they could, for instance (and this is a case which actually occurred), alter the basis on which the assessment of the land revenue had been made, and largely reduce the income derived by the Government from the land, but they could carry out no improvements, great or small, for which the actual expenditure of money was required. If it became necessary to spend 20*l.* on a road between two local markets, to rebuild a stable that had tumbled down, or to entertain a menial servant on wages of 10*s.* a month, the matter had to be formally reported for the orders of the Government of India. No central authority could possibly possess the knowledge or find the time for the efficient performance of such functions throughout so vast a tract of country. The result was complete absence of real financial control, frequent wrangling between the supreme and provincial Governments, and interference by the former not only in financial but in administrative details with which the local authorities were alone competent to deal. Under these circumstances, as General Strachey wrote at the time, 'the distribution of the public income degenerated into something like a scramble, in which the most violent had the advantage, with very little attention to reason; as local economy brought no local advantage, the stimulus to avoid waste was reduced to a minimum, and as no local growth of the income led to local means of improvement, the interest in developing the public revenues was also brought down to the lowest level.'

In 1867 definite proposals were made by General Strachey for the reform of this system, and in 1871 they were adopted by Lord Mayo, who was then Viceroy. They were based on the principle that there was only one means by which local economy and efficient financial administration could be secured; that each provincial Government must be made responsible for the management of its own local finances; a certain income capable of expansion by good administration was in each case to be assigned, and, subject to some general conditions, the manner in which that income might be expended on the various branches of the public service was to be left to the provincial Government to determine.

The system of financial decentralisation inaugurated by Lord Mayo was largely developed during the viceroyalty of Lord Lytton, and a similar policy has been followed by his successors. The effect has been felt throughout the whole system of Indian administration. While no useful powers of financial control have been surrendered by the central Government, the provincial Governments have been freed from vexatious interference which weakened their authority and efficiency, and their relations towards the Government of India have become more harmonious. They are entrusted with the management of those branches of the revenue which depend for their productiveness on good administration, and they have now a direct and, so to speak, a personal interest in rendering that management as efficient as possible, because they know that a large portion of any increase of income that may be obtained will be at their disposal for useful expenditure within their own provinces.

The financial arrangements between the supreme and provincial Governments vary in detail, but are in each case similar in principle. Some branches of the public administration are obviously imperial rather than provincial in their nature. The Government of India must, for instance, be responsible for the military defence of the Empire, for payment of the interest on the Public debt, and for the charges to be met by the Home Government. Some departments, such as the Post Office, Telegraphs, and Mint, must be managed throughout India on a uniform system, and are more conveniently controlled by the central authority. Receipts and charges under the following heads are treated wholly or chiefly as imperial—Opium, Salt, Customs, Tributes from Native States, Post Office, Telegraph, Mint, the Public Debt, Railways, and Army Services. The revenues from Land, Stamps, Excise, Assessed Taxes, and other sources, are shared in varying proportions between the imperial and provincial Governments. In 1886-87, out of a total gross revenue of 77,300,000*l.*, the provincial Governments were entrusted with the expenditure of 21,000,000*l.* From this income they had to provide for the greater part of the expenditure incurred on the various departments of the civil administration intrusted to them; for the collection of the land revenue, for the courts of justice, jails, police, education, medical services, civil buildings and roads, and for a multitude of other charges.

An arrangement is made under which each provincial Government receives for a specified term, usually for five years, certain revenues from which it has to meet certain charges. The amount in each case is regulated by the estimated requirements of the province. Subject to general rules and conditions, the detailed management of the assigned revenues and services is left to the provincial Governments; they have the benefit of any economies that they can effect; and they receive either the whole or a share of any increase of revenue which may accrue during the period of the arrangements between them and the Government of India. There is under ordinary circumstances a steady growth in the productiveness of the revenues administered by the provincial Governments. For example, between 1882 and 1887 there was an increase under the heads of Land Revenue, Stamps, and Excise, of about 1,900,000*l.*, and of this sum the provincial Governments received about 900,000*l.* They have thus, if their management be good, an increasing income to meet increasing demands for material and administrative improvements. When the time for a new arrangement arrives, the imperial Government takes such share as it thinks fit to claim in the increase of the revenue which has accrued.

I have already quoted the opinion of Sir Henry Maine on these measures of decentralisation. I believe with him that no more important and successful reforms have been made in Indian administration since the transfer of the government to the Crown. But they have not reached their final limits. I have repeatedly insisted that the primary fact lying at the root of all knowledge about India is the immense diversity of the countries and peoples which it comprises, but it is a fact which centralisation of the Government ignores. While our empire was being gradually built up, concentration and centralisation in the administration were often inevitable. Now that it has been constituted on a firm and peaceful basis, decentralisation is an essential condition of progress. The time will come when, in regard to nearly all the ordinary matters of internal administration, each great province of India will be virtually almost a separate state. Not only will this result be obtained without the sacrifice of any part of that supreme authority of the central Government which it is essential to maintain, but we shall gain a largely increased measure of political security. No central Government, as Sir Henry Maine has observed, entrusted with the charge of such an unexampled undertaking as the rule of India, can escape serious occasional errors. 'Under a centralised Government there is danger of generalising a local mistake. Localised, a mistake can be connected with comparative ease; it becomes dangerous in proportion to the area of its diffusion.'[1]

It has been said truly that India has become one of the great powers of the world. A few figures will show what she has become financially, and they will illustrate the remarkable changes of the last fifty years.[2]

In 1840, the gross revenues of India were 21,000,000*l.*; in 1857, the year before the assumption of the Government by the Crown, they were 32,000,000*l.*; in 1886, they were 77,000,000*l.* In 1840 the total value of the

[1] *The Reign of Queen Victoria*—'*India*,' vol. i. p. 515.

[2] Except when reference is made to expenditure incurred in sterling in England, all the figures that follow represent rupees converted into pounds at the conventional rate of two shillings to the rupee. They are really tens of rupees, not pounds sterling. The symbol now officially adopted in the Indian accounts to represent ten rupees is Rx. I have retained the old system as being more intelligible to English readers. It will be understood that the exchange value of the sovereign varies with the gold price of silver. See page 117.

foreign trade was 20,000,000*l.*; in 1857 it was 55,000,000*l.*; in 1886 it was 163,000,000*l.* Equally remarkable figures might be given for the public expenditure. I will give one example only; in 1840 the gross expenditure on account of all classes of public works in India hardly exceeded 200,000*l.*; in 1857 it had risen to nearly 3,000,000*l.*; in 1886, including the cost of working the railways, it was about 30,000,000*l.*

It is true that few of these figures are really comparable, but I give them to illustrate the magnitude of the changes that have taken place in India. One fact is sufficient to show that it is only for this purpose that such comparisons can usefully be made. Since 1840, six great provinces, covering some 450,000 square miles, with a population of nearly 50,000,000, have been added to the empire.

The immense growth of the revenues has been in no degree due to increased taxation. If, without going back to a time with which no comparisons are possible, we compare the revenues of British India in 1886 with those of twenty-five years before, we shall find that under almost every head there has been a diminution rather than an increase in the public burdens. The land revenue, measuring it by its incidence on the area assessed, is everywhere lighter than it was. The salt duties were generally higher than they are now. Heavy customs duties were levied in the former period on every article of import and export, whereas now there is almost absolute freedom of trade.

I do not propose in these lectures to speak of the present financial position of India, of surpluses, deficits, and so forth. The amount of the public income and expenditure is affected in all countries by circumstances which are constantly changing. But I shall describe the principal sources from which the revenues are derived, and give some of the more important facts connected with Indian taxation, trade, and economical interests.

The gross annual revenues of British India at the present time amount to more than 77,000,000*l.*, but it would be a mistake to suppose that this sum represents the amount taken from the people by taxation. The State in India has resources which render heavy taxation unnecessary, and there is certainly no country in the world possessing a civilised Government in which the public burdens are so light. The taxation falling annually on the population of British India is less than 2*s.* per head. If we were to include the land revenue it would be about double that amount, but this would be no more reasonable than, in a similar calculation for our own country, to reckon as taxation a large proportion of the rent paid to private landholders.

In 1886–87, out of a gross income of 77,337,000*l.*, only 20,684,000*l.* was raised by taxes properly so called; 56,653,000*l.* was derived from other sources. If we compare these figures with the corresponding figures of the English revenues, we find that, in the latter case, in 1886–87, out of a total revenue of 90,000,000*l.*, 75,000,000*l.* was derived from taxation, and only 15,000,000*l.* from other sources. In England, taxation supplies five-sixths, and in India not much more than one-fourth of the public income. The difference is really greater, for the Indian figures include not only the receipts of the imperial Government, but those derived from provincial and local sources of revenue throughout India, excepting taxes raised in municipalities for the service of the towns.

The following table shows the actual gross revenues of India for 1886–87 under each of the principal heads:—

Sources of Revenue		Receipts, 1886–87	
		£	
Gross revenue derived from sources other than taxation	Land revenue	23,055,724	
	Opium	8,942,976	
	Forests	1,103,970	
	Tributes from Native States.	695,415	
	Interest	670,548	
	Post-office, Telegraph, Mint.	2,027,482	
	Receipts by civil departments and miscellaneous .	2,309,932	
	Railways	14,477,759	
	Irrigation works. . . .	1,656,705	
	Buildings and roads . .	727,574	
	Receipts by military departments	985,003	
			56,653,088
Gross revenue derived from taxation	Salt	6,657,644	
	Stamps	3,751,280	
	Excise	4,375,174	
	Provincial rates . . .	2,099,861	
	Customs	1,246,293	
	Assessed taxes	1,354,735	
	Registration	299,059	
			20,684,046
Total gross revenue . .		. .	77,337,184

Many of these receipts do not represent sources of net revenue. In the Indian accounts the gross receipts in every branch of the administration are entered, whether net revenue is yielded or not. For example, the Government lends money to Native States and to various public bodies, and receives from them payments of interest; these, amounting to nearly 700,000*l.*, are shown among the gross receipts; but on the other side of the account there is an entry of more than 4,000,000*l.* for interest on the ordinary public debt. So again, the Government received from railways and irrigation works more than 16,000,000*l.*, and this sum is shown as gross revenue, but the expenditure from revenue in the same year on those classes of works exceeded the receipts by nearly 2,000,000*l.* Under other heads, representing real sources of net revenue, the expenses of collection are shown on the other side of the account. Thus, for instance, more than 23,000,000*l.* is entered as the gross amount of the land revenue, but nearly 3,500,000*l.* appears under expenditure as charges of collection. There are other receipts called 'departmental,' but with one or two exceptions I need not refer to them, or to receipts under heads which do not show a net income. Setting off against expenditure receipts of this kind, and deducting from the gross revenues the charges of collection, the actual net revenue of British India in 1886–87 was 44,736,000*l.*

I shall now explain what are the great sources of revenue.

The most important of all is the Land revenue, which yields a gross amount of about 23,000,000*l.* a year.

From time immemorial the ruling power throughout India has been entitled to a share of the produce of every acre of land, and this share is the so-called land revenue.

Mr. Fawcett, in his 'Manual of Political Economy,' has described the land revenue of India in a passage which I cannot do better than quote :—

'The Government in India exercises over a great portion of the soil the same rights of property as those which an English landlord exercises over his own estate. The Government in India takes the place of individual landlords, and the cultivators of the soil rent their land from the Government instead of from private landholders. . . As far as the cultivators of the soil are concerned, it can be a matter of no consequence whatever to them whether they pay a land tax to the Government, or whether they pay rent to private landowners. Hence a land tax is no harder upon the cultivator; nor does this impost cause any loss to the rest of the community. It, therefore, follows that a land tax, so long as it does not exceed a rack-rent, cannot increase the price of products raised from the land, for those who grow the products would not sell them cheaper if they paid rent to a private landlord instead of paying the same amount to the Government in the form of a land tax. A land tax consequently differs from all other taxes, for it possesses the excellent quality of providing a large revenue for the State without diminishing the wealth of any class of the community. Those, therefore, are completely in error who quote the aggregate amount of taxation which is raised in India in order to prove how heavily the people of that country are taxed. At least 20,000,000*l.* per annum is obtained in India by the land tax, but it would be as unreasonable to consider this amount as a burden laid upon the people as it would be to consider that the whole rent which is paid to English landlords in this country is an impost levied on the cultivators of the soil.'[1]

Instead of giving opinions of my own to the same effect, I will make another quotation from Mr. J. S. Mill:—

'A large portion of the revenue of India consists of the rent of land. So far as this resource extends in any country, the public necessities of the country may be said to be provided for at no expense to the people at large. Where the original right of the State to the land of the country has been reserved, and its natural—but no more than its natural—rents made available to meet the public expenditure, the people may be said to be so far untaxed; because the Government only takes from them as a tax what they would otherwise have paid as rent to a private landlord. . . . It is, of course, essential that the demand of revenue should be kept within the limits of a fair rent. Under the native Governments, and in the earlier periods of our own, this limit was often exceeded. But, under

[1] *Manual of Political Economy*, 5th edit. p. 568.

the British rule, in every instance in which the fact of excessive assessment was proved by large outstanding balances and increased difficulty of realisation, the Government has, when the fact was ascertained, taken measures for reducing the assessment. The history of our government in India has been a continued series of reductions of taxation; and in all the improved systems of administration the object has been not merely to keep the Government demand within the limits of a fair rent, but to leave a large portion of the rent to the proprietors. . . Thus, by far the largest item in the public revenue of India is obtained virtually without taxation, because obtained by the mere interception of a payment which, if not made to the State for public uses, would generally be made to individuals for their private use.'[1]

In the last fifty years there has been a very large increase in the land revenue of British India. The gross amount received in 1836–37 was 12,300,000*l.*; in 1856–57 it was 18,000,000*l.*; in 1886–87 it was 23,000,000*l.*; but it must not be supposed that the burden on the land has become heavier. The truth is that the process, described by Mr. Mill as 'a continued series of reductions of taxation,' has gone on during this period without intermission. The increase of land revenue has been mainly due to the extension of the empire. Since 1840 there has been an addition of about 450,000 square miles of territory, with, taking no account of Upper Burma, 6,000,000*l.* of land revenue. In our older provinces the growth of the land revenue has been entirely the result of increase in the area of cultivation and in the value of agricultural produce, and in no instance has it been due to enhancement of the incidence of the Government demand. Thus (I am now quoting from Mr. Cunningham),

[1] *Memorandum of the Improvements in the Administration of India*, 1858.

'in Madras the area assessed increased from 9,750,000 acres in 1850 to 20,000,000 in 1875–76, and, though the land revenue is 1,000,000*l.* sterling higher, its incidence per acre is reduced by 4½*d.* on dry land and 5*s.* on irrigated land. Similarly, in Bombay, the assessed area has increased from 12,500,000 acres in 1856 to 20,300,000 in 1875–76, and an increase of 750,000*l.* in the land revenue has resulted, notwithstanding an average reduction of 4½*d.* per acre in the assessment. In the same manner, in the North-Western Provinces, where the land revenue is calculated on the supposed value of the rental, the share of the rent claimed by the Government has much decreased. . . . In the Punjab it is notorious that the land revenue is infinitely lighter than that in any previous period, and the fact is corroborated by the enormous increase in the price of land since it passed under our rule from the cruel rack-renting of the Sikh Government.'[1]

There has never, so far as our knowledge goes, been a Government in India that has taken so small a share in the profits of the soil as that taken by ourselves. This is true of every province of British India. Under all preceding Governments, and under Native Governments to this day, there has been, in the words of Mr. Thomason, 'no other limit to the demand upon the land than the power of the Government to enforce payment and the ability of the people to pay.'

Under the system laid down by Akbar, and carried into effect in the year 1582 by the famous settlement of Tódar Mal, the sovereign was held to be practising a wise moderation when he fixed his share of the gross produce of the land at 33 per cent., but this was much less than was ordinarily demanded. The Maráthas took at least one-half; and the same proportion was ordinarily assumed to be their proper share by the Governments that preceded us in Madras. The result of the minute

[1] *British India and its Rulers*, p. 141.

inquiries made towards the end of the last century showed that the Native rulers in Bengal usually took about 54 per cent. In the Punjab, when we first occupied the province, it was found that the share of the gross produce taken by the Sikh Government was from 40 to 50 per cent. Elphinstone, in his 'History of India,' thus sums up the facts in regard to the land revenue under Native Governments: 'The sovereign's full share is now reckoned at one-half. A country is reckoned moderately assessed if he only takes one-third;' and in one of his minutes, referring to the Deccan, he says that it seems to have been 'the original principle in all settlements for the Government to take half and leave half to the cultivator.'

Compare the foregoing facts with the following.

Instead of sweeping off the whole or the greater part of the surplus profit of the land, our Government never takes more than a fixed share, which falls at an average rate of from 3 per cent. to 8 per cent. of the gross outturn. In the Punjab, in tracts which are fertile and protected by irrigation, and in which the Sikh Government would have taken not less than 50 per cent., we take less than 17 per cent.; the average demand for the province is 5·6 per cent. In Bombay, the highest assessment on the most productive land is 16 per cent.; the average for the province is 7·6 per cent. Many of the Native States of Bombay have been surveyed and settled on the system adopted by our Government, and their rates are always 10 to 15 per cent. higher than in the British districts. In Madras, the average demand is now 6·3 per cent. In the North-Western Provinces, where the basis of the assessment is the rental of the land, and not the gross produce, our Government, at the beginning of this century, took 90 per cent. of the rent. We took the same proportion under the permanent settlement in Bengal. In the North-Western Provinces and Oudh the share of the State is now 50 per cent. of the rental, an amount estimated to be equivalent to 7·8 per cent. of the gross produce.[1]

In Bengal the incidence is much less, but this has been the result of special causes, to which I shall again refer.

Although the demands made upon the land by the British Government are much lighter than those of the Governments that preceded it, it must be remembered that the principles on which our demands have been regulated are altogether different from theirs, and comparisons between the two are sometimes misleading. While our policy has been to encourage the growth of private property in land, and to take for the State only a moderate share of the rental or produce, former Governments hardly recognised the existence of such property, and frequently took from the cultivator an amount as large as the full rack-rent which might have been taken by a private landlord, or the whole of the surplus profit after the expenses of cultivation had been defrayed. The cultivator was entitled to subsistence; everything else belonged to the State.[2] This is often the assumption in Native States at the present time. In the words of Mr. J. S.

[1] These figures, showing the proportions of the gross produce taken as revenue, are taken, for the most part, from the Report of the Indian Famine Commissioners.

[2] 'The following maxim is believed to express the ruling idea of the revenue system maintained under the Emperor Akbar:—"There shall be left for every man who cultivates his land as much as he requires for his own support till the next crop be reaped, and that of his family, and for seed. This much shall be left to him; what remains is land-tax, and shall go to the public treasury."'—Sir E. Buck's *Statistical Atlas of India*, p. 22.

Mill: 'Except during the occasional accident of a humane and vigorous local administration, the exactions had no practical limit but the inability of the peasant to pay more.' At the same time, when the peasant has no rights of property, and cultivates as a rent-paying tenant, it cannot always be assumed that he pays less under our system than he paid before, when there was no private landlord between him and the State.

An interesting investigation was made by the late Mr. Edward Thomas, in his 'Revenue Resources of the Moghul Empire,' into the question of the amount of the revenue derived from the land and other sources by the Moghul Emperors; but the materials which he was able to collect were very imperfect, and it is difficult to say what confidence should be placed in conclusions based upon them. The revenues doubtless reached their highest point under Aurangzeb. Mr. Thomas tells us that two manuscripts in the British Museum, copies apparently of official documents, give the land revenue of the empire for 1664–65 at 26,743,000*l.* and 24,056,000*l.* Bernier, about the same time, gave the amount as 22,593,000*l.*; his details for the various provinces differ greatly from those in the Museum manuscripts, and Bernier himself describes his list as 'ce mémoire que je ne crois pas trop exact ni véritable.' Towards the end of the seventeenth century a Venetian physician, Manucci, was employed at the Court of Aurangzeb, and an account of much that he learned there is to be found in Catrou's 'Histoire générale de l'Empire du Mogol' (Paris, 1702). A list is given, on Manucci's authority, of the amount of the land revenue in each province in 1697, when Aurangzeb's empire was much larger than it had been thirty years before. The total reaches the sum of 38,719,000*l.* Whether these figures represent the demand or the collections is not stated, but no doubt the former is intended. Three manuscripts in the India Office Library give the amount of Aurangzeb's land revenue at sums varying between 34,187,000*l.* and 34,641,000*l.*; the years to which they refer are not stated, and although the totals do not much differ, the discrepancies in the details are great.

Considering that the land revenue of the British Government amounts only to 23,000,000*l.*, drawn from a more extensive empire than that of Aurangzeb, the sums said to have been received or demanded from the land by the latter seem at first sight to deserve little credit. It seems to me, however, by no means impossible that even the largest amount mentioned may be approximately correct, because, as I have just explained, no comparisons are really possible between the land revenue of former Governments and our own. The 38,000,000*l.*, or whatever may have been the actual amount of Aurangzeb's revenue from land, included not only all that we now take as land revenue, but the greater part of the profit that we leave to private proprietors. For example, the rental of the landholders of Bengal is now probably not less than 20,000,000*l.*, of which only about 4,000,000*l.* is taken by the State. If a ruler like Aurangzeb were to take our place, nearly the whole sum would be claimed by him which is now intercepted by the zemindars.[1]

[1] The views above stated seem to me to accord with Manucci's remarks in the following passage. After detailing the revenues of Aurangzeb he says:—'On est étonné sans doute d'une si prodigieuse opulence, mais il faut considérer que tant de richesses n'entre dans les trésors du Mogol que pour en sortir tous les ans, du moins en partie, et pour couler une autre fois sur ses terres. La moitié de l'empire subsiste par les libéralités du prince, ou du moins elle est à ses gages. Outre ce grand nombre d'officiers et de

Although the land revenue of India is not derived from taxation, but is a portion of the rent or produce reserved by the State, in accordance with immemorial custom, the land is not entirely exempt from taxation. It is liable to certain rates which vary in the different provinces, but which are everywhere light. Deducting about 500,000*l.* shown under this head, but applied to payments for village services which have nothing to do with taxation, they yield about 2,500,000*l.* a year. They are mainly applied to local purposes, such as the construction and maintenance of roads, schools, hospitals, and dispensaries.

soldats qui ne vivent que de la paye, tous les paysans de la campagne, qui ne labourent que pour le souverain, sont nourris à ses frais, et presque tous les artisans des villes, qu'on fait travailler pour le Mogol, sont payés du trésor impérial. On conjecture assez quelle est la dépendance des sujets, et par conséquent, quelle est leur déférence pour leur maître.'

Although I see nothing incredible in the amount which Aurangzeb's land revenue is said to have reached, the evidence given by Mr. Thomas to support the opinion that the total revenue of the empire was 77,438,000*l.* seems to me quite insufficient. It is arrived at by doubling the amount of the land revenue, and is based on the following passage from Catrou's work. After enumerating the miscellaneous sources of revenue, he says, on Manucci's authority: 'Tout ce casuel de l'empire égale, à peu près, ou surpasse même, les immenses richesses que l'empereur perçoit des seuls fonds de terre de son domaine.' Another Italian traveller, Careri, writing in 1695, says: 'I was told that the Mogul receives from only his hereditary countries 80 crores of rupees (80,000,000*l.*) a year.' There is apparently no other authority, excepting these general statements, for the conclusion that the total revenues of Aurangzeb approached 80,000,000*l.*, and I cannot think that they deserve credence. This question of the amount of the revenues of the Moghul Emperors has been carefully considered by Sir W. Hunter. He abstains from giving any final judgment, but is clearly of opinion that the matter remains open to much doubt. As he has observed, it is probable that 'the purchasing power of silver, expressed in the staple food-grains of India, was two or three times greater than now.' He has also noticed that these conversions into sterling are made at the nominal rate of ten rupees to the pound, whereas the actual rate was then eight or nine rupees to the pound. Consequently, the figures given above, which profess to represent Aurangzeb's resources, would have to be considerably increased.—See Sir W. Hunter's *Imperial Gazetteer of India*, Art. 'India,' p. 298.

Next to the land revenue, the most productive source of the public income in India is Opium. It yielded in 1886–87 nearly 9,000,000*l.*, almost the whole of which was derived from opium exported to China.

More than one-half of this revenue is obtained from opium produced and manufactured in our own territories under a strict system of State monopoly; the rest is obtained from a customs duty levied on opium produced and manufactured in Native States and exported from Bombay.

In Bengal, Behár, the North-Western Provinces and Oudh, the cultivation of the poppy is not allowed except on the condition that the whole of the produce shall be sold to the Government. Notice is given every year that the Government will be prepared to purchase crude opium at a certain specified price. The price offered varies according to the quantity of opium required, and the area of the poppy crop varies with the inducement which this price holds out to the cultivator. The opium is manufactured at Government factories, and sold by auction in Calcutta to the highest bidders.

The poppy is also largely cultivated in the Native states of Central India. The British Government interferes in no way with the production or manufacture, but the opium cannot reach the sea without passing through our territories, and we levy a heavy duty on every chest of opium exported.

I do not propose to discuss the vexed question of the morality of the system under which the Indian Government derives revenue from the consumption of opium in China. I shall merely state the conclusions to which my own study of the subject has led me.[1]

The first thing to be learned is this, that, although the finest opium consumed in China is Indian, China does not depend on India for her supply. It is a common but complete mistake to suppose that the prohibition of the export of opium from India would have the result of putting a stop to opium-smoking in China. If the supply of opium from India were to cease, the richer classes in China would be deprived of a luxury which they prize, but, so far as the general population was concerned, the consumption of opium would remain much as it was before. Long before Indian opium went to China, opium was consumed there; no one can say how long the custom of opium-smoking has prevailed. A single province of Western China produces more opium than the whole of India; the cultivation is carried on, so far as the Chinese Government is concerned, with perfect freedom, and it is constantly and rapidly increasing. The population of China practically depends for its supply on the opium produced at home.

If, therefore, all that is said about the ruin of the Chinese by opium were true, the prohibition of imports from India would afford no remedy. But it is certainly not true. Excess in opium, so far as the individual consumer is concerned, may probably be as bad as excess in alcohol; it cannot be worse, and its effects upon his neighbours are comparatively harmless. Used in moderation, as the vast majority of Chinese smokers use it, there is no reason to believe that opium is

[1] A more complete account of the opium revenue is given in *The Finances and Public Works of India*, by Sir John and General Richard Strachey.

injurious. I do not doubt that the people of France, and Italy, and Spain are, on the whole, better for their wine, and that the people of England and Germany are better for their beer. Neither do I doubt that, on the whole, the Chinese are better for their opium.

It is often said that the Chinese Government views the opium trade with dislike and desires its abolition. Whatever may once have been the case, it undoubtedly now desires that the trade should flourish, because it derives from duties on Indian opium a large and highly prized revenue. It has officially disclaimed any wish to see the imports from India diminished. Its real and reasonable object, for which it has long been striving, has been to obtain for itself a larger share of the profit derived by a foreign State from the consumption of opium by Chinese subjects.

For many years past an import duty has been levied by China on all opium brought from India or elsewhere. Apart from this duty, the amount of which is regulated by treaty, transit duties, and more or less irregular exactions, called *lekin*, have been levied upon opium at varying rates, and at various places, on its passage from the port of entry to its destination in the interior of the country. These duties were formerly collected by the provincial authorities, but the proportion that reached the imperial treasury was very uncertain. It was said that one-half of the amount went into the pockets of the collectors. The Chinese Government had long been anxious that a different system should be introduced, and it proposed to our Government that, in addition to the ordinary import duty, a supplementary duty, at a uniform rate, should be levied, in lieu of *lekin*, when the opium was imported. They proposed to issue to purchasers, for opium on which the whole of these duties had been paid, certificates which would protect the drug from all other demands in its progress from the port of entry to the interior. This arrangement was accepted by our Government, and, as one of the provisions of the Chefoo Convention, it came into force in February 1887. Opium, instead of being liable to a fixed duty of 30 taels [1] per chest, with a further indefinite liability for *lekin*, now pays altogether 120 taels per chest, the whole of which is collected by the Chinese Customs authorities and goes directly into the imperial treasury.

If the anticipations of the Chinese Government are fulfilled it will receive a large increase of revenue. The financial results to India can only be shown by experience; but if there should be a loss of revenue, which may not improbably happen, it will still be true that it was right and politic on the part of our Government to receive in a liberal spirit the reasonable representations of China.

In those parts of India where opium intended for export to China is produced, little or no opium is consumed. In the Punjab, however, there has always been a large consumption of opium, chiefly in the form of a decoction of poppy-heads called *post.* Its use is general among the Sikhs, who are prevented by religious prejudices from smoking tobacco. They are physically the finest race in India, and it would be difficult to find in any part of the world a more manly and more vigorous people.

1,104,000*l.* was received in 1886–87 under the head of Forests. This revenue is derived from the sale of

[1] The value of the tael in English money varies according to the relative price of silver and gold. Its value in 1887 was about 4*s.* 10*d.*

timber and other produce from the Government forests; but the greater part of it is spent on forest conservancy and other charges, and the net income was only 383,000*l.* Before the transfer of the Government to the Crown, practically nothing had been done towards the preservation of the forests of India, which are very extensive and valuable, and their destruction was rapidly going on. In 1861 a separate Forest department was created. Up to 1885 about 50,000 square miles of forests had been demarcated, and strictly reserved for the benefit of the State, under the management of officers who have received special scientific instruction in forestry in Europe. The creation and development of this department, for the protection of a valuable source of the public wealth, must be counted among the important reforms of modern times in India.

The Tributes and contributions from Native States are fixed by treaties, and yield nearly 700,000*l.* a year. They are chiefly paid for the maintenance of troops locally required. The Government of India is responsible for the preservation of peace throughout the whole of India, and the contributions that it receives from the Native States are an insignificant return for the services that it renders.

The revenue yielded by the Post Office and Telegraphs is slightly exceeded by the expenditure. The Government has not aimed at making a profit from the Post Office. The receipts have increased from 177,000*l.* in 1856–57 to 1,154,000*l.* in 1886–87, but they have been largely devoted to the improvement of the postal service. There is no country where the rates of postage are so low, or where the Post Office is better managed. The number of letters, newspapers, and parcels passing through the post was 38,000,000 in

1856 and 239,000,000 in 1886. There could hardly be a more striking illustration of the progress of the country.

The construction of telegraph lines was commenced in 1850. In 1886 there were 82,000 miles of wire in India, and more than 2,000,000 messages were delivered. The net receipts from the telegraphs now give a fair return on the capital expended in their construction.

LECTURE IV.

TAXATION IN INDIA—FOREIGN TRADE—HOME CHARGES.

REVENUE DERIVED FROM TAXATION—THE SALT TAX—SOURCES OF SUPPLY OF SALT—FORMER SYSTEM OF LEVYING DUTIES—THE INLAND CUSTOMS LINE—ITS ABOLITION—THE PRESENT SYSTEM—RESULTS OF RECENT REFORMS—THE POLICY THAT SHOULD BE FOLLOWED—THE STAMP REVENUE—EXCISE ON SPIRITS AND DRUGS—MISREPRESENTATIONS ON THIS SUBJECT—PRINCIPLES OF EXCISE ADMINISTRATION—ASSESSED TAXES—THE INCOME TAX—REGISTRATION—CUSTOMS DUTIES—THE DUTIES ON COTTON GOODS—FREE TRADE IN INDIA—ABOLITION OF IMPORT DUTIES—THE RESULTS—EFFECT OF REMISSION OF DUTIES ON COTTON GOODS—EXPORT DUTY ON RICE—THE GROWTH OF THE FOREIGN TRADE OF INDIA—CONDITIONS UNDER WHICH THE TRADE IS CARRIED ON—IMPORTS OF GOLD AND SILVER—EXCESS OF EXPORTS OVER IMPORTS—CHARGES IN ENGLAND ON ACCOUNT OF INDIA—THE MANNER IN WHICH THESE CHARGES ARE MET—THE CURRENCY—FALL IN THE GOLD VALUE OF SILVER—THE LOSS BY EXCHANGE—SERIOUS CONSEQUENCES AND CAUSES FOR ANXIETY.

TAXES, properly so-called, yielded altogether in India, in 1886–87, a gross revenue of 20,684,000*l*. Among them the most important is the tax on salt. It gave in 1886–87 a gross amount of 6,658,000*l*.

The system under which the Salt duties are levied varies in different parts of India. Bengal and Assam, with more than 70,000,000 of people, obtain nearly the whole of their salt from England. There are hardly any local sources of supply for these provinces except the sea, but on the greater part of the coasts of Bengal salt cannot be made cheaply by solar evaporation; the climate is damp, and the difficulty is increased by the vast quantity of fresh water brought to the Bay of Bengal by the Ganges and Bráhmaputra. There are no protective duties, and the locally produced salt cannot compete with that imported from Cheshire. Owing to the fact that the exports from India are largely in excess of the imports, freights to India are very low, and salt costs little to import. The tax in Bengal is levied as an import duty at the port of entry.

In Madras and Bombay, on the other hand, although the facilities for communication with England are equally great, English salt does not compete with that produced locally, for the manufacture of salt from the sea is an easy process. The duty in Madras is collected partly under an excise system, and partly under a monopoly, by which all salt is manufactured for the Government and sold at a price which gives a profit equal to the duty. In Bombay the duty is levied as an excise.

The North-Western Provinces and Oudh, and parts of the Central Provinces and of the Punjab, derive their chief supply of salt from lakes or springs impregnated with salt in the Native States of Rájputána. The salt is prepared by solar evaporation at works controlled by the Government. Further north, the greater part of the Punjab is supplied from rock-salt, which is found in inexhaustible quantities. The salt is extracted and sold by the Government, the duty being included in the selling price.

Until 1882–83, the amount of duty varied in different provinces. It was higher in the Bengal Presidency than in Madras and Bombay. So long as there were no railways and few roads, the inconvenience of these different rates was not much felt; but as communication improved, it became more and more impossible to prevent salt taxed at a lower rate from coming into provinces where the tax was higher, and a system gradually grew up in India to which, for extraordinary folly, it would be hard to find a parallel.[1]

In 1843 the establishment of a customs line was commenced, and by 1870 it had extended itself across the whole of India from a point north of Attock, on the Indus, to the Máhánadi, on the borders of Madras, a distance of 2,500 miles. Along the greater part of its length it was a huge material barrier, which Sir M. E. Grant Duff, speaking from personal observation, said could be compared to nothing else in the world except the Great Wall of China; it consisted principally of an immense impenetrable hedge of thorny trees and bushes, supplemented by stone walls and ditches, across which no human being or beast of burden or vehicle could pass without being subjected to detention and search. If this customs line had been put down in Europe, it would have stretched, in 1869, from Moscow to Gibraltar; as late as 1879, when it was abolished, it was still more than 1,500 miles long, a distance as great as that from London to Constantinople. It was guarded by an army of officers and men, some 12,000 in number, divided into beats which were constantly patrolled by night and day, and watched from 1,700 guard-posts. It may easily be imagined what obstruction to trade, what abuses and oppression, what annoyance and harassment to individuals, took place. The interference was not confined to the traffic passing into the British provinces, for an export duty of a most objectionable character, not abolished until 1878, was levied on all sugar passing from British territory into Native States, and sometimes from one part of British territory to

[1] The following account of the Inland Customs line is taken from *The Finances and Public Works of India.*

another. Obstructions were offered to the traffic from whichever direction it came.

It was impossible, without great loss of revenue, to get rid of this inland customs line while the salt tax was levied at different rates in different provinces, and until we had the means of controlling the manufacture and taxation of salt produced in Native States and brought into our own territories.

The first steps towards a better system were taken by the Government of Lord Mayo in 1869. An amicable arrangement was made with the Native States of Jaipur and Jodhpur, under which we acquired the sole right of manufacturing salt at the Sámbhar salt lake, the chief of the salt sources of Rájputána, and from which a large proportion of the supply of Northern India is derived. The same policy was followed during Lord Northbrook's administration, and an important reduction was made in the length of the customs line in its southern section, where it passed through British territory only.

At last, in 1879, under the Government of Lord Lytton, this system, which had been one of the opprobria of British rule, finally disappeared. In 1878, Lord Lytton declared the maintenance of the inland customs line to be a great political and commercial scandal, and it will always be a cause of satisfaction to me that I was able to help him in getting rid of it.

The abolition of the customs line was rendered possible by two measures. By the first the duties throughout India, although not quite equalised, were made to approximate so nearly that salt could not profitably be taken from one province to another. By the second measure agreements were entered into with the Native States of Rájputána, under which the

British Government obtained leases and control of all the more important sources of salt manufacture. Liberal compensation was given to the chiefs of the Native States for loss of revenue.

The equalisation of the salt duties throughout India, at a reduced rate, was completed in 1882 under the Government of Lord Ripon. The duty was then fixed at two rupees per maund (82 lbs.), or about four shillings per cwt. This is equivalent to an annual tax of about fivepence per head of the population.[1]

This is the only obligatory tax which falls upon the masses of the population in India, and, although they are very poor, it cannot be said that the additional price which they have to pay for their salt is felt as an appreciable burden. The case was different twenty or thirty years ago, when high duties and, still more, the absence of means of communication made it difficult for the poorer classes in some parts of India to obtain a sufficient supply of salt. In 1877 the Government declared that its policy would aim at giving to the people throughout India the means of obtaining an unlimited supply of salt at the cheapest possible cost; that the interests of the people and of the public revenue are identical, and that the only just and wise system is to levy a low rate of duty on an unrestricted consumption. This principle has been acted upon ever since with satisfactory results. The consumption has steadily increased, and the combined effect of reduction of duty, the extension of railways, and the general improvement in the means of communication, has been to make salt cheaper in the greater part of India than it had

[1] In January 1888, in consequence of financial pressure, the duty was raised to two and a half rupees per maund.

ever been before, while the revenue is larger than before the reform of the old system was begun.

Unfortunately the temptation is always great in times of financial pressure to have recourse to the easy expedient of increasing the duty on salt. The vast majority of the people throughout India are probably unaware even of the existence of the tax; but it is on them—that is, on the poorer classes—that the actual burden falls. The masses remain unmoved and silent, while the small and wealthier minority, who alone can make their voices heard, give loud approval to measures which impose no appreciable obligation upon themselves. No efforts consistent with financial prudence should be spared to reduce to the utmost the price of salt throughout India, and thereby to stimulate consumption. A time of extreme political emergency may come when a large and immediate addition to the revenues is necessary, and when fresh direct and unpopular taxation cannot wisely be imposed. Under such circumstances, the tax on salt might without serious objection be temporarily increased, for the Government would thus be able to obtain, by a small increase of duty, large additional resources, almost without the knowledge of the people. Salt ought to be looked on as the last great financial reserve, to be drawn upon in case of urgent necessity, but not otherwise.

Under existing conditions in India a moderate tax upon salt is open in principle to little objection. The reasons for this conclusion were summed up by the Duke of Argyll, when Secretary of State for India, in a passage which I cannot do better than quote:—

'On all grounds of general principles, salt is a perfectly legitimate subject of taxation. It is impossible in any country to reach the masses of the population by direct taxes. If they are to contribute at all to the expenditure of the State, it must be through taxes levied upon some articles of universal consumption. If such taxes are fairly adjusted, a large revenue can thus be raised, not only with less consciousness on the part of the people, but with less real hardship upon them than in any other way whatever. There is no other article in India answering this description upon which any tax is levied. It appears to be the only one which, at present, in that country can occupy the place which is held in our own financial system by the great articles of consumption from which a large part of the imperial revenue is derived. I am of opinion, therefore, that the salt tax in India must continue to be regarded as a legitimate and important branch of the public revenue. It is the duty, however, of the Government to see that such taxes are not so heavy as to bear unjustly on the poor by amounting to a very large percentage upon their necessary expenditure. The best test whether an indirect tax is open to this objection is to be found in its effect upon consumption.'[1]

The Stamp revenue is derived partly from stamps on commercial papers, and partly from fees, levied by means of stamps, on proceedings in the judicial courts. It amounted in 1886–87 to 3,751,000*l.*, of which more than 1,000,000*l.* was derived from commercial stamps, and about 2,500,000*l.* from court fees.

The revenue under the head of Excise is derived from duties on spirits and intoxicating drugs. The people of India generally are extremely abstemious; the consumption of spirits is for the most part confined to the lower classes, but even among them there is, in the words of the Government of India, 'a condition of things which, if it existed in England, would be regarded almost as a millennium of temperance. Drunkenness in the English sense of the term hardly exists in India.' There has been a large and steady increase in the excise revenue. In 1870 it was less than 2,250,000*l.*; in 1880

[1] Despatch to Government of India, January 21, 1869.

it was 2,840,000*l.*; and it was 4,375,000*l.* in 1886–87. Benevolent people in this country, carried away by the enthusiasm of ignorance, have found in such figures as these the opportunity for indignant protest against the wickedness of a Government which, with the object of obtaining revenue, affords, in defiance of native opinion, constantly increasing facilities for drinking. There is no foundation for such assertions. The sole cause of the increase of revenue has been improved administration and the suppression of illicit distillation and sale. I quote from a despatch of the Government of India the following summary of the facts:—

'Few subjects have of recent years obtained greater attention at the hands of the Government than questions relating to excise administration. In each of the three larger Governments the excise system has, within the last six or seven years, been completely examined in its operation and in its effects. These examinations have been made under the instructions of the local Governments and in direct communication with us, and the principles on which they have been based, and which have been unanimously accepted by all the authorities concerned, have been these: that liquor should be taxed and consumption restricted, as far as it is possible to do so without imposing positive hardships upon the people and driving them to illicit manufacture. The facts now placed on record show that in this policy the local Governments have been completely successful, and that the great increase of excise revenue in recent years, which has been taken as evidence of the spread of drinking habits, really represents a much smaller consumption of liquor, and an infinitely better regulated consumption, than the smaller revenue of former years. . . .

'There is not the slightest reason to imagine that in the days of native administration the Indian populations refrained from indulgence in a practice which it requires the constant watchfulness of the British administration to prevent. Under the Mohammedan administration which immediately preceded the British rule, the facilities for drinking were very much greater than have ever since existed, and the prevalence of drinking habits was quite as much complained of. The reports of the Chief Commissioners of the Central Provinces and of Assam prove that it is precisely those tribes and races which have been the least accessible to the influences of British rule which are most addicted to intoxicating drinks and drugs. We have at the present day ample evidence on this very point in the conflict between the British and Native excise systems wherever British and Native territory meet. These are the only points where the British system breaks down, because the restrictions imposed upon manufacture and consumption on the British side of such frontiers are not met by equivalent restrictions on the other side. One of the main difficulties which the excise authorities have to meet is that of excluding from British territory the more lightly taxed and more easily obtained spirit available in Native States.

'It is only by strong preventive establishments that illicit distillation can be prevented. The great increase in the revenue does not mark the extension of drinking habits, but is the result of a great and general increase in the rate of tax, which it would have been entirely impossible to realise but for the great improvement in preventive measures which has accompanied it. In fact, the ability of the Excise department to prevent illicit distillation is the only limit which is imposed in practice to increase in the rate of taxation.'

There is hardly a province in British India in which, during the last ten years, there has not been a decrease in the number of liquor shops and in the consumption of liquors.

The next head of Indian taxation is that of Provincial Rates, which I have already mentioned.

In 1859, the year after the transfer of the government to the Crown, Mr. James Wilson was appointed financial member of the Governor-General's Council. The heavy charges incurred in the suppression of the mutinies and the reorganisation of the administration rendered the imposition of fresh taxation necessary, and in 1860, under the advice of Mr. Wilson, a general Income tax was imposed. It was levied at the rate of 4 per cent., or rather more than 9½*d.* in the pound, on all incomes of 500 rupees and upwards, and at half that rate on incomes between 200 and 500 rupees. It yielded in 1861–62 a net revenue of nearly 2,000,000*l.* Many changes have from time to time been made in the system thus introduced. The direct taxation of incomes has several times been wholly or partially abolished, and several times it has been restored. Sometimes there has been a general tax upon all incomes, sometimes a licence tax on professions and trades, and sometimes on trades only. In 1877–78 the question of direct taxation was forced into prominence by the necessity of making provision against the financial dangers caused by the liability to famine to which the greater part of India is from time to time subject. Taxes which were called licence taxes, but which were really in the nature of taxes on income, were then imposed throughout India on the commercial and trading classes, and additional rates were placed on the land in some of the provinces. In 1886 a further step was taken. An Act was then passed imposing a tax on all incomes derived from sources other than agriculture. The rates already levied on land remained unaltered, and the licence taxes were removed. This Act affects no income below 500 rupees; on incomes of 2,000 rupees and upwards, it falls at the rate of 5 pies in the rupee, or about 6¼*d.* in the pound; and on incomes between 500 and 2,000 rupees at the rate of 4 pies in the rupee, or 5*d.* in the pound. The poorer classes are not touched. An income of 50*l.* a year seems very small to us in Europe, but to a native of India, in his own country, it is almost as large an income as 500*l.* would be here. I hope it may now be assumed, after many years of contest, that an income tax has been finally accepted as a permanent source of revenue in India. The amount yielded by the income tax in 1886-87 was 1,355,000*l.*

There is no country where a general tax upon incomes is more just than in India; but there has been much difficulty in imposing and maintaining it, because it has been opposed by the richest and most powerful classes, who alone can make their voices heard. It has long been a reproach to our administration that they have borne no fair proportion of the public burdens. The official classes, in the absence of direct taxation, contribute almost nothing. The mercantile and professional classes derive, from the security which they enjoy, greater benefits from our government than any other part of the community, but they have paid almost nothing for its support, except when direct taxation has been imposed upon them. Even the land, although it provides so large a portion of the public revenues, sometimes fails to contribute anything like an adequate amount; the most notorious example of this fact is seen in Bengal, where the zemindars, the richest class in the richest province of the empire, not only, in consequence of the mistakes of the last century, pay an altogether insufficient sum as land revenue, but remain in great measure exempt from taxation. Much has been said about the unpopularity of an income tax in India. It is undoubtedly disliked by those who have to pay it; but out of the 200,000,000 people in British India, less than 300,000 are liable to the tax, and no such term as unpopular can reasonably be applied to it. I do not undervalue the fact that the small minority on which the income tax falls is politically the most influential section of the whole community, but its discontent is a lesser evil than the injustice of allowing it almost entirely to escape taxation.

The revenue under the head of Registration is not very important in amount. It is derived from fees levied on instruments brought for registration; in some cases, when immovable property above a certain value is affected, the registration of documents is obligatory, in other cases it is optional.

I have gone through all the heads of taxation except Customs. I propose to give in some detail the history of late legislation on this subject, because a nearer approach to complete freedom of trade has been made in India than in almost any other country, and the results have been extremely important.

Until 1860 nearly everything imported into India was taxed at the rate of 10 per cent. *ad valorem.* On some articles the rate was much higher. Almost everything exported paid a duty of 3 per cent. In 1864, the general rate of duty on imports was reduced to 7½ per cent., and in 1875, under the Government of Lord Northbrook, to 5 per cent. Many exemptions from export duty were made from time to time, and in 1875 the only exports still taxed were rice, indigo, and lac.

The application to the Indian customs tariff of free trade principles might have been long delayed but for the fortunate accident that the interests of a great British industry were affected. Cotton goods were among the articles on which import duties were imposed. The English manufacturers complained loudly that the practical result was to levy a protective duty to their detriment in favour of cotton manufactures rapidly growing up in India. After a long and acrimonious discussion, the question at issue so far as the principles at stake were concerned, was decided on May 31, 1876, in a despatch to the Government of India from the Marquis of Salisbury, who was then Secretary of State for India. He showed that there was no conflict between the interests of India and of England, and that while the abolition of these duties would give legitimate relief to a great British industry, it was a measure still more urgently required in the interests of India. He said that while the duties had the effect of checking the import of British manufactures, they were at the same time exposing to future injury an Indian industry which it was of the first importance should rest upon sound foundations, which there was every reason to believe would rapidly increase, and which ought not to be allowed to grow up under influences which experience had shown must be injurious to its healthy and natural development. 'Whether (he wrote) the question be regarded as it affects the consumer, the producer, or the revenue, I am of opinion that the interests of India imperatively require the timely removal of a tax which is at once wrong in principle, injurious in its practical effect, and self-destructive in its operation.'

In the following year (July 11, 1877), a resolution was adopted by the House of Commons, without a division, that 'the duties now levied upon cotton manufactures imported into India, being protective in their nature, are contrary to sound commercial policy, and ought to be repealed without delay so soon as the financial condition of India will permit.'

Famine and other causes of financial difficulty prevented immediate action, but in the financial statement, March 1878, an important step not only towards the abolition of the duties on cotton goods, but towards the complete freedom of trade was announced. A declaration on the part of the Government of India was then made by myself of the principles which it was intended to carry out gradually as circumstances allowed :—

'It is not necessary to discuss the advantages to a country of free trade, and the disadvantage of protective duties. It is sufficient to say that these have been admitted for many years by the statesmen who, of whatever party, have guided the policy of the United Kingdom. . . . The principles on which the customs legislation of the United Kingdom has been based are now admitted axioms by all who recognise the theoretic advantages of free trade. These principles are, as regards imports :

'1. That no duty should exist which affords protection to native industry; and, as a corollary, that no duty should be applied to any article which can be produced at home without an equivalent duty of excise on the home production ; also, that no duty should be levied except for purely fiscal purposes.

'2. That, as far as possible, the raw materials of industry and articles contributing to production should be exempt from customs taxation.

'3. That duties should be applied only to articles which yield a revenue of sufficient importance to justify the interference with trade involved by the machinery of collection.

'As regards exports : That duties should be levied on those commodities only in which the exporting country has practically a monopoly of production.

'These principles are of general application, but in the case of India they possess a peculiar significance. India is a country of unbounded material resources, but her people are a poor people. Its characteristics are great power of production, but almost total absence of accumulated capital. On this account alone the prosperity of the country essentially depends on its being able to secure a large and favourable outlet for its surplus produce. But there is a special feature in the economic conditions of India which renders this a matter of yet more pressing, and even of vital importance. This is the fact that her connection with England, and the financial results of that connection, compel her to send to Europe every year about 20,000,000*l.*

sterling worth of her products without receiving in return any direct commercial equivalent. This excess of exports over imports . . . is really the return for the foreign capital, in its broadest sense, invested in India, including, under capital, not only money, but all advantages which have to be paid for, such as the intelligence, strength, and energy on which good administration and commercial prosperity depend.'

Excluding the duties levied on salt and liquors, which corresponded to the internal excise duties imposed on those articles, the Indian import duties yielded at that time (1876–77) 1,275,000*l.*; and 811,000*l.* of this was derived from cotton goods. Apart from the latter sum there remained, therefore, only 464,000*l.* levied from a multitude of articles, many of which yielded an insignificant revenue. It was clear that after the abolition of the duties on cotton goods it would be impossible to maintain the rest of the import tariff, and the intention was declared of getting rid of all import duties as soon as the state of the finances permitted. The first step was at once taken, in March 1878, by the remission of duties on a great number of minor articles, and on some of the coarser descriptions of manufactured cotton goods. In the following year, in March 1879, a more important measure was adopted by the resolution to remit the duty on all so-called grey cotton goods, except those of the finer qualities.

None of the previous steps towards the abolition of customs duties had been taken by the Government without difficulty, and this further measure, which it was obvious must lead before long to the destruction of the whole fabric of the customs tariff, met with much opposition. Popular opinion in India has always, in regard to questions of fiscal reform, been obstructive and ignorant; and the fact that the abolition of customs duties would be favourable to English manufacturers was enough, in the belief of many, to prove that the party purpose of obtaining political support in Lancashire, and not any care for the interests of India, was the real motive of the Government. This opposition, as I have said elsewhere, satisfied Lord Lytton that he must carry out the measure himself, or acquiesce in nothing being done at all. He believed that the essential interests of India required it, and he was not to be deterred by the imputation of base motives. The case was one of those which had either to be settled by a bold and enlightened Viceroy, or be allowed to drift on, to the serious discredit of the Government and injury of the country. The measure was held by Lord Lytton to be so necessary that it could not rightly be delayed, and it was carried into effect on March 13, 1879. This step was taken by Lord Lytton, in opposition to the opinion of a majority of his Council, but on the advice of Sir John Strachey, the financial member. It was approved, on April 4, 1879, by the House of Commons in the following resolution :—

> 'That the Indian import duty on cotton goods, being unjust alike to the Indian consumer and the English producer, ought to be abolished, and this House accepts the recent reduction in these duties as a step towards their total abolition, to which her Majesty's Government are pledged.'[1]

If the object in view had been the reduction and not the total abolition of import duties, a different method would have been adopted in dealing with these duties. The result of the plan actually followed was, as had been foreseen and desired, the speedy collapse of the whole fabric of the customs tariff. It soon

[1] *Finances and Public Works of India*, p. 287.

became obvious that it was not reasonable that certain cotton goods should be admitted free while others of almost the same character in everything but name remained liable to duty. Both manufacturers and importers complained, and, as the condition of the Indian finances had by this time become highly prosperous, it was impossible to justify the retention of the remaining duties on the finer qualities of goods; and, as I have already explained, when the cotton duties were given up, the rest of the import duties must go with them.

The history of these proceedings, and the forecast of the future which had become inevitable was summed up in the year 1881 in the following passage which I quote from the 'Finances and Public Works of India:'—

'The policy followed by the Government of India during the viceroyalty of Lord Lytton was one of absolute free trade, without reservation or qualification, and financial necessities alone prevented that policy from being carried out to the fullest extent. These proceedings have rendered inevitable the almost total abolition of customs duties, which of all Indian taxes are probably the worst. The cotton duties are virtually dead, and the other import duties cannot long survive them. How long a period may elapse before such a consummation is reached cannot be predicted; but the time is not very far distant when the ports of India will be thrown open freely to the commerce of the world.

'The people of India consume at present hardly any foreign luxuries; and cotton goods, which are among the necessaries and not among the luxuries of life, are the only articles of foreign production which come largely into their consumption. There is no present possibility of deriving a large customs revenue from anything else. . . . The reforms which have been described will be remembered hereafter in the economical history of India, and they will be set down among the honourable titles of Lord Lytton's and Lord Salisbury's administration. They will be remembered, not only because they were the first application to India of the principles of free trade, but also because they have been carried out in a manner which has made the adoption of any other policy virtually impossible in the future, and has rendered it almost a matter of certainty that, within a short period of time, the absolute freedom of Indian commerce will be accomplished.

'The authors of this book may be pardoned for recollecting the part they have taken in this work, and while on public grounds they must regret the almost universal opposition and disapproval in spite of which the policy they have so long maintained has been carried out, they cannot pretend that their personal satisfaction in the success which has been gained already, and in the greater future success which is inevitable, has been diminished by such considerations.

'Non tam portas intrare patentes
Quam fregisse juvat.'[1]

This was written early in 1881, and in March 1882 the anticipations of the authors were verified by the abolition of all the remaining import duties, on the advice of Sir Evelyn Baring, by the Government of Lord Ripon.

In January 1886 the financial member of the Governor-General's Council, Sir Auckland Colvin, gave, in the Legislative Council, the following summary of the results that followed :—

'The value of imports of manufactured goods, treasure, and Government imports apart, which in the ten years before 1878–79 averaged 35,000,000*l.*, was, in 1884–85, 53,000,000*l.* The average of the four years from 1878–79, when the first duties were remitted, to 1881-82, the year before the final abolition, was 47,000,000*l.*; the average of the three years from 1882–83 to 1884–85 has been 51,000,000*l.* The percentage of increase from 1878–79 to 1881–82 was 28; from 1878–79 to 1884–85

[1] *The Finances and Public Works of India*, by Sir John Strachey and Lieut.-General Richard Strachey.

it has been 45. If we remember that during this period prices have been steadily falling, and that these figures represent value, not quantities, the real increase will be much greater. I am not so foolish as to suppose that the great growth of our imports since 1878–79 is due solely or mainly to the abolition of the import duties. It is due to a variety of causes. It is partly due to the increase in our exports; it is partly due to the cause to which so much of the increase of our exports is due—namely, to the extension of our railways, and to the consequent improvement in the distribution and cheapening of commodities; it is due to the forcing of accumulated stocks, owing to the fall of prices in England, upon the Indian market; it is very largely due to the fall of prices in England; but, unquestionably, it is also partly due to the abolition of import duties.'

The first serious remission of duty on cotton manufactures was made in March 1879. In the four years preceding that date, the average annual value of the imports of cotton goods was 18,760,000*l.*; in the four years following the complete abolition of the duty, and ending with March 1886, it was 24,690,000*l.* In 1886–87 the value of cotton goods imported into India rose to 28,674,000*l.*, but in that year the trade is said to have been stimulated by causes of temporary operation. The prices of cotton goods have greatly fallen since the Indian import duties were remitted, and the increase in the quantities imported has been still more striking than the increase in value. In 1877–78, before the first remission of duty, the number of yards of cotton piece-goods imported into India was 1,358,700,000; in 1886–87 it was 2,155,400,000. English cotton goods constitute in value nearly one-half of the whole import trade of India.

Large as the increase of these imports has been, there is no doubt that it would have been larger but for the rapid growth in India, and especially in Bombay, of the manufacture of all but the finer qualities of cotton goods. In the ten years following 1876 the number of the Indian mills was nearly doubled. In 1877 they employed 1,289,000 spindles, and in 1886 this number had risen to 2,261,000. Not only do their products come largely into the local markets, but a very important export trade in cotton yarns and piece-goods has sprung up from India to China and other countries of Asia, and is fast increasing. The value of this trade rose from 1,000,000*l.* in 1876–77 to 4,200,000*l.* in 1886–87. In the former year China received its principal supplies of yarn from England; in the latter year the exports from India were much larger than those from England. Thus, the anticipations expressed by Lord Salisbury in 1876 have been fulfilled. Far from any injury having been caused to Indian manufacturers by the removal of protective duties, a great industry, the prosperity of which is to India a matter of extreme importance, has been rapidly growing up, exposed to none of the influences which threatened to interfere with its natural development. The advantage that the manufacturers of England have obtained has been great, but that obtained by India has been still greater.

With one exception, to which I shall presently refer, India has now done everything in her power to establish complete freedom of commercial intercourse between the two countries. England cannot say the same; she still maintains her duties on Indian tea and coffee, deriving from the former, at a rate of 50 per cent. on its value, more than 1,000,000*l.* sterling a year. India already supplies nearly one-half of the tea consumed in England.

I have spoken of the total abolition of duties on imports, but there are two articles on which they are still necessarily imposed, because the same articles are subject to an internal excise duty. One of them is salt, which is liable to an import duty at the same rate at which excise duty is levied; liquors are the other. Arms and ammunition are also subject to a duty which, on all the cheaper qualities, is prohibitory, but this is imposed for purely political reasons, it being inexpedient to allow the free import of arms into India.

So far as the import trade is concerned, the principles of free trade have been carried out in India more completely than in Great Britain or in any other country. Nothing more in this direction remains to be done; trade is absolutely free.[1] The same cannot be said of the exports. One export duty still remains, that on rice, chiefly grown in Burma. The revenue taken from the land in Burma is very small, and Burma and India had, for many years, something approaching to a monopoly of the supply of rice to Europe. This rendered the results less injurious than they would otherwise have been; but the tax is one that cannot, on economical grounds, be defended, and I fear that the reasons, such as they were, that were formerly given in its defence are no longer applicable. Since 1880 there has been no increase in the trade, and the fall of prices in Europe has made it possible to use other grains in place of rice in the manufacture of starch and for distillation. The only excuse for the maintenance of this tax has been its productiveness; during the five years ending with 1886, the average revenue yielded by it was about 700,000*l.* The duty is levied at the rate of 3 annas per Indian maund of 82 lbs., or about 4½*d.* per cwt.

[1] Unfortunately, these statements regarding the complete freedom of the import trade of India have ceased to be strictly accurate, for in January 1888 an import duty was imposed on petroleum.

The development in recent years of the foreign trade of India has been very great, and it affords a remarkable illustration of the increase in the material wealth of the country. In 1840 the total value of the seaborne trade was about 20,000,000*l.*; in 1857, the year before the transfer of the Government to the Crown, it was 55,000,000*l.* in 1876–77 it was 114,000,000*l.*; in 1886–87 it exceeded 163,000,000*l.* The foreign trade of India is now about equal to that of Great Britain fifty years ago. It is carried by 11,000 vessels, with a tonnage exceeding 7,000,000 tons, of which more than 6,000,000 are British. The tonnage employed in the foreign trade of Great Britain in 1840 was smaller than that employed in the trade of India at the present time. More than two-thirds of the whole trade of India passed in 1886–87 through the Suez Canal.

The expansion of trade has been more rapid in India during the last ten years than in any other country in the world. Between 1873 and 1884 the foreign trade of Great Britain was stationary, and even suffered a slight diminution; the trade of France and of Germany increased by about 7 per cent., and that of the United States by 21 per cent., while the increase was 60 per cent. in India.

As might be expected in a country easily accessible by sea alone, and shut out from the rest of Asia, along nearly the whole of its frontiers, by almost impassable mountains or other formidable obstacles, the trade carried by land from and into India is comparatively insignificant; nor, except perhaps on the side of Burma, can these conditions be expected to change, because, when physical difficulties are overcome, the countries beyond are scantily peopled and extremely poor.

The conditions under which the foreign trade of India is carried on are peculiar.

It is probable that out of the 200,000,000 people inhabiting British India not less than 180,000,000 are wholly or mainly dependent upon agriculture for support. Great manufacturing industries have no existence except when, to some extent, they have been established by European capital or under European influence.

There is hardly one of the principal agricultural staples of the world which is not or may not be produced in India. The products both of the temperate and tropical zone find, in one or more of the regions within her boundaries, the climate, soil, and all other conditions that they require. The power of cheap agricultural production in India, and her capacity for supplying to other countries food-stuffs and raw materials for manufacture, are practically unlimited, while the capacity of Europe to consume is, or may become, as large as that of India to produce.

Almost everything that the people of India desire to meet their simple requirements is produced at home. This is true even of the comparatively rich, to the great majority of whom the wants and luxuries of European life are unknown. It is not so much the general poverty of the people, as the peculiar and slowly changing character of the social and industrial conditions under which they live, that confines within narrow channels their demands for the productions of other countries. The only articles of general consumption which they can often obtain from abroad more cheaply than they can produce them, are clothing, simple metal manufactures, and metals as materials for their own industries. But there is one other important demand that cannot be supplied except from foreign sources. There has always been a flow into India of the precious metals, and centuries of disorder and oppression, the lessons of which are not soon forgotten, have led the people to invest their savings in what seems to them the safest form. Large quantities of gold and silver are thus constantly required for the purpose of hoarding. These hoards are often kept in the shape of personal ornaments. It often surprises Englishmen to see the profusion of gold and silver bangles and other jewellery with which the women even of the humbler classes deck themselves on occasions of festivity. In the five years ending with 1886–87, the value of the net imports of gold into India was more than 22,000,000*l.*, and that of the net imports of silver more than 44,000,000*l.* Although the greater part of the silver is converted into rupees, which constitute the basis of the metallic currency of India, the proportion of the silver imports which comes into circulation as money is much smaller than that which is hoarded. Gold is not a legal tender, nor is it used as money; there is virtually no coinage of gold, and the gold that is imported is hoarded.

Taking together the imports of merchandise and treasure, the value, at the present time, of the imports into India falls short of the value of the exports by about 17,000,000*l.* a year. For this excess India receives no direct commercial equivalent, but she receives the equivalent in another form.

English capital to a very large amount has been, and is still being, invested in India by the State and by private individuals in railways, irrigation works, and industrial enterprises, and interest on these investments has to be remitted to England. In addition to this, large sums are required in England for what are really investments for India of another kind. It is an inevitable consequence of the subjection of India that a portion of the cost of her Government should be paid in England. The maintenance of our dominion is essential in the interests of India herself, and, provided that she is not compelled to pay more than is really necessary to give her a thoroughly efficient Government, and in return for services actually rendered to her, she has no reason for complaint. The charges to be met in England are numerous: interest has to be paid on sterling debt incurred for India in this country; there are charges for the civil and military administration, furlough allowances, pensions, payments to the English Government for British troops, stores of every kind required for use in India, railway material, and so forth. The charges which the Secretary of State for India has to meet in England necessarily vary much from year to year. I will take a single year as an illustration. In 1884–85 the net expenditure in England was 16,250,000*l.* Of this sum, more than 2,500,000*l.* was for interest on ordinary debt; 4,750,000*l.* for interest on railway capital; 3,500,000*l.* for army charges; 1,500,000*l.* for civil pensions and leave allowances. The cost of the Secretary of State's administration, including all the establishments connected with the India Office and the Home Government of India, was about 200,000*l.* Stores of the value of more than 1,000,000*l.* were sent to India, and 2,500,000*l.* was spent in England as capital outlay on railway and irrigation works.

I must briefly notice the manner in which the payments due by India to England are made. The average amount by which the exports from India annually exceed the imports is about 17,000,000*l.* This sum has to be paid in coin in India for the produce exported. The process by which this is done is as follows.

The exporter from India sells his Indian produce in Europe; to pay for it in India he must either send silver to that country, or he must purchase bills on India in London. The chief demand for remittances of money from India is that of the Secretary of State; he draws bills on the Government treasuries in India, and it is mainly through these bills, which are paid in India out of the public revenues, that the merchant obtains the money that he requires in India, and the Secretary of State the money that he requires in England.

It is this process which is sometimes represented as one by which India is being constantly drained of her resources, and forced to pay a crushing tribute to England. Such assertions are unfounded. England receives nothing from India except in return for English services rendered or English capital expended. The payments made by India are the result and the evidence of the benefits which she derives from her connection with England. In place of constant anarchy, bloodshed, and rapine, we have given to her peace, order, and justice; and, if our Government were to cease, all the miseries from which she has been saved would inevitably and instantly return. Her payments in England are, as I have already said, nothing more than the return for the foreign capital in its broadest sense which is invested in India, including as capital not only money, but all advantages which have to be paid for, such as the intelligence, strength, and energy on which good administration and commercial prosperity depend. India derives from these investments benefits far outweighing in value the price that she has to pay, and it is through the excess of her exports over imports that she meets her liabilities.

The remittances on account of interest on English

capital invested in useful public works in India obviously involve no real charge to India, because such investments give to her a far larger profit than the interest sent away. Thus, for example, about 200,000,000*l.* has been spent in India on railways and irrigation works, and that sum has been provided partly by State loans or from revenue, and partly through companies receiving a guarantee of interest. The railways give a gross income of, say, 18,000,000*l.*, which is paid, in the first instance, into the Government treasuries; the greater portion of this sum is spent in India itself in wages and working expenses, and about 5,000,000*l.* is sent to England as interest on the capital expended. The persons who voluntarily pay the 18,000,000*l.* for the use of the railways are largely benefited by them, and would have had to pay much more had they been obliged to use ruder means of conveyance. It has been not unreasonably calculated that India now derives from her railways, conducted for the most part with English capital, a benefit of 50,000,000*l.* or 60,000,000*l.* a year. The payment of 5,000,000*l.* in England indicates, under such circumstances, no drain upon India, but a transaction which has conferred upon her enormous benefits. The same may be said of the smaller investments in tea, coffee, indigo, cotton mills, and other industries, mainly supported by British capital, the interest remitted on account of which implies the enrichment and not the impoverishment of the country.[1]

Gold being the standard of value in England, the payments which India has to make in this country must be made in gold. The standard of value in India is silver, and silver constitutes primarily the metallic currency. Gold is not a legal tender. The paper

[1] *Finances and Public Works of India*, pp. 315 and 104.

currency is established on a silver basis, notes being convertible on demand into silver coin.

Before 1871 the fluctuations in the value of silver in relation to gold were comparatively small. The exchange value of the Indian rupee was seldom much less than two shillings. In consequence, principally, of changes in the monetary systems of France and Germany, the causes, after 1871, no longer operated which had maintained throughout the world, at an almost uniform ratio, the value of silver to gold. Of these causes I do not propose to speak, but, after they ceased to act, depreciation followed in the value of silver in relation to gold. One of the consequences was that when India had to buy the gold required for the discharge of her obligations in England, she had to give for it an increased number of silver rupees, for gold in India and silver in England are merely articles of merchandise.

When the rupee was worth 2*s*., you could get 100*l*. in England for 1,000 rupees paid in India; in 1887, when the rupee was worth 1*s*. 5*d*., the same number of rupees produced 70*l*. 17*s*.

It is easy to understand what a serious matter this becomes when the Government of India has to purchase with its depreciated silver the large amount of gold required for meeting its liabilities in England. Every penny by which the rupee falls in value makes a difference of more than 1,000,000*l*. in the amount which India has now to pay within the year. Assuming that 14,000,000*l*. has to be provided annually in England to meet the Home charges, by means of remittances from India, the fall in the gold value of silver since 1871–72 involves an additional annual payment by India of 60,000,000 rupees. In other words, taxation to that amount is now being levied in India over and above what would have been necessary if these changes in the relative value of gold and silver had not taken place. Without going back so far as 1871–72, I may add that in the two years ending with March 1888 the charge thrown upon India on this account has increased by more than 20,000,000 rupees—or in conventional sterling 2,000,000*l.* It is, at the same time, so impossible to foresee the course of the exchanges that the Government cannot estimate, within a sum which may amount to many millions of rupees, the probable expenditure of the year. Its most careful anticipations are liable at any time to be completely upset by causes absolutely beyond its control. Such a condition of things is not only fatal to financial and to administrative efficiency and progress, but, if it be suffered to continue, it may lead to political consequences of the utmost gravity.

How, apart from the interests of the Government and the taxpayers, the economical interests of Indian producers and traders have been affected by these changes in the relative value of the precious metals, is a question into which I shall not enter. The last few years have been a period of much prosperity in India. Prices in India itself have hitherto hardly been affected, and, looking at what has occurred in Europe, we may believe that India has gained no small advantage from the comparative stability of her silver standard in relation to commodities other than gold. However this may be, there can be no question regarding the serious nature of the difficulties in which the Government is involved. No one can say where this continuous depreciation of silver is to stop, or when we shall see the end of the constantly recurring increase in the liabilities of the Government which follows as the inevitable result.

Recourse has already been had to taxes that are economically objectionable and which place fresh burdens upon the poorer classes, and we are perilously near the time in which we may be called on to adopt measures which may be politically dangerous or inexpedient. We have hitherto never introduced into India any strange and unpopular taxation affecting the masses of the population. If we were to change this policy, and were to impose heavy burdens of a kind hitherto unknown, our position might become very different to what it has been in the past. Our difficulties would be seriously increased if such burdens were to meet charges from which the Indian taxpayer derived no benefit, the nature of which he was unable to understand, and which were the direct result of the existence of a foreign dominion. But the truth is that, for such a state of things as that which exists, no readjustment of Indian taxation could afford a remedy. Even if India were a country like Great Britain, where the public revenues, in case of necessity, can almost at any moment be largely increased, she would find, while her standard of value differed from that of England, and while the gold value of silver continued to fall, no relief from pouring into the bottomless pit of her treasury constantly increasing supplies of silver.

I do not now propose to discuss any of the measures by which it has been suggested that relief might be afforded, but no language that I could use would be too strong to express my sense of the gravity of this question. There is no Indian authority who does not feel that, if it be allowed to drift on in the future as it has drifted in the past, we may some day find ourselves in a position not only of extreme financial difficulty but of political peril.

LECTURE V.

PUBLIC WORKS—THE PUBLIC DEBT—FAMINE INSURANCE.

MR. J. S. MILL ON THE DUTIES OF GOVERNMENTS—FAMINES IN INDIA—NECESSITY FOR ROADS, RAILWAYS, AND CANALS—ABSENCE OF ROADS UNDER NATIVE GOVERNMENTS—THEIR CONDITION UNDER THE EAST INDIA COMPANY—MEASURES TAKEN BY LORD DALHOUSIE—RAILWAY CONSTRUCTION—CREATION OF PUBLIC WORKS DEPARTMENT—PROGRESS UP TO 1887—IRRIGATION WORKS IN NORTHERN INDIA—CANALS OF MOHAMMEDAN SOVEREIGNS—THE GANGES AND OTHER CANALS—THEIR VALUE—IRRIGATION WORKS IN CENTRAL AND SOUTHERN INDIA AND IN SINDH—EXPENDITURE ON RAILWAYS AND IRRIGATION WORKS—THE MANNER OF PROVIDING FUNDS—GUARANTEED COMPANIES—POLICY OF BORROWING FOR INVESTMENT IN PUBLIC WORKS—BARRACKS AND HOSPITALS FOR BRITISH TROOPS—THE PUBLIC DEBT—DIVISION INTO ORDINARY AND PUBLIC WORKS DEBT—INCREASE OF DEBT OWING TO THE MUTINIES OF 1857—SUBSEQUENT DECREASE OF ORDINARY DEBT—INVESTMENTS OF THE GOVERNMENT IN RAILWAYS—RAILWAYS CONSTRUCTED BY GUARANTEED COMPANIES—THE FINANCIAL RESULTS OF THE POLICY OF BORROWING FOR PUBLIC WORKS—EXPENDITURE FROM REVENUE ON PUBLIC WORKS—INSURANCE AGAINST FAMINE—THE POLICY ADOPTED.

THE duties of the Government in India go far beyond those which we expect from a Government in countries like our own.

'In the particular circumstances of a given age or nation,' writes Mr. J. S. Mill, evidently with India especially in his mind, 'there is scarcely anything really important to the general interest which it may not be desirable, or even necessary, that the Government should take upon itself, not because private individuals cannot effectually perform it, but because they will not. At some times and places there will be no roads, docks, harbours, canals, works of irrigation, hospitals, schools, colleges, printing presses, unless the Government establishes them; the public being either too poor to command the necessary resources, or too little advanced in intelligence to appreciate the end, or not sufficiently practised in conjoint action to be capable of the means. This is true, more or less, of all countries inured to despotism, and particularly of those in which there is a very wide distance in civilisation between the people and the Government, as in those which have been conquered and are retained in subjection by a more energetic and more cultivated people.'[1]

But for our Government, hardly any of these requirements of civilised life would now be supplied in India, and in India there are special reasons which make the duty which thus falls upon the Government extraordinarily urgent.

Lord Macaulay did not speak too strongly when he said that, excepting only the inventions of the alphabet and the printing press, no inventions have done so much for the moral and intellectual progress of man as those which abridge distance and improve the means of communication.

Roads, railways, and canals, and other works and appliances which facilitate communication are necessary in India, not only for reasons universally applicable, but because they are required to save the people from calamities of which, in Europe at the present time, we have happily little experience. In India, the very existence of the people depends on the regular occurrence of the periodical rains; and when they fail through a wide tract of country, and, still worse, when they fail in successive years, the consequences are terrible. The greater part of India is liable periodically to this danger, but the country is so vast that it never happens that all parts of it suffer at the same time. Improvements in the economical condition of the people, and especially more diversity of occupation,

[1] *Principles of Political Economy*, vol. ii. p. 551.

can alone bring complete safeguards, and render general famine, in its extremest form, through a great tract of country, impossible. But this must be a long and gradual process. Meanwhile, it has been found by experience that although the entire prevention of famines, the most destructive of all calamities, is beyond the power of any Government, we can do much to mitigate them by removing obstacles which hinder commercial intercourse, and which diminish the productiveness of the land. The instruments by which we can do this are roads, railways, and canals. If, to give one illustration, you read the history of the great Indian famine of 1877–78, you will find ample proof of the incalculable value of such works. Without them, millions of people must have been left to perish without the possibility of relief.

It has only been within the last thirty or forty years, and especially since the transfer of the Government from the East India Company to the Crown, that we have at all recognised the duties which thus fall upon us. Before that time, India was, to a great extent, governed on principles that might have commended themselves to a beneficent Oriental ruler rather than to modern Englishmen. Even an enlightened man like Sir Charles Metcalfe could maintain, fifty years ago, that India required no roads; and in fact there were none. No Native prince ever made a road. Before the establishment of our Government there was not a road deserving the name in all India. Under the Native Governments that preceded us (I am quoting from the Indian Famine Commissioners), nothing more was done than to plant trees along each side of the track used as a road, and occasionally to throw up earth on it when it passed through a depression; such bridges as existed were made at the private expense of civil magnates or governors desirous of leaving a name behind them.

The graphic description which Lord Macaulay has given of the highways of England in the time of Charles II. is almost exactly applicable to those of India as I remember them in my youth. On the best lines of communication in England, he tells us, it was often hardly possible to distinguish the road at all, or to avoid losing one's way in the dark; the mud lay deep on the right and left, and only a narrow track of firm ground rose above the quagmire; it happened almost every day that coaches stuck fast until a team of cattle could be procured to tug them out of the slough; when the floods were out, passengers perished in the attempt to cross, or narrowly escaped being swept away, or had to wander across meadows, and ride to the saddle-skirts in water. The markets were often inaccessible during several months. 'The fruits of the earth were sometimes suffered to rot in one place, while in another place, distant only a few miles, the supply fell far short of the demand.' When Prince George of Denmark went to visit Petworth he was six hours in going nine miles, and it was necessary that a body of sturdy hinds should be on each side of his coach, in order to prop it up; an unfortunate courtier who was one of the party complained that during fourteen hours he never once alighted, except when his coach was overturned or stuck fast in the mud. All this, which I have borrowed from Lord Macaulay, is precisely what might have happened to Indian travellers, on the most frequented highways of the country, little more than thirty years ago, if they trusted themselves to wheeled vehicles. But practically, for people who could afford it, the only means by which a long journey could be accomplished was to be carried by men in a palanquin. A dák journey, as it was called, of a thousand miles was, to an Englishman at least, a process of misery which in these days can hardly be understood. I remember Lord Lawrence telling me that when he was a young man he was thought to have performed an extraordinary feat, because, travelling day and night, he reached Delhi a fortnight after leaving Calcutta, a journey for which, at the present time, twenty-four hours are thought too long. Throughout a great part of India it was only in the dry season that travelling was possible without extreme difficulty, and, during three or four months of the year, trade, excepting where water-carriage was available, came altogether to a standstill. As Colonel Chesney says in his 'Indian Polity:'

> 'The Court of Directors, until almost the termination of their existence, did not recognise the prosecution of public works as a necessary part of their policy. The construction of a road or canal was regarded by them, in their earlier days, much in the same light that a war would be—as an unavoidable evil, to be undertaken only when it could not be postponed any longer, and not, if possible, to be repeated.'

In 1836–37, the year preceding the Queen's accession, the total expenditure of the Government on roads and buildings in India was 81,000*l.*; and before 1850 the expenditure on all classes of public works, other than barracks, hospitals, and public offices, never reached 400,000*l.* in the year. In 1886–87 the outlay on railways and irrigation works, by the State or by companies guaranteed or subsidised by the Government, was 10,417,000*l.*, and on roads, public buildings, and other public works 5,202,000*l.* Speaking in 1858,

Mr. Bright said that in a single English county there were 'more travelable roads than in the whole of India, and the single city of Manchester, in the supply of its inhabitants with the single article of water, has spent a larger sum of money than the East India Company spent in the fourteen years from 1834 to 1848 in public works of every kind throughout the whole of its vast dominions.' I do not doubt that Mr. Bright's statement was substantially not far from correct.

In the last years of the East India Company, however, and especially during the vigorous Government of Lord Dalhousie, matters began rapidly to improve. Under the enlightened rule of Mr. Thomason, one of the wisest of Indian statesmen, great progress was made in the North-Western Provinces in the construction of metalled roads, and bridges, and other useful works; and his example was vigorously followed by his successor, Mr. John Colvin, and in the Punjab by the Lawrences. The grand trunk road from Calcutta to the North was rapidly pushed on. In 1854 the Ganges Canal, the greatest irrigation work in the world, was opened, though not completed.

People had become alive to the fact that without the material appliances which facilitate and cheapen the means of communication and production there could be no rapid progress either in the condition of the people or in the efficiency of the Government. In 1853 the necessity of constructing railways to connect the chief provinces and cities of India was declared by Lord Dalhousie in a Minute which laid the foundation of the existing system of railway communication. Three great lines were soon afterwards commenced: the East Indian Railway, from Calcutta towards the Northern Provinces; the Great Indian Peninsular Railway, and the Madras

Railway, starting respectively from Bombay and Madras, and running through Western and Southern India. These lines were constructed by private companies, under a guarantee from the Government of a minimum return of 5 per cent. on the capital expended.

In 1854 a separate Department of Public Works was for the first time created under the Government of India. In 1856–57 the outlay on public works, exclusive of the sums spent on railways by the guaranteed companies, had risen to nearly 2,250,000*l*.

The mutinies of 1857 brought fresh and the strongest possible proof of the necessity for improved means of communication. When peace was restored, and the Government was transferred to the Crown, the construction of public works went on with increased speed, and from that time to this there has been constant progress. Considering the vast extent of India and the fact that almost everything has been done by the Government, and almost nothing by unaided private enterprise, we may be well satisfied with the work that has been accomplished.

The contrast in this respect between the India of the present time and the India of thirty or forty years ago is astonishing. I have told you what it was formerly. Railways now connect the principal districts and cities; the great rivers are bridged; the country has been covered with roads, and there is no considerable town without its telegraph office. In March 1888, 14,383 miles of railway were open, and 2,487 more were under construction or sanctioned. In 1887 more than 95,000,000 passengers and more than 20,000,000 tons of goods were carried on the Indian railways. The time, however, is distant when it will cease to be true that the provision of increased means of communication is one of the chief duties that rest on the Government of India.

There is another result of the construction of railways in India that I must not omit to mention. They have increased, to a degree that is hardly calculable, our military strength; and so long as we retain our maritime supremacy, and the determination to maintain our empire, it will, we may reasonably hope, be impossible that any combination of hostile powers should dangerously threaten our dominion.

I must now refer to works of another kind, hardly second in importance, in some parts of India, to those of which I have been speaking.

In Northern India, even in good seasons, artificial irrigation is a necessity for the successful cultivation of many of the more valuable crops, and when there is a general failure of the periodical rains there is no other means by which drought and scarcity can be prevented. A large portion of Northern India is now protected by canals of greater magnitude than any that exist in other countries of the world. This is especially true of the tract in the North-Western Provinces called the Doáb, lying between the Ganges and Jumna, and containing more than 10,000,000 people. Owing to its geographical position, which made it the chief centre of the Moghul Empire, and to the industry of its numerous population, it has been for centuries one of the most important countries of India.

Long before our time some of the Mohammedan sovereigns had undertaken works on the western bank of the Jumna, with the object partly of irrigation, but still more with that of affording a supply of water to the city and imperial palaces of Delhi. A canal, the course of which is not very clearly known, was made by Firoz Toghlak, as far back as 1351 A.D., and more important works from the Jumna were constructed by Akbar and by Sháh Jehán in the sixteenth and seventeenth centuries. An elaborate system appears to have been in force for regulating the distribution of the water. The orders of Akbar provided 'that all parties, rich or poor, weak or strong, shall share alike;' and directed, for the comfort of travellers, 'that on both sides of the canal trees of every description, both for shade and blossom, shall be planted, so as to make it like the canal under the tree in Paradise, and that the sweet flavour of the rare fruits may reach the mouth of everyone, and from these luxuries a voice may go forth to travellers, calling them to rest in the cities, where their every want will be supplied.'[1] Not long after the death of Aurangzeb, when the empire was rapidly broken up, the canals of the Moghul sovereigns ceased to flow, and it was not until 1817, after these provinces had passed under the British Government, that their restoration and improvement was commenced. Later on, an examination of historical records led to a result which deserves to be noticed. Describing the excavations for the canal of Firoz Toghlak, the historian Ferishta mentions incidentally that the workpeople employed upon them found, near the foot of the hills, quantities of giants' bones. 'To minds familiar with discoveries in fossil geology the old chronicle had a gleam of significance,' and the investigations which followed led to the discovery, by Falconer and Cautley, of the gigantic fossil remains now in the British Museum.[2]

Little of the old irrigation works of our predecessors is retained in the existing canals. Practically, all of these

[1] *Calcutta Review*, 'Canals of Irrigation,' 1849. [2] *Ib.*

have been made by ourselves, and the often-repeated statement, prompted, I suppose, by that strange inclination to depreciate their own achievements which often besets Englishmen, that the old canals have been more profitable than those constructed by ourselves, has not the least foundation of truth.

The most important of these works are those which distribute the water of the Ganges through the districts of the Doáb. In the winter and spring, before the Ganges has been swollen by the melting of the snow in the Himálaya, and when water is urgently required for agricultural operations, nearly the whole visible stream of the great river at Hardwár, where it leaves the mountains, is thrown into an artificial channel. The works on the first twenty miles of its course are in a high degree remarkable, for the canal intersects the drainage of the lower Himálaya, and has to be carried across rivers which often become furious torrents, bringing down enormous floods. These obstacles have been overcome by various methods, with a skill of which our Indian engineers may well be proud. One torrent flows harmlessly in a broad artificial bed over the canal which runs below; over another, still more formidable, with a bed more than two miles wide, the canal, which is virtually the whole Ganges, is carried by an aqueduct. Some 200 miles lower down, the Ganges has again become a large river, and nearly all its water is again diverted into a second canal. The two canals together are capable of discharging nearly 10,000 cubic feet of water per second; the ordinary supply of each is more than double the volume of the Thames at Teddington in average weather, and this great body of water is distributed over the country by a number of smaller channels, for the irrigation of the land. The length of the main channels exceeds 1,000 miles, and there are more than 4,000 miles of distributories.

Three canals of smaller dimensions, but which in any other country would be looked on as works of great magnitude, distribute in a similar way nearly the whole of the water brought by the Jumna from the Himálaya. In Behár, the border province of the Bengal Lieutenant-Governorship, which in its physical character closely resembles the adjoining provinces of the north-west, another great canal is taken from the river Són.

There are other important irrigation canals in Orissa and in Bengal; but in the latter province irrigation is not ordinarily so essential as in countries farther north, where the climate is drier and the seasons are more precarious.

The following facts, which I take from the Report of the Indian Famine Commissioners, will give some idea of the value of the irrigation works of the North-Western Provinces:—

'Up to the end of 1877–78 the capital outlay on completed canals had been 4,346,000*l.* The area irrigated in that year was 1,461,000 acres, the value of the crops raised on which was estimated at 6,020,000*l.* Half the irrigated area was occupied by autumn crops, which, but for irrigation, must have been wholly lost, and it may be safely said that the wealth of these provinces was consequently increased by 3,000,000*l.*; so that three-fourths of the entire first cost of the works was thus repaid to the country in that single year.

In the Punjab, works of equal importance have been, or are being constructed, to utilise the waters of the Sutlej, the Rávi, and other rivers, and their value has been as great as in the North-Western Pro vinces.

'During the droughts of 1877–78,' Mr. Cunningham tells us, 'their benefits were extended to 1,333,000 acres, the greater portion of which would, but for canal irrigation, have been absolutely barren. During this period the land irrigated by the two principal canals produced good grain to the amount of 300,000 tons, worth 2,000,000*l.* sterling, and enough to keep 1,800,000 people for a year; while the non-food crops—sugar, dyes, spices, &c.—were reckoned to be worth another 1,000,000*l.* In other words, the value of the crops saved by the two canals in a single season was more than equal to the entire cost (2,260,000*l.*) of the completed system.'[1]

Different systems of irrigation prevail in other parts of India. In Central and Southern India, large tracts of country are dependent for their supply of water on lakes or reservoirs, known by the not very appropriate name of tanks. These are in some cases natural lakes, but oftener they have been formed by the construction of dams of masonry or earth across the outlets of valleys in the hills, and they are fed sometimes by rivers and sometimes by the rainfall of a more or less extensive area. They vary in size from ponds irrigating a few acres, to lakes of several miles in circumference. Some of them are works constructed in times of which we have no historical record.

These are not the only means of irrigation in Southern India. Works hardly inferior in importance to those of the North-Western Provinces and Punjab but on a different system, have been carried out by the British Government in the Madras presidency, for utilising the waters of the Godáveri and Kistna rivers. At the head of each of the deltas which they form

[1] *British India and its Rulers*, p. 134.

before they reach the sea, a great weir, or, as it is locally called, an *anicut*, is thrown across the river, which is diverted into irrigation canals and distributing channels, some of which are also used for navigation. A large area, with a population of nearly 2,000,000, thus obtains complete protection against failure of rain; and these works have not only been in the highest degree beneficial to the people, but very profitable to the State. In the famine of 1876–77 these irrigated tracts produced rice to the value of 5,000,000*l.*, a large part of which was available for the relief of suffering districts. Without canal irrigation there would have been no crops at all, and the value of the produce in a single year was four times as great as the whole of the capital expended on the canal works by the Government. Further south, in Tanjore, works of a different kind provide the means of utilising through a large tract of country, in the delta of the Káveri, almost the whole water supply of that river. In Northern India the ordinary rental of land is doubled by irrigation, and it is often more than quadrupled in Madras.

In the province of Sindh another system prevails. Little rain falls there, and without irrigation there would be no cultivation. In the same way that agriculture in Egypt depends on the inundation of the Nile, it depends in Sindh on the floods brought down by the Indus in the season of the periodical rains. There is great room for further improvements, but the existing irrigation renders the province fairly prosperous, and gives the means of subsistence to 2,000,000 people.

Altogether there are, in India, under the management or supervision of the British Government, some 28,000 miles of canals and distributories, irrigating more than 10,000 square miles. They far surpass all similar works in other countries, and no public works of nobler utility have ever been undertaken in the world.

Up to the present time about 200,000,000*l.* has been spent on railways and irrigation works in India. Nearly the whole of this outlay has taken place since the transfer of the Government to the Crown, and by far the greater part of it during the last twenty years. In spite of the efforts of the Government and all encouragement which it could legitimately give, little private capital has hitherto been forthcoming without a guarantee of interest for railways in India. Almost their whole cost has been provided either directly by the Government, or by English companies aided by a guarantee. Up to the end of 1885–86 about 155,600,000*l.* had been spent on railways; of this sum 102,500,000*l.* was supplied by the guaranteed companies, and 53,100,000*l.* by the State. Under the terms of the contracts, the Government is entitled at certain periods to purchase the guaranteed railways, and it has already exercised this power in some cases. In addition to the expenditure on guaranteed and State railways, about 3,000,000*l.* has been spent on lines constructed by companies with more or less assistance from the Government, and about 5,000,000*l.* has been spent on railways in Native States.

Irrigation works have cost about 28,300,000*l.*; nearly the whole of these have been constructed by the Government itself.

I must briefly explain the system under which the funds for this great expenditure have been supplied.

When, after the mutinies of 1857, the obligation of providing numerous works of improvement had been recognised, it became evident that the ordinary revenue could not furnish the means of meeting the necessary outlay. The financial difficulties involved by the suppression of the mutinies were great, and for some years afterwards the necessity of providing barracks and hospitals for the largely increased force of British troops was so urgent that the progress of other works was crippled. Since 1857 more than 30,000,000*l.* has been given from the revenue for military works in India.

In 1864 the principle was accepted, that for the construction of works of irrigation it was right to supply by loan the funds which could not be otherwise provided. This conclusion first took a practical shape in 1867–68, during the Government of Lord Lawrence, in accordance with a scheme drawn up by General R. Strachey. It was clear that only a comparatively small part of the necessary outlay could be met from the revenues; the rest was to be supplied by loans. No project was to be taken up which did not promise to be fairly remunerative within a reasonable time; it was believed that the earnings would before long more than cover the interest on the borrowed capital, and that no ultimate charge would fall on the general revenues. In 1869, General Strachey proposed to extend this system to the development of railways. His plans were adopted by Lord Lawrence, and the first steps were taken by Lord Mayo in 1870 for carrying them into effect.

I will not describe the various phases through which this policy has passed. The main principle, that railways and irrigation works in India may wisely, and without financial danger, be constructed with borrowed money, has been consistently carried out, partly by the Government itself, and partly through the agency of companies assisted by a guarantee of interest or by subsidies from the State. Up to 1885–86 the expenditure incurred in pursuance of this policy was 165,683,000*l.*

Of this sum, 91,845,000*l.* forms part of the State debt, and 73,839,000*l.* represents the capital of guaranteed and assisted companies.

It will be understood from what has been said that this subject is closely connected with that of the public debt.

The public debt of India amounted in 1885–86 to 166,511,000*l.* The debt is divided for purposes of account into two parts—the ordinary debt, similar in character to the public debt of other countries, and the public works debt, consisting, as I have explained, of money invested in railways and works of irrigation. The ordinary debt, in 1885–86, was 74,666,000*l.*, and the public works debt was, as above stated, 91,845,000*l.*

In 1857, just before the outbreak of the mutinies, the public debt of India was 51,378,000*l.* The task of suppressing the mutinies and the reorganisation of the administration added, in the next five years, more than 42,000,000*l.* to the debt; and the result of these and other borrowings was that in 1862 the total amount of the debt was 97,037,000*l.* In 1886 it was 166,511,000*l.* Thus, in the twenty-four years that elapsed after the suppression of the mutinies and the cessation of the extraordinary expenditure immediately due to them, the debt was increased by 69,474,000*l.* This increase resulted entirely from the policy of borrowing for investment in railways and irrigation works. Apart from such investments, the public debt in the period I have mentioned not only received no increase, but was reduced by nearly 19,000,000*l.* This will appear the more remarkable when it is remembered that India during this time suffered from a succession of serious famines, involving an expenditure of nearly 15,000,000*l.* for their relief, that a net sum of 12,250,000*l.* was spent on wars in Afghánistán and Egypt, and that a large increase of charge has been caused by the fall in the gold value of silver.

Up to the end of 1885–86 the investment of the Government from borrowed funds in State railways was 67,223,000*l.*, and in irrigation works 24,622,000*l.*; these two sums together make up 91,845,000*l.*, the total amount of the debt invested in public works.

The existing State railways have for the most part been constructed directly by the Government, but there have been some exceptions. Between 1879 and 1886, the Government, under the terms of the original contracts, exercised in several cases its power of purchasing the railways constructed by companies. These railways then became State lines; their debenture liabilities became State debts; and their capital is now represented by State terminable annuities. In 1886 the debt incurred by the purchase of guaranteed railways exceeded 10,250,000*l.* The most important of the undertakings thus purchased was the East Indian Railway, the great line connecting Calcutta with Delhi and the Northern Provinces. The transaction has proved very advantageous to the State. In 1885–86 it brought to the public revenues, after meeting all charges, including interest on borrowed capital, a clear profit of 614,000*l.* The purchase was chiefly made by creating an annuity for seventy-four years. At the end of that term, when the transaction is complete, the Government will come into the receipt of a clear yearly income which it has been estimated cannot be less than 2,500,000*l.* In this and in some other cases the working of the line is not managed directly by the Government, but through a company under a working lease.

I have still to speak of the railways constructed by companies with a guarantee of interest, or with other assistance from the State. The total capital expenditure incurred under this system, excluding the lines purchased by the State, was, at the end of 1885–86, 73,839,000*l.*, and this represents the sum to which, at that time, guarantees in one form or another extended.

The rate of guaranteed interest was, in the case of the older lines, 5 per cent., and the Government bound itself to make good any sum by which the net traffic receipts, after paying all working expenses, fell short of the amount necessary to provide interest at that rate. The later contracts have been more favourable to the Government.

The true measure of the burden of public debt is the annual charge thrown upon the revenues by the payment of interest. Let us see what the financial results of the policy of borrowing for investment in public works, judged by this test, have been.

In 1862–63 the total net charge upon the revenues of India on account of debt of every description was 4,978,000*l.*; in 1885–86 the same net charge was 2,894,000*l.*, a reduction of 2,084,000*l.*

The net charge on account of the ordinary debt diminished by 1,785,000*l.* On the public works debt there was no net charge at all. After paying all charges, including interest on borrowed capital, and the annuities for the purchased railways, the State railways and irrigation works yielded a profit of 264,000*l.* to the revenues of India. If we leave out of the account works still under construction, the profit was much larger.

These results are exclusive of those obtained through

the guaranteed railway companies, and, to render my explanation complete, they must be included. In 1862–63 the payments to these companies, to make up the difference between the guaranteed interest and the earnings, amounted to 1,607,000*l.*, and in 1885–86 to 1,027,000*l.*

It thus appears that the total net charge to the State on account of debt of every description, including that invested in public works, and also including the sums paid for guaranteed interest to railway companies, was 6,585,000*l.* in 1862–63, and 3,921,000*l.* in 1885–86, a reduction of 2,664,000*l.*

The financial results would be much more favourable but for the fact that many of the railways are incomplete, and that there are many on which the receipts have not nearly reached the amount which may be ultimately expected. Some of them have been constructed for the special purpose of giving protection against famine to poor and remote districts, and with little prospect of profit. Others are required for military reasons connected with the defence of the north-western frontier; no works are more necessary, but they are not likely to give much commercial return. It is probable that, for some years to come, these causes will make the general financial results of railway construction in India seem less successful than they really deserve to be considered.

There is another cause which diminishes the direct profit from Indian railways. The effect of the fall in the gold value of the rupee has been in this respect very serious; the earnings of the lines are in silver, but the greater part of the interest on the capital expenditure, the annuities paid in respect of guaranteed railways purchased, and nearly the whole of the payments to the guaranteed companies, have to be paid in gold.

In 1886–87 these gold payments amounted to 5,284,000*l*. To provide this sum India had to pay nearly 20 millions of rupees more than would have been required if the rupee had retained its old value of 2*s*. But for this loss by exchange the Indian railways, even in their present often incomplete condition, would have given a return of nearly 5½ per cent. on their capital cost, and would have yielded a net revenue to the State of 798,000*l*., instead of involving, as they did, a net charge of 1,189,000*l*.

I have said enough to show that, in spite of all drawbacks, the policy of borrowing for investment in productive public works has been highly successful, and that it has conferred most important benefits on the country.

I have hitherto spoken only of those public works which give a direct return in cash on the money spent upon them. Since the transfer of the Government to the Crown there has also been a very large expenditure from revenue on works which, although some of them do not come into that class, are of high utility. Within this period, nearly 150,000,000*l*. has been devoted to roads and bridges, telegraphs, hospitals, barracks and military works, colleges, schools, and other public buildings and minor works of irrigation and navigation. Twenty thousand miles of telegraph lines have been constructed, and I cannot tell you how many thousand miles of roads.

Before I leave the subject of public works there is one other matter to which I must refer. I have pointed out that, in addition to the reasons which in other countries render the construction of railways necessary, they are required in India because without them it is not possible to give adequate relief on the occurrence of the famines to which India is from time to time exposed through the failure of the periodical rains. In some provinces the provision of irrigation works is not less important. Thus, the question of the construction of railways and canals is closely connected with that of the measures which the Government ought to take for the prevention and relief of famine.

It was not until 1874, when Lord Northbrook was Viceroy, that it was recognised that, since famines could not be looked on as abnormal and exceptional calamities, it was essential that provision against the grave financial obligations which they involve should be made as one of the ordinary charges of the State. 'Whatever means,' Lord Northbrook said, 'we may take to obviate or mitigate them, it must, under present circumstances, be looked upon as inevitable that famines will from time to time occur;' he concluded that to meet them merely by borrowing would be financially ruinous, that it was necessary to reserve in prosperous times a substantial surplus of revenue over expenditure, and that, if this surplus were devoted to the reduction of debt, or to preventing the increase of debt for the construction of productive public works, there would be no objection, when famine occurred, to meeting from borrowed money charges to the full extent to which debt had been reduced or prevented.

In 1877–78 measures were taken by the Government of Lord Lytton for giving practical effect to these principles.

Between 1873 and 1878 the actual expenditure on the relief of famine, including remissions of land revenue, was nearly 16,500,000*l*. This was a period of exceptional disaster, and the Government came to the conclusion that, taking an average of years, it might safely be assumed that the annual charge for relieving famine was not likely to exceed 1,500,000*l*. It was determined, therefore, that in addition to that necessary margin of revenue over expenditure which a prudent administration always desires to maintain, a surplus of 1,500,000*l*. must every year be provided on account of famine relief alone, and that this sum, when the country was free from famine, must be regularly devoted to the discharge of debt, or to the prevention of debt which would otherwise have been incurred for the construction of railways and canals. The practical result of such a plan would be to store up, in times of prosperity, resources by means of which, when famine occurred, it would be possible to meet the heavy obligations of the State. If, for example, this policy were followed during a period of ten years in which there was no famine, debt at the end of that time would have been reduced or prevented to the extent of 15,000,000*l*., and, if serious famine then occurred, 15,000,000*l*. might be borrowed for its relief without placing the country in a worse position financially than that of ten years before.

The original scheme under which 1,500,000*l*. was to be annually devoted to the reduction or prevention of debt was subsequently modified. It was determined that a portion of this sum should be directly expended on the construction of railways and canals required for the protection of districts specially liable to drought and consequent scarcity, and that the rest of it should be applied to reducing the amount of the annual borrowing for public works.

This policy of insurance against famine was simple in its nature, but it has been constantly misunderstood. It has often been supposed that a separate fund was constituted, into which certain revenues were to be paid, and which could only be drawn upon for a specified purpose. No such impracticable notion was ever entertained, and every idea of the kind was from the first repudiated by the Government, and by myself, who was responsible for the original scheme. The 'Famine Insurance Fund,' of which people have often talked, never existed. The intention was nothing more than the annual application of surplus revenue to the extent of 1,500,000*l.* to the relief of actual famine, or to the reduction or prevention of debt.

In March 1887 it was determined to suspend temporarily the operation of the famine insurance scheme. In consequence of the heavy expenses incurred on account of the annexation of Upper Burma, the increase of military charges consequent on the advance of Russia, the fall in the gold value of silver, and other causes, it became clear that the expenditure of the ensuing year must largely exceed the revenue; and to cover the otherwise inevitable deficit the Government had to choose between the imposition of fresh taxation and the stoppage for a time of the annual grant from revenue for famine insurance. It was resolved that the latter was the lesser evil, but it was declared that the aim of the Government will be to obtain again as soon as possible the necessary surplus, and to devote it to the purposes to which under the famine insurance scheme it was assigned.

LECTURE VI.

THE LAWS AND THE ADMINISTRATION OF JUSTICE.

THE FOUNDATIONS OF THE EXISTING JUDICIAL SYSTEM—REGULATIONS AND ACTS—THE LAWS AND THE COURTS BEFORE THE TRANSFER OF THE GOVERNMENT TO THE CROWN—REGULATION AND NON-REGULATION PROVINCES—THE INDIAN LAW COMMISSION—LORD MACAULAY AND THE PENAL CODE—THE PROGRESS OF CODIFICATION—SIR HENRY MAINE ON THE INDIAN CODES—SIR JAMES STEPHEN ON THE INDIAN PENAL CODE—THE ESTABLISHMENT OF HIGH COURTS—THE CODE OF CRIMINAL PROCEDURE—CONSTITUTION OF THE CRIMINAL COURTS—CRIMINAL JURISDICTION OVER EUROPEAN BRITISH SUBJECTS—CHANGES IN THE LAW IN 1884—THE CODIFICATION OF THE CIVIL LAW—HINDU AND MOHAMMEDAN LAW—CHAPTERS OF THE CIVIL CODE ALREADY ENACTED—SIMPLIFICATION AND CONSOLIDATION OF THE LAW—THE CODE OF CIVIL PROCEDURE—CONSTITUTION OF THE CIVIL COURTS—CIVIL JURISDICTION OVER EUROPEANS—THE 'BLACK ACT' OF 1836—LORD MACAULAY—THE NATIVE JUDGES—DEFECTS IN THE EXISTING JUDICIAL SYSTEM.

ALTHOUGH much had been done by Warren Hastings to reform and organise all branches of the public service, the main foundations of the existing administration of justice in India were laid in the time of Lord Cornwallis. In 1793 the issue of formal and definite legislative enactments began in the series of laws known as the Bengal, Madras, and Bombay Regulations. Since 1833 the term 'Regulation' has ceased to be used; the laws are called, as in England, 'Acts.' These Regulations and Acts, and such Acts of Parliament as apply to India, constitute, apart from Hindu and Mohammedan law, of which I must speak separately, the civil and criminal law of British India.

Before the transfer of the Government to the Crown, the administration of criminal justice was in an unsatisfactory condition. The police was often oppressive, inefficient, and corrupt. In the greater part of British India, the criminal law and procedure were a jumble based on the old Mohammedan law, eked out and rendered tolerable by the Regulations and Acts of our own Government, by fragments of English law, and by the decisions and intructions of the superior courts. Civil justice was in a worse condition. The law was only to be found in a wilderness of enactments and 'circular orders' of the courts, and as the number of these increased they became in course of time, as Mr. Cunningham says, 'hopelessly unwieldy, entangled, and confusing. Human diligence shrank from the task of searching amid the voluminous provisions of obsolete or repealed legislation for a germ of living law, and grave illegalities not unfrequently occurred, owing to the ignorance which the chaotic condition of the statute-book rendered almost inevitable.'[1]

These difficulties were increased by the devotion of the superior Indian courts of that time to technicalities which survived long after they had ceased in England to be seriously mischievous. Even in the later years of the East India Company, the civil courts often seemed to be intended rather for the performance of certain forms and ceremonies than for the administration of justice.

While this was the condition of the law and procedure, the expansion of the empire was in more or less constant progress, and when new provinces were annexed the Government shrank from taking the judicial system of the older provinces as a model. Apart from such reasons, when the people had never been accustomed to anything but personal rule of the roughest

[1] *India and its Rulers*, p. 203.

sort, it was often necessary, on the first introduction of our Government, to concentrate executive and judicial authority in the same hands. Government by regular course of law cannot be substituted in a moment for a Government of irresponsible power. Moreover, the simpler forms of administration were much cheaper.

It thus came to pass that there were two systems in force—one in the older provinces, and the other in the territories which had more recently come into our possession. The former were called 'Regulation,' and the latter 'Non-Regulation' provinces. A Non-Regulation province was one to which the old Regulations and Acts in force in the Regulation provinces had not been extended, in which fewer officers were employed, and in which executive and judicial functions were, to a great extent, exercised by the same persons. Bengal, the North-Western Provinces, Madras, and Bombay, were Regulation provinces; the Punjab, Oudh, the Central Provinces, and British Burma, were Non-Regulation.

It is a mistake, though a common one, to suppose that in the more advanced of the Non-Regulation provinces, as, for example, in the Punjab, when the Government was transferred to the Crown, the administration was conducted in a rough and ready way, in accordance with our officers' own notions of equity, unhampered by law. The Government of the Punjab, in 1860, really deserved better than the Government of the North-Western Provinces or of Bengal, so far as the judicial administration was concerned, to be called a Government by law. In the former case the laws, though simple, were rational, intelligible, and certain; in the latter case the system was so chaotic that there was virtually almost no law at all. When the admirable codes of law and procedure, of which I shall presently speak, were introduced, less change had to be made in the system of administering criminal and civil justice in the Non-Regulation than in the Regulation Provinces.

The superiority of the administration which was so marked in the Non-Regulation Provinces towards the close of the East India Company's Government ceased before many more years had passed. Improvement in the older provinces went on rapidly, and, although differences in the form of the administration still exist, the distinctions between Regulation and Non-Regulation Provinces have become much less important than they were. Excepting Burma, a few wild hill tracts on the frontiers alone remain outside the pale of the codes of law and procedure which apply to the whole of British India.

The first steps towards the simplification and improvement of the law were taken in the time of the East India Company, but they led to little practical result before the transfer of the Government to the Crown. In 1833 it was provided by the Act of Parliament which renewed the Company's charter that a fourth member of Council should be appointed, in concert with a Commission, for the purpose of preparing a body of law for British India. Lord Macaulay was appointed member of Council, and the first subject taken up was the preparation of a Penal Code. This work fell chiefly upon Lord Macaulay, and it was completed by him while he was in India, between 1834 and 1838. The code remained as a mere draft for twenty-two years, and it was not until 1860 that it became law. During this interval it was revised from time to time by Lord Macaulay's successors, and especially by Sir Barnes Peacock, the last Chief Justice of the Supreme Court of Calcutta. 'The long delay in the enactment of the Penal Code,' writes Sir James Stephen, 'had thus the singular but most beneficial result of reserving a work which had been drawn up by the most distinguished author of the day for a minutely careful revision by a professional lawyer, possessed of as great experience and as much technical knowledge as any man of his time. An ideal code ought to be drawn by a Bacon and settled by a Coke.'[1]

Although many valuable recommendations for the improvement of the criminal and civil law were made by the Commission of which Lord Macaulay was a member, the Penal Code was the only important result of its labours. In 1853, when the Company's charter was again renewed[2] a fresh Commission was appointed in England, and this was followed in 1861 by a third Commission, for the purpose of preparing a body of substantive law for India, 'and also to consider and report on such other matters relating to the reform of the laws of India as might be referred to them by the Secretary of State.' To these two Commissions, whose work continued until 1870, and to the eminent men who since the time of Lord Macaulay have held the office of legal member of Council, we owe the succession of excellent laws which have been passed by the Indian Legislature, and which form chapters in a system of codified law. This system is not yet complete, but there is no country where the work of codification has made greater progress. 'British India,' writes Sir Henry Maine, 'is now in possession of a set of codes which approach the highest standard of excellence which this species of legislation has reached. . . . In form, intelligibility, and in comprehensiveness, the Indian codes stand against all competition.'[3]

[1] *History of the Criminal Law*, vol. iii. p. 300. [2] 16 and 17 Vic. c. 95.
[3] *The Reign of Queen Victoria—'India,'* vol. i. p. 503.

The Penal Code, which became law in 1860, was followed in 1861 by the Code of Criminal Procedure. Substantially, the whole criminal law of British India is contained in these two laws.

In regard to the merits of the Indian Penal Code no one can speak with higher authority than Sir James Stephen, and in forming his judgment he has not only had the advantage of his English experience, but of personal knowledge gained by observation in India. He has pronounced it to be 'by far the best system of criminal law in the world,' and I cannot doubt that he is right in his prediction that it will prove the most remarkable and lasting monument of Lord Macaulay, its author. The authority of his other writings is hardly as indisputable as it was, but his Penal Code has (in Sir James Stephen's words) 'triumphantly supported the test of experience for upwards of twenty-one years, during which time it has met with a degree of success which can hardly be ascribed to any other statute approaching the same dimensions.'

I cannot do better than continue my quotation :—

'The Indian Penal Code may be described as the criminal law of England freed from all technicalities and superfluities, systematically arranged, and modified in some few particulars (they are surprisingly few) to suit the circumstances of British India. . . . It is practically impossible to misunderstand the Penal Code, and, though it has been in force for more than twenty years, and is in daily use in every part of India by all sorts of courts and amongst communities of every degree of civilisation, and has given rise to countless decisions, no obscurity or ambiguity worth speaking of has been discovered in it. . . . Since its enactment it has been substantially the only body of criminal law in force in India, though a few other statutes contain penal provisions on various special subjects. I have already expressed my opinion that the Indian Penal Code has been triumphantly successful. The rigorous administration of justice of which it forms an essential part has beaten down crime throughout the whole of India to such an extent that the greater part of that vast country would compare favourably, as far as the absence of crime goes, with any part of the United Kingdom, except perhaps Ireland in quiet times, and apart from political and agrarian offences. Apart from this, it has met with another kind o success. Till I had been in India I could not have believed it to be possible that so extensive a body of law could be made so generally known to all whom it concerned in its minutest details. I do not believe that any English lawyer or judge has anything like so accurate and comprehensive and distinct a knowledge or the criminal law of England as average Indian civilians have of the Penal Code. Nor has all the ingenuity of commentators been able to introduce any serious difficulty into the subject. After twenty years' use it is still true that any one who wants to know what the criminal law of India is has only to read the Penal Code with a common use of memory and attention.'[1]

Until 1861 the Supreme Courts established by Royal Charter in Calcutta, Madras, and Bombay exercised original criminal and civil jurisdiction over all classes within the limits of the three Presidency towns. The principal criminal and civil courts established by the Company's Government in the Mofussil (as everything outside the Presidency towns was termed) were called respectively the Sudder Nizámat and Sudder Diwáni Adálat. They were the supreme courts of appeal, and capital sentences were referred to the Nizámat Adálat for confirmation.

In 1861 these Supreme and Sudder courts were abolished by Act of Parliament,[2] and in substitution for them High courts with both criminal and civil jurisdiction were established, one for each of the provinces of Bengal, Madras, Bombay, and the North-Western

[1] *History of the Criminal Law*, vol. iii. p. 332.
[2] 24 and 25 Vic. c. 104.

Provinces. For parts of India not included in either of those provinces, High courts were formed under other names by the legislative authority of the Government of India; in the Punjab there is a Chief court, with three judges; in the other provinces the chief appellate authority is an officer called the Judicial Commissioner. The judges of the High courts are partly English barristers and partly members of the Indian Civil Service, and there are usually in each court one or more Native judges chosen from the Native judicial service or from the pleaders. The High courts in each province are the courts of appeal from the District courts, criminal and civil, and their decisions are final, except in certain civil cases in which an appeal lies to the Judicial Committee of the Privy Council in England. Sentences of death require the confirmation of the High court.

The High courts exercise constant supervision over all the subordinate courts. Elaborate returns are regularly sent to them at short intervals, showing in great detail the business disposed of, and, as the whole of the evidence in every case, or a memorandum of its substance, has to be taken down by the judges or magistrates with their own hands, and a record made of every order that is passed, the High courts are able, by examining the returns, by sending for proceedings, and by calling for explanations, as well as from the cases that come before them in appeal, to keep themselves acquainted with the manner in which all the courts are discharging their duties.

The Code of Criminal Procedure, which became law in 1861, has been recast and amended from time to time, but in essential respects it has not been much altered. It is in force throughout British India, although a few of its provisions have, in some parts of the country, been modified to meet special requirements. Among all the laws of India there is no one more important than this, which regulates the machinery by which peace and order are maintained, and by which crime is prevented and punished. It describes the constitution of all the criminal courts; it defines the powers which each court can exercise; it classifies the offences under the Penal Code or other laws which each judge or magistrate can try; it regulates the manner in which police investigations are to be carried on; the powers of the police to make arrests with or without the warrant of a magistrate; the proceedings to be taken for keeping the peace and for preventing unlawful assemblies; for the removal of public nuisances; the manner in which accused persons are to be brought before the magistrate, in which inquiries and trials are to be held, in which evidence is to be heard and recorded, in which commitments to the superior courts are to be made; it contains rules for the trial of cases with juries and assessors, for the admission of appeals, for the revision of sentences and orders by the superior courts, and for many other matters more or less directly connected with criminal procedure. As Sir James Stephen said in one of his speeches in India, this code is really the principal means through which the practical everyday business of governing the empire is carried on. The system which it lays down is complete, efficient, and successful.

In every province there are a certain number of divisions, in each of which a Court of Session is established, presided over by a Sessions judge. Additional, joint, and assistant Sessions judges may be appointed. Every sessions division consists of a certain number of districts, to each of which a magistrate, called the District magistrate, is attached. Any number of subordinate magistrates that may be required are appointed in the district, subject to the general control of the District magistrate. In the towns of Calcutta, Madras, and Bombay there are magistrates called Presidency magistrates. To enable a magistrate or judge to exercise jurisdiction over European British subjects, he must be appointed a justice of the peace, and a justice of the peace must himself be a European British subject. There are certain exceptions to this rule. The judges of the High courts, the Sessions judges, District magistrates, and Presidency magistrates are justices of the peace *ex officio*, and the law does not require that they shall be European British subjects.

A High court may pass any sentence authorised by the Penal Code or other law. All trials before the High court are by jury.

A Sessions judge may pass any sentence authorised by law, but sentences of death are subject to confirmation by the High court. All trials before the Court of Session are either by jury or with assessors.

There are three classes of magistrates:—

(1) Courts of Presidency magistrates, and of magistrates of the first class, in which District magistrates are included; they can pass sentences of imprisonment not exceeding two years, and of fine not exceeding 1,000 rupees. In cases which they are not competent finally to decide, they commit for trial to the Court of Session or High court.

(2) Courts of magistrates of the second class. They can pass sentence of imprisonment not exceeding six months, or of fine not exceeding 200 rupees.

(3) Courts of magistrates of the third class. They

can pass sentences of imprisonment not exceeding one month, or of fine not exceeding 50 rupees.

In certain cases and under certain restrictions, magistrates of the first class, or, if specially so empowered, magistrates of the second class, can pass sentences of whipping.

Excepting the High courts, the judges of which are appointed by the Crown, all the judges and magistrates are appointed by the Provincial Governments.

While the substantive criminal law is the same for all classes, certain distinctions of procedure have always been maintained in regard to criminal charges against European British subjects.[1] Until 1872, excepting in trivial cases, a European British subject could only be tried or punished by one of the High courts. The result was often a complete denial of justice, for prosecutors and witnesses might have to travel for many hundred miles before a case could be heard. This state of things was remedied in 1872, when the Code of Criminal Procedure was re-enacted, in accordance with the proposals of Sir James Stephen, who was legal member of Council. It was then provided that European British subjects should be liable to be tried for any offences by magistrates of the highest class, who were also justices of the peace, and by judges of Sessions courts; but it was necessary, in both cases, that the magistrate or judge should himself be a European British subject. A magistrate might pass sentence of

[1] The following definition of the term 'European British subject' is given in the Code of Criminal Procedure:—'European British subject' means—(1) any subject of Her Majesty born, naturalised, or domiciled in the United Kingdom of Great Britain and Ireland, or in any of the European, American, or Australian Colonies or Possessions of Her Majesty, or in the Colony of New Zealand, or in the Colony of the Cape of Good Hope or Natal; (2) any child or grand-child of any such person by legitimate descent.'

imprisonment for three months and fine of 1,000 rupees; a Sessions judge might imprison for one year, and fine. Cases requiring severer punishment were referred to the High court. In the towns of Calcutta, Madras, and Bombay, the Presidency magistrates were justices of the peace by virtue of their offices, and, whether they were Europeans or Natives, they could try and punish European British subjects.

Matters remained in this position until 1883, when the Government of India considered that the law regarding jurisdiction over European British subjects required alteration. The Covenanted Civil Service, recruited in England under a system of open competition, has been open since 1853 to Europeans and Natives alike. It has been provided by Parliament that certain offices, and among them the greater number of the principal judicial and magisterial offices, shall be held by members of that service. In 1883 there were only twelve Natives in the Covenanted Civil Service, but a few of them had reached a stage when, in the ordinary course of promotion, they would become District magistrates and judges in the Courts of session. Under the Code of Criminal Procedure no Native holding one of these offices could try any charge against a European British subject. The Government considered that the law in this respect ought to be altered. It was stated that 'the Government of India had decided to settle the question of jurisdiction over European British subjects in such a way as to remove from the code, at once and completely, every judicial disqualification which is based merely on race distinctions.'

This declaration, made in uncompromising terms, provoked a storm of indignation on the part of the European community throughout India. It was not confined to the non-official classes, but extended almost equally to the servants of the Government; it reached a point at which it threatened to become a cause of serious political anxiety, and nothing could be more lamentable than the animosities of race that were aroused, the prejudices, the bitterness and bad feeling between Europeans and Natives that were excited.

I shall reserve for another occasion the observations which I may wish to make on the general subject of the employment of Natives of India in posts of importance. I shall now say a few words only in connection with the unhappy controversy to which I am referring.

No one can desire more strongly than myself the removal in India of disqualifications on account of difference of race, so far as this is compatible with the security of our dominion and with good administration, and no one can be more satisfied than I am that it is unreasonable that a Native of India, who, by his own capacity and merit, has risen to high judicial office, should not be as completely trusted as an Englishman. I consider that the Native judge of a Court of session ought to exercise the same jurisdiction over Europeans and over everybody else which he would exercise if he were an Englishman. I therefore sympathise with the object which the Government of India had in view, but I think that the form in which its proposals were made was unfortunate. I have always believed that, if matters had been more discreetly managed, every amendment of the law that was essential might have been made without objection on the part of the European community.

The controversy ended with the virtual though not avowed abandonment of the measure proposed by the Government. Act III. of 1884 extended rather than diminished the privileges of European British subjects charged with offences, and left their position as exceptional as before. The general disqualification of Native judges and magistrates remains; but if a Native be appointed to the post of District magistrate or Sessions judge, his powers in regard to jurisdiction over European British subjects will be the same as those of an Englishman holding a similar office. This provision, however, is subject to the condition that every European British subject brought for trial before the District magistrate or Sessions judge has the right, however trivial be the charge, to claim to be tried by a jury of which not less than half the number shall be Europeans or Americans. No such claim can be made by Natives charged with offences, and it is a claim which could not be made by an Englishman in any magistrate's court in his own country. The Legislature has virtually declared that the summary powers of the European District magistrate over European offenders shall be taken away, not because this was held to be in itself desirable, but because such powers could not be given to a District magistrate who is a Native. While this change was made in the powers of District magistrates, the law in regard to other magistrates remained unaltered. All English magistrates of the first class, outside the Presidency towns, other than the District magistrate, are appointed to be justices of the peace, and they exercise jurisdiction over European British subjects as they did before; but no Native magistrates in similar positions can be appointed to be justices of the peace or exercise such jurisdiction. There are many districts in which it may happen, when a charge against a European British subject comes before a District magistrate, that a sufficient number of Europeans and Americans cannot be found to constitute a jury; the case must then, under the orders of the High court, be transferred for trial to another district where a jury can be formed. Thus, opportunity is offered for the occasional revival of the old scandals and denials of justice and hardship which were common before 1872, when the trial of European British subjects could only take place before the High courts, and complainants and witnesses were liable to be sent away to great distances from their homes. It is true that this is not likely often to occur in practice, because the District magistrate, to whom alone these new provisions of the law apply, will usually take care to try in his own court no charge against a European British subject, but will transfer it, as he can always do, to one of his European subordinates, whose summary powers of dealing with such cases have not been touched. The law has certainly not been changed for the better, but for practical purposes it remains much as it was before Act III. of 1884 was passed. The only other change was that District magistrates trying European British subjects with a jury were authorised to pass sentence of imprisonment, which may extend to six months, or fine which may extend to 2,000 rupees, or both.

I am afraid that the result of all this has been that we must leave to a distant future the hope that the Government of India will be able to place the law regarding jurisdiction over European British subjects on a satisfactory footing.

The codification of the criminal law of British India is complete. The codification of the civil law is a far more difficult task. Both Hindus and Mohammedans are in possession of great bodies of law, parts of which are believed by them to be of more or less divine origin, containing elaborate instructions on every sort of subject affecting property, inheritance, and the relations of life. Unless Native customs and feelings and prejudices are repugnant to humanity and justice, we are bound to respect them, and the mere suspicion that we desired to interfere with them might be politically dangerous. No one is likely to attempt to codify the Mohammedan law, and there is no single body of Hindu law that is generally recognised; it differs in different provinces, and is constantly modified by local and personal custom. A large part of the substantive civil law is, therefore, and must remain, untouched by our legislation. Those branches, however, both of substantive and adjective law, where these difficulties do not apply have been dealt with in a comprehensive manner. Codes relating to contracts, negotiable instruments, transfer of property, trusts, easements, and other subjects, evidence, limitation, and a complete Code of Civil Procedure, have already been enacted, and these, with certain exceptions saving local and other usages and customary rights, are generally applicable throughout British India. Another important chapter of the Civil Code, the Succession Act of 1865, contains the law of intestate and testamentary succession; but the greater part of it applies only to Europeans, East Indians and some other classes domiciled in British India, and has no application to Hindus or Mohammedans. Subject to the serious exceptions that I have noticed, there is hardly any country in which the laws are contained in so small a compass, in which they are so excellent both in substance and in form, and in which they are so easily intelligible.

The codification and simplification of the law has been one of the greatest reforms of modern times in India. There has been a prevalent but mistaken notion that India, during the last ten or twenty years, has been suffering from over-legislation. Speaking generally, the result of recent legislation, apart from that which must always be required to meet current wants of the day, has been greatly to reduce the body of the law, to get rid of obsolete enactments, and to consolidate and simplify the laws in force. Many illustrations of what has been done in this direction might be given. Thus, the law under which the civil courts in Bengal were constituted had formerly to be searched for in thirteen Regulations and Acts scattered over seventy-seven years; now it is to be found in one short Act of thirty-eight sections. I remember Sir James Stephen giving to the Legislative Council in India ocular demonstration of the nature of the process that had been going on, by pointing to a series of huge volumes which contained the law as it used to be, and which the table before him could scarcely hold, and then showing us a few octavo volumes which contained all the existing Acts of the Legislature.

I cannot say that the practical administration of justice has been as successful in the civil as in the criminal courts, but the improvement has been great since the transfer of the Government to the Crown.

Before 1859 the procedure was extremely complex and technical, the delays and opportunities for corruption and fraud were endless, the Native judges were often very imperfectly educated, and their integrity was sometimes open to grave suspicion. They were so miserably paid that to expect any high standard of honesty or efficiency was unreasonable. In 1859 the Code of Civil Procedure was enacted, and it has from time to time been amended. It has rendered the procedure of the courts simple and reasonable; the position of the Native judges has been greatly improved; they are now a well-educated class, with a good knowledge of law, and highly paid, and an immense change has taken place in their character and competency.

The constitution of the civil courts, below the High court of which I have already spoken, varies somewhat in different provinces; but in Bengal, the North-Western Provinces, Madras, and Bombay, it is substantially uniform. There are usually three classes of courts: District judges, Subordinate judges, and Munsifs or Subordinate judges of the second class. The Judge exercises a general control over all the courts in his district, and hears certain classes of appeals. The Subordinate judge can try, subject to some restrictions, cases of any value. The jurisdiction of the Munsif varies. In some provinces he can hear suits not exceeding 5,000 rupees, in others his powers are more limited. Appeals lie to the High court from the decisions of the District judge. There are also Small Cause courts, which decide cases of small amount without appeal. In the Punjab, the Central Provinces, and Oudh, the system is somewhat different, but it need not now be described.

Until the year 1836, European British subjects were under the jurisdiction of the Supreme Courts alone. It was then decided, by Act XI. of 1836, that they should be made amenable to the civil courts of the Company, and that in this respect no distinctions should be maintained between them and the Natives of India. This measure, commonly known as the 'Black Act,' was received in Calcutta with the furious opposition described by Lord Macaulay, the history of which is familiar to the readers of his life. Lord Macaulay was then a member of the Governor-General's Council, and to him is mainly due the honour of having insisted upon passing this wise and necessary law. The opposition of the Europeans, although to the last degree violent, was virtually confined to Calcutta, and as the number of the English outside the Presidency towns was then comparatively small, the outcry against the Government was less formidable than that of 1883. I quote from a minute of Lord Macaulay the following description of the state of things that then prevailed:—

'Till the passing of Act XI. of 1836 an Englishman at Agra or Benares who owed a small debt to a native, who had beaten a native, who had come with a body of bludgeon-men and ploughed up a native's land, if sued by the injured party for damages, was able to drag that party before the Supreme Court of Calcutta (a distance perhaps of 1,000 miles), a court which in one most important point—the character of the judges—stands as high as any court can stand, but which in every other respect I believe to be the worst in India, the most dilatory, and the most ruinously expensive. . . . The expenses of litigation in England are so heavy that people sit down quietly under wrongs and submit to losses rather than go to law, and yet the English are the richest people in the world. The people of India are poor, and the expenses of litigation in the Supreme Court are five times as great as the expenses of litigation at Westminster. An undefended cause which might be prosecuted successfully in the Court of King's Bench for about 8*l.* cannot be prosecuted in the Supreme Court under 40*l.* Officers of the court are enabled to accumulate in a few years, out of the substance of ruined suitors, fortunes larger than the oldest and most distinguished servant of the Company can expect to carry home after thirty or forty years of eminent service. I speak of Bengal, where the system is now in full operation. At Madras, the Supreme Court has, I believe, fulfilled its mission. It has done its work. It has beggared every rich native within its jurisdiction, and is inactive for want of somebody to ruin.'

Since 1836 no distinctions of race have been recognised in the civil courts throughout India. At the present time, Native judges preside over the great majority of the courts; excepting the higher appellate tribunals, almost the whole administration of civil justice is in their hands. They exercise jurisdiction in all classes of civil cases over Natives and Europeans alike, and no word of objection on the part of the latter is ever heard. The Lord Chancellor did not give the Native judges too high a character when he said in the House of Lords in 1883, as the result of his experience of Indian cases appealed to the Privy Council, that 'in respect of integrity, of learning, of knowledge, of the soundness and satisfactory character of the judgments arrived at, the judgments of the Native judges were quite as good as those of the English.' I think that the highest authorities in India would even go further, and say that, excepting the High courts, the Native judgments are the better of the two. In disposing of business of this sort, superior knowledge of the language and habits of the people gives to the Native many advantages over the Englishman.

Notwithstanding the great improvement that has taken place, the system under which civil justice is administered cannot be said to be altogether satisfactory. It is often difficult for an ignorant population to understand, and it is too mechanical and rigid in its operation. For the more difficult class of cases it is excellent, but for the mass of the judicial business in India the machinery is too elaborate for the work. Out of 1,500,000 suits annually decided by the courts, not much less than one-half are for sums under 2*l.*, and 1,250,000 of them are for sums under 10*l.* I am afraid there is much truth in a remark of Sir Lepel Griffin, that our courts are more mysterious to an Indian peasant than the maze at Hampton Court to an uninstructed visitor. They are also too expensive. Heavy stamp duties still exist; they were originally imposed partly as a means of obtaining revenue to meet the expenses of the courts, and partly under the unfortunate notion, not yet altogether exploded, that needless litigation is encouraged by making recourse to the courts cheap and easy.

LECTURE VII.

EDUCATION IN INDIA.

THE FIRST ESTABLISHMENT OF COLLEGES IN BENGAL—CONTROVERSY BETWEEN THE ADVOCATES OF ORIENTAL AND ENGLISH STUDY—LORD MACAULAY IN 1835—THE EXISTING SYSTEM OF HIGHER EDUCATION—NEGLECT OF PRIMARY EDUCATION—SYSTEM LAID DOWN BY LORD HALIFAX—ITS MAIN FEATURES—THE INDIAN UNIVERSITIES—COLLEGES—TECHNICAL EDUCATION—CHARACTER OF COLLEGIATE INSTRUCTION—MISSIONARY INSTITUTIONS—EDUCATION OF MOHAMMEDANS—THEIR DISLIKE OF EXISTING SYSTEM—SIR SYAD AHMAD KHAN—THE COLLEGE ESTABLISHED BY HIM—THE EDUCATION OF NATIVE CHIEFS AND NOBLES—THE MAYO COLLEGE—SECONDARY EDUCATION—HIGHER AND MIDDLE SCHOOLS—PRIMARY EDUCATION—ITS PROGRESS—FEMALE EDUCATION—LADY DUFFERIN'S ASSOCIATION—EXPENDITURE ON EDUCATION—GENERAL RESULTS—EXTREME IGNORANCE OF THE PEOPLE—SMALL NUMBER OF HIGHLY EDUCATED MEN—NUMBER OF OFFICERS IN THE PUBLIC SERVICE WHO HAVE PASSED UNIVERSITY EXAMINATIONS—THE DANGERS OF THE PREVAILING IGNORANCE—DISREGARD OF ORIENTAL LITERATURE—DEFECTS OF EXISTING SYSTEM—SIR HENRY MAINE ON THE EFFECTS PRODUCED BY THE STUDY OF ENGLISH LITERATURE—THE WANT OF A HISTORY OF BRITISH INDIA—THE INACCURACY AND BAD FAITH OF MILL'S HISTORY—LITTLE ABOUT INDIA TAUGHT IN OUR COLLEGES.

IT was only during the later times of the East India Company's Government that the promotion of education in India was considered one of the duties of the State. The encouragement, however, of Oriental learning had long, to some extent, been acknowledged to be a matter of importance, both for its own sake, and because a knowledge of Mohammedan and Hindu law was necessary in the civil and criminal courts. To Warren Hastings belongs the honour of having founded, in 1782, the first college in Bengal, and it was maintained for some years at his expense. It was especially intended to encourage the study of Arabic and Persian literature and Mohammedan theology, 'to qualify the Mohammedans of Bengal for the public service, chiefly in the courts of justice, and to enable them to compete on more equal terms with the Hindus for employment under Government.' In 1791, a college with similar objects, but 'designed to cultivate the laws, literature, and religion of the Hindus, and specially to supply qualified Hindu assistants to European judges,' was established at Benares. A few more institutions of a similar kind were founded, but as time went on the demand for other forms of education rapidly increased. A long controversy took place, in which there was much exaggeration on both sides, between the advocates of Oriental and English study; the former desired to give more liberal help to students of Sanskrit, Arabic, and Persian, and to encourage the production of literary and scientific works in the Oriental languages; the latter maintained that all the higher branches of knowledge should be taught through the medium of English alone. The controversy virtually ended in 1835 with a minute by Lord Macaulay, who was then a member of the Governor-General's Council in Calcutta. Nothing could exceed the contempt which in his picturesque sentences he poured forth on the whole literature of the East.

'The question before us,' he wrote, 'is simply whether, when it is in our power to teach this language—English—we shall teach languages in which, by universal confession, there are no books on any subject which deserve to be compared to our own; whether, when we can teach European science, we shall teach systems which, by universal confession, wherever they differ from those of Europe, differ for the worse; and whether, when we patronise sound philosophy and true history, we shall countenance, at the public expense, medical doctrines which would disgrace an English farrier, astronomy which would move laughter in the girls at an English boarding-school, history abounding with kings thirty feet high and reigns thirty thousand years long, and geography made up of seas of treacle and seas of butter.'

The influence of Lord Macaulay was irresistible. The Government of Lord William Bentinck decided that 'the great object of the British Government ought to be the promotion of European literature and science among the natives of India, and that all the funds appropriated for the purpose of education would be best employed on English education alone.' Although some of the old institutions were allowed to go on teaching in a feeble way the classical languages of the East, the conclusion virtually arrived at was that Oriental studies required no encouragement from the State.

During the next ten or fifteen years a good deal of progress was made in the establishment of colleges and schools by the Government and by missionary societies. Very little was thought at that time about primary education for the masses of the people. Education, it was said, would gradually 'filter downwards.'

So far as higher education is concerned, the principles laid down in 1835 have been in the main adhered to ever since.

There were some exceptions to the general neglect of primary education which followed the measures taken in 1835. In the North-Western Provinces, in particular, their wise and enlightened Lieutenant-Governor, James Thomason, laid the foundations of a great system of elementary village schools; but it was not until 1854 that the duty of the State in regard to this matter was distinctly recognised. In that year orders, for which Lord Halifax (then Sir

Charles Wood) was mainly responsible, were sent by the Court of Directors to India, and the despatch containing them has been not improperly called 'the charter of education in India.' I shall quote, from the Report of the Indian Education Commission of 1883, a summary of its contents; it will show the system on which the Government has been working ever since:—

'The immediate aims of the Government were the same as those to which the attention of every European State was first directed when organising its system of public instruction. The existing schools of all kinds were to be improved and their number increased, systematic inspection was to be established, and a supply of competent teachers was to be provided. But in India the attitude of the State to national education was affected by three conditions to which no European State could furnish a parallel. In the first place, the population was not only as large as that of all the European States together that had adopted an educational system, but it presented, in its different provinces, at least as many differences of creed, language, race, and custom. Secondly, the ruling power was bound to hold itself aloof from all questions of religion. Thirdly, the scheme of instruction to be introduced was one which should culminate in the organisation of a literature and science essentially foreign. While, therefore, on the one hand, the magnitude of the task before the Indian Government was such as to make it almost impossible of achievement by any direct appropriation from the resources of the empire, on the other, the popular demand for education—so important a factor in the success of the European systems—had to be created. The Government adopted the only course which circumstances permitted. It was admitted that "to imbue a vast and ignorant population with a general desire for knowledge, and to take advantage of the desire when excited to improve the means for diffusing education among them, must be the work of many years; as a Government, we can do no more than direct the efforts of the people, and aid them wherever they appear to require most assistance."'

Under the orders of 1854, supplemented by later instructions, a separate Department of Public Instruction was constituted. Universities were to be founded in Calcutta, Madras, and Bombay; institutions for training teachers for all classes of schools were to be established; the number of Government colleges and high schools was to be increased; new middle schools were to be created; efforts were above all to be devoted to the development of elementary education with the object of 'conveying to the great mass of the people, who are utterly incapable of obtaining any education worthy of the name by their own unaided efforts, useful and practical knowledge, suited to every station in life.' The English language was to be the medium of instruction in the higher branches of education, and the vernacular languages of the country in the lower, and English was to be taught wherever there was a demand for it. The extension of education in the higher branches, would, it was thought, be mainly effected by applying the system of grants-in-aid; the resources of the State were to be so devoted as to assist those who could not be expected to help themselves, while it was hoped that the richer classes would gradually be induced to provide for their own education. The system of grants-in-aid to private institutions was to be based on entire abstinence from interference with the religious instruction given in the schools; aid was to be given, within certain limits, to all schools which imparted a good secular education and were under competent management; all aided schools were to be open to inspection by Government officers. This system has been put into practice throughout British India. Every province has its separate Educational Department under an officer called the Director of Public Instruction, with a large staff of officers, colleges, schools, and grants-in-aid.

The three universities of Calcutta, Madras, and Bombay were established in 1857; a fourth was established at Allahabad for the North-Western Provinces in 1887. Their constitution is similar to that of the London University; they have a Chancellor, Vice-Chancellor, and Senate, with a governing body; they are examining bodies only, but by their examinations they control the course of study throughout the greater part of India, in the colleges affiliated to them. In 1882 a university was established at Lahore for the Punjab, and this is not only an examining but a teaching body also.

The entrance examination for matriculation is open to all. The subjects are English, a classical or vernacular language, history, geography, mathematics, and, in Madras and Bombay, elementary physical science. The usual age of the candidates is between sixteen and eighteen, and, according to the estimate of the Education Commission, the standard of knowledge required is about that which at the age of sixteen an English boy of average intelligence will be found to possess. Success in this examination admits a student to any of the affiliated colleges.

The college course does not much differ in the various provinces. After two years, a student may present himself for the first examination in Arts, the subjects being English, a classical language (Oriental or European), history, mathematics, logic, and, if he so desires, a branch of natural science. Two years later, he may present himself for the B.A. degree. Degrees are conferred in Arts, Law, Medicine, and Civil Engineering. The M.A. degree completes the college course; the examination is held in one or more of the following subjects: languages, history, mental and moral philosophy, mathematics, pure and mixed, and physical science. The proportion of students who go beyond the entrance examination is not large, and the number who obtain degrees is small.

Taking the three universities of Calcutta, Madras, and Bombay together, in the ten years ending with 1886, out of 75,047 candidates, 27,545 passed the entrance examination. During the same time there were 3,457 B.A., and only 365 M.A. graduates.

Some very useful colleges have been established for special objects, such as the study of medicine and surgery and engineering.

The medical colleges deserve particular notice, for no educational institutions in India have been so remarkably successful. There are nearly 1,500 hospitals and dispensaries in British India in charge of Native surgeons educated in our colleges and schools. Among all the benefits conferred upon the people by our rule, there is perhaps no one more highly and universally valued than this. Surgery is an art for which Natives of India have a remarkable aptitude; many of the Native surgeons are extremely skilful, and they often perform difficult operations in a manner that would not discredit the surgeons of London or Paris. More than 10,000,000 patients are treated every year at the Indian hospitals and dispensaries.

Little has hitherto been done in India towards the establishment of institutions for technical instruction, but a beginning, especially in Bombay and Madras, has been made. This is a want which in England is only slowly beginning to be supplied, and we see in India the reflection of English indifference. The neglect is especially to be regretted in regard to the chief of Indian arts, Agriculture. The recent establishment of Agricultural Departments, to which I shall again refer, will, it may be hoped, lead to the recognition of the importance of applying scientific knowledge to the processes of Indian agriculture, and to the provision of means of agricultural instruction.

In regard to the general scope and character of collegiate instruction in India, I cannot do better than quote the account given in the Report of the Indian Education Commissioners:—

'The system is now almost uniform throughout India. Purely Oriental colleges must be excepted. These, however, are so few in number that they scarcely enter into a consideration of collegiate education in its modern development. The college of to-day aims at giving an education that shall fit its recipient to take an honourable share in the administration of the country, or to enter with good hope of success the various liberal professions now expanding in vigorous growth. The English and Oriental classics occupy an important place in the collegiate scheme. In history, philosophy, mathematics, and physical science, English is the medium of instruction, and the passport to academic honours. . . . The affiliated colleges are of two grades: those whose students go no farther than the first Arts examination, and those in which they proceed to the B.A. and M.A. degrees. The strength of the teaching staff varies with the wealth of the institution, the number of the students, and the class of examinations for which candidates are sent up. Thus, the Presidency College in Calcutta has a Principal, eleven Professors, and two teachers of Sanskrit and Arabic. This staff provides for lectures being given in all the various subjects of all the examinations. A smaller college will be content with a Principal, two Professors, a Pandit, and a Maulavi. In their scheme of discipline, and in the academic life of their students, Indian colleges have but little analogy to those of the older of the English universities, their resemblance being closer to those of Scotland and Germany. Residence in college buildings is not only not generally compulsory, but the colleges are few in which any systematic provision is made for control over the students' pursuits out of college hours. Boarding-houses are indeed attached to certain institutions, and their number increases year by year. But unless the student's home be at a distance from the collegiate city, and he have no relatives to receive him, it is seldom that he will incur the expense which residence involves. Two principal reasons account for this feature in our system. First, the initial outlay upon buildings is one from which Government and independent bodies alike shrink. For so poor is the Indian student that it would be impossible to demand of him any but the most moderate rent—a rent perhaps barely sufficient to cover the cost of the annual repairs. The second obstacle lies in the religious and social prejudices which force class from class. Not only does the Hindu refuse to eat with the Mussulman, but from close contact with whole sections of his own co-religionists he is shut off by the imperious ordinances of caste. Experience, however, has already proved that the barriers of custom are giving way. In the North-Western Provinces and the Punjab, where the residential system has been widely tried, the success has been considerable, and nothing but want of funds stands in the way of a fuller development. In the more important Bombay colleges, also, a considerable number of the students are in residence; in Bengal and Madras the system has been less fully recognised.'[1]

Although an important share in higher education is taken by the institutions established by private effort, with the help of grants-in-aid from the State, there is no present probability of the arrival of the time, to which many have looked forward, when it may be possible for the State to devote nearly the whole of its efforts to the encouragement of primary instruction, leaving the main provision of the means of higher education to private institutions, aided and supervised by the Government. But it would be difficult to give too much honour to the work of secular education which has been undertaken by private agencies, and especially by Protestant and Roman Catholic missionaries. In 1882 there

[1] *Report of the Indian Education Commission*, p. 273.

were in British India 4,732 institutions of various kinds conducted by Protestant missionaries, with 188,000 scholars.

The success of the measures for the promotion of higher education has been more marked among Hindus than among Mohammedans. In many parts of India, Mohammedans, especially those of the upper classes, have always been disinclined to accept the education offered in our schools and colleges, and frequent complaint has been made that they are consequently unable to compete on equal terms with Hindus for employment under Government. Feelings of religious intolerance sometimes tend to make the Mohammedans refuse to admit the necessity of western knowledge, but apart from such reasons, and (in the words of the Indian Education Commission),

'Apart from the social and historical conditions of the Mohammedan community in India, there are causes of a strictly educational character which heavily weight it in the race of life. The teaching of the mosque must precede the lessons of the school. The one object of a young Hindu is to obtain an education which will fit him for an official or a professional career. But before the young Mohammedan is allowed to turn his thoughts to secular instruction, he must commonly pass some years in going through a course of sacred learning. The Mohammedan boy, therefore, enters school later than the Hindu. In the second place, he very often leaves school at an earlier age. The Mohammedan parent belonging to the better classes is usually poorer than the Hindu parent in a corresponding social position. He cannot afford to give his son a complete education. In the third place, irrespectively of his worldly means, the Mohammedan parent often chooses for his son while at school an education which will secure for him an honoured place among the learned of his own community, rather than one which will command success in the modern professions or in official life. The years which the young Hindu gives to English and mathematics in a public school, the young Mohammedan devotes in a Madrasa to Arabic and the law and theology of Islam. When such an education is completed, it is to the vocation of a man of learning rather than to the more profitable professions that the thoughts of a promising Mohammedan youth naturally turn.'[1]

It must not be assumed from the fact that the Mohammedans look with little favour on our system that they are always less alive to the value of education than Hindus. In the North-Western Provinces, for instance, there are 80,000 pupils receiving education in private schools, and 28,000 of these are Mohammedans; thus the Mohammedan section of the population furnishes, in proportion to its numbers, four times as many pupils as the Hindu. In spite of the disadvantages under which the Mohammedans are placed by their dislike of the education given in our colleges, they hold, in the North-Western Provinces and Oudh, in proportion to their total numbers, a much larger number of offices in the service of the Government than the Hindus. But this is not the case in the greater part of India; as a rule, the share of the Hindus in public employments much exceeds that of the Mohammedans.

These difficulties in regard to the higher education of Mohammedans have been similar in kind to those which have frequently arisen in Europe. That education should be severed from religion is an idea as repugnant to a good Mohammedan as it is to many Christians. There is now little use in discussing whether we have not carried out too rigidly in India the principle of holding ourselves aloof from all concern with the religious education of the Mohammedans. No similar questions arise with Hindus, for their religion is not one that can be taught, or that they desire to see

[1] *Report*, p. 505.

taught; it has no fixed dogmas and tenets; in Sir Alfred Lyall's words, it is 'a troubled sea, without shore or visible horizon, driven to and fro by the winds of boundless credulity and grotesque invention.' It may be true that it would have been right and politically wise to show greater sympathy with the belief and habits of thought of our Mohammedan subjects, and to treat more respectfully a literature and philosophy which they highly and naturally prize, but it was and is practically impossible for any English Government to act in these matters on any other rule than that which has been adopted. We cannot teach the doctrines of Islam.

Thus it has come to pass that the colleges of the Government, those in the hands of Hindus, and those conducted by missionaries, are all unacceptable to the Mohammedan who desires that his son shall be instructed in his own faith, and in the classical languages of his people.

There was a man among the Mohammedans of Northern India who believed that this difficult problem could be solved. Syad Ahmad Khan, or, to give him his present title, Sir Syad Ahmad Khan, belongs, as his name betokens, to an ancient family that claims to be descended from the Prophet. His ancestors came into India from Central Asia, and held high office under the Moghul Emperors. I am proud to call him my friend, and there is no man for whom I feel a more true respect. His son, Syad Mahmud, was formerly a member of this university, and is now one of the judges of the High Court at Allahabad. It was soon after the mutinies of 1857 that I first knew Syad Ahmad Khan at Morádabad. He was then one of the most distinguished of our Native judges, bearing, at a time when Native courts of justice were often far from immaculate, a character as high as that of any Englishman. He was in the prime of life, a man of noble presence, honoured by all our countrymen for the loyalty and courage with which he had devoted himself to our cause, when our Government had been swept away, and not one Englishman remained in Rohilkhand.

Syad Ahmad Khan, although he did not possess the power of fluent speech in English, had made himself well acquainted with our language. He was in every respect a thoroughly enlightened man, alive to the value of European knowledge, and to the fact that unless the Mohammedans could accept the results of western civilisation there was no hope for them in the future. He felt that after a century of British rule there was still little sympathy between the Mohammedans and ourselves, and that nothing but the better education of his countrymen could bring the two races into more friendly relations. This education could not be supplied by the State; it must be supplied by the Mohammedans themselves, in a manner consistent with the dictates of their religious belief.

Syad Ahmad Khan, like the friends of knowledge and progress in other countries, had to bear the open or covert opposition of many of his countrymen. His doctrines were declared to be unorthodox and dangerous, nor were Englishmen wanting whose opinions had been cast in moulds of a sort similar to those approved by Mohammedan bigotry, and who looked with little favour on Syad Ahmad Khan's innovations. For he, a Mussulman, declaring that he reverently accepted the authority of the Christian Scriptures, had dared to enter into critical dissertations of their meaning, and to appeal to them for evidence of the mission of Mohammed.

Syad Ahmad Khan has always been a sincere believer in his own religion. He has claimed for it that it shall not be judged by the opinions of the ignorant and the bigots, or by those of its enemies of another faith, but that it shall be interpreted in the liberal spirit in which wise Christians interpret theirs. According to his belief, the faith of Islam, properly understood, is the friend of truth and progress in every branch of human knowledge.

With this conviction Syad Ahmad Khan devoted himself to the establishment of a college for the higher education of Mohammedans. He has given to this object for the last five-and-twenty years every effort of his life, and the whole of his worldly means. He was joined by some influential friends; as time went on, hostile prejudices and opposition diminished; munificent endowments were offered, and help and encouragement came not only from Mohammedans, but from Hindus and Englishmen In 1883, the college founded by him at Aligarh, in the North-Western Provinces, had made such progress that the Indian Education Commissioners wrote of it in the following terms:—

'It is in some respects superior to any educational institution in India, and one which bids fair to be of the greatest importance from a political as well as from an educational point of view. . . . It is the first expression of independent Mussulman effort which the country has witnessed since it came under British rule. The Aligarh Society has set an example which, if followed to any large extent, will solve the problem of national education; and it is difficult to speak in words of too high praise of those whose labours have been so strenuous, or to overrate the value of the ally which the State has gained in the cause of education and advancement.'

The college receives a grant-in-aid from the Government. It has an English principal, who not long ago was a member of the University of Cambridge, and seven Native professors, three of whom are Masters of Arts. The schools attached to the college have an English head-master, and Native teachers of English, Arabic, Persian, and Hindi. Religious instruction is given to Mohammedan students, both Sunni and Shiah, in Arabic or Persian, as a part of the daily exercise; but although the college was primarily intended for Mohammedans, so much sympathy and generosity were displayed by Hindu friends, that its secular classes have been thrown open to Hindus also. In regard to scholarships and prizes, the rules of the college show no partiality to Mohammedans, and separate boarding-houses are provided for Hindu students. The college is affiliated to the Allahabad University, and, with the schools attached, contains some 300 students.

'The business of the college,' says the Report of the Education Commission, 'is managed by two committees; one, composed of Native and European gentlemen, dealing with matters of instruction only; the other, composed entirely of Native gentlemen, which regulates the general concerns of the institntion. Much of the popularity of the college is due to the provision for the residence of students belonging to families of the upper classes. The rooms of the first-class boarders are scarcely less comfortable than those of an under-graduate at Oxford or Cambridge, and the Mussulmans take their meals together in a dining-hall.'

I will finish this account of Syad Ahmad Khan's college with his own words, addressed especially to his English friends, assembled at Aligarh in January 1877, when Lord Lytton, the Viceroy, laid the foundation-stone of the new buildings.

'The personal honour,' he said, 'which you have done me assures me of a great fact, and fills me with feelings of a much higher nature than mere personal gratitude. I am assured that you, who upon this occasion represent the British rule, have sympathies with our labours, and to me this assurance is very valuable, and a source of great happiness. At my time of life it is a comfort to me to feel that the undertaking which has been for many years, and is now, the sole object of my life, has roused, on the one hand, the energies of my own countrymen, and, on the other, it has won the sympathy of our British fellow-subjects and the support of our rulers; so that when the few years I may still be spared are over, and when I shall be no longer amongst you, the college will still prosper, and succeed in educating my countrymen to have the same affection for their country, the same feelings of loyalty for the British rule, the same appreciation of its blessings, the same sincerity of friendship with our British fellow-subjects as have been the ruling feelings of my life.'

Syad Ahmad Khan's task is by no means completed. Although the college has found liberal supporters, and has made extraordinary progress, the Mohammedan community is generally poor, and if more money were forthcoming the benefits of the college might be very greatly extended. The income is insufficient, and to complete the college buildings a considerable sum is wanted. There are many people in England anxious to assist, if they knew how, the work of Indian progress. Let them send their help to Sir Syad Ahmad Khan's college. They could find no more certain way of doing good.[1]

When the Indian universities were first established, Lord Canning expressed the hope that the time was near when the nobility and upper classes of India would think that they had not had the dues of their rank

[1] Sir Syad Ahmad Khan was for some years a member of the Council of the Governor-General for making laws and regulations. He is now a member of the Legislative Council in the North-Western Provinces, and the Queen has recognised his great services by conferring on him the dignity of Knight Commander of the Star of India.

unless they passed through the course of the university. This expectation has not been fulfilled. The upper classes, even where no religious objections have existed, have for the most part kept themselves aloof. India being a country where the influence of birth and position is extremely great, this is unfortunate, but there is nothing in the fact that is surprising. The princes and chiefs and great landholders of India have never, with rare exceptions, been educated. To be absolutely illiterate usually involves, even at the present time, no discredit; sometimes, indeed, it is held positively honourable, because to be anything else would be a violation of immemorial custom. Native chiefs and nobles have shown, with comparatively rare exceptions, no disposition to send their sons to our colleges, because they attach little value to education, and are afraid of social contamination.

A good beginning has, however, been made in this matter, through the institution of special colleges. The most important of these is the Mayo College at Ajmir, established by desire of Lord Mayo for the education of the sons and relatives of the chiefs, nobles, and principal families of Rájputána. Many of them have sent their sons to the college. It has been liberally endowed by the principal chiefs, and receives a grant-in-aid from our Government.

'English, Sanskrit, Hindi, Persian, Urdu, arithmetic, algebra, Euclid, history, and geography are now among the studies of the college. It is not desired to make these young chiefs great scholars, but to encourage in them a healthy tone and manly habits. To this end the training they receive is admirably adapted. If at the outset the chiefs displayed no great alacrity in sending their relatives, and if some of these looked with dislike upon their new phase of life, the experience of the past seven years has almost entirely dissipated the earlier reluctance. All the principal States have erected boarding-houses for their own cadets.'[1]

Institutions with similar objects have been established at Lahore, and in several other places. There is no doubt that in this respect progress is being made, and the rising generation will be better informed than its predecessors.

The Government and aided institutions in British India for higher education in connection with the universities numbered 111 in the year 1886, with nearly 11,000 scholars.

The systems followed in different provinces in respect of secondary education vary so much that no description would be generally applicable. There is usually at the head-quarters of every district a Government Higher school, where English and the subjects required for the entrance examinations at the universities are taught. Many schools of a similar kind have been established by missionaries, and receive grants-in-aid. In most of the smaller towns there is a Middle school, giving an education intermediate between that given in the higher and primary schools, and English is sometimes taught. In 1886 there were 4,400 Government and aided institutions of various kinds for secondary education in British India, with 420,000 scholars.

There were formerly many advocates in India of what was called 'the downward filtration' theory of education. They believed that it was wiser to concentrate our efforts on the higher education of a few rather than attempt the task of giving elementary education to the masses of the population, but for many years past the

[1] *Report of Education Commission*, p. 482.

Government has adhered to the only true principle, that while the importance of giving every legitimate encouragement to higher education must be fully recognised, the main duty of the State lies in providing means of primary instruction to the classes which can make no provision for themselves. I need not enlarge on the magnitude of such an undertaking in India. Anything like compulsory education is out of the question. Even if unlimited funds were available, it would be impossible to succeed, except by slow degrees, and by steady perseverance through a long course of years, in educating any large proportion of 200,000,000 people, nearly the whole of whom are now totally illiterate, and filled to a degree which can hardly be exaggerated with the prejudices of ignorance, and caste, and superstition. It was an almost inevitable consequence of the difficulty of such an undertaking that the Government, notwithstanding the principles that it had laid down for its guidance, should spend too large a proportion of the available funds on higher education, the results of which were more immediately apparent, and too little on the extension of elementary instruction.

In some parts of India there have been, from time immemorial, large numbers of village and local schools, in which instruction of an elementary kind is given. In the Hindu schools the instruction is chiefly or wholly secular; the Mohammedan schools have a religious character. In Bengal, in particular, these indigenous schools have always been numerous. In Bombay, on the other hand, it was found that in 90 per cent. of the villages there were no schools at all. The measures taken by the Educational departments have been much affected by facts of this nature. In Bengal and in Madras the existing system of primary instruction is in a great measure based on the indigenous schools, which receive grants-in-aid from the State; in Bombay, in the North-Western Provinces and the Punjab, on the other hand, the primary schools are mostly provided by the Government at the cost of local funds, raised by rates on the land. In Burma, where a larger proportion of the population can read and write than in any part of India, primary education, according to the ancient custom of the country, is almost entirely in the hands of the Buddhist monks.

Reading, writing, arithmetic, and sometimes a little mensuration, are taught in the primary schools.

In 1886, taking together all classes of primary schools—Government, aided, and private—there are said to have been in British India about 120,000 institutions, with nearly 2,900,000 scholars. Among them were 5,200 girls' schools, with about 250,000 scholars.

It is considered that about 20 per cent. of the population are of an age to require elementary instruction. It cannot be asserted that the figures which I have given are altogether to be accepted; but assuming them to be approximately correct, there ought to be in British India about 21,000,000 boys at school instead of less than 3,000,000, and 20,000,000 girls instead of little more than 200,000.

Women in India take a larger and more active share in the practical business of life than is usually supposed; they often manage estates and large commercial concerns, and show extreme acuteness and intelligence. An example of their administrative ability is seen in the Native State of Bhopál, which for two generations has been ruled by women. But the idea that women, or at any rate respectable women, ought to receive a school education, or any of the instruction that is proper for boys, is one that is almost unknown in India, even among that small section of the population that has been powerfully affected by Western habits of thought. Not unfrequently it is considered that to be able to read and write is an accomplishment which a modest woman had better be without. These prejudices, the custom of marrying girls when they are mere children, and, among all but the poorer classes, the seclusion in which women live, render it impossible for the Government to take any very active steps for the encouragement of female education. Nothing except the growth of more reasonable views among the Natives themselves can bring about much improvement.

In spite of these obstacles, the last ten years have seen some progress in female education. Remarkable instances have not been wanting in which Native ladies have attained literary and academic distinction; several have passed the University Entrance Examinations, and two or three have obtained degrees. The instruction afforded has been chiefly of an elementary character. The progress has been especially marked in Southern and Western India, where the women are less secluded than in the North. While in 1871 there were about 10,000 girls receiving school instruction in Madras, the number had risen to 59,000 in 1886. In Bombay, the number similarly increased from about 9,000 to 49,000. In Bengal, the number of girls at school was 5,900 in 1871, and 80,000 in 1886.

Much of this progress has been due to the missionary societies. The girls in their schools are far more numerous than in those of the Government, and zanána missions connected with the societies give more or less secular instruction in a considerable number of Native families. The example given by English ladies who have devoted themselves to teaching in the zanánas is being followed by Natives themselves, who are often unwilling to admit avowedly Christian influences into their families. The Report of the Indian Education Commission states that

> 'in Calcutta, Madras, and Bombay, and in many large cities of India, it is now possible for a wealthy native to obtain instruction for the ladies of his family within his own house. A distinct class of zanána agencies on a secular basis is springing up, conducted by committees of native gentlemen, or by mixed committees of Natives and Europeans, with the object, in some cases, of imparting education in zanánas without any element of religious teaching; in others, of testing by periodical examinations, and encouraging by records, the home-education of governesses. These agencies are already doing useful work, although on a comparatively small scale, and the commission trusts that they will receive a still larger measure of sympathy and co-operation from English ladies in India.' [1]

In connection with the subject of female education I must mention the admirable scheme initiated by the Countess of Dufferin for supplying female medical aid to the women of India. I have referred to the success of the medical colleges established by the Government, and to the great aptitude shown by Natives of India in the practice of surgery and medicine. The country is covered with hospitals and dispensaries; but the women of India are shut off from the benefits brought by European science to their doors, because their customs make it impossible to allow the professional attendance of men. A lamentable amount of unnecessary suffering is the consequence. The association that has been founded, and which has already made remarkable progress, has for its objects the provision, on a large scale, of the means of teaching and training

[1] *Report* p. 535.

women in India to act as doctors, hospital assistants, nurses, and midwives; the establishment, under female superintendence, of dispensaries and hospitals for the treatment of women and children; the opening of female wards under female superintendence in existing hospitals and dispensaries; the provision of female medical officers and attendants for existing female wards; and the supply of trained nurses and midwives for women in hospitals and private houses. It has been laid down as a fundamental rule of the association that it shall be absolutely unsectarian in its aims and conduct, and that no one of its servants shall ever be allowed to proselytise or interfere in any way with the religious belief of the people. The success of this most excellent movement will largely depend on the encouragement that it may receive from the Government and from local authorities. There is no reason to fear that this will be wanting.

In 1885–86 the total expenditure of the State on education was 2,420,000*l*., of which about 1,200,000*l*. was contributed from imperial, provincial, and municipal funds, and the rest was derived from fees, endowments, and other sources. In every province a considerable sum is raised by rates on the land for local purposes, and in almost every instance a share of it is devoted to education. Some, but not many, of the towns contribute liberally from municipal resources.

It will be understood from the account which I have given that although progress has been made during the last thirty years, a very small proportion of the population of India has received even elementary instruction.

The information given by the census of 1881 is incomplete; but out of about 116,500,000 males for whom returns are furnished, only 10,500,000, including those under instruction, were recorded as being able to read and write, and 106,000,000 as illiterate. At the same time, out of a female population of 111,800,000, no less than 111,400,000, were illiterate; only about 400,000 could read and write or were being instructed.

If we turn to higher education I am afraid that the numerical results are not much better. The number of Natives of India who can be called highly educated according to a European standard is extremely small. I have already mentioned that in ten years only 365 graduates passed the M.A. examination in all the Indian universities. Sir Henry Maine tells us that in the twenty years ending with 1883 not more than 5,000 M.A. and B.A. degrees were given altogether.

> 'I will assume,' he says, 'that every man who has taken a Bachelor of Arts degree is sufficiently educated to have valuable ideas on politics; and for the purpose of including all who in any sense can be called educated men, I will multiply the total by five. That gives 25,000 Indian gentlemen of an education and age to take an interest or a part in politics. But the population of all India—of British India and of the dependent states —is rather over 250,000,000 souls. Thus the proportion of the educated element to the rest of the population is as 25,000, which is probably much above the mark, is to 250,000,000, which is below the true total.' [1]

I have no doubt that Sir Henry Maine was right in his belief that 25,000 is much above the actual number of Indian gentlemen who can be called educated, and among the 123,000,000 of Hindu and Mohammedan women in India there are probably not 500 to whom that term could properly be applied. Sir M. E. Grant

[1] *The Reign of Queen Victoria—'India,'* vol. i. p. 526. It is shown by the report of the Public Service Commission 1886-87, Appendix M, that the actual number of M.A. and B.A degrees given in the twenty years ending with 1883 was 4,526, or less than Sir Henry Maine's estimate.

Duff has estimated that in Madras—probably, as he says, the most educated and Anglicised part of India—the proportion of graduates to the population is thirty-eight to a million. It will be understood that I am now speaking of those only who have received an English education. The number of Brahmans who are more or less learned in ancient Sanskrit literature is considerable, although there are not many great scholars; but, with rare exceptions, they have no acquaintance with any branches of Western knowledge.

The Natives of India who have learned enough English for ordinary clerical work, and for many employments in which a knowledge of our language is required, are numerous. They hold almost all the minor appointments in the Government offices; they are a highly useful, efficient, and unassuming class, but they have, as a rule, no pretensions to be called educated men. The great majority of the young men at our higher schools and colleges go there because it is a certain way of getting on in life. It is a very successful way, both for themselves and their employers, but they are as a rule content with the minimum amount of English education which enables them to perform their work. A certain number of them continue their studies and are more ambitious. They often obtain employment in the executive service, and in some provinces they supply a large proportion of the Native judges. I have already said how high a character these officers have earned for their attainments and integrity. Some of them have reached, as judges of the High courts, the highest judicial rank which anyone, whether he be Native or English, can attain in India. Many practise at the bar with as great success as Englishmen; others are professors and masters in the colleges and schools, or are in charge of the numerous hospitals and dispensaries. Out of 1,696 graduates of the Calcutta University between 1871 and 1882, 1,155 are known to have entered the public service, or to have become lawyers, or doctors, or civil engineers. In 1882, out of 971 graduates at Madras, 796 were holding remunerative employment in various professions. In 1887, in Bengal, among 623 Native officers holding the principal posts in the executive and judicial services, 542 had either passed the entrance or first arts examination or had taken degrees. In Madras and Bombay, more than 50 per cent. of posts of the same class were filled by men with similar qualifications. In Northern India English education has made less progress and the proportion is smaller.

The facts that I have given show how small an impression has hitherto been made on the enormous mass of Indian ignorance. Among all the dangers to which our dominion in India is exposed, this ignorance is the greatest. So long as it continues, no one can say what unreasoning panic may not spread like wildfire through the country, or what may be its consequences. No one now doubts that the mutiny of the Bengal army, whatever it may subsequently have become, had its real and sole origin in a panic of this kind, in the general and honest belief of the soldiers that our Government intended to destroy their caste, which involved everything that was most valuable to them in this world and in the next. It is hardly less true now than it was in 1857 that we are liable at all times to such dangers as this. Ignorance is their foundation, and there is no safeguard against them except the increased knowledge of the people. We must not undervalue, however, the progress that has been made; nor, when we remember how short a time has elapsed since our own country, under far less difficult circumstances, began to recognise the necessity of elementary education, ought we hastily to blame the Government in India for not having accomplished more. Four years before the Queen's accession no public money was granted in England for elementary schools. In 1885 the grants by Parliament and from rates had risen to 4,000,000*l*. In the whole of India excepting the North-Western Provinces, when the Government was transferred to the Crown, there were only some 2,000 Government and aided elementary schools, with less than 200,000 scholars. When we consider that in 1886 there were more than 70,000 of these schools, and more than 2,500,000 scholars, we must admit that things are better than they were.

I have spoken of the controversy of 1835, which, under Lord Macaulay's influence, ended with the decision that English literature and science must be the basis of higher education in India. Very little science was taught in those days even in England; and still less in India; and it was the study, not of English science, but of English classical literature, that was practically encouraged. As Sir Henry Maine has often pointed out, the strict and sober tests of truth which modern science can alone supply were exactly the element that was wanting in the education of Orientals, and especially of Hindus. Native thought and literature, as he says, 'is elaborately inaccurate; it is supremely and deliberately careless of all precision in magnitude, number, and time.' 'The Indian intellect stood in need, beyond everything else, of stricter criteria of truth. It required a treatment to harden and brace it, and scientific teaching was exactly the tonic which its infirmities called for.' Even at the present time, although matters in this respect are somewhat better than they were, science holds a very secondary place in the Indian universities; the progress of literary education has been considerable, but no sufficient encouragement has been given to the study of science and its application to the industrial arts. We may find an illustration of the truth of Sir Henry Maine's remarks in the remarkable success achieved by Natives of India whose professions have a more or less scientific, exact, and practical basis. This is especially the case with those who have devoted themselves to the study and practice of European surgery and medicine, and to that of Anglo-Indian law, the character of which is eminently accurate and precise. The best results of English education in India are seen in the Native surgeons and in the Native judges; the worst results are seen in those whose education has been merely literary. Natives have not been successful as engineers. As a rule, they dislike physical exertion that can be avoided. A good engineer must be himself a master of mechanical arts, always ready in case of necessity to make use of his own hands, and this is usually not agreeable to the educated Native, especially in Bengal and Southern India.

No one will doubt that it was right to encourage the study of the English language. For a Native of India there is plainly no other key by which he can unlock the stores of Western knowledge, and without it he cannot hope to take any prominent part in the higher branches of the public administration. Whether it was right, apart from the higher claims of science, to assign to the classical literature of England the almost exclusive position which it has held in the Indian educational system, and almost to ignore the existence of the literature of the East, is another matter.

I think that the views of Warren Hastings and Sir William Jones were nearer the truth than those of Lord Macaulay. If they could have taken part in the discussions of 1835, they would have said that while the study of English classical literature would be most valuable to Hindus and Mohammedans, it was not less desirable that they should study the literature of their own people and kinsmen. A Hindu would often reap more advantage from the Máhábhárata and the plays of Kálidása than from Paradise Lost and Hamlet and Othello. A Mohammedan youth would appreciate the noble poetry of Arabia more than that of England; the Sháhnámeh would be more profitable to him than translations of Homer, and he would probably learn more wisdom from Omar Khayyám than from European philosophers. No one will now sympathise with the contempt with which Lord Macaulay treated the ancient literature of the East. Whatever may be its value in comparison with our own, it abounds in works which rank among the remarkable achievements of human genius.

Sir Henry Maine has pointed out with admirable truth the consequences in India of the fact that English classical literature towards the end of the last century was 'saturated with party politics.'

'This,' he says, 'would have been less serious if at this epoch one chief topic of the great writers and rhetoricians—of Burke and Sheridan, of Fox and Francis—had not been India itself. I have no doubt that the view of Indian government taken, at the end of the century, by Englishmen whose work and speeches are held to be models of English style, has had deep effect on the mind of the educated Indian of this day. We are only now beginning to see how excessively inaccurate were their statements of fact and how one-sided were their judgments.'[1]

[1] *The Reign of Queen Victoria—'India,'* vol. i. p. 506.

These remarks point to what I have long believed to be a serious misfortune to our Indian Government—the non-existence of any history of British India which is trustworthy and complete in its facts, and which at the same time possesses the essential quality of literary excellence. Since the earlier part of the present century the old stories of the crimes by which the establishment of our power in India was attended have been passed on from one author to another. A few students know that for the most part these stories are false, and (to use the words of Sir Alfred Lyall) that 'the hardihood and endurance of the men who won for England an empire were equalled only by the general justice and patience with which they pacified and administered it.' These calumnies have caused, and still are causing, no little mischief both in England and in India. Thousands of excellent people are filled with righteous indignation when they read of the atrocious acts of Clive and Hastings, the judicial murder of Nandkumár, the extermination of the Rohillas, the plunder of the Begums. No suspicion of the truth reaches them that these horrors never occurred, and the fear can hardly be repressed that there may be some foundation even now for charges of Indian misgovernment and oppression. Disparagement of their own countrymen has always been one of the common failings of unwise Englishmen, those 'birds of evil presage who at all times have grated our ears with their melancholy song.' They find in the supposed crimes of the founders of our Indian empire an unfailing source of invective and obloquy. This false history is systematically taught by us, and believed by the educated Natives of India to be true. It is impossible that this should not have a serious effect on their feelings towards their English rulers.

We owe to Sir James Stephen, to whom India owes many other debts for good service, 'the first attempt (I am quoting the words of Sir Henry Maine) to apply robust, careful, and dispassionate criticism to this period of history.' One at least of the imaginary crimes to which I have referred—the judicial murder of Nandkumár by Impey and Hastings—will hardly again appear in sober history.

The great criminal in this matter was James Mill, whose history, 'saturated,' if history was ever so saturated, 'with party politics,' is ordinarily accepted to this day as the standard and veritable history of British India. His 'excessive dryness and severity of style,' Sir James Stephen says, 'produce an impression of accuracy and labour which a study of original authorities does not by any means confirm. . . . His want of accuracy is nothing to his bad faith. My experience is, that when he makes imputations, especially on lawyers, he ought always to be carefully confronted with the original authorities.'[1] I should have hesitated, even on such authority as that of Sir James Stephen, to accuse an historian not only of inaccuracy but of bad faith if I did not feel that I had qualified myself to form an independent opinion on the subject.

I have personally had occasion to investigate the facts of perhaps the worst of the crimes of which Hastings has been accused, the sale and extermination of the Rohillas. Several years of my Indian service were passed in the province of Rohilkhand. When I was first sent there, men were still living who remem-

[1] *The Story of Nuncomar and the Impeachment of Sir Elijah Impey*, vol. ii. p. 149.

bered having heard in their childhood the story of Háfiz Rahmat, the great Rohilla chief, of his defeat by the English, and his death. I went to Rohilkhand without a doubt of the truth of the terrible story told by Burke and Mill, and by Lord Macaulay in his famous essay, but I soon changed my opinion. I found myself in the midst of a population by which the history of those times had not been forgotten, and of which an important and numerous section consisted of Rohillas, the children and grand-children of the men whose race was supposed to have been almost exterminated. I was in frequent communication with a Rohilla prince who ruled over a considerable territory which his ancestor owed to Warren Hastings, and which had been in the possession of his family ever since. No one had ever heard of the atrocities which to this day fill Englishmen with shame. Later in life I was able to undertake an examination of the original authorities on the Rohilla war, and I can hardly express in moderate language my indignation at the misrepresentations, the suppression of truth, the garbling of documents of which I found that Mill had been guilty. The English army was not hired out by Hastings for the destruction of the Rohillas; the Rohillas, described by Burke as belonging to 'the bravest, the most honourable and generous nation on earth,' were no nation at all, but a comparatively small body of cruel and rapacious Afghán adventurers who had imposed their foreign rule on an unwilling Hindu population, and the story of their destruction is fictitious. It was unfortunate that Lord Macaulay accepted Mill as an authority deserving the fullest confidence. There is not an important fact in his essay on Warren Hastings which is not taken from Mill's History. I share the admiration which Sir James Stephen has expressed for the services rendered to India by Lord Macaulay, and of him I shall speak no word of disrespect. But it is a misfortune that he was thus misled. I fear that the time is distant when English people will cease to accept his brilliant essays as the chief sources of their knowledge regarding the establishment of our empire in India.

There remains one subject, connected with our system of education, to which I have not referred. It is matter for great regret that almost nothing of our knowledge of ancient or modern India, whether of its languages or its history, its people or its institutions, has been derived from the colleges and universities of our Government. They succeed in giving a more or less good imitation of an ordinary English education, but the young men of India learn in them very little about their own country. An unfortunate result is often seen in the want of sympathy shown by English-speaking Hindus, and especially by Bengális, for the poorer and less instructed classes of their countrymen, in their love for the emptiest platitudes of political discussion, and in their persistent refusal to grapple with those terrible social questions which are always confronting us in India, and in which lie the chief difficulties of our Government. This is a subject to which I shall return in another lecture.

LECTURE VIII

AN INDIAN PROVINCE.

REASONS FOR DESCRIBING AN INDIAN PROVINCE—THE NORTH-WESTERN PROVINCES AND OUDH—THEIR SITUATION, AREA, POPULATION, LANGUAGE, AND HISTORY—ASPECT OF THE COUNTRY—THE AGRICULTURAL POPULATION—CITIES—MANUFACTURES—DELHI AND AGRA—THE MONUMENTS OF THE AFGHÁN AND MOGHUL DYNASTIES—RACES OF MEN—ARYANS AND NON-ARYANS—THE RELIGIONS OF THE PEOPLE—HINDUS AND THE HINDU RELIGION—SIR ALFRED LYALL'S ASIATIC STUDIES—ILLUSTRATIONS OF THE RELIGION OF AN INDIAN PROVINCE—MR. IBBETSON'S REPORT—CHARACTERISTICS OF BRAHMANISM—SUPERSTITIONS AND CUSTOMS—CASTE—ERRONEOUS IDEAS REGARDING IT—ITS TRUE CHARACTER—THE REVERENCE FOR BRAHMANS—CASTE NOT CONFINED TO HINDUS—CASTE AMONG INDIAN MOHAMMEDANS—THE DISTRIBUTION OF MOHAMMEDANS IN INDIA—SMALL DIFFERENCE BETWEEN THE MAJORITY OF MOHAMMEDANS AND HINDUS—THE MORE ORTHODOX MOHAMMEDANS THOSE OF FOREIGN DESCENT—THE MOHAMMEDANS NO CAUSE FOR POLITICAL ANXIETY—EFFECTS OF ENGLISH EDUCATION—CONVERTS TO MOHAMMEDANISM.

If anyone were to propose to give in a few lectures an adequate description of all the countries of Europe—their geography, their climates, their governments and systems of administration, the character and customs and languages and religions of their inhabitants—his undertaking would not be more impossible than that of giving within the same limits an adequate description of India; nor, however much those limits might be exceeded, do I believe that for the latter task any man living possesses the necessary knowledge. I think that if I endeavour to give some account of one of the great provinces, noting, as I go on, points which in other Indian countries differ or correspond, I may be able to convey more accurate information than by any other plan that I could follow. This will be especially true in regard to the public administration; for notwithstanding my warnings about the danger of generalisations, the main structure of the government throughout British India has been built up on not very various lines.

I propose to take as my example of an Indian province the North-Western Provinces and Oudh. I choose them because I know them best. A large part of my Indian service was spent in them, and I have been, as Lieutenant-Governor and Chief Commissioner, at the head of their administration.

These provinces lie within the great Indo-Gangetic plain. They comprise nearly all the upper portion of the basin of the Ganges and Jumna, from their sources in the Himálaya to the borders of Bengal. They are one of the most homogeneous of the great provinces of India, in the aspect of the country and in the condition and character of their inhabitants. They cover about 82,000 square miles, and contain about 33,000,000 people.

Oudh, excepting on the north, where its boundary is the Himálayan State of Nepál, is surrounded by districts of the North-Western Provinces. It contains 24,000 square miles, and more than 11,000,000 people.

Physically, there are no important differences between the North-Western Provinces and Oudh, the whole forming together one continuous alluvial plain, broken only by the rivers which intersect it; but politically, the two provinces have been, until some years ago, under separate administrations. Oudh became British territory in 1856; it was partially amalgamated with the North-Western Provinces in 1877; and although there are still many differences in the revenue and judicial systems of the two provinces, they have become virtually a single province under a Lieutenant-Governor, whose head-quarters are at Allahabad. The united province covers 106,000 square miles, with a population of 44,000,000. Its area is not much smaller, and its population is larger than that of Great Britain and Ireland. If we exclude the mountainous and thinly-peopled districts of the Himálaya, there is no country in Europe excepting Belgium in which the population is so dense. The average number of persons to the square mile in Belgium is 485, and in England and Wales, 446; in the North-Western Provinces and Oudh it is 460. No other Indian province is so thickly peopled; in Bengal, which most nearly approaches it, the average number to the square mile is 360.

Throughout this great tract, although there are many differences of dialect, the people generally speak the same language, Hindi. The mixed language called Urdu, or Hindustani, which has become a *lingua franca*, very generally understood throughout a great part of India, grew up in the Northern provinces in the time of the Mohammedan sovereigns. Its grammar is mainly Hindi, while in its vocabulary there is a large admixture of Persian and Arabic, the languages of the Mussulman invaders. Urdu is the literary and official language of the North-West; it is commonly spoken in the towns and by the upper classes, and especially by the Mohammedans.

This has been for ages the most famous part of India. In pre-historic times it was the Central or Middle land, the Madhya-desha of the sacred books of the Hindus and of the ancient poets, the abode of the solar and lunar races, and of the gods and heroes of the Máhábhárata and Rámáyana. To say nothing of the more or less mythical cities of which little but the names remain, this tract contains the most holy places of India—Benares, Ajodhya, Kanauj, Muttra, and many others. It was here that Buddha was born and preached and died, and it was from this centre that his creed spread over a great part of the Eastern world. In more modern times Hindustan was the chief seat of the Mohammedan power. Delhi and Agra became the capitals of the Afghán and Moghul sovereigns, and although the great majority of the population always remained Hindu, there was for many centuries no part of India in which Mussulman authority and organisation were so complete. In our own times this has been politically the most important portion of our Indian Empire. 'To the native imagination,' as Mr. Keene has observed, 'Hindustan is still the centre of India, and Delhi is still the metropolis.'[1]

I referred in my last lecture to the unfortunate fact that the history of British India has still to be written, and to the inaccuracy of the well-known history of James Mill. I gave one illustration, taken from the story of the sale of the Rohillas by Warren Hastings, and their destruction. Some other events connected with the history of the last century which have impressed themselves indelibly on the minds of Englishmen occurred in the North-Western Provinces and Oudh, and have been almost equally misrepresented; but this is a subject into which I cannot now enter.

The North-Western Provinces came into our possession between 1775 and 1803. Until 1833 they were governed from Calcutta as a part of the so-called Bengal

[1] Keene's *Moghul Empire*.

presidency; in that year a separate government under a Lieutenant-Governor was constituted for them. These provinces and Oudh were the principal scene of the mutinies of 1857. Before that year the seat of the Government of the North-Western Provinces was at Agra; it was then transferred to Allahabad, and has remained there. Delhi, which until 1857 had belonged to the North-Western Provinces, has been since that time under the Government of the Punjab.

Sir Henry Maine, referring to Northern India, has spoken of the monotony of life and ennui 'caused by its ungenial climate and the featureless distances of its plains,' and he quotes the words of the Emperor Baber, the founder of the Moghul dynasty, on closing the history of his conquest:—

> 'Hindustan is a country that has few pleasures to recommend it. The country and towns are extremely ugly. The people are not handsome. The chief excellency of Hindustan is that it is a very large country, and that it has abundance of gold and silver.'

I cannot deny that immense tracts in Northern India, and precisely those of which English travellers see the most, deserve, for a portion of the year, the epithets of monotonous and featureless and ugly. There is, for the most part, no luxuriance of vegetation; during the hot dry months, when the crops have been cut everything is burnt up by the fiery winds; the ground is almost everywhere highly cultivated, but all is brown and arid. At other seasons, although a country so absolutely flat can hardly escape being monotonous, there is, the towns apart, as much to admire in the plains of Northern India as in those of France, and more than in those of Northern Germany.

I spoke in my first lecture of the great physical

differences between this part of India and Bengal. In the rainy season and winter, travelling along the railway through the central parts of the North-Western Provinces, a distance of more than 500 miles. the whole country through which you pass is a continuous sheet of rich cultivation, studded with groves of mango, the most valuable of the fruit-bearing trees of India, a constant succession of thriving villages, many prosperous towns, and not a few great and famous cities. It would be difficult to find in any part of the world, on so large a scale, a more striking prospect of industry and quiet contentment; and if, judging by a European standard, the traveller sees few signs of wealth, he sees almost none of extreme poverty. Nearly the whole of the agricultural population is collected in villages, between which stretch the wide unbroken fields. There are few of those scattered homesteads which are so often seen in Europe. This feature of rural life, a consequence of the universal insecurity which until the present century had prevailed from time immemorial, is common throughout India.

In the North-Western Provinces and Oudh, as everywhere else in India, the mass of the population is agricultural, and the number of non-agriculturists is smaller than would be supposed from the figures of the census. A large proportion of the people returned as engaged in trades and employments are village servants and village shopkeepers who belong in fact to the agricultural community. It is probable that 90 per cent. of the whole population are so closely connected with the land that they may properly be called agricultural.

There is, however, no part of India in which large cities and towns are so numerous. Lucknow has 260,000 inhabitants; Benares, 200,000; Agra, Allahabad, and Cawnpore, 150,000 each; and eight other towns have populations of from 50,000 to 100,000. Trade is active. The exports consist almost entirely of agricultural produce, wheat and other food-grains, ghee, oilseeds, sugar, and indigo; the imports are chiefly European manufactured articles, piece-goods, metals, drugs, and salt. Manufactures of general commercial importance there are none, excepting in a few instances in which they have been established by Europeans, but large numbers of people throughout the country are employed in domestic handicrafts. The coarser cotton cloths which form the ordinary clothing of the poorer classes are chiefly of home manufacture. Some of the textile fabrics, as the kinkhábs, or gold brocades of Benares and the embroideries of Delhi,[1] are costly and beautiful.

I cannot speak at any length of the splendid works of architectural and decorative art which are found in these provinces, and which surpass everything of the kind in India. Except in Athens, nothing has ever been built more beautiful than the Táj.

'Perhaps in the whole world,' says Mr. Fergusson, 'there is not a scene where nature and art so successfully combine to produce a perfect work of art as within the precincts of this far-famed mausoleum. . . . No words can express the chastened beauty of that central chamber, seen in the soft gloom of the subdued light that reaches it through the distant and half-closed openings that surround it. Used as a Barah Durrie, or pleasure-palace, it must always have been the coolest and the loveliest of garden retreats; and now that it is sacred to the dead it is the most graceful and the most impressive of the sepulchres of the world.'[2]

[1] I speak of Delhi as if it were still included in the North-Western Provinces, but since the mutinies of 1857 it has been transferred to the Punjab.

[2] Fergusson's *History of Indian and Eastern Architecture*, pp. 575, 598.

I doubt whether any European palace can show anything equal in beauty to the audience-halls of the Moghul emperors. No portals approach in magnificence those of Fatehpur Sikri and Delhi. Giotto's campanile is not a more perfect work than the great minaret of the Kootub.

In this part of India the most splendid architectural monuments are those left by the Mohammedan sovereigns. Simple and admirable in general design, they are still more remarkable for the faultless taste of their decoration. Nothing has ever surpassed the surface ornamentation of stone carving with which some of the buildings of the Afghán dynasties are covered, or the later and still more beautiful inlaying with precious stones adopted by the Moghuls. There seems no doubt that the art of pietra dura decoration was introduced into India by Italians, but the masters were far surpassed by their pupils. The process was applied in a new and independent style, and there is nothing in Italy in this sort of decoration that can be compared, in beauty of design, or colour, or effect, with the work found in the palaces and tombs of India. The Oriental artists of the Mohammedan sovereigns had at their disposal unbounded wealth, unlimited labour, and the most lavish profusion of precious materials, but nothing is more remarkable in their finest works than the sobriety and refinement of their taste.

I will not tell you any of the stories of British vandalism which has ruined or suffered to perish some of the most admirable works of Oriental architecture, or of the general decadence in which European influences have helped to involve the beautiful arts of India. I trust that we have seen the worst. Our English governors have, I hope, become generally alive to the disgrace which, in past times, our countrymen have too well and too often deserved for their barbarous destruction or ignorant neglect of works of priceless artistic or historic value. Whatever may be the case elsewhere in India, no such reproach now attaches to the North-Western Provinces.

I do not propose to say more than a few words about the races from which the population of these and other Indian provinces has been derived. Our knowledge of these subjects is still in its infancy. How far the ordinary theories regarding the invasion or immigration, some thousand years ago, of the Aryans into India will ultimately be accepted, I cannot tell. They have been based on the assumption that language is the test of race. Because there is an intimate relation between the languages of Greeks, Romans, Germans, Celts, and Hindus, we have been taught that all these peoples are branches of one great Aryan race, and in particular that Englishmen and Hindus are derived from a common stock. We are told that the Aryans first came from the North-West into the Punjab and the Northern provinces, and that they gradually spread themselves over a great part of India; that in the north, under the Aryan domination, the Hindu polity and religion grew up, as they are described in the ancient literature, and that the languages of the people show to this day how complete was the subjugation of the country by the Sanskrit or Prákrit-speaking immigrants. When the Aryans penetrated further south into regions more difficult of access, they could not, we are told, displace or absorb the people in actual occupation; and these aboriginal or non-Aryan races, classed as Dravidian, Kolarian, or under other names, are still represented in great numbers and distinguished by fundamental differences of language and customs. Some of the fragments of these non-Aryan races are now, Sir William Hunter writes, 'in the same stage of human progress as they were described by Vedic poets more than 3,000 years ago. . . . The bolder or more isolated of the aboriginal races have kept themselves apart, but by far the greater portion submitted in ancient times to the Aryan invaders, and now make up the races of the Hindus.'[1] Sir William Hunter estimates that the aboriginal or semi-Hinduised tribes number more than 20,000,000. They are found, for the most part, in the table-land of the southern peninsula, and in the Himálaya. In the Indo-Gangetic plain, the occupation of the country by the Aryans, and the absorption of the non-Aryan element of the population, were virtually complete. These are the ordinarily accepted facts.

Out of 44,000,000 people in the North-Western Provinces and Oudh, about 38,000,000 are, according to the census of 1881, Hindus, and about 6,000,000 are Mohammedans. Practically, the whole population is included in these two classes; there are 13,000 Christians, a few Buddhists, Jews, and others. The division between Hindus and Mohammedans does not help us much, however, in this or in any other province, towards understanding what the religions of the people really are.

I do not propose to give any description of modern Hinduism in the forms in which it is practised by the less ignorant classes. The subject is one on which it is easy to find information. But there are some points connected with it which I wish to notice.

The religion of the agricultural population, which

[1] *Imperial Gazetteer of India*, Art. 'India.'

includes the vast majority of the inhabitants of the Indian continent, has little resemblance to the more orthodox forms of Hinduism, which are alone, for the most part, described in books. I laid great stress in my first lecture on the fact, which lies at the very root of all knowledge about India, that neither India as a whole nor any Indian country possesses, according to European ideas, any sort of unity, political, social, or religious. This is especially true of the religion of the Hindus. There are 190,000,000 people that we call Hindus, but the term Hindu is one of which no definition is possible.

Excepting the wild tribes which have not yet been engulfed in the ocean of Brahmanism, everyone in India is called a Hindu who is not a Mohammedan or a Christian, or a professor of some other recognised creed.

If you wish to learn what Hinduism really is, I must refer you to Sir Alfred Lyall's 'Asiatic Studies.' There is no work which throws such light on modes of Indian life and thought, and on religious and social and political phenomena, or which so admirably illustrates the survival in India of ancient conditions of society. In regard to the religion of the Hindus, I know nothing that can be compared in value and interest with Sir Alfred Lyall's book.

The term 'Hindu' is not, he says, 'a national, or even a geographical denomination, but signifies vaguely a fortuitous conglomeration of sects, tribes, hereditary professions and castes.' The Hindu religion is 'a religious chaos.' . . . 'I doubt whether anyone who has not lived among Hindus can adequately realize the astonishing variety of their ordinary religious beliefs, the constant changes of shape and colour which these beliefs undergo, the extraordinary fecundity of the superstitious sentiment.' Hinduism is 'a tangled jungle of disorderly superstitions, ghosts, and demons, demi-gods, and deified saints, household gods, tribal gods, local gods, universal gods, with their countless shrines and temples, and the din of their discordant rites—deities who abhor a fly's death, and those who delight still in human victims.'[1]

If a religion be a creed with certain distinctive tenets, Hinduism is not a religion at all. The sacred books of Sanskrit literature represent in no way the religion of the masses of the people. It is true that the sanctity of the Vedas is an accepted article of faith among Hindus who have heard of their existence, but they have nothing to do with the existing popular beliefs. Even the Purános, and other comparatively late works, which Elphinstone says may be called the scriptures of modern Hinduism, have little practical connection with the religion of the great majority of the population. Some of their gods and goddesses, indeed, have almost everywhere, in one form or another, places among the recognised deities. Millions of pilgrims flock to the shrines of Vishnu and Siva, and Krishna and Ráma are loved from one end of India to the other, but the everyday life of the ordinary Indian peasant is little affected by thoughts of the great gods of Hindu mythology. You will understand that I am now speaking of the rural population. In the larger towns there is much more of the Hinduism that we read about in books.

Sir Alfred Lyall has given in his first chapter an interesting description of the religion of an Indian province, taking his illustrations mostly from Berár, in

[1] *Asiatic Studies*, p. 2.

Central India. I will not quote them because they are easily accessible, but I will read to you some passages from an excellent report by Mr. Ibbetson, of the Civil Service, on the census of 1881 in the Punjab. It follows closely on the lines of Sir Alfred Lyall's work, and its facts are applicable in their general character, although not in all their details, to the provinces of which I am more particularly speaking.

Hinduism—or, to give it its more appropriate name, Brahmanism—is, as Mr. Ibbetson says, a sacerdotalism rather than a religion.

> 'The veneration for Brahmans runs through the whole social as well as religious life of a Hindu peasant, and takes the practical form of either offerings or food. No child is born, named, betrothed, or married; nobody dies or is burnt; no journey is undertaken, or auspicious day selected; no house is built, no agricultural operation of importance begun, or harvest gathered in, without the Brahmans being feed and fed; a portion of all the produce of the field is set apart for their use; they are consulted in sickness and in health, they are feasted in sorrow and in joy. But with the spiritual life of the people, so far as such thing exists, they have no concern. Their business as Brahmans is to eat and not to teach. . . . The sacerdotal despotism has altogether overshadowed the religious element, and the caste system has thrust its roots so deep into the whole social fabric that its sanction is social rather than religious. A man may disbelieve in the Hindu Trinity; he may invent new gods of his own, however foul and impure; he may worship them with the most revolting orgies; he may even abandon all belief in supernatural powers, and yet remain a Hindu; but he must reverence and feed the Brahmans, he must abide by caste rules and restrictions, he must preserve himself from ceremonial pollution, and from contact and communion with the unclean on pain of becoming Anathema Maranatha.'

This universal acceptance of Brahmans, and the recognition of their divine right to be fed by the rest of the community, is the one link between the countless shapes of Hinduism; this, to the great majority of Hindus, constitutes in practice the chief part of their religion.

Sir Alfred Lyall was the first to explain clearly the process which has been going on, and which, wherever opportunity offers, goes on still, by which Brahmanism brings within its pale almost all the forms of worship with which it comes into contact, and adopts without objection all sorts of strange gods and demons. There can be no doubt that his statement is strictly accurate that the people who every year become Brahmanists in India outnumber all the converts to all other religions put together.[1]

With regard to the worship of the gods, the important matter to the mass of the population is the propitiation of the tribal or other deity who attends to the affairs of your own particular caste or occupation, and of the local gods and ghosts and saints and demons who haunt every hill and grove and village. Their names are often unknown, or little cared for, outside the limits of their personal or territorial authority, and their numbers are countless. These powers, for the most part malevolent, go on multiplying or perishing; they are maintained or degraded according to their deserts; frequent miracles, the stream of which in India is never-ending, support the faith of their devotees or transfer it to some new object; and all of them are readily accepted as worthy of veneration or fear by the Brahmans; the gates of the Hindu Pantheon are never shut. These local gods and evil powers are at all times on the alert to resent and punish neglect and disrespect. Little is to be hoped from them, but everything is to be feared.

[1] *Asiatic Studies*, p. 101.

Every disease and every misfortune is more or less dependent on their influence, and the life of the Indian peasant is bound up with the observances required to give a certain amount of security against this ever-present danger.

In the Indian superstitions there is almost always a grotesque element. I will give a few examples of them; they will not necessarily be applicable to any one extensive tract, for custom in regard to these matters is infinitely various, but they will not on this account be less characteristic.[1]

The most dreaded of the minor deities in Northern India are those who cause special diseases. The small-pox goddess, Sítala, is the eldest and most formidable of seven fatal sisters. She is worshipped by women and children only, and enormous numbers of them attend her shrines. She usually rides on a donkey, and therefore it is proper to give a feed of grain at her shrine to the donkey of the village potter, first waving the grain and white cocks over the head of the child to be protected. At the same time black dogs are fed, fowls, pigs, goats, and cocoa-nuts are offered. An adult who has had small-pox must let a pig loose for Sítala, or he will be attacked again. If an epidemic of small-pox appears in the village, the goddess is punished by the cessation of all worship and offerings, but so long as the disease is absent nothing is too good for her. She is easily frightened or deceived, and when a woman has lost

[1] I have taken these illustrations of prevalent superstitions from Mr. Ibbetson's *Report on the Census of the Punjab*, from Sir Henry Elliot's *Races of the North-Western Provinces*, and from the *Report on the Settlement of Bareilly* by Mr. Moens. I have often given the words of the original authors, but so much has been omitted or altered that I have not marked all my borrowings as quotations, and it has therefore to be explained that nearly all that is said on this subject is due to the authorities that I have named, and especially to Mr. Ibbetson's most interesting Report.

a son by small pox, and fears that another may be attacked, it is desirable to let the goddess understand that the second son is of no value, and, as evidence of this, to send him round the village in a dust-pan, or to dress him in old rags borrowed from the neighbours.

Everything is to be feared from the malevolent dead. A man who has died a violent death, or without sons, is dangerous, and it is prudent to erect a shrine to him. One of these ghosts of great fame in the Delhi territory is Teja. He was taking milk to his aged mother when a snake bit him in the nose. He begged to be allowed to take the milk to her, and then came back to be again bitten and killed. These evil ghosts are especially dangerous to women and children after eating sweetmeats, and a pinch of salt should be taken as a precaution. They are fond of going down your throat when you yawn. They cannot set foot on the ground, so it is wise in haunted places to sleep on the ground and not on a bed.

The Evil eye is more common and dangerous than the gettatura of Naples. Its malignant influence may even be exercised by inanimate objects. I have myself been officially obliged, in one of the Hill districts, to interfere on behalf of a considerable population, to give protection against a small white house newly built in a conspicuous situation, the owner of which sorrowfully admitted that, through no fault of his own, it was undoubtedly bringing ruin on his neighbours. Sir Alfred Lyall has given examples of the worship of inanimate objects of strange appearance. I knew a case in which the sight of a distant mountain peak of peculiar form had caused for many years the complete abandonment of a village and of a rich tract of cultivated land.

Good and bad omens are innumerable. Two water-pots, one on the top of the other, are especially fortunate if they be left to the right in passing; and the same rule is applicable to cows and antelopes; a snake, on the other hand, should be passed on the left.

The superstitious ceremonies observed at births and marriages are curious.

'If,' writes Mr. Ibbetson, 'a boy be born, a net is hung over the doorway, a chain stuck on to the wall, and a fire lighted on the threshold, which is kept up night and day to prevent evil spirits from passing. The swaddling-clothes should be borrowed from another person's house. On the night of the sixth day the whole household sits up and watches over the child, for on that day his destiny is determined, especially as to immunity from small-pox. If he go hungry on that day he will be stingy all his life. None of these precautions are taken on the birth of a girl.'

No agricultural operations can be carried on without the performance of certain ceremonies, and the superstitions connected with them are endless. I will give one or two illustrations. This is the manner in which the planting of sugar-cane is commenced in Rohilkhand. When the ground is ready, the plough is worshipped and decorated. This goes first, and is followed in the same furrow by a second. Behind this comes the sower, wearing silver ornaments, a necklace of flowers, a red mark on his forehead, and lamp-black on his eyelids. Before beginning his work he is regaled with ghee and sweetmeats. He strews the bits of sugar-cane into the furrow at intervals of about a foot. He is called the elephant. Behind him comes a second man, called the crow, who picks up any bits which have not fallen into the furrow. A third man, called the donkey, supplies the elephant with sugar-cane from a basket tied to his waist.

It is a fortunate omen if a man on horseback comes into the field while this is going on. When the work is done, all who have been engaged in it go to the house of the cultivator of the field and have a dinner, composed of pulse, milk and spices, rice, and cakes of unleavened bread. In some districts, the wife of the elephant follows with a ball of cotton. At some unexpected moment he turns on her, and after a sham contest bears her to the ground. The cotton, being forced out of her hand, spreads upon the ground, and the parties present exclaim, 'May our sugar-cane grow and spread like this cotton.' Not the least essential part of this and all other proceedings is that the Brahmans must be fed and proper offerings given to them.

Mr. Ibbetson gives some examples of the superstitions regarding cattle. Nothing connected with them, such as butter or leather, must be bought or sold on Saturday or Sunday. The manner in which, when cattle-plague first appears in a village, it can be cast out, and transferred to the next village in the East, is curious. All fieldwork, grinding, and cooking are stopped on Saturday morning, and on Sunday night a procession takes a buffalo skull, a lamb, sticks of the *siras* tree, butter-milk, fire, and sacred grass to the boundary, over which they are thrown, while a gun is fired three times to frighten away the disease. 'Last year a man was killed in an affray resulting from an attempt to transfer the plague in this manner. A villager in Gurgáon once captured the cattle-plague in its material shape, and would not let it go till it promised never to remain where he or his descendants were present; and his progeny are still sent for when murrain has fastened on a village, to walk round it and call on the plague to fulfil its contract.'

Great power over milch-cattle is exercised by the Singhs, or snake-gods, and the milk of the eleventh day after calving is sacred to them. These Singhs have a widespread reputation among the villagers of Northern India. Those best known are the black, green, and grey Singhs; but dead men have a way of becoming snakes, so their numbers multiply, and shrines must be erected to them. If a peasant sees a snake he will salute it, and if it bites him he or his heirs will build a shrine to prevent similar occurrences in future.

Among the delusions about modern India which it seems impossible to kill, the belief still survives that although there have been many changes in the system of caste, it remains true that the Hindu population is divided into the four great classes described by Manu: Brahmans, Kshatriyas, Vaisyas, and Sudras. In India itself this notion is fostered by the more learned among the Brahmans, who love to make themselves and others believe in the continuous existence of a divinely constituted organisation. To what extent the religious and social systems shadowed forth in the ancient Brahmanical literature had an actual existence it is difficult to say, but it is certain that little remains of them now. The Brahmans maintain their exceptional position; but no one can discern the other great castes which Manu described.

Excluding the Brahmans, caste means for the most part hereditary occupation, but it also often signifies a common origin of tribe or race. India, in the words of Sir Henry Maine, is divided into a vast number of independent, self-acting, organised social groups—trading, manufacturing, cultivating. 'In the enormous majority of instances, caste is only the name for a number of practices which are followed by each one of a multitude of groups of men, whether such a group be ancient and natural or modern and artificial. As a rule, every trade, every profession, every guild, every tribe, every class, is also a caste; and the members of a caste not only have their special objects of worship, selected from the Hindu Pantheon, or adopted into it, but they exclusively eat together, and exclusively intermarry.'[1]

Mr. Kitts, in his interesting 'Compendium of the Castes and Tribes of India,' compiled from the Indian Census Reports of 1881, enumerates 1,929 different castes. Forty-seven of these have each more than 1,000,000 members; twenty-one have 2,000,000 and upwards. The Brahmans, Kunbis (agriculturists), and Chumárs (workers in leather) are the only three castes each of which has more than 10,000,000; nearly 15 per cent. of the inhabitants of India are included in these three castes.

The distinctions and subdivisions of caste are innumerable, and even the Brahmans, who have this in common, that they are reverenced by the members of all other castes, are as much divided among themselves as the rest. There are nearly 14,000,000 Brahmans; according to Mr. Sherring, in his work on 'Hindu Tribes and Castes,' there are more than 1,800 Brahmanical subdivisions; and it constantly happens that to a Brahman of some particular class or district the pollution of eating with other Brahmans would be ruinous. They are numerous almost everywhere; Oudh is one of their especial strongholds. In that province they number more than 1,250,000, and constitute one seventh of the Hindu population.

[1] *Village Communities*, p. 219.

'Every one of them,' writes Mr. Benett, 'is invested with a reverence which no extreme of abject poverty, no infamy of private conduct, can impair, and which is beyond anything which a mind not immediately conversant with the facts can conceive. They are invariably addressed with the titles of divinity or highest earthly honour. The oldest and highest of the members of other castes implore the blessing of the youngest and poorest of theirs; they are the chosen recipients of all charity, and are allowed a licence in their private relations with the inferior castes which would be resented as a deadly injury in any but themselves.'

The Brahmans have become so numerous that only a small proportion can be employed in sacerdotal functions, and the charity which it is a duty to bestow upon them could not, however profuse, be sufficient for their support. They are found in almost every occupation. They are soldiers, cultivators, traders, and servants; they were very numerous in the old Sepoy army, and the name of one of their subdivisions, 'Pánde,' became the generic term by which the mutineers of 1857 were commonly known by the English in India. The number of Brahmans in the public service at the present time is very large. Out of 1,866 of the chief executive and judicial offices held by Hindus in 1887, 904 were held by Brahmans.

'Their number (I am quoting from the Report of the Public Service Commission) is sixfold that of any other Hindu caste, except the Kayasths—who, however, are only half as numerous as the Brahmans—and it represents a proportion of about 35 per cent. on the total number of persons employed in these branches of the public service. This is especially noteworthy when it is remembered that the number of males of the Brahman caste bears a proportion of only between 7 and 8 per cent. to the total male Hindu population of British India.'

It is remarkable that the Brahmans, with rare exceptions, have never aspired to actual sovereignty.

The ordinary assumption that caste in India is an institution peculiar to Hindus is altogether erroneous.

'Caste,' writes Mr. Kitts, 'is not necessarily conterminous with religion. Among the 185 largest castes or tribes in the Punjab, there are only forty-three the members of which belong all of them to the same large religious body. In Bombay and Berár members of the same castes are found, some of whom are Jains, while others are Vaishnava Hindus, and here the difference of religion is not even a bar to intermarriage. Converts to Islam commonly retain their old caste name. A complete list of castes and tribes cannot be confined simply to the Hindu religion.'[1]

Mr. Ibbetson, in his Report on the census in the Punjab, shows how completely it is true that caste is a social and not a religious institution. Conversion to Mohammedanism, for instance, does not necessarily affect the caste of the convert.

This brings me to the general subject of Mohammedanism in India.

In the North-Western Provinces and Oudh, out of a total population of 44,000,000, about 6,000,000 are Mohammedan.

There has been much misapprehension about the Indian Mohammedans. We are sometimes warned that there are 50,000,000 of them, many of them disaffected, and we are told of possible dangers to our rule. In regard to this matter there are two facts of primary importance. The first is, that among all the countries of India, there are only two in which the Mohammedans are very numerous; the second is, that the larger proportion of these so-called Mohammedans are so ignorant of the religion to which they nominally belong, and so little devoted to any of its tenets, that they might almost

[1] *Compendium of the Castes and Tribes of India.*

as properly be counted among the innumerable classes of Hindus.

Throughout the long strip of country, for the most part scantily peopled, in the valley of the Indus, below the mountains of AfgháFnistán and Baluchistán that form the western frontier of India, the great majority of the population has been for many centuries Mohammedan. This tract, varying in breadth to a maximum of about 400 miles, extends some 800 miles, from beyond Pesháwar on the north, through the plains of the Western Punjab and Sindh to the sea. Although within the geographical limits of India, it has no resemblance to any other Indian country. It contains a population of 9,000,000 or 10,000,000, of which between 6,000,000 and 7,000,000 are Mohammedan. The dominant races of Patháns and Baluchis are of foreign origin, but the majority of the population consists of the descendants of Hindu or aboriginal tribes, who long ago accepted, more or less, the religion of their conquerors.

In the eastern and richer and more populous parts of the Punjab, Mohammedans, real or nominal, are also numerous, but their faith was never generally adopted. There are between 6,000,000 and 7,000,000 of them, descended mostly from converts from Hinduism.

Excepting these countries, on the northern and western frontiers of India, the only great Indian province in which a very large proportion of the population embraced Mohammedanism was Lower Bengal. Out of 36,000,000 people in Bengal Proper, nearly 18,000,000 are Mohammedans. In the eastern districts of the delta of the Ganges, and beyond the Brahmaputra to the eastern limits of India, they constitute the great bulk of the agricultural population. Nothing is known historically of the time or manner in which this religious conversion occurred. But the conversion was nominal rather than real.

Thus, some 31,000,000, or more than three-fourths of the whole number of Mohammedans, are found on the western and eastern borders. In the rest of India, containing 196,000,000 people, there are only 19,000,000 Mohammedans. The progress of the Mohammedan religion in India generally has therefore been far smaller than might be supposed from the bare statement that it is professed by 50,000,000 people, and that progress will seem still smaller when the true character of Indian Mohammedanism is understood.

The great majority of the Mohammedans of India hardly deserve that name. They differ little from their Hindu neighbours in religion or customs, and they maintain similar distinctions of caste. I will read to you the description given by Mr. Ibbetson of the Mohammedans of the Eastern Punjab:—

'The Mussulman Rájput, Gujar, or Jat is, for all social, tribal, political, and administrative purposes, exactly as much a Rájput, Gujar, or Jat as his Hindu brother. His social customs are unaltered, his tribal restrictions are unrelaxed, his rules of marriage and inheritance unchanged; and almost all the difference is that he shaves his scalp-lock and the upper edge of his moustache, repeats the Mohammedan creed in a mosque, and adds the Mussulman to the Hindu wedding-ceremony. . . . The local saints and deities still have their shrines, even in villages held wholly by Mussulmans, and are still regularly worshipped by the majority, though the practice is gradually declining. The women especially are offenders in this way, and a Mussulman mother who had not sacrificed to the small-pox goddess would feel that she had wantonly endangered the life of her child. The Hindu family priests are still kept kept up and consulted as of old, and Brahmans are still fed on the usual occasions, and in many cases still officiate at weddings side by side with the Mohammedan priests. As for superstitions, as distinct from actual worship, they are wholly untouched by the change of faith, and are common to Hindu and Mussulman. A brother officer tells us that he once entered the rest-house of a Mohammedan village in Hissar, and found the headmen refreshing an idol with a new coat of oil, while a Brahman read holy texts alongside. They seemed somewhat ashamed of being caught in the act, but, on being pressed, explained that their Mulla had lately visited them, had been extremely angry in seeing the idol, and had made them bury it in the sand. But now that the Mulla had gone they were afraid of the possible consequences, and were endeavouring to console the god for his rough treatment. The story is at any rate typical of the state of the Mohammedan religion in the villages of the Delhi territory.'[1]

In these matters, I may add, the Hindus are ready to meet the Mohammedans more than half way. The Brahmans have no sort of scruple in accepting Mohammedan saints as proper objects of veneration, and nothing is commoner than to see the lower classes of Hindus taking an active part in Mohammedan ceremonies, and beating their breasts at the Moharram like good Mussulmans.

Similar accounts might be given of the agricultural Mohammedans in other Indian countries. There is no more reason to suspect these so-called Mohammedans of disaffection, or to look upon them as a source of possible political danger, than would be the case if they were called Hindus. For the most part they are quiet peasants, the descendants of Hindus, nominally converted. The Mohammedan sovereigns usually treated their subjects, in matters of religion, with great tolerance; but more or less pressure was from time to time brought upon Hindus to induce them to embrace the faith of the ruling power. This was especially the case in the time

[1] *Report on the Census of* 1881 *in the Punjab*, p. 143.

of Aurangzeb, the most bigoted of the Mohammedan emperors. The change of faith was often little more than nominal, and took place to an extent just sufficient to save the joint property of the village community from molestation. One section of the brotherhood would become Mohammedan, while the rest remained Hindu. The change of religion had little practical result, nor did it affect the rules of caste or the social life of the community.

There is, of course, in India a large and very important body of Mohammedans of a different type, descended, with little or no admixture of the Hindu element, from former invaders or immigrants, and holding with more or less orthodoxy the tenets of their faith. The Mohammedan population of the towns, whatever may have been its origin, is usually far less Hinduised than that of the country villages. In the North-Western Provinces, only 7 per cent. of the Hindu population live in the towns, while 25 per cent. of the Mohammedans are found there. In the agricultural districts, with a total population of 40,000,000, less than 4,500,000 are Mohammedan, or about 111 among every 1,000 persons; but in the towns, with a total population of 4,250,000 nearly 1,500,000, or one-third of the inhabitants, is Mohammedan. This fact tends to make the political importance of the Mohammedans greater than it would otherwise be. In many of the towns much religious animosity prevails between Mohammedans and Hindus, and this has often led to sanguinary affrays. Among the agricultural population the members of the several creeds, if creeds they can be called, usually live together very peaceably.

When a Mohammedan who has been virtually a Hindu in his customs and religious observances rises in the world he begins to assume foreign titles to respect. He calls himself Khán, or Shaikh, or even Saiyad, a descendant of the Prophet.

'In the Punjab,' writes Mr. Beames, 'where the process of conversion has been carried out on a very large scale, there used to be a proverbial couplet to this effect, supposed to be spoken by a convert,—

> Last year I was a weaver, this year I am a Shaikh,
> Next year, if grain is dear, I shall be a Saiyad,—

meaning that if he sold his crops well he should be wealthy enough to assume this latter title.'[1]

The chief classes of Mohammedans claiming foreign descent are the Saiyad, Moghal, Pathán, and Shaikh. Among these the Shaikhs are the most numerous, but the great majority of them are the descendants of Hindu converts. Politically, the Patháns, people of Afghán origin, are the most important. During the Mohammedan dynasties, and especially while the empire was breaking up, they poured into India as adventurers and soldiers of fortune, ready to sell their swords to the highest bidder. Their unscrupulous violence and courage gave them great influence, and they were the only Mohammedan foreigners who permanently established themselves in the plains of India in large numbers. These were the people, who, under their Indian name of Rohillas, fought against us in the time of Warren Hastings. The story of their cruel extermination has become an accepted fact of history, but, as I have already said, it is fabulous.

Recollections of their old dominion, and the splendid monuments which testify to the magnificence of their former sovereigns, have exercised a powerful influence

[1] Elliot's *Races of the North-Western Provinces*, vol. i. p. 185.

in keeping alive among the higher classes of Mohammedans in Northern India feelings of pride in their religion and race; but their social and political importance has diminished since the mutinies of 1857, when many of their chief families became implicated in rebellion, and suffered in consequence. They still, however, hold a more influential position in the country than their mere numbers would give them; they are more generally energetic than Hindus, and possess greater independence of character. In perfection of manner and courtesy a Mohammedan gentleman of Northern India has no superior.

It is not possible to say what proportion of the 50,000,000 Mohammedans may be held to represent the classes once dominant in India. Sir George Campbell, whose knowledge entitles him to speak with unusual authority, thinks that on an outside estimate we may assume them to be 5,000,000. Whatever be the actual number, it is comparatively small, and this is the only section of the Indian Mohammedans which at the present time has much political importance. It doubtless includes many who feel for us and our Government a deep and fanatical dislike, but it also includes a large number of men who, perhaps above all others in India, deserve our confidence and respect. It is a mistake to suppose that the better classes of Mohammedans are as a rule disloyal; there are no people to whom such a term is less applicable. It is remarkable that English education, which not unfrequently seems to develop and bring into prominence the least admirable qualities of the feebler races of Hindus, seldom leads to such results among Mohammedans. Education does not dispose the more vigorous Mohammedan to indulge in the foolish political agitation, the thinly veiled sedition, and the scurrility which have charms for the effeminate Bengáli ; it makes him more manly, independent, and self-reliant, and a more loyal citizen.

The fears that are sometimes expressed that we may see in India a general outburst of Mohammedan fanaticism, and a simultaneous rising of millions of Mohammedans against our power, seem to me, therefore, not only groundless but absurd. So far as any elements of political danger from the Mohammedans exist, they are completely nullified by the fact that the feelings of all true Mohammedans towards idolatrous Hindus are far more hostile than towards Christians, and any religious outburst on their part would be met by Hindus with equal animosity and with greater strength. The truth plainly is that the existence side by side of these hostile creeds is one of the strong points in our political position in India. The better classes of Mohammedans are already a source to us of strength and not of weakness, and a continuously wise policy might, I believe, make them strong and important supporters of our power. They constitute a small but energetic minority of the population, whose political interests are identical with ours, and who, under no conceivable circumstances, would prefer Hindu dominion to our own.

I have laid much stress on the fact that the majority of Indian Mohammedans differ little from Hindus ; but I must add that there has undoubtedly been a growing tendency during the last half century towards the purification of their faith from Hindu superstitions and from Brahmanical influence. We may hope that with the increase of knowledge and civilisation this progress towards a nobler religion will continue. It has been said that in some parts of India Mohammedanism is at the present time making many converts. It is not possible to give statistics that have any value, but I have no reason to believe that any considerable change in this direction is going on.

LECTURE IX.

AN INDIAN PROVINCE (*continued.*)

AGRICULTURE IN NORTHERN INDIA—ERRONEOUS BELIEFS REGARDING CONSUMPTION OF RICE IN INDIA—SIR HENRY MAINE ON MR. BUCKLE'S GENERALISATIONS—MILLETS THE CHIEF FOOD OF THE PEOPLE—THE AGRICULTURAL YEAR—THE BEGINNING OF THE RAINY SEASON—THE SUMMER AND AUTUMNAL CROPS—THE WINTER CROPS—IRRIGATION FROM CANALS AND WELLS—ROTATION OF CROPS—TEA CULTIVATION—THE LAND REVENUE—TENURES OF LAND—SETTLEMENTS OF THE LAND REVENUE IN SOUTHERN AND NORTHERN INDIA—VILLAGE COMMUNITIES—CLASSES OF CULTIVATORS—AMOUNT AND INCIDENCE OF THE LAND REVENUE—THE SYSTEM OF SETTLEMENT IN NORTHERN INDIA—THE TRIGONOMETRICAL, TOPOGRAPHICAL, AND REVENUE SURVEYS—CADASTRAL SURVEYS—PRINCIPLES OF ASSESSMENT—THE SETTLEMENT OFFICER—THE RECORD OF RIGHTS—VILLAGE ACCOUNTANTS—MAINTENANCE OF ACCURATE RECORDS—RECENT REFORMS IN THE SYSTEM OF SETTLEMENTS—REPORTS OF SETTLEMENT OFFICERS—THE GREAT VALUE OF SURVEY AND SETTLEMENT OPERATIONS—SETTLEMENTS IN OUDH—THE TÁLUKDÁRS—LORD CANNING'S PROCLAMATION—CONFISCATION OF THE RIGHTS OF VILLAGE PROPRIETORS AND CULTIVATORS—MEASURES TAKEN BY LORD LAWRENCE—RECENT IMPROVEMENTS—CONDITION OF OUDH—CREATION OF AGRICULTURAL DEPARTMENTS—IMPORTANCE OF THEIR DUTIES.

CONTINUING my sketch of matters of interest in the North-Western Provinces, which I have taken as my example of an Indian province, I shall speak in this lecture of subjects connected with agriculture, the greatest of Indian industries.

During the winter, a large part of Northern India has a climate as cold as that of spring in the south of Europe, and the time between October and April is sufficiently long to bring to maturity many of the chief agricultural products of the temperate zone. During the summer months, on the other hand, the crops are those of the tropics, or of a kind that do not suffer from excessive heat. There is thus in the productions and processes of agriculture a variety of which we have no example in Europe.

I am afraid that the belief that the people throughout India live generally upon rice is almost as prevalent in England as ever. There could be no more complete delusion. Rice, in the greater part of India, is a luxury of the comparatively rich. It is grown where the climate is hot and damp, and where there are ample means of irrigation ; it is a valuable crop in a great part of India, but it is only in Lower Bengal and in parts of Madras and Bombay, in districts where the conditions of soil and climate are suitable to its abundant production, that it forms the ordinary food of the people, or enters to an important extent into the consumption of the poorer classes. Out of the whole population of India it is probable that not more than a fourth part live upon rice.

The mistaken notions that prevail on this subject doubtless had their origin, as Sir Henry Maine has observed, in the fact that the English have in a great measure obtained their ideas about India from what they have seen or heard on its coasts. Because the ordinary food of the people in Lower Bengal is rice it was assumed that it was the ordinary food throughout India. Sir Henry Maine has drawn from this an instructive illustration of the danger of over-bold generalisations—a danger, as I have more than once remarked, which cannot be too carefully guarded against in regard to a multitude of Indian questions. 'Mr. Buckle,' he says, 'in the general introduction to his "History of Civilisation," has derived all the distinctive institutions of India, and the peculiarities of its people, from their consumption of rice. From the fact he tells us, that the exclusive food of the natives of India is of an oxygenous rather than a carbonaceous character, it follows by an inevitable law that caste prevails, that oppression is rife, that rents are high, and that customs and law are stereotyped.' This is as if an Indian traveller, landing on the west coast of Ireland, and finding that the people lived on potatoes, were to assume that potatoes were the ordinary food throughout Europe, and were to base upon the fact conclusions regarding the conditions of society in Germany and Spain.

Excepting in the rice-consuming countries that I have named, millets form the chief food of the population throughout almost the whole of India, and they furnish also the most important of the crops used as fodder for cattle. Pulses of various kinds are largely consumed. Little or no meat is eaten by the poorer classes, and the pulses supply the nitrogenous element which is required. Meat, however, is commonly eaten by Mohammedans when they can afford it, and the great majority of Hindus who abstain from it do so because it is an expensive luxury, rather than from religious scruples.

The millets and pulses which form the chief food-supply of the people flourish throughout the greater part of India. In the damper and more tropical regions they are cultivated in the drier months of the warm winter; in the drier countries where the winter is comparatively cold, they are the principal crops of the summer.

In Northern India the agricultural year begins with the periodical rains which, as I explained in my first lecture, are established towards the end of June. The crops of the cold season are cut in March and April, after which comes a period of about two months, when, owing to the intense heat and drought, agricultural operations are almost at a standstill. Towards the middle or end of June the heat reaches its extremest point. Midnight is hardly less oppressive than midday, except that during the day a fiery wind blows strongly from the west. Vegetation is burnt up ; hardly a sound of animal life is heard. All day and all night, except for a short time about sunrise, when there is a slight fall in the temperature, you will, if you are wise, keep every door and window closely shut to bar out the raging heat. Sometimes, but less frequently in the North-Western Provinces than in the Punjab, there comes one of those remarkable atmospheric disturbances known as dust-storms, when the day becomes as dark as the darkest night, the violent winds which accompany them occasionally bringing destructive hail or torrents of rain.

Among all the phenomena of nature, there are few more impressive than those which usher in the rainy season in Northern India. It is not only of heat and discomfort that one has to think. Until rain falls the fields cannot be ploughed for another harvest, and the danger of drought and famine, if the coming of relief should be too long delayed, cannot be forgotten. The telegrams with news of the progress of the monsoon from the sea are every day eagerly expected, as in time of war news of the progress of a campaign.

In India, and in regions of the earth lying under similar geographical conditions, within the tropics or in their neighbourhood, all meteorological phenomena recur with a regularity and an intensity unknown in Europe, and, if their normal course be seriously interrupted, the consequences have a significance which in temperate climates it is not easy to appreciate. The vital importance for good or evil of the variations of the seasons is, of course, obvious in other countries, but in India it is brought home to everyone with extraordinary strength and vividness. Not a year passes in which it is not clear to almost the whole population that the very existence of the country as a dwelling-place for man depends on the regular sequence of the seasons. In Europe drought or floods may cause misery and loss, but they can hardly lead to absolute ruin over thousands of square miles, and to many millions of people, such as that which has not unfrequently happened in India from failure of the periodical rains.

In favourable years the rains have usually set in about the middle of June on the Bombay coast and in Bengal; they travel up gradually towards Northern India, where they arrive about a fortnight later, and you may often trace their advance from one day to another. At last, when the heat has become greater than ever, the clouds begin to collect, and there comes down a deluge, almost always accompanied by thunder and lightning. When the rain is plentiful and all goes well, nothing can be more wonderful than the change which comes almost instantaneously over the whole face of nature. Under the influence of the tropical heat and abundant moisture, within a time that may be measured by hours rather than days, the country that was like a desert begins to look like a garden. The rapidity of the progress of vegetation is astonishing, and the manner in which animal life suddenly reappears is not less wonderful. You are reminded of the description of Aaron and the magicians stretching forth their hands over the streams and over the ponds and bringing up frogs which covered the land of Egypt.

As soon as the rain has sufficiently moistened the ground, the fields are ploughed and the summer and autumnal crops are sown. All these are included under the general name of *kharíf*. The most widely-cultivated, and the most important to the poorer classes, since they furnish to them and to their cattle the principal means of subsistence, are the millets called *juár* and *bájra* (*Sorghum vulgare*, and *Pennisetum typhoideum*). In districts where the climate is damp and irrigation easy, rice is extensively grown at this season. Sugar-cane is another crop of much importance; in no other part of India is it so valuable as in the North-Western Provinces; it may be classed among the hot-weather crops, since it remains on the ground nearly throughout the year, and its growth mainly depends on the heat and moisture of the summer. Some of the pulses, maize, indigo, and cotton are also cultivated at this season of the year.

The rains are over in Northern India towards the end of September, and in the following month the autumn crops are for the most part cut.

In October and November, when the excessive heat and moisture have passed away and the cold season has begun, the soil and climate become suitable for the agricultural products of temperate latitudes, and the winter crops, known under the general name of *rabi*, are sown. Between November and March it would be difficult to find a more delightful climate for Englishmen than that of Northern India. The nights and mornings are cold and even at times frosty, and the days pleasantly warm. After Christmas there is almost always a short season of moderate rain, which is of much importance to the growing spring crops.

The chief agricultural staples of Northern India at

this period of the year are wheat and barley. They occupy nearly 60 per cent. of the whole food-producing area in the North-Western Provinces. Wheat from the North-Western Provinces and Punjab has already become an important source of supply to England, and, as the means of communication are extended and cheapened, it will, it may be expected, become still more important hereafter. To what extent Indian wheat may ultimately compete in the English market with wheat from America is a question on which I will not speculate, but there is no doubt that India is capable, under favourable conditions of price, of providing a very large and increasing supply. Wheat in the Punjab is a still more important crop than in the North-Western Provinces. It is also extensively grown in parts of Central India, Bombay, and the Northern Deccan, and in those countries, as well as in Northern India, it forms the chief article of food among the richer classes. Barley is largely consumed by those who cannot afford to eat wheat. Various kinds of pulses, tobacco, opium, linseed, and mustard, are widely cultivated at this season. Oil-seeds are one of the chief articles of export from India to Europe. The principal winter crops are harvested in March and April.

Although, as furnishing the chief means of subsistence to the mass of the population, the first importance must be assigned in this part of India to the summer crops, which are dependent on the periodical rains, the more valuable products, on which the people have mainly to rely for increase of wealth and prosperity, and for the means of paying their revenue and rent, are those grown in the winter. Even in favourable seasons artificial irrigation is necessary for their successful cultivation. The rental of irrigated land in Northern India is usually double that of land dependent on the season alone.

I have already given some account of the magnificent irrigation canals constructed by the British Government, surpassing in magnitude and usefulness all other works of the kind in the world. In Northern India it is for the crops of the cold season that they are especially valuable. Important as they are, the wells constructed by the villagers themselves are more important still. In the great alluvial plain, water can almost everywhere be found from ten to forty feet from the surface of the ground. If the soil be solid, a well can often be dug for a few shillings; if sandy strata have to be passed through, the well must be lined with masonry, and costs much more. In the North-Western Provinces and Punjab, a large proportion of the cultivated area is constantly irrigated from wells during the winter months, and the number of wells is usually a good index to the condition of the agricultural population. Unfortunately, although the value of well-irrigation, under ordinary circumstances, cannot be overestimated, the supply of water in extremely dry seasons often fails, and wells cannot give the complete protection against drought and famine which is afforded by canals drawn from the great rivers.

Within the time at my disposal I can say little about Indian methods of agriculture. The implements are simple, but the persevering industry of the people is great. The experienced officers of the Agricultural department in the North-Western Provinces have satisfied themselves that wheat and barley, under good cultivation, yield a produce equal in quality and quantity to that usually obtained in many countries of Europe or America, however inferior the result may be if the comparison be made with the produce of carefully and scientifically treated land in England.[1]

The system of rotation of crops is simple. In the richer and better-manured lands two crops are often raised from the same land within the year. In the rainy season maize or indigo is grown, or some other crop that can be cut before it is too late to plough for the spring harvest, and wheat or barley is sown in October or November. On the greater part of the land the usual plan is to raise one crop only. In the first year millets are grown in the rainy season, and after the crop has been cut the land will be left fallow for nearly a year, until the following October, when it is ready for sowing wheat or barley. This will be cut in March or April, and when the rains begin in June it will be followed by another crop of millets.

There is another product of Northern India that I must mention. Some fifty years ago, in the time of Lord William Bentinck, the Government began the attempt to introduce the cultivation of tea. Gardens were established in the Himálayan districts of the North-Western Provinces, and men were brought from China to superintend operations. For many years the result was doubtful, and if the experiment had been in other hands than those of the Government, which could afford to wait, it would have been abandoned as hopeless. At last, when experience had shown what was required and what was to be avoided, the success became so great that action of the Government was no longer necessary, and the field was left to private enterprise. This was the beginning of the great tea industry of India, which now supplies nearly one half of the tea consumed in Great Britain. The hill districts of Eastern Bengal

[1] *Field and Garden Crops, North-West Provinces.*

have since proved more favourable to the abundant production of tea than those of the North-Western Provinces.

Except where the State has alienated its rights in favour of individuals, or of religious or charitable institutions, or otherwise, private rights in land have always been subject in India to the superior rights of the sovereign.

I have described in a former lecture[1] the nature of the land revenue. I have shown that it must not be looked upon as taxation, but as the share of the produce to which, from time immemorial, the State, as the chief proprietor of the land, has been entitled; that no Government in India has ever taken so small a share as that which we demand; and that the rate at which the land revenue falls has gone on constantly diminishing. It has been the policy of our Government to encourage, by the limitation of its demand, the growth of private property in land; to define for a term of years or in perpetuity the shares of the produce or rent which the private landholder and the State shall respectively receive, and to give security to the former that improvements made by him on the land shall not lead to an increased demand by the Government. The interests connected with the land possess an altogether paramount importance. The variety of tenures and agricultural customs is infinite, but there is no part of India in which the condition of the people and the success or failure of the administration are not intimately affected by the manner in which the rights and responsibilities of the State and of individuals in the land are regulated.

One warning in connection with these subjects must

[1] Lecture III., p. 75.

be borne in mind. Such terms as 'property in land,' 'proprietor,' and 'tenant' have to be used in default of others more appropriate; but since private proprietorship in land has hardly existed in India in the form in which it exists in England, misconception easily arises. It has happened not unfrequently, especially in Bengal and in Oudh, that English ideas of property, derived from a different condition of things, have exercised a pernicious influence on the interests of the actual occupants of the land.

What is technically called a 'Settlement of the land revenue' consists in the determination of the share of the produce or rental to which the State is entitled, and in the record of all private rights and interests in the land.

The systems for the assessment of land revenue may, speaking generally, be said to fall into two great divisions, one being in force in Southern and the other in Northern India.

In the Madras and Bombay provinces the land is for the most part in the possession of peasant proprietors, with every one of whom the Government enters into a separate engagement. The tenure is called *ryotwári*.[1]

'The tenure of the ryot in Southern India (I am quoting from the Report of the Indian Famine Commissioners) is as secure and simple as can well be conceived. He holds his land in proprietary right, subject to the payment of the assessed revenue, which is fixed for a period of thirty years. He has the option of resigning his entire holding, or any individual field, at the end of the agricultural year. His improvements cannot be made a ground for increasing his assessment at the

[1] The meaning of the term *ryot* in Southern India is different from that which it bears in the North. In the former case it means the private owner of the land; in the latter case it means a cultivating tenant who has often no permanent rights at all.

time of the periodical settlement. He can sell, mortgage, or let his land to anyone without requiring the consent of the Government, and at his death the land descends to his children according to the rules of inheritance.'

The land is marked off by the Survey department into fields or blocks, on each of which the Government demand is assessed. In Bombay a valuation is made of every field, under a minute system of investigation, in regard to soil, produce, situation, markets, prices, past history, selling and letting value, and other particulars, and the demand of the Government is fixed at a rate estimated to fall at from 3 to 16 per cent. of the gross produce, the general average being 7·6. The assessments are made for thirty years.

In Madras, by an elaborate system of classification, experiment, and inquiry, an estimate is made of the average annual value of the produce of the plot to be assessed. After deducting the cost of cultivation and making a large allowance for vicissitudes of season, one half of the net profit is taken as the share of the Government—an amount held to be equivalent to an average rate of 6·3 per cent. of the gross produce.

In Northern India the system is different. The Government revenue is assessed, not on each field or block, but on the whole of the land included within the boundaries of the village. The village is the unit of assessment. The Government has usually no dealings with individual cultivators. There is often a class of landholders intermediate between the Government and the cultivator; they receive rent in cash, or in a share of the produce, and they pay a portion of this rent as land revenue to the Government. Often, in Bengal and in Oudh, and sometimes in the North-Western Provinces, these proprietors, under the name of Zemindars, or Tálukdárs, hold very large estates.

In a large part of the North-Western Provinces, and still more commonly in the Punjab, the land is held by small proprietors, cultivating their own land wholly or in part, and associated together in those village communities of which Sir Henry Maine has given so interesting an account.

'These communities are represented by an elected or hereditary head, and are jointly responsible for the payment of the Government revenue due from the entire village. Sometimes all the land is held in common, and the proceeds are thrown together and divided among the sharers by village custom. Sometimes the proprietors all have their separate holdings in the estate, each paying the quota of revenue due from his plot, and enjoying the surplus profits of it.'[1]

As I explained in my third lecture, the share of the rental to which the State, as chief proprietor of the land, is held to be entitled, was formerly much larger than it is now. At the beginning of the present century, in the North-Western Provinces, it was 90 per cent.; it was afterwards 66 per cent.; and for the last thirty years it has been 50 per cent. This is considered equivalent to about 7·8 of the gross produce.

The manner in which the Government revenue, assessed on the village as a whole, is to be distributed among the shareholders is usually settled by themselves. Any proprietor may demand the separation of his property from the rest of the village, but so long as the village estate remains undivided, the ultimate responsibility for the payment of the Government revenue rests jointly on the whole community. In the Punjab

[1] *Report of Indian Famine Commission*, Part II., p. 110.

the village proprietors themselves cultivate the greater part of the land. In the North-Western Provinces a larger proportion of it is cultivated through tenants paying rent. It is a conseq ıence of this fact that the average standard of comfort among the agricultural classes is lower than in the Punjab.

Whatever be the tenure of land, the system of agriculture throughout India is one of *petite culture*. In the words of Sir Edward Buck, you may consider that almost the whole country is split up into millions of five-acre farms. The holders of these farms are small proprietors or tenants, either paying revenue directly to the State or rent to an intermediate landlord.

Tenants are almost everywhere divided into two classes. A large proportion of them possess, according to immemorial custom, a right of permanent and hereditary occupancy in the land so long as they pay the rent that is due. The amount of their rent mainly depends on local custom, not on competition; and it can only be enhanced on certain grounds specified by law. A tenant of this class can only be ousted by decree of court, on proof of non-payment of rent; and without a decree of court the landlord cannot obtain a higher rent. The principal ground of allowable enhancement is that the tenant is paying at a lower rate than that usually paid by neighbouring tenants of the same class for land of equal value. This class of cultivators possesses, in fact, limited rights of property, and these rights may accrue by mere lapse of time. A tenant who, by himself or his ancestors, has held during twelve years uninterrupted occupation of the same land acquires a permanent right of occupancy.

Cultivators of this class are usually far better off than those who have no such privileges. 'Whenever,' say the Indian Famine Commissioners, 'inquiry has been made, it has been found that in all matters relating to material prosperity, such as the possession of more cattle, better houses, and better clothes, the superiority lies on the side of the occupancy tenant, and as a rule they hold larger areas of land. About 70 per cent. of the cultivated land in the North-Western Provinces is tilled either by the proprietors themselves, or by tenants with these rights.'

Below this class come the tenants-at-will. They constitute a very large class, but they are less numerous than the tenants with occupancy rights. The tenant-at-will can be evicted at the close of any agricultural year, and the amount of his rent depends on the bargain he can make with his landlord. Below the tenants come the agricultural labourers, the poorest section of the community, depending on wages usually paid in kind. Although they constitute a large class, they are happily far less numerous than the tenants.

The land revenue in the North-Western Provinces and Oudh amounted in 1886–87 to 5,763,000*l.* The rental is about 13,000,000*l.*; but this does not represent a sum actually paid, because a large number of the cultivators pay no rent, being themselves proprietors.[1]

The first step towards a settlement of the land revenue is an accurate survey. The great Trigonometrical survey was commenced early in the century and has now extended its network of triangles over the whole of India. Its operations, in the measurement of an arc of

[1] The average incidence of the land revenue per cultivated acre is Rs. 1 14a. 8p. in the North-Western Provinces, and Rs. 1 8a. 5p. in Oudh; the corresponding rate in Madras is Rs. 1 12a. 6p, and in Bombay, Rs. 1 0a. 9p. At the conventional rate of two shillings to the rupee, these sums are, in English money:—North-Western Provinces, 3*s.* 10*d.*; Oudh, 3*s.* 0*d.*; Madras, 4*s.* 2*d.*; Bombay, 3*s.* 1½*d.*

the meridian, and in affording data for determining the figure of the earth, have possessed the highest scientific value, and have served as the basis of innumerable useful undertakings. On it has been founded the Topographical survey, which delineates the geographical features of the country, and the Revenue or Cadastral survey, which provides maps of villages, estates, and fields. The latter is the basis of every settlement of the land revenue. Each village has its maps, showing its boundaries and principal features and every field. There are, it is said, more than 30,000,000 fields and plots in the North-Western Provinces, all of which have been measured and mapped.

The settlement of the amount to be paid annually as land revenue in the North-Western Provinces and Oudh, and in the greater part of British India, excepting Bengal, is usually made for a term of thirty years, during which time there can be no increase, under any circumstances, in the Government demand. Of the permanent settlement in Bengal, made nearly a century ago, I shall have to speak again. It was also applied to Benares and to three other districts of the North-Western Provinces, bordering on Bengal, and it is still in force. In the rest of Northern India this misfortune has been escaped.

The thirty years' assessment is made on the assumption that the amount payable to the State is a fair average sum which, taking one year with another, can be paid without difficulty during the term of the settlement, the profits of good years covering the losses of bad; but in practice, when unusual calamities of season occur, the Government is never backward in allowing the temporary suspension or permanent remission of its demand.

The responsibility for the proper supervision of all arrangements connected with the periodical assessments of the land revenue rests, in the first instance, on the settlement officer. His duty is both fiscal and judicial; he has to determine the amount of the Government demand, and to make a record of all existing rights and responsibilities in the land. He has a large staff of experienced subordinates, almost all of whom are Natives of the country, and the settlement of the district assigned to him is a work which has usually required several years of constant work. The reforms consequent on the recent establishment of Agricultural departments will, however, lead, as I shall presently notice, to much simplification of the settlement officer's proceedings, and to much greater rapidity in the completion of the settlements. All the work of the settlement officer is liable to the supervision of superior officers; the assessments proposed by him require the sanction of the Government before they become finally binding; and his judicial decisions may be reviewed by the civil courts.

It is the duty of the settlement officer to make a record of every right which may form the subject of future dispute, whether affecting the interests of the State or of the people. The intention is to alter nothing, but to maintain and place on record that which exists.

One of the necessary results of these proceedings is the prevention of litigation and of crime. In the words of Mr. Thomason, the settlement officer

'comes among the people as their friend and peacemaker rather than as their judge. He does not ordinarily interpose between two parties when their passions are inflamed by the animosity of a fierce dispute or the anxiety of a protracted lawsuit; his first object has been to fix a moderate assessment, and to lay restrictions on a right possessed by the Government, which they all acknowledge and consider sacred, and for moderation in the exercise of which they are grateful. Having successfully accomplished this, and thereby conferred on them a new and valuable property, he calls upon them, whilst their minds are calm and their best feelings brought into action, to come to an agreement on all points likely to produce disputes among them; he then reduces the terms of the agreement to record, and gives to the record the stamp of judicial authority.'[1]

A most elaborate system was long ago contrived for the preparation and maintenance of the record of rights. Every field, as I have explained, is shown in the village maps, and it has a number corresponding with a register or field-book. In this are entered the area of the field, the crop, whether or not it is irrigated, the rent payable for it, and other particulars. A rent-roll is prepared for every village, showing the fields and area of each cultivator's holding, the length of time for which he has held, the rent which he has to pay, and the person to whom it is payable. A list is also drawn up showing the proprietors of land in the village, the share of each, and the amount of revenue for which each is responsible.

Until not long ago it was a weak point in the land revenue system of Northern India, that no sufficient provision existed for maintaining the accuracy of the records prepared at the time of the settlement with so much labour. It is obviously not enough to make a record of facts connected with the land at any given time; the constant revision of the record is necessary, so that it may always represent the actual condition of things.

Every village or circle of villages in Northern India has, according to ancient custom, among the servants of the community, a local accountant or notary called

[1] Directions to Revenue Officers.

the Patwári, and on him the responsibility primarily rests for the maintenance of the village records. In the North-Western Provinces and Oudh there are about 31,000 patwáris, each of whom has charge of three or four villages. It was found extremely difficult in practice to ensure the accuracy of the patwári's papers. Maps and records, prepared at the cost of the State with the utmost care, frequently lost the greater part of their value by failure to maintain them up to date. This had long been recognised as a serious evil. Public and private interests alike suffered from the frequent inaccuracy of the official registers.

The establishment in 1875 of a separate department of Land Records and Agriculture, of which I shall again speak, has made it possible effectually to remedy these defects, and to ensure the constant correction of the village records.

I quote from an official report the following account of the manner in which this is done :—

'Changes occur every year under nearly all the heads of the record which the patwári has to prepare. Field boundaries are altered; waste land is brought under cultivation; parts of holdings are relinquished by tenants; tenants are ejected; new tenancies are created; rents are raised or lowered; proprietors die and their lands are divided among the heirs; sales and mortgages take place; irrigation and crops vary perpetually with season and market. All such changes are carefully noted every year by the patwári in the map and in his annual record. Abstracts of each year's record are made for each village and tabulated, and these again are compiled for each sub-division of the district. In this way the agricultural resources of every village, sub-division, and district can at any time be ascertained.

'To render these records accurate, and to enforce their punctual preparation, a very rigorous system of supervision and testing is necessary. This is effected through Native inspectors called Kánungos. There is in each district a staff of these officers, whose duty it is to supervise and check the field work of the patwáris, to test their annual entries, and verify changes recorded by them. There are nearly 1,200 kánungos of various grades in these provinces. In every district there is a special training school, through which the patwáris are required to pass and qualify according to prescribed standards.'

These measures for ensuring the accuracy of the village records have also led to very important improvements in the system under which settlements are periodically revised.

The policy of fixing for all time the demand of the State upon the land has been—I trust, finally—abandoned. We have had sufficient evidence of the folly of such a policy in the consequences to which, after nearly a century's trial, it has led us in Bengal. It has nevertheless always been felt that there were serious evils connected with the system under which settlements were made in Northern India for a term of years. Whatever care be taken, operations of survey and inquiry and record cannot be carried on continuously for several years without harassment of the agricultural classes, and without causing uneasiness and discontent. When the term of the settlement approached its close, not only was a check placed on improvements, but positive deterioration was to be feared, because the people were apprehensive that signs of prosperity might lead to enhancement of the Government revenue.

The necessity for elaborate local investigations ceases when the village records are accurately maintained, and in a great part of the North-Western Provinces these are now so trustworthy that when a new settlement is necessary they can be used as a sufficient basis for the revision of the assessment.

An official paper gives the following account of the system under which settlements are now made in the North-Western Provinces:—

'These most valuable and successful reforms, carried out under the direction of the Department of Land Records and Agriculture, which have laid the foundations of all the recent improvements in the revision of land assessment, were originally devised and inaugurated by Sir Edward Buck. In the districts about to be brought under settlement, the annual correction of the village maps has made them so nearly accurate as to render a fresh survey unnecessary, and the rent-rolls compiled by the Patwáris, under the supervision of the Kánungós, are sufficiently correct to serve as the basis of assessment. For the costly and troublesome temporary establishments which used to be employed has been substituted this ordinary and permanent agency, and the results have been, that proceedings which would have lasted at least ten years under the old system will now be carried out in three years, and probably at less than a quarter of the expense. The first duty of the settlement officer is to verify the rent-roll drawn up by the village accountant; and unless he has grounds for believing that the rents are fraudulently understated, or that for any other reason they are very much below the rents paid in similar circumstances in the same neighbourhood, he accepts them as the basis of his assessment, and fixes the Government revenue at half the rental. He is forbidden to take prospective assets into account, and in every case the assessment will rest on the ground of actuals. In assessing land cultivated by the proprietors themselves, for which no true rent is paid, he applies a rate which is 25 per cent. lower than the rent paid by tenants in the same village.'

No enhancement of the Government demand can be made on account of increased value given to the land by wells or other permanent improvements made at the expense of the owner or occupier.

The importance of the reforms that have thus been carried out, and which are due to the formation of the provincial Agricultural department, can hardly be overstated. They have brought about a complete revolution in the system under which settlements were formerly made. The administration will be strengthened; the interests of the agricultural population will be better protected; the efficiency of the courts will be increased, because they will have access to trustworthy records of the rights of all persons interested in the land; the expenses of litigation will be reduced; and the saving of money to the Government will be very large.[1]

The Reports of the settlement officers constitute, in the words of Sir Henry Maine, 'a whole literature of very great extent and variety, and of the utmost value and instructiveness.' I have now before me one of these Settlement Reports, a folio volume of more than four hundred pages. I doubt whether there is any English county of which you could find so minute a description. Physical geography, climate, history, castes, religions, communications, population, commerce, condition of the people, education, agricultural statistics, systems of cultivation, tenures of land, history of past and present settlements, rates of rent and revenue—there is hardly a subject of interest in regard to which the results of long and patient investigation have not been recorded. This is the class of authorities to which we must go if we desire to learn the truth about the condition of the people.

Excepting in Bengal, where nearly a century ago a permanent settlement of the land revenue was made without surveys, and on data to which at the present time we should attach no value, systems of settlement

[1] It has been estimated that the saving in the cost of settlement operations which these reforms have made possible in the North-Western Provinces and Oudh will amount, in the period of thirty years for which the settlements are made, to 1,187,000*l*.

as careful and elaborate as that which I have been describing exist in all the chief provinces of British India. The plans followed in the Punjab and in the Central Provinces are based, for the most part, on those of the North-Western Provinces. In Southern India, where the prevailing tenures of land are different, the systems of assessment are, as I have already said, different also. Under one system or another, cadastral surveys have been made and registers of rights and possession have been prepared, which, notwithstanding inevitable imperfections, are probably more complete than any that exist in any other country. Much in the existing land revenue system of Northern India is due to the great Akbar; it assumed almost its present form under the East India Company; it owes much of its perfection to James Thomason,[1] one of the most enlightened men that have administered an Indian province; and its efficiency has gone on increasing since the transfer of the government to the Crown. No greater and more beneficent work has ever been undertaken than these vast operations, extending over several hundred thousands of square miles, designed to protect the interests of more than 100,000,000 of people.

The system adopted in the North-Western Provinces has formed the basis of the settlements in Oudh; but in the latter province there are some exceptional facts which I must notice.

In speaking of Bengal I shall have to refer to the unfortunate mistakes which led to the confiscation of the rights of a large proportion of the peasantry. The story of the settlement in Oudh is in some respects hardly less lamentable.

[1] Mr. Thomason was Lieutenant-Governor of the North-Western Provinces from 1843 to 1853.

I shall have occasion, in another lecture, to refer to the condition of Oudh in 1856, when it became British territory. The Tálukdárs were the great landlords, and about two-thirds of the province were included in their estates. Some of them belonged to families which had been in possession for centuries, and their claims to be recognised as proprietors could not rightly be denied. Some had been officials or revenue contractors, intermediate between the Native Government and the village proprietors; by their ability or rapacity they had often become holders of large estates, and had managed to appropriate to themselves more or less completely the rights of the old occupants.

On the annexation of Oudh in 1856, the Tálukdárs were treated neither with discrimination nor justice. In the first settlement of the land revenue, claims were often ignored which ought to have been admitted, and when the mutinies of 1857 occurred the majority of the Tálukdárs went into open rebellion. I will not give in any detail the history of what followed. A proclamation was issued by Lord Canning, confiscating to the British Government, with a few exceptions, all landed property in Oudh. His object, regarding which there was at first much misunderstanding, was to get rid of all the obligations involved by the settlement of 1856, to obtain a *tabula rasa* which would give the opportunity of repairing the injustice with which many of the Tálukdárs had been treated, and of restoring their estates on condition of loyal submission. This purpose was effectually carried out, but unfortunate consequences followed. After the mutinies there came over the British Government and its officers, almost throughout India—happily, for a short time only, but long enough to do much injury—a flood of reactionary opinions, and all the experience of the past seemed forgotten. Permanent settlements of the land revenue were to be introduced; great landlords were to be created or their growth encouraged, in the belief that they would become devoted supporters of our Government; the system of dealing with small village proprietors and communities was pronounced politically unwise; the rights of tenants were declared to have no existence, or at any rate must not be strengthened to the detriment of the landlord.

When Oudh was reoccupied after the mutinies, in 1858, it offered a fine field for the application of such opinions. 'The maintenance,' the Government of India wrote to the Secretary of State in November 1859, 'of a landed aristocracy in India, where it exists, is an object of such importance that we may well afford to sacrifice to it something of a system which, while it has increased the independence and protected the rights of the cultivators of the soil, has led to the exhaustion or decay of the old nobility.' India is doubtless not a country in which it would be wise to ignore the consideration due to families whose position and claims may have been recognised for centuries, and which in the eyes of the people still retain their titles to honour, and in the settlement of 1856 many of the Tálukdárs received scant justice. But the injustice that followed the new arrangements was worse. The ancient rights of multitudes of small proprietors and cultivators, rights often older and more undoubted than those of the Tálukdárs, were swept away or ignored; the Tálukdárs not only recovered their estates, but they received, in many cases, extravagant privileges to which they themselves made no pretensions, and solemn promises that those privileges should be maintained were given by the Government. It is true that, under the orders of

Lord Canning, all subordinate rights in the land which had been actually enjoyed before the annexation of the province were to be preserved; but the onus of proof lay upon those who claimed them. In consequence of the orders of confiscation, followed by the grant of full rights of property to the Tálukdárs, the legal presumption was *primâ facie* that the right of the Tálukdár was complete and that other rights in the land had been extinguished. Anarchy prevailed in Oudh before annexation, and it was difficult for an ignorant peasant to prove that he had enjoyed at that time rights independent of those of the Tálukdár. The fate of the tenants was as bad as that of the small proprietors. With rare exceptions, rights of occupancy in the land were declared to have no existence in Oudh. Lord Lawrence, when he became Viceroy, was anxious that remedies should, so far as was possible, be applied, to diminish the injustice which had been done. I was myself, as Chief Commissioner of Oudh, one of the agents through whom he acted, but I look back with no satisfaction on such amount of success as was gained. Public opinion in India was still going through the phase of admiration for artificially created aristocratic institutions; and, both in his own Council and in England, Lord Lawrence met with such strong opposition that it was impossible to do much. He did all that seemed at the time practicable, but it may be a question whether it would not have been better to have done nothing; for although protection was given to an important class of small proprietors, and to a small class of tenants, it may be feared that the measures that were taken tended to give greater strength to a vicious system.

About two-thirds of the land in Oudh are owned by 272 great landlords, the Tálukdárs, and one-third by proprietors of small estates, or by the sharers in village communities. The greater part of the province is cultivated by tenants possessing no permanent rights. Custom has gradually been giving way to competition in the determination of rents. Much, however, has been lately done to improve the position of cultivators. The Tálukdárs have been wise enough to see that resistance on their part to inevitable reforms is, in their own interest, bad policy, and they have concurred in legislation to render the condition of tenants less precarious. Under an Act passed in 1886, important checks have been placed on enhancement of rent and eviction. Sitting tenants are now, as a general rule—with, however, certain unfortunate exceptions—entitled to continue in undisturbed occupation of their holdings, at present rates, for periods of seven years; and on the expiry of each period they are entitled to renewal at a rent not exceeding by more than 6¼ per cent. that formerly paid. In all cases compensation is due to tenants before they can be evicted.

In spite of all our mistakes and shortcomings in Oudh, the condition of the people generally is undoubtedly far better than it was before the establishment of our Government. There has been a great increase of cultivation, the means of communication have been immensely improved by the construction of roads and railways, new markets have been opened, the prices of agricultural produce have risen, and the cultivators, although usually very poor, are better fed, better clothed, and better housed than they were.

In speaking of the system under which the assessments of land revenue are periodically revised, and under which land records are maintained, I referred to the improvements that have followed the creation of a separate department for the control of this branch of the administration. I must return for a moment to this subject.

Lord Mayo was the first Governor-General who gave practical recognition to the value of the study of questions connected with Indian agriculture.

'For generations to come,' the Government of India wrote in 1870 to the Secretary of State, 'the progress of India in wealth and civilisation must be directly dependent on her progress in agriculture. Agricultural products must long continue the most important part of the exports, and the future development of Indian commerce will mainly depend upon the improvement in the quantity and quality of existing agricultural staples, or on the introduction of new products, which shall serve as materials for manufacture and for use in the industrial arts. . . . There is perhaps no country in the world in which the State has so immediate and direct an interest in such questions. The Government of India is not only a Government but the chief landlord. The land revenue, which yields more than 20,000,000*l.* of her annual income, is derived from that portion of the rent which belongs to the State and not to individual proprietors. Throughout the greater part of India, every measure for the improvement of the land enhances the value of the property of the State. The duties which in England are performed by a good landlord fall, in India, in a great measure, upon the Government. Speaking generally, the only Indian landlord who can command the requisite knowledge is the State.'

In 1870, a separate Department of Agriculture and Commerce was created under the Government of India.

It was foreseen by Lord Mayo that this central department of control would be able to do comparatively little until working departments with similar objects had been established under the local Governments. In 1875, when I was myself Lieutenant-Governor, the first provincial department of Agriculture was created in the North-Western Provinces, and the example has since been followed in the other provinces of British India.

These departments are still in their infancy, and mistakes have not been infrequent, but they have already led to most valuable reforms. I do not doubt that much will ultimately be done, by the application of more scientific methods, towards the actual improvement of Indian agriculture, but up to the present time the chief work undertaken has been the improvement of the land revenue administration, the better organisation of the system for maintaining accurate land records, and the reform of the methods under which the land revenue is assessed. I have shown some of the advantages which have been already obtained in the North-Western Provinces.

LECTURE X.

AN INDIAN PROVINCE (*continued*).

THE CIVIL ADMINISTRATION—THE COVENANTED AND UNCOVENANTED SERVICES—THE EMPLOYMENT OF NATIVES IN THE CIVIL ADMINISTRATION—AN INDIAN DISTRICT—THE MAGISTRATE AND COLLECTOR OR DISTRICT OFFICER—HIS FUNCTIONS—SUBDIVISIONS OF DISTRICTS—THE TAHSILDARS—THE JOINT, ASSISTANT, AND DEPUTY MAGISTRATE AND COLLECTOR—THE POLICE—JAILS—HOSPITALS—SANITATION—PUBLIC WORKS—EDUCATION—MUNICIPALITIES—LOCAL SELF-GOVERNMENT—COMMISSIONERS OF DIVISIONS—THE REVENUE BOARD—HEADS OF DEPARTMENTS—THE LIEUTENANT-GOVERNOR—THE LEGISLATIVE COUNCIL—THE JUDICIAL COURTS—THE RESULTS OF BRITISH ADMINISTRATION—CONDITION OF THE PEOPLE—EMIGRATION—CHARACTER OF THE PEOPLE—CRUEL CUSTOMS—CRIME—INFANTICIDE—CRIMINAL TRIBES.

I NOW propose to give a sketch of the manner in which the administration of an Indian province is carried on, taking, as before, the North-Western Provinces and Oudh as my example. In regard, however, to many matters connected with this subject, I have little to add to what has been already said. I have given in previous lectures some account, more or less generally applicable to the whole of British India, of the constitution of the provincial Governments, of the system under which justice is administered, of the measures taken to encourage education, of the railways and works of irrigation, and of the principal sources of the public income. I shall now speak more particularly of some of the executive branches of the provincial administration, to which I have hitherto made little reference. I will begin by describing the constitution of the Civil Service.

The Civil Service of India is usually but not very accurately said to consist of two great divisions: the Covenanted and the Uncovenanted Service. The Statute of 1793[1] reserved to the former all the principal civil offices under the degree of member of Council, but the provisions of that law were modified in 1861. An Act of Parliament passed in that year[2] enumerates the offices which, under ordinary circumstances, can only be held by covenanted civilians. It includes the offices of the civil Secretaries and Under-secretaries, the head of the Account department, the Civil and Sessions judges, Magistrates and Collectors of districts in Regulation provinces, Joint and Assistant magistrates and collectors, members of the Board of Revenue, Commissioners of Revenue, and others. Persons not belonging to the covenanted service can only be appointed to these offices, under special circumstances, with the approval of the Secretary of State, and of a majority of his Council.[3]

The requirements of these statutes have been in one important respect modified by subsequent legislation.

Parliament during the last fifty years has from time to time enacted measures with the avowed object of giving to the Natives of India a larger share in the administration. The Act of 1833[4] declared that 'no Native of the said territories, nor any natural-born subject of His Majesty resident therein, shall by reason only of his

[1] 33 Geo. III. c. 52.

[2] 24 & 25 Vic. c. 54.

[3] The meaning of the term 'covenanted' is as follows: The superior servants of the East India Company were obliged to enter into covenants, under which they bound themselves not to engage in trade, not to receive presents, to subscribe for pensions for themselves and their families, and other matters. This custom has been maintained. Successful candidates, after passing their final examinations, enter into covenants with the Secretary of State before receiving their appointments.

[4] 3 and 4 Will. IV. c. 85.

religion, place of birth, descent, colour, or any of them, be disqualified from holding any place, office, or employment under the said Company.' While the door seemed thus to be opened to Natives, it was practically shut upon them by the enactments which reserved most of the chief offices to members of the covenanted service. Until 1853 the first appointments to that service were made by the directors of the East India Company by nomination, and no Native of India was ever nominated. In 1853,[1] the nomination system was abolished, and the service was thrown open to public competition. A few Natives have from time to time been successful in the competitive examination, but, this being held in London, they obviously have serious difficulties to meet. In 1887 the covenanted service comprised 890 members, of whom only 16 were Natives.[2] In 1870 another measure was therefore enacted by Parliament with the object of giving to the Natives other means of rising to high offices. It was declared 'expedient that additional facilities should be given for the employment of Natives of India of proved merit and ability in the Civil service of Her Majesty in India,' and that subject to rules to be laid down by the Governor-General in Council, with the sanction of the Secretary of State and Council, such Natives might be appointed to any of the offices reserved by law to the members of the covenanted service. Nothing could be done towards carrying out these provisions until rules had been made in the manner prescribed, and for

[1] 16 and 17 Vic. c. 95.

[2] These figures include officers on leave and others. The number of offices held by covenanted civil servants in India is 765, about one to every 1,000 square miles, and one to every quarter of a million of the population. I take these and other figures from the Report of the Indian Public Service Commission, 1886–87.

nearly ten years the Act remained almost a dead letter. In 1879, when Lord Lytton was Viceroy, rules were laid down, under which, when they had come into full operation, a sixth part of the whole number of offices reserved to the covenanted Civil service would be held by Natives of India. The principle of open competition being clearly unsuitable in India, appointments were to be made by selection, tests of qualification being supplied by special examinations. About fifty Natives have been appointed under these rules; but as the system has not passed out of the experimental stage, and will probably be modified, I will not now describe it further. These Native gentlemen, although not technically members of the covenanted Civil service, virtually belong to it. I reserve for another lecture my remarks on the general question of the employment of Natives in important posts. I am now describing the state of things that actually exists.

I have already explained the difference between Regulation and Non-Regulation provinces.[1] It is only to the former that the Act of Parliament reserving certain offices for members of the covenanted service fully applies. In the Non-Regulation provinces some of these offices are held either by covenanted civilians, or by officers of the Staff Corps, or by members of the Uncovenanted service.

The so-called Uncovenanted service has no existence as a single and separate body. Every public servant employed in the civil administration, who does not belong to the covenanted Civil service or to the Army is an uncovenanted officer. Thus, the great majority of civil officers are included under this term.

It was long ago laid down as a maxim, in regard

[1] Lecture VI., p. 145.

to the employment of European officers in the more important branches of the service, that the first selection of young men shall not be made in India, but shall rest with the authorities in England, while, after the first selection, those authorities shall exercise no interference. The distribution of offices, and all questions of appointment and promotion, are left absolutely to the Governments in India. 'It is a historical fact (I am quoting from an official paper) that the observance of this wholesome rule has more than anything else conduced to the purity of Indian patronage, and to its general freedom from party and political bias.'

There are some branches of the administration for which it is hardly possible to find properly qualified Natives. The time may come when this will no longer be true, but at the present time the Civil engineers and the superior officers in the Educational, Public Works, Telegraph, and Forest services must, as a general rule, be Englishmen. The first appointments to the superior Educational service are made, by selection, by the Secretary of State for India; officers of the other services that I have named are chosen in England by competitive examination, and go through a special course of instruction at the Royal Indian Engineering College at Cooper's Hill, which, although open to others, is maintained primarily for this purpose.

With these, and some other exceptions, all appointments to civil offices are made by the Governments in India, and the rule has been laid down and acted upon that, as far as possible, qualified Natives are to be employed, in preference to Europeans, in every branch of the administration.

Out of the total number of civil *employés* in India, 90 per cent. are Natives, but of course the great majority of these are in minor posts. Excluding the 765 offices held by covenanted officers, there are about 2,600 persons in the superior grades of the executive and judicial branches of service, and very nearly all of these are Natives. Thus, although the higher offices of control are held by Englishmen, the greater part of the actual administration is in Native hands. This is often ignored in discussing the question of the admission of Natives to a larger share of public employment. The organisation of our great and highly efficient Native Civil service is one of the most successful achievements of the British Government in India. Native officers manage most of the business connected with all branches of the revenue, and with the multifarious interests in land. Natives dispose of the greater part of the magisterial work. The duties of the Civil Courts, excepting the Courts of Appeal, are almost entirely entrusted to Native judges. A Native judge sits on the Bench in each of the High Courts. For many years past, Native judges have exercised jurisdiction in all classes of civil cases, over Natives and Europeans alike. I have already stated my belief that, as a rule, their work is quite as good as that of the English judges. Twenty years ago, the Native Civil service was badly paid, comparatively inefficient, and not always trustworthy. In these respects there has been a great change. Nothing in the recent history of India has been more remarkable than the improvement that has taken place in the standard of morality among the higher classes of Native officials. Much of this has certainly been due to the fact that their position and salaries are far better than they were, and that temptations to corruption have been removed, but I do not doubt that much has been due to their better education. Another powerful cause has been in silent and constant operation. The Native officials have had before them, through a long course of years, the example of the irreproachable integrity of the Englishmen employed in the higher ranks of the public service. Living in an atmosphere of official uprightness has made Native judges and magistrates upright also.

Although the salaries given to Natives in posts of importance are ordinarily less than those given to Englishmen, they are very liberal, and they do not err on the side of being too small. With the exception of England, there is no country in Europe in which judicial and executive officers receive salaries equal to those given in the Native Civil service of India.[1] At

[1] It is difficult to compare salaries in countries where the conditions of life and the official duties to be performed are very different. Subject to this warning, which, however, tells strongly in favour of what I have said regarding the salaries paid to natives of India, I give the following facts. In Bengal a Native High Court judge receives 5,000*l.* a year. The salaries of the Native subordinate judges range from 720*l.* to 1,200*l.*, and those of the Munsifs (the lowest class of judges) from 300*l.* to 480*l.* The salaries of the higher grades in the executive service are not very dissimilar. In Algeria, the highest judicial officer, the First President of the Court of Appeal, who is always a Frenchman, receives 720*l.*, with a furnished house. No other judge has more than 400*l.* The Juges de Paix, also Frenchmen, receive from 108*l.* to 160*l.* a year, with furnished houses. The salary of no Mohammedan judicial officer, a native of Algeria, exceeds 60*l.* The Préfet of Algiers receives 1,000*l.*, and two other Préfets receive 800*l.*; each Préfet has also a travelling allowance of 200*l.* a year and a furnished house. No Sous-Préfet has more than 360*l.* In France itself the salaries of the higher judicial and executive officers are smaller than those given to Natives in India. For instance, the First President of the Cour de Cassation receives 1,200*l.* In the Cour d'Appel, the salaries of the First Presidents range from 600*l.* to 1,000*l.*, and of the other Presidents from 300*l.* to 550*l.* In the Tribunaux de Première Instance the salaries of the judges are from 144*l.* to 800*l.* The Juges d'Instruction receive from 115*l.* to 384*l.*; the Juges de Paix from 72*l.* to 320*l.* In many cases these salaries are supplemented by the grant of furnished houses and by various allowances, usually of small amount. A comparison between the salaries given to officers of the executive service in India and in France would show similar results. The great majority of the Préfets in France, who hold offices second in importance to hardly any in the country, receive less than Native Deputy Magistrates of the higher grades in Bengal.

the same time, I do not doubt that much remains to be done in throwing open to Natives a larger proportion of the offices now reserved for Englishmen. This is a question to which I shall refer in another lecture. I now come back to the subject of the administration of an Indian province.

Throughout British India the District, technically so called, is the unit of administration. Every province is divided into Districts, each of which has its separate organisation. A province is a collection of Districts; and without a clear conception of a District no one can understand how the actual government of India is carried on. In the details of District organisation there are great differences in different provinces, but the general principles on which the administrative system is based are much the same everywhere, and the account which I am about to give of a District in the North-Western Provinces is, in many respects, generally applicable to the whole of British India.

The North-Western Provinces and Oudh are divided into forty-nine districts, each of which is a compact tract, having usually an area of 1,500 or 2,000 square miles, and a population of 750,000 to 1,500,000. This is about the area and population of one of the larger English counties. In some provinces, and especially in Madras, the districts are much more extensive.

In India, where an absolute government is administered by a small body of foreigners far more advanced in civilisation than the people of the country itself, the most essential condition of safety to the rulers, and of good government to the people, is that authority should be strong, and authority cannot be strong unless it is concentrated. In every district of British India the Government has its representative in whom all executive authority centres. This officer, in the North-Western Provinces, in Bengal, in Madras, and in Bombay, is called the Magistrate and Collector, or Collector alone; in the Punjab, in Oudh, in Burma, and in the other so-called Non-Regulation provinces, he is called the Deputy Commissioner. The term 'District Officer,' by which he is often known, is applicable in both cases. The name Collector conveys to English ears a very false idea. A collector in England is a petty officer who collects rates and taxes; in India he is, in many respects, the most important officer in the whole administrative hierarchy.

I borrow from Sir William Hunter the following description:—

'The district officer, whether known as collector-magistrate or as deputy commissioner, is the responsible head of his jurisdiction. Upon his energy and personal character depends ultimately the efficiency of our Indian Government. His own special duties are so numerous and so various as to bewilder the outsider; and the work of his subordinates, European and native, largely depends upon the stimulus of his personal example. His position has been compared to that of the French *préfet*, but such a comparison is unjust in many ways to the Indian district officer. He is not a mere subordinate of a central bureau, who takes his colour from his chief and represents the political parties or the permanent officialism of the capital. The Indian collector is a strongly individualised worker in every department of rural well-being, with a large measure of local independence and of individual initiative. As the name of collector-magistrate implies, his main functions are twofold. He is a fiscal officer, charged with the collection of the revenue from the land and other sources; he is also a revenue and criminal judge, both of first instance and in appeal. But his title by no means exhausts his multifarious duties. He does in his smaller local sphere all that the Home Secretary superintends in England, and a great deal more, for he is the representative of a paternal and not of a constitutional Government.

Police, jails, education, municipalities, roads, sanitation, dispensaries, the local taxation, and the imperial revenues of his district are to him matters of daily concern. He is expected to make himself acquainted with every phase of the social life of the natives, and with each natural aspect of the country. He should be a lawyer, an accountant, a financier, and a ready writer of state papers. He ought also to possess no mean knowledge of agriculture, political economy, and engineering.'[1]

All this signifies, not that he is expected to be omniscient, but that the magistrate and collector is the principal officer of Government in every branch of the executive administration of the district. As the local representative of the Government, through whom all the orders and measures of the ruling power are issued and made known to the people, and on whom the Government depends for information of every serious matter that occurs, he holds a position of great and exceptional importance. If the district officer is weak and incapable, authority and law in the district are weak also; if he is strong and competent, they are respected. Every cause which tends to diminish his influence lessens the authority of the Government, whether that cause be shortcomings of his own, or the injudicious action of his superiors. At the same time, it must not be supposed that he has any irresponsible and arbitrary power; all his more important duties are strictly regulated either by law or by rules laid down by the Government, and all his proceedings are subject to supervision and, when necessary, to correction.

His duties as collector differ in different provinces, according to the system on which the land revenue is assessed, the prevailing tenures of land, and other local

[1] *Imperial Gazetteer of India*, Art. 'India.'

circumstances. Thus, in Bengal, where the Government demand has been fixed in perpetuity, and where no attempt has been made to maintain accurate records of existing rights in the land, the duties of the collector are less important and difficult than in the temporarily settled provinces.

In the North-Western Provinces, the collector, as Mr. Thomason writes, 'in order properly to discharge his duties, must possess the most complete knowledge of the landed tenures in his district, and of everything which tends to affect the interests of the agricultural population.' He has to act in many capacities. He supervises the arrangements for securing the payment at the appointed times of the land revenue, the excise upon spirits, the revenue derived from stamps, and the assessment and collection of the income tax. He is personally responsible for the care of the Government treasury at the head-quarters of the district, and for the punctual preparation and submission of the public accounts. The records and registers affecting landed property are deposited in his office; and, in connection with the Agricultural department of which I spoke in my last lecture, the duty rests upon him of maintaining in a condition of efficiency the elaborate system laid down for their preservation and correction. He decides judicially, subject in many cases to an appeal to the Civil courts, disputes regarding rent, and other questions between landlords and tenants.

'Nothing can pass in the district of which it is not his duty to keep himself informed, and to watch the operation. The vicissitudes of trade, the state of the currency, the administration of civil justice, the progress of public works, must all affect most materially the interests of the classes of whom he is the constituted guardian. Officious interference in matters beyond his immediate control must be avoided, but temperate and intelligent remonstrance against anything which he sees to be wrong is one of his most important duties.'[1]

I need hardly say that the district officer cannot administer personally the details of all this business. He has at his disposal a large staff of officers, English and Native, through whom the work is carried on. An efficient district officer watches every department of the administration; he is always ready to intervene, but he does not occupy himself with the details of business which his subordinates are as competent as himself to transact. His duties of supervision are so onerous and important that he ought, as Mr. Thomason has said, to do nothing that he can make others do for him.

Every district is partitioned, for the convenient administration of business, into a number of subdivisions, often corresponding with those that existed before our time. Each revenue subdivision is in charge of a Native officer of high standing, called in the northern provinces a Tahsildár, and in Southern India a Mamlatdár. He superintends the collection of the revenues, and all business connected with the land. The Tahsildárs are the principal agents of the collector in the interior of the district, and their duties, on a smaller scale, are almost as various as those of the collector himself. They are chosen with care, and are an intelligent and excellent class of public servants. 'The satisfactory administration of the subdivision,' the Famine Commissioners write, 'the proper carrying out of the details of government, the protection of the people from hardships and oppression, the detection of abuses, and the general well-being of the community, very greatly depend upon the integrity, zeal, and

[1] *Directions for Collectors, N.W.P.*, p. 184.

ability of the Tahsildár.' There are usually five or six Tahsildárs in each district of the North-Western Provinces.

The district officer is also the chief magistrate of the district; but the title of magistrate is hardly, according to English ideas, more appropriate than that of collector. He exercises, it is true, magisterial functions, but he is a great deal more than a magistrate. The responsibility for the protection of life and property throughout the district, for the maintenance of the public peace, and for ensuring obedience to the laws, rests ultimately upon him. He exercises supreme authority over the police, and all the magisterial courts and the gaols are under his supervision. In one capacity or another, he possesses all the authority necessary to make him, in the eyes of the people, the representative of the Executive Government.

The first place on his staff is held by the Joint Magistrate and Deputy Collector; in the Non-Regulation Provinces he is called Assistant Commissioner. He is always an officer of considerable length of service and experience. The territorial or other limits of his jurisdiction are determined by the district officer; the extent of his executive authority mainly depends on the amount of confidence placed in him by his superior; but in respect of cases heard by him as a magistrate, his powers are almost the same as those of the district officer himself. Next below him comes the Assistant Magistrate and Collector; if the district be large and the work heavy, there may be more than one officer of this grade. No assistant is invested with any powers or receives promotion until he has given evidence of his competency by passing examinations in the Native languages and in law. The magistrate and collector, the joint magistrate and deputy collector, and the assistant, are all, with rare exceptions, Englishmen belonging to the covenanted Civil service. The other chief officers of the executive staff are the Deputy Collectors and Deputy Magistrates; they are almost always Natives. There are several in each district, some of them at the head-quarters, and others in the interior of the district.

I have spoken in a previous lecture[1] of the Code of Criminal Procedure which defines the various classes of magisterial and other criminal courts, and the powers which each class of officers can exercise.

The system under which the police is administered differs in different provinces, but its general organisation throughout India is based on a law passed in 1861, and the manner in which its duties are to be performed is laid down in great detail in the Code of Criminal Procedure. Every district is divided into a number of police divisions, each of which is in charge of a police officer, almost always a Native, with a force of constables, clerks, and other subordinates. Every village or circle of villages has, according to the ancient custom of the country, its chaukidár, or watchman, whose duty it is to report all occurrences falling within the cognisance of the police.

Under the Native Governments that preceded us there was, outside the towns, hardly any police at all, and the responsibility for preserving the peace and for the detection of serious crime rested on the proprietors of land. This responsibility still attaches to them by law, and various old regulations define their obligations for reporting, preventing, and detecting crime. It was inevitable that as the administration became more

[1] Lecture VI., p. 150.

regular, and more completely organised, the difficulty of enforcing general responsibilities of this kind would become greater, and the assistance practically given by the landholders in matters of police is usually small.

At the head-quarters of every district there is an officer called the District Superintendent of police. He is, with rare exceptions, an Englishman, and sometimes an officer of the army. He supervises, with the help of his staff of inspectors and others, and subject to the general control of the magistrate of the district, all police arrangements, and is responsible for the efficiency and good behaviour of the force. The law gives to the district officer a general power over the police of the district, but the interference which he practically exercises varies in different provinces. In the North-Western Provinces and Oudh his supreme authority and responsibility have been carefully maintained; but in some other provinces (unfortunately, as I think) his powers have been so strictly limited that the police has become virtually a separate department, administered by the District Superintendent, under the orders of the Inspector-General of police, at the head-quarters of the Government.

The character of the police in India varies much. Before the transfer of the Government to the Crown, no branch of the administration was in greater need of reform. The police was often oppressive and corrupt. The traditions of police management in India tended to encourage much that was bad. Under all Native Governments, past and present, torture has been avowedly or tacitly permitted, and has been looked upon as a natural and legitimate means of obtaining evidence. The people, for the most part, will not protect themselves, but have been accustomed, from time immemorial, to submit unresistingly to all official action. Under such circumstances it has always been difficult to guard against abuses. The improvement has been great. There is little violent crime, and the protection to life and property is as complete as in almost any European country. But there can be no doubt that Sir James Stephen is right when he gives, as a result of his personal experience in India, the opinion that 'no part of the institutions by which India is governed requires more careful watching in order to prevent the police, which is designed for the protection of the people, from becoming a means of petty oppression. The Code of Criminal Procedure is full of provisions intended to guard against this and at the same time to make the police efficient for their purpose.'[1]

Every district has its gaol, and there are central prisons in convenient situations. There are few countries in Europe where the gaols are so well looked after. A great Indian prison is a model of cleanliness and good management. Every district has also its engineer establishments for the construction and maintenance of roads, bridges, and other public works and buildings; its telegraph and post-offices; its schools and hospitals. More than 250 hospitals and dispensaries have been established in the North-Western Provinces and Oudh, and more than 2,000,000 patients are treated in them every year. I have already spoken of these institutions, and of the great skill of many of the Native surgeons. They are highly valued by the people, and for the most part are supported by voluntary local subscriptions, the Government supplying only the Native doctor and European medicines. Each district has a European

[1] *History of the Criminal Law of England*, vol. iii. p. 331.

officer, called the Civil Surgeon, who supervises all the medical establishments.

I wish that I could give as satisfactory an account of the progress of sanitary improvement, but the prejudices and ignorance of the people make even simple reforms difficult. Much has been done to improve the sanitary condition of the larger towns, but there is little reason to believe that the country generally is less liable than in former times to virulent attacks of epidemic cholera and fever. There is, indeed, one respect in which progress has been made. Smallpox has always been extremely fatal in Northern India, but a large part of the North-Western Provinces is now becoming well protected by vaccination. The prejudices and suspicions of the people have gradually been giving way, and vaccination is extended with constantly increasing success. In the Himálayan districts, in particular, smallpox, which thirty years ago sometimes decimated the population, has been almost extirpated. A staff of vaccinators is maintained by the Government in every district of the North-Western Provinces and Oudh. It is only in a few of the larger cantonments that vaccination has been made compulsory. The whole sanitary department of the province is under the control of an officer called the Sanitary Commissioner.

I will not again speak of the public works constructed by the British Government in Northern India. I have already given some account of the great canals of irrigation, and have shown the immense improvement that has taken place in the provision of means of communication.[1] All the principal towns and districts are now connected by railways, and the country is well supplied with roads and bridges.

[1] Lecture V., pp. 125–132.

I described in a previous lecture[1] the system of education followed in the Indian universities, colleges, and schools. The villages in the districts of the North-Western Provinces are grouped together in small circles, each of which has its Government school, affording elementary instruction to the poorer classes of the agricultural population. These schools teach, in the language of the country, reading, writing, arithmetic, and a little geography and mensuration. Although they are so numerous that the means of primary education are almost everywhere within reach, they contained in 1886 only about 200,000 scholars. Besides these there were nearly 80,000 scholars in so-called indigenous schools, which have no connection with the Educational department of the Government.

In each revenue subdivision there is a school, teaching, in the vernacular language, grammar, geography, Indian history, arithmetic, algebra, geometry, mensuration, and the elements of natural science. At the head-quarters of the district there is always a Government school of a superior kind, in which English is taught, and in many of the larger towns there are good schools conducted by private agencies, chiefly by missionaries, receiving grants-in-aid from the Government. These schools often give an education up to the standard of the entrance examination of the university.

I have already spoken of the colleges, of which there are six in these provinces. Until 1887 the direction of higher education was in the hands of the University of Calcutta, but in that year a university was established at Allahabad, to which the colleges of the North-Western Provinces and Oudh have been affiliated. Like the

[1] Lecture VII., p. 164.

other Indian universities, with the exception of that at Lahore, it is not a teaching body.

For the management of local affairs every large town has its municipality, the members of which are chiefly natives of the place not in the service of the Government. There are 109 of these municipalities in the North-Western Provinces and Oudh, and more than 3,000,000 people live within their limits. These non-official bodies co-operate usefully with the Government authorities in the management of the roads, conservancy, schools, hospitals, and in all the local business. Many of the Native members are honorary magistrates, often associated in Benches. More than a quarter of the less serious criminal cases brought to trial in the North-Western Provinces are decided by the unpaid Native magistracy.

In almost all cases a large majority of the members of the municipal boards are elected by the townspeople. The voting qualification depends on amount of income, house-rating, and contribution to municipal taxation. The rules under which elections are conducted are framed by the Provincial Government, and vary according to local circumstances. The chairman is usually the magistrate of the district, but in this matter the boards have generally the power of making their own choice. The income of the municipalities of the North-Western Provinces and Oudh amounted in 1886 to 270,000*l.*, the greater part of which was raised by octroi duties on articles brought into the towns for consumption.

There are similar boards in the rural districts. An electoral body is nominated by the Government, and this body chooses from its own members not less than three-fourths of the board. The magistrate of the district is the chairman. These boards levy no rates, but local funds and grants from the provincial revenues are assigned for the local duties entrusted to them.

During the last few years much has been done throughout India in the direction of local self-government, but the systems in force are still to a great extent in a tentative stage. It cannot be said that the people usually take much interest in such matters; they care nothing for sanitation, or for any of the modern improvements to which we attach importance, and if they were left to please themselves they would ordinarily prefer that their towns and villages should remain in the condition with which their forefathers were content. No taxation is more unpopular in India than direct taxation for local purposes. People can understand that they must contribute towards the expenses of the State, for the maintenance of the army, for the courts of justice, and so forth; but that they should be made to pay for the drainage of their streets, and for so-called improvements which we tell them will diminish mortality and disease, is a thing of which they fail to see the necessity or justice. Nevertheless men are often found among the Native members of the municipalities who are sufficiently enlightened to understand the value of the work in which they are engaged, and glad to help in performing it.

Including the cities of Calcutta, Bombay, and Madras, there were in 1886 in British India 750 municipalities, with an income of 3,500,000*l*., and a population, within municipal limits, of 14,500,000.

I must now speak of the manner in which the executive authorities of the districts are brought under the control of the Provincial Government.

The forty-nine districts of the North-Western Provinces and Oudh are grouped together into eleven Divisions, technically so called, each of which is in charge of an officer called the Commissioner. In matters connected with the revenue in all its branches, and with the executive administration generally, he exercises powers of supervision over the proceedings of the district officers, but he does not interfere in the details of the business entrusted to them. In certain cases appeals lie to him, and nothing of importance can happen without his knowledge, because all communications between the district officers and the Government pass through his hands.

A similar system prevails in other parts of British India, with the exception of Madras, where there are no Commissioners. In that province the district officers communicate directly with the Government, except in revenue matters, on which they make their reports through the Revenue Board.

Besides the commissioners of divisions, there is a large staff of officers at Allahabad, the seat of the Provincial Government, through whom the executive business of the province is supervised, reported on, and submitted for the orders of the Lieutenant-Governor. The members of the Revenue Board are entrusted with the duty of supervising the proceedings of the collectors and commissioners in matters connected with the land, and the collection and management of the public revenues. The term 'board' has become, in this and other provinces, a misnomer. It has been found in India, as elsewhere, that, as Bentham expressed it, almost every board is a screen, efficient for hiding what ought to be known, and for avoiding individual responsibility. Each member of the Revenue Board has now his own separate duties.

The departments of Police, Jails, Education, Medical Services, Public Health and Vaccination, Agriculture and Commerce, Forests, Meteorology, Registration, Stamps and Excise, and Public Works have all, under one title or another, their respective heads, who act as the advisers of the Lieutenant-Governor. They make their reports and receive their orders through the Secretaries to the Government.

Authority, in every branch of the public service excepting the judicial, is centralised in the Lieutenant-Governor, subject only to the paramount authority of the Governor-General in Council. Excepting the Viceroy, no officers in India are entrusted with so large a measure of personal power as the Lieutenant-Governors of the great Indian provinces. They have no executive councils. Their nominal dignity is less than that of the Governors of Madras and Bombay, but the territories ruled by the Lieutenant-Governors are in no way inferior in political importance, and, in the case of Bengal and of the North-Western Provinces, they have larger populations and larger revenues. The checks against the wrongful exercise by the Lieutenant-Governor of arbitrary power are, however, complete. There is no branch of the administration in which he is not bound either by positive law, or by the standing orders of the Supreme Government, or by the system which has gradually grown up under his predecessors. Any great changes which he may desire to introduce must first receive the approval of the Governor-General in Council. He can impose no new taxation; his powers of sanctioning fresh expenditure, although large, are carefully restricted; and he has no control over the military forces in his province. As I have already explained, the Government of India keeps the army in its own hands throughout Bengal and Northern India.

Until 1887 the Lieutenant-Governor of the North-Western Provinces had no Council for legislative purposes, and all laws required for the North-Western Provinces and Oudh were passed in the Council of the Governor-General. He has now a Legislative Council similar to those in Madras, Bombay, and Bengal, the constitution of which I described in a former lecture.[1]

There are other departments of the administration which, as I before explained, are under the control of the Supreme and not of the Provincial Government, because they deal with matters of imperial interest, common to the whole of India; among these are the Post Office and Telegraph, the Survey, the Public Accounts and Currency.

Before leaving this part of my subject I must repeat that no one can understand how the actual government of India is carried on until he has obtained a proper appreciation of the facts which I stated in the earlier part of this lecture. The unit of administration in every province of British India is the district; every district has its own organisation; the province is a collection of districts, with the addition of the strong central authority of the Provincial Government which controls and gives unity to the whole; the machinery by which this central authority is exercised is efficient and complete; nothing of public importance can occur in any district or in any village, information regarding which is not immediately laid before the Government of the province.

I have now spoken of the executive administration only. The courts of justice, as in other countries

[1] Lecture II., pp. 36, 37.

possessing civilised systems of government, are independent of the executive power; the Government, like its subjects, is amenable to the law, and, like them, may be sued in the courts.

I have already given a general account of the system under which the administration of justice in India is carried on.[1] In the North-Western Provinces each district has a Civil Judge, a member of the covenanted Civil Service, who also presides over the court of Session.

The district is divided into a convenient number of sections, in each of which there are courts of civil jurisdiction, subordinate to the court of the Judge. There are two classes of these courts; those of the Munsifs, who try suits up to the value of 1,000 rupees; and those of the Subordinate judges, who try them, with certain restrictions, to any higher amount. Appeals lie in the smaller cases to the Judge, and in cases for more than 5,000 rupees to the High court. There are also Small-cause courts, which decide petty cases without appeal. Out of more than 200 Subordinate judges and Munsifs in the North-Western Provinces there are only two or three who are not Natives.

In the North-Western Provinces, the High court, which has its seat at Allahabad, consists of a Chief Justice and four Puisne Judges, all appointed by the Crown. One of the Judges and the Chief Justice are chosen from the English Bar, two of the Judges are members of the covenanted Civil Service, and one of them is a Mohammedan gentleman, once a member of Cambridge University.

The Lieutenant-Governor appoints the district judges, and possesses in criminal cases the power of

[1] Lecture VI., p. 143.

pardon, but he has no control over the judicial administration.

I shall speak in another lecture of some of the results of this elaborate system of government. I must now say something regarding the material condition of the people.

It is easy in almost every country to find examples of extreme poverty, and it is easy in India. The day labourer is often little better than an hereditary bondsman, and in bad seasons his condition is miserable. It would be hard to discover people living in a worse state of moral and physical degradation than that of the lowest classes of Mohammedans in many of the towns of Northern India. I shall have to give you some account of the unhappy condition of a large section of the peasantry in Behár, who live under the curse brought on Bengal by the mistakes of the last century. It is easy for the Indian pessimist to take cases of this kind, which are not rare, and then, by a bold generalisation, to assume that extreme poverty and misery are the normal condition of the agricultural population throughout India. You might as reasonably, on evidence of the condition of the poorest classes in the West of Ireland, or in the worst slums of the great cities of England, conclude that the rural and town population of our own country are universally wretched and degraded.

Referring to Northern India, I have already said that there is no country in which more complete and trustworthy information has been placed on record in regard to every subject affecting the agricultural population.

The immediate requirements of life are easily satisfied in the climate of India, and if you compare the physical ease and comfort of the average Indian peasant with that existing among the same class in the greater part of Europe, I cannot doubt (I am now quoting the conclusions of the Indian Famine Commissioners) that 'the advantage would probably be greatly in favour of the former, although his life may be shorter and subject to greater risks.'

The great majority of Indian agriculturists have the advantage of possessing, either as peasant proprietors or as cultivators with occupancy rights, permanent interests in the land. The condition of the people mainly depends on the degree in which these interests exist. This is always shown in a striking manner when seasons of drought occur. The first to suffer are the field-labourers, who live on the wages of their labour. If the rainy season fails, the land cannot be cultivated, and they are thrown out of employment. The next to suffer are the tenants-at-will, with no fixed rights and little credit. Where, on the other hand, the land is cultivated by the proprietors themselves, or by tenants with hereditary rights, it is only when drought is unusually severe and prolonged that these classes require help, for they have stocks of food and money to fall back upon, and they have credit with the money-lenders.

The field-labourers, when they have no permanent and hereditary employment in their villages, and who depend on wages paid usually in kind, are the only class in the condition of which it is probably true that there has been no general improvement. They are often worse off than in the times when there were no roads and railways, and when the value of agricultural produce was lower. To the menial servants of an Indian village a rise in prices does not bring increased wages, and they are usually too ignorant and helpless to think of bettering their condition by going elsewhere for employment, which would not in these days be difficult to find. But these are exceptions. Unless the seasons be especially unfortunate, the ordinary life of the Indian peasant is far from unhappy.

The fact that he has very little money has often led to mistaken conclusions on the part of English writers. Their ordinary supposition is that the Indian, like the English peasant, buys all that he requires for his support, but nothing could be more erroneous. As a rule, he derives from the land which he himself owns or cultivates most of the necessaries of life for himself and his family.

'He retains,' in the words of Mr. T. H. Thornton, 'so much of his produce as he requires for seed and home consumption, and disposes of the surplus only, and this surplus he does not ordinarily sell in open market, but makes over to the village *banya*, or shopkeeper, with whom he has an account current for cash advanced and goods supplied. To attempt to give a money value to these primitive transactions, and formulate the financial condition of the peasantry in terms of cash receipts and payments, must be a very hazardous undertaking.'

Little money passes through the hands even of the well-to-do Indian peasant. He need buy little or nothing except the simple implements of husbandry, cooking-vessels, clothing, sweetmeats, and tobacco; and all these together will not cost him many shillings in the year. In the provinces of which I have been more particularly speaking, his mud-walled cottage affords clean and, according to his ideas, comfortable shelter. He has not much clothing, but much is not wanted; even in the winter he suffers little from the cold. Under ordinary circumstances, he has sufficient food of the only kind that he desires, the produce of his own fields or garden, his millets and lentils, his barley or his rice, his much-appreciated *ghee*, made from the milk of cows or buffaloes, the vegetables, spices, and condiments of which in a hot climate there is no lack, and as much tobacco, sugar, and sweetmeats as he can afford to buy. His wife has often her holiday attire and her silver ornaments, for after providing the necessaries of life there is frequently something left for simple luxuries and for buying jewellery, the latter the most common form of hoarding. If, as is usually the case, he drinks no spirits, the only tax that he has to pay is about fivepence a year for salt, for himself and each member of his family. The improvement in the condition of the people in Northern India within my own recollection has been obvious. As one of the settlement officers observes, the vessels used by the peasantry forty years ago were almost always earthen; now they are of brass; their clothing is better and they have more of it; 'now every tenant dresses like a Brahman or zemindar of old days.' One of the most experienced officers of the North-Western Provinces has declared, as the result of his inquiries and observation, his belief that the landowning classes are, speaking generally, four or five times as rich as they were at the beginning of the century; 'everywhere', he says, 'there has been an extraordinary rise in the value of land, and the great advance in wealth and prosperity of the agricultural classes is too plainly evident to be called in question.'

Similar improvement has taken place in the greater part of British India. It has been estimated by competent observers that in the Punjab the value of land has more than sextupled in value in the last five-and-twenty years. In many parts of Bombay the progress has been remarkable. I have now before me the report of the revision of settlement in one of the divisions of Kandésh. It shows that in the course of thirty years the population increased 40 per cent.; there was an increase of 70 per cent. in the area of cultivation; the number of substantial houses was three times larger; the number of carts belonging to the peasant proprietors doubled; there was a great increase in agricultural stock, and in all the signs of prosperity; whereas thirty years ago trade could hardly be carried on except on the backs of bullocks, the country is now intersected by a railway and by roads, and the local value of agricultural produce is double what it was. In the Bombay Presidency, even in the last ten years, the area under wheat cultivation has increased by about 69 per cent., and this has not been at the expense of other crops, for the acreage under the grains that supply the ordinary food of the people has increased also.[1]

In a previous lecture[2] I showed the enormous progress in the trade of India during the last thirty years; progress which it is not possible should have taken place without a corresponding development of the wealth and industry of the country.

Gloomy forebodings have been not uncommon in regard to the difficulties to which India may be exposed in a not very distant future from the pressure of population on food. In some Indian countries the population is already denser than in almost any part of Europe, and there can be little doubt that it is rapidly increasing. Among the checks on the growth of population which formerly existed—war, pestilence, and famine—the first has ceased, and the last has lost some at least of its

[1] Speech by Sir. J. B. Peile in Bombay Legislative Council, July 14, 1886.
[2] Lecture IV., p. 111.

power. Whether the rate of mortality has diminished is less certain; cholera and smallpox and fever seem as rife as ever. No obligation, both for men and women, is more universally recognised than that of marriage at the earliest possible age. Emigration across the sea makes small progress, and the time must be very distant in which it can afford an outlet of much importance to the surplus population of India. In the ten years ending with 1885 there were 164,000 emigrants.

In spite of all this, it is probable that before the growth of population becomes a serious question, increase in the productiveness of the soil, increase of cultivation, which already goes on rapidly, and changes in the habits of the people will have supplied a remedy. Railways, and improved communications, and increasing wealth are bringing about great changes. Not long ago it was hardly possible to emigrate from one part of India to another; in 1887 there were more than 95,000,000 passengers on the railways. Bengal furnishes the labourers required by Assam for its tea-plantations, and Burma receives every year a large number of immigrants from Southern India. When the people become less unwilling to leave their own provinces for countries where the conditions of life are easier, and when diversity of occupation increases, they will find ample space within the limits of the Indian continent. Exclusive of Bengal, for which there are no statistics, there are said to be in India some 80,000,000 acres of unoccupied land fit for cultivation—an area exceeding that of the United Kingdom. The land actually under cultivation would, with improved methods, support a far larger population, and already, in some parts of India, important manufacturing industries are growing up.

I must now say something about the character of the people in the provinces which I have been attempting to describe.

English officers will tell you that they would not hesitate to lead their Sikhs and Patháns and Gúrkhas against any European enemy. We could not go so far as this in speaking generally of the population of the North-Western Provinces and Oudh; but the people are by no means wanting in manliness and courage, and some classes furnish excellent soldiers. In regard to their other qualities it is dangerous to generalise. In the North-Western Provinces and Oudh there are 4,600,000 Brahmans, 3,700,000 Rájputs and Játs, more than 5,000,000 of the menial caste Chamár, and so on. You could find no country in Europe in which the differences between the various sections of the population are as great.

A Hindu gentleman of great intelligence once said to me that while he fully admitted the superiority of the English not only in the arts of civilised life, but in many noble qualities, there was one virtue, on which the English especially prided themselves, in which they seemed to him inferior to his own countrymen. 'The English,' he said, 'seem to think that honesty consists in not telling a lie in answer to a direct question. Almost all of us tell lies when it seems convenient to do so; but, in my opinion, in the particular quality of honesty we are better than the English.'

There was a good deal of truth in the contention of my Hindu friend. If lying be the test of dishonesty, it would be hard to equal the dishonesty that you meet with in India. I have heard one of the most eminent of our judges doubt whether the perjury that goes on in his court in England could be surpassed in India; but

I think he is wrong, and that in this matter the Indian courts would easily carry off the palm. Nevertheless, if I were asked what was the most striking characteristic of the people of Northern India, I should say it was their honesty. I will read to you what Mr. Benett of the Indian Civil Service has written about this, because he has well expressed what I think :—

'Writing two centuries before Christ, of the Hindus in the kingdom of Patna, an educated Greek selected as the leading feature in their character their honesty and integrity in the ordinary relations of life; and, paradoxical as it may sound to most English ears, it is probable that this is almost as true of the Hindu village of to-day as it was of the Buddhist court of two thousand years ago. Even among our own servants no one can fail to have been astonished at the absolute safety with which large sums of money may be entrusted to their keeping, when theft would be almost impossible of detection and would secure them comfort for the remainder of their lives. In the higher ranks, the well-paid and educated office-clerks are faithful and trustworthy beyond any other class of men who can be procured for their responsible duties. What has been said applies to their relations with foreign masters, for whom they can rarely feel any affection, and who not unfrequently regard them with a suspicion which would be itself enough to make most men dishonest. In their relations with their own people the quality is far more conspicuous. Trade transactions involving enormous sums are carried through with a want of precaution which we should consider idiotic, but which is justified by the rarity of breaches of faith. In a country where writing is an art as common as it is with us, large debts are contracted every day on nothing but the verbal security of the borrower; and if there may be occasional repudiation in our courts, the fact that that security is still considered sufficient is ample proof that the debts are honourably acknowledged among the parties themselves. In such cases limitation is never thought of, and families who have emerged from poverty will discharge debts contracted by their ancestors a century back, of which no other record exists but an entry in the money-lender's private ledger. Their whole system postulates an exceptional integrity.'[1]

No people are more charitable. It is true that the Indian idea of charity is often very different from ours, and it is affected so strongly by caste considerations that it sometimes seems to us to pass into cruelty. But there is hardly any class that is not, according to its means and according to its own ideas, kind-hearted and benevolent. Nothing is more remarkable in times of scarcity than native charity, although it is often too indiscriminate to be wise. The people generally are extremely industrious. Although uneducated and superstitious to a degree unknown in the most ignorant countries of Europe, the agricultural classes are certainly not inferior in intelligence to the peasants of our own country.

All classes are polite but not servile in their manners; it would be impossible to surpass the finished courtesy of a Mohammedan gentleman.

I must leave this part of my subject. I spent in Northern India the best and not the least interesting portion of my life. It is impossible to live among its people without feeling for them a deep regard, and, assuming that our dominion does not perish before the proper time has come, I cannot doubt that their future will be fortunate.

I have been describing a peaceful, contented, and well-disposed society, deserving in a high degree the respect and affection of its rulers, but it must not be forgotten that we shall have a very incomplete idea of India if we look only at what we see upon the surface. The more we learn about India the more we become alive to the fact that we are, to use Sir James Stephen's

[1] *Introduction to the Oudh Gazetteer*, by Mr. W. C. Benett, C.S., p. 28.

expression, the representatives of a belligerent civilisation, which has to wage constant warfare against strange barbarisms, horrid customs, and cruel superstitions, ancient survivals, ready at any moment to start into activity. The material progress of India, and the changes in the system of British administration during the last fifty years, have been extraordinarily great, but the vast mass of the population remains (in the words of Sir Henry Maine) 'an energetic expression of the Past, hardly affected by its contact with the Western world.'

If you look at the criminal statistics of the North-Western Provinces, which are as carefully collected as in any country of Europe, you will come to the conclusion that there is less crime than in England, and that the people are astonishingly peaceable and honest. The conclusion will be true; but if you inquire more deeply you will find strange facts that these statistics do not show. You will find, for instance, that in the North-Western Provinces there are more than 200,000 people belonging, not to barbarous tribes like the Patháns on the Afghán frontier,[1] nor to the outcasts and scum of the community, but to classes of honourable and comparatively civilised men, who are living under the restraint of special penal laws, because from time immemorial they have killed their female children. Among all the races of India, there is none more noble than the Rájput; and among the Rájputs, the first rank belongs to the Chauháns—the *sangre azul*, as they have been called, of Indian chivalry. No men in India are so proud of their lineage, and they trace their descent, not

[1] The following is extracted from an official report of 1887:—'According to the Pathán code of honour, murder under certain conditions is not a crime but an obligation. 2,000 murderers are believed to be at large in the Pesháwar district.' In this case also a special law has been put in force.

from mortal ancestors, but from the sacred fire called forth on the summit of Mount Ábu, by one of the sages of the Vedas, to destroy the demons who were persecuting the Brahmans and depriving the gods of their sacrifices. These people are numerous in the North-Western Provinces. In the district of Mainpuri there are 30,000 of them, and not many years ago it was discovered that among them there was not a single girl. Every daughter that was born was killed. The higher the rank of the family the more constant and systematic was the crime.

'There is at Mainpuri,' wrote Mr. Raikes, the magistrate of the district in 1850, 'an old fortress which looks far over the valley of the Eesun River. This has been for centuries the stronghold of the Rája of the Mainpuri Chauháns, whose ancient blood represents the *crême de la crême* of Rájput aristocracy. Here, when a son, a nephew, a grandson, was born to the reigning chief, the event was announced to the neighbouring city by the loud discharge of wall-pieces and matchlocks; but centuries had passed away and no infant daughter had been known to smile within these walls.'[1]

This is not rhetoric but the statement of a fact. In 1856 special inquiries were instituted. It was found that this practice of infanticide, although especially prevalent among the Rájputs, was by no means confined to them, and it was common not only in the North-Western Provinces but in Oudh, the Punjab, and in parts of the Bombay presidency. Numbers of villages were visited where there was not a single girl, and where there had never been one within the memory of man. Of one large Rájput community on the borders of Oudh it was officially reported that 'not only are there no girls to be found now, but there never have

[1] *Notes on the North-Western Provinces of India*, 1852.

been any, nor has such an event as the marriage of a daughter taken place for more than two hundred years.' In 1869 another investigation showed that there was little change for the better. This was the sort of report:—In seven villages, 104 boys, and 1 girl; in twenty-three villages 284 boys, and 23 girls; in other villages, the marriage of a girl an entirely unknown ceremony; and so on.

I cannot now describe the marriage customs of the Rájputs, but there is a very interesting account of them in Sir Alfred Lyall's 'Asiatic Studies.' A Rájput cannot marry a woman who does not belong to a Rájput family, but at the same time he cannot marry one of his own class.

'The custom makes marriage difficult by narrowing the field of selection; for neither can a man go very far among strange tribes to seek his wife, nor a father to seek a husband for his daughter; so that a poor man often does not marry at all, while a rich man of high birth is besieged with applications for his hand, in order that the stigma of an unmarried daughter may at least be formally removed.'[1]

Thus, while an unmarried daughter is looked upon in India as hopelessly disgraced—and this is true of almost all classes and not of Rájputs only—a son-in-law cannot always be found unless the father of the girl is prepared to pay highly, and the marriage of a daughter may mean the ruin of a family. Rather than incur this danger, the Rájput prefers that his daughter should perish. But a far more powerful reason is immemorial custom, which Manu declares to be 'transcendent law and the root of all piety.' These people have gone on killing their children generation after generation because their forefathers did so before them, not only without a

[1] *Asiatic Studies*, p. 220.

thought that there is anything criminal in the practice, but with the conviction that it is right.

For many years past measures have been taken in the North-Western Provinces for the prevention of this crime. For a long time, in the days when our civilisation was less belligerent than it has since become, it was thought that the best hope of success lay in the removal of the causes which appeared to lead to its commission, and especially in the prevention of extravagant expenditure on marriages; but although these benevolent efforts were undoubtedly useful, their practical results were not great, and it gradually became clear that it was only by a stringent and organised system of coercion that these practices would ever be eradicated.[1] In 1870 an Act of the Legislature was passed which enabled the Government to deal with the subject. A system of registration of births and deaths among the suspected classes was established, with con-

[1] While this book was passing through the press an account reached England of some interesting proceedings in Rájputána. In March 1888 the representatives of all the ruling chiefs met together and agreed to rules limiting the expenditure on marriages. These rules were declared binding on Rájputs of all ranks except the chiefs themselves. Many previous attempts, with the view of suppressing the motives to infanticide in Rájputána, have been made and have failed, and, even if the chiefs were anxious to enforce such rules, their power to do so would be more than doubtful. I fear that the sanguine hopes that have been expressed in regard to the results of this movement are not likely to be fulfilled. The chiefs at the same time agreed that no boy under eighteen and no girl under fourteen shall hereafter be married. It is impossible to anticipate that this rule, passed with the avowed object of preventing child marriages, can have any immediate or important effect on one of the most prevalent and most lamentable of Indian customs, by which thousands of girls, hardly out of their infancy, are every year condemned to lives of perpetual widowhood. The incident is nevertheless interesting. The proposal, we are told, was made spontaneously by the aged chief of Bundi, and we may hope that the Agent to the Governor-General in Rájputána is right in the belief which he has stated, that it 'shows at all events that a feeling is getting abroad, even among those who are the greatest upholders of ancient customs, against the evils caused by these marriages.'

stant inspection and enumeration of children; special police-officers were entertained at the cost of the guilty communities, and no efforts were spared to convince them that the Government had firmly resolved that it would put down these practices, and would treat the people who followed them as murderers. Although the time is, I fear, distant when preventive measures will cease to be necessary, much progress has been made, and there are now thousands of girls where formerly there were none. In the Mainpuri district, where, as I have said, there was, not many years ago, hardly a single Chauhán girl, nearly half of the Chauhán children at the present time are girls; and it is hoped that three-fourths of the villages have abandoned the practice.

In an official statement made by the Government of the North-Western Provinces in 1887 it is said that in those districts in which the Rájput clans are scattered and greatly mixed with other classes of the population, and where the support of clan feeling and clan custom is comparatively weak, there is reason to think that infanticide has almost ceased. In other districts where the Rájputs are found in large and homogeneous communities, the suppression of the crime is much more difficult. In 1887 there were still, in the North-Western Provinces, more than 200,000 people, in twenty-eight districts, subject to the special provisions of the law. There can be no doubt that if vigilance were relaxed the custom would before long become as prevalent as ever.

It would be a mistake to suppose that the British Government receives, in the performance of duties of this kind, any help or sympathy from other classes of Hindus who have never practised such crimes. Interference with ancient custom is an abomination to a Hindu, whether it be his own custom or not.

I will give another illustration of the strange conditions that still exist in India, and of the difficulties with which we have to contend. Much of the crime that is committed is carried on by tribes of criminals as their regular and legitimate occupation, not only with no thought of criminality, but in the belief that in following the custom of their forefathers they are acting in the only way that is right. I will not repeat the well-known story of the Thugs, the professional murderers who practised their trade over a great part of India. They have been extirpated by the British Government. The professional Dacoits, associated for the purposes of violent gang-robbery, have also, at least in our own provinces, nearly ceased to exist. Other criminal organisations, with which it is more difficult to deal, abound to this day.

The following quotation from an official report will show what these professional criminals are. You will see that they have no resemblance to the habitual criminals of Europe.

'We all know that trades go by castes in India; a family of carpenters will be a family of carpenters a century or five centuries hence, if they last so long; so with grain-dealers, blacksmiths, leather-makers, and every known trade. A carpenter cannot drop his tools and become a dealer in grain or anything else. If we keep this in mind when we speak of "professional criminals," we shall realise what the term really means. It means that the members of a tribe whose ancestors were criminals from time immemorial are themselves destined by the usages of caste to commit crime, and their descendants will be offenders against the law until the whole tribe is exterminated or accounted for in the manner of the Thugs. Therefore, when a man tells you he is a Badhak, or a Kanjar, or a Sonoria, he tells you, what few Europeans ever thoroughly realise, that he is an offender against the law, has been so from the beginning, and will be so to the end; that reform is impossible, for it is his trade, his caste—I may almost say his religion—to commit crime.'

Here is the account of one of these tribes called Barwárs. Their head-quarters are in the district of Gonda, in Oudh, where they inhabit forty-eight villages, and number a thousand families. They have little to do with agriculture; they live quietly and honestly at their homes for some months of every year, and the rest of their time is spent in wandering, in small gangs, over distant parts of the country, plundering everything they can find. But they may not steal cattle; they may despoil the temples of the gods; they may rob even the goddess Debi, one of the special objects of their worship. The only sacred places that they may not touch are the temple of Jaganáth in Orissa, and the shrine of a certain Mohammedan martyr. They have a regular organisation, under duly chosen chiefs; every child goes through a form of religious initiation on the twelfth day of his life; if a man of the tribe gives up his thieving profession he is excommunicated and disgraced. The time for starting on their predatory expeditions is settled by the astrologers, and the plunder brought home is divided according to fixed rules, after $3\frac{3}{4}$ per cent. has been set aside, to be distributed in certain proportions among their gods. Each family has in its house an altar, dedicated to the special tutelary god of the tribe, Panch Puria, a god not recognised by other classes; on a certain day in August a fowl must be sacrificed on the altar, and thin cakes of bread must be baked, and these offerings have then to be given to a Mohammedan fakeer, who goes from house to house beating a kettledrum.

These Barwárs are by no means one of the most important of the criminal tribes. Some are devoted to cattle-stealing, others are dangerous robbers. In Gurgáon, one of the frontier districts of the Punjab, the official reports tell us of a large isolated British village, surrounded by Native territory, inhabited almost exclusively by some 2,000 people of the Mina tribe. Their sole occupation is, and always has been, plunder in the Native States, and in distant parts of British India; they give no trouble at home, and, judging from criminal statistics, it would be supposed that they were an honest community. They live amid abundance, in substantial houses, with numerous cattle, fine clothes and jewels, and fleet camels to carry off their plunder; and, it is added, 'there is no end to their charity.'

In the North-Western Provinces alone there are said to be twenty-nine different tribes who, without any notion of criminality, have from time immemorial made crime their sole serious occupation; and they are probably not less numerous in other parts of India where less is known about them.

There is a special law for dealing with these classes. Registers are kept showing all the members of the tribes; they can be compelled to live within certain local limits, and prevented from leaving those limits without permission, and they may be arrested if they are found beyond them. In some cases, the measures taken have been more or less successful, but the difficulties are great, and a long time must elapse before we see the end of the criminal tribes of India.

LECTURE XI.

NATIVE STATES.

AREA, REVENUES, AND POPULATION OF NATIVE STATES—MEANING OF THE TERM 'NATIVE STATE'—PREVALENT MISTAKEN IDEAS—NATIVE STATES NOT NATIONALITIES—NATIVE PRINCES OFTEN FOREIGNERS—THE ENGLISH HAVE DESTROYED NO ANCIENT DYNASTIES—DIFFERENT CLASSES OF NATIVE STATES—THE MOHAMMEDAN AND MARATHA STATES—THEIR FOREIGN CHARACTER—ANCIENT DYNASTIES PRESERVED BY THE BRITISH—MYSORE—TRAVANCORE—THE STATES OF RÁJPUTÁNA AND THE PUNJAB—THE GOVERNMENTS OF NATIVE STATES—THE PERSONAL DESPOTS—THE TRIBAL CHIEFS—ANTIQUITY OF INDIAN FAMILIES—THE SUPREMACY OF THE BRITISH GOVERNMENT—OUR RELATIONS WITH NATIVE STATES—ASSUMPTION BY THE QUEEN OF TITLE OF 'EMPRESS OF INDIA'—SIR HENRY LAWRENCE ON NATIVE STATES AND BRITISH RESIDENTS—THE CHARACTER OF NATIVE RULERS—FREQUENT NECESSITY FOR BRITISH INTERVENTION—THE ANNEXATION OF OUDH—CONDITION OF OUDH BEFORE ANNEXATION—BARODA—DEPOSITION OF THE GAIKWÁR—GWALIOR AND INDORE—THE STATES OF CENTRAL INDIA—SIR LEPEL GRIFFIN ON MISRULE IN NATIVE STATES—DESIRE OF THE BRITISH GOVERNMENT TO MAINTAIN THE NATIVE STATES—THEIR MISRULE THEIR SOLE DANGER—THE CONDITIONS ESSENTIAL TO THEIR PRESERVATION—THE RESTORATION OF MYSORE TO NATIVE RULE—TERMS ON WHICH THE TRANSFER WAS MADE—THE RESULTS—THE NECESSITY OF MORE GENERAL APPLICATION OF SIMILAR PRINCIPLES—THE ARMIES OF THE NATIVE STATES.

THE Native States of India cover an area of more than 500,000 square miles, and contain a population of about 55,000,000. Their total revenues are estimated at about 17,000,000*l.* Counting them all, there are several hundreds of them, but the great majority are so insignificant in extent, and their rulers have so little authority, that they do not deserve the name of States. The largest, that of the Nizam of Hyderabad, has an area of 82,000 square miles, and a population of nearly 10,000,000; Gwalior, 29,000 square miles, and a population of 3,000,000; Mysore, 25,000 square miles, and 4,000,000. Several others have between 1,000,000 and 3,000,000 people.[1]

Excepting the Himálayan State of Nepál, which since 1815 has been enabled by its geographical position to maintain a constant attitude of complete but friendly isolation, no Native State within the limits of India has any real independence; but, subject to this general fact, their rulers have every degree of power and importance, from the petty chief with little or no political authority to princes with large revenues and considerable armies, with whose internal administration, under ordinary circumstances, we hardly interfere.

I am obliged to use the term 'Native State,' but this expression only signifies a State not directly administered by Englishmen. We might with as much propriety apply the term 'Foreign States' to some of the principal Native States of India, for their rulers

[1] The following list shows the area and population of the principal Native States:—

	Sq. miles	Population	Religion and race of ruler
Hyderabad. (The Nizam)	81,800	9,840,000	Mohammedan
Bhopál	6,900	955,000	
Baháwalpur	15,000	573,000	
Gwalior. (Sindhia)	29,000	2,990,000	Hindu. Maratha
Indore. (Holkar)	8,400	1,050,000	
Baroda. (The Gaikwár)	8,600	2,190,000	
Mysore	24,700	4,190,000	Hindu
Travancore	6,700	2,400,000	
Jaipur	14,500	2,500,000	Hindu. Rájput
Jodhpur	37,000	1,750,000	
Oodepur	12,700	1,500,000	
Rewah	10,000	1,300,000	Hindu. Bhagela
Patiála	5,900	1,500,000	Sikh

are as much foreigners to the people that they govern as we are ourselves. The term 'Native States' is apt to convey the idea that they are Indian nationalities existing in the midst of our great foreign dominion. This, indeed, is the popular English belief. It is assumed that in our conquest of India we imposed our rule on peoples that had previously been governed by princes of their own race, that we took the place of ancient native dynasties which we destroyed, and that, having kept for ourselves the more valuable provinces, we have, for one reason or another, allowed some portions of India to retain their Native governments. No suppositions could be more contrary to fact. When, after the death of Aurangzeb in 1707, the Moghul Empire was breaking up, a scramble ensued for the fragments, and this lasted through the greater part of the last century. The chief competitors during the latter half of the struggle were the Maráthas, the Mohammedan powers of Southern India, and the English. The larger share of the gain fell to the English, but our competitors had no better titles than our own. All alike were foreigners in the countries for which they were contending.

Those who desire to learn the truth on this subject should read Sir Alfred Lyall's 'Asiatic Studies,' to which I have so often referred, and Professor Seeley's admirable book 'The Expansion of England.'

'One of the popular notions in England and Europe' (I am quoting from Sir Alfred Lyall) 'regarding the establishment of the English empire in India is that our conquests absorbed nationalities, displaced long-seated dynasties, and levelled ancient nobilities. These are some of the self-accusations by which the average home-keeping Englishman justifies to himself the indulgence of sitting down and casting dust on his head whenever he looks back upon the exploits of his countrymen in India—an attitude which is observed by foreigners with suspicion or impatience according to their insight into English character. Yet it would be easy to prove that one important reason why the English so rapidly conquered India was this, that the countries which fell into our hands had no nationalities, no long-seated ruling dynasties, or ancient aristocracies, that they had, in fact, no solid or permanent organisation of the kind, but were, politically, treasure trove, at the disposal of the first who, having found, could keep. The best proof that in these countries the English destroyed no organised political institutions is the historical fact that in the countries which they annexed none such had been left for them to destroy. On the other hand, where indigenous political institutions of long standing still exist, it is the English who have saved them from destruction.'[1]

The principal Native States of India may be roughly divided into two classes. The first comprises the States possessing the largest measure of independence, and the most important of these are the Mohammedan and Marátha States which survived the struggles of the close of the last and the beginning of the present century. Their rulers are in all cases foreigners. None of these States are much older than our own dominion; the principal officials are usually as foreign as the chiefs; the armed force mainly consists of foreign mercenaries; and there is no closer sympathy between the people and their rulers than that which exists in the British territories. I have repeatedly pointed out how misleading are such terms as 'Natives of India,' 'People of India,' and other general expressions; and this warning is especially necessary in regard to the 'Native States.' It can never be assumed that because the chief of a Native State is a so-called 'Native of India' he has any rights differing in kind from our own. If a question arises whether our own administration or that of

[1] *Asiatic Studies*, p. 181.

a Native ruler is to be preferred, Englishmen usually suppose that the choice must lie between giving to the people the foreign government of the English or the national government of their own countrymen. For instance, there was much discussion not long ago whether we ought to restore to the Nizam the districts of Berár which had been assigned to us, and which have been for many years under British administration. Few had any suspicion of the fact that the Mohammedan Government of Hyderabad would be as foreign as our own to the people of Berár, who are Hindus having nothing in common with their former rulers.

The Nizam holds the first place among the Native princes of India. The founder of the ruling family was one of Aurangzeb's viceroys; in 1724 he was virtually independent. Nearly the whole population is Hindu, but Hindus have no share in the administration; every thing is in the hands of Mohammedan foreigners. The army chiefly consists of foreign mercenaries. There is no part of India in which the people have less sympathy with their rulers, men of other countries and of another faith. Frequent interference by the British Government has been necessary; the misfortune is that it has not been more complete and efficacious. Excepting sometimes for a short period, no Government in India has been more shamelessly corrupt than that of the Nizam. The Hyderabad State is the chief surviving relic of Mohammedan supremacy in India. With the not very important exceptions of Bhopál and Baháwalpur, the other States under Mohammedan rulers, about twenty in number, are politically insignificant. The population of the so-called Mohammedan States is altogether about 14,000,000, but of this number at least 12,000,000 are Hindus. Even in Hyderabad, where the Mohammedans have been in power for centuries, there are less than 1,000,000 of them to 9,000,000 Hindus. Thus a very small proportion of the 50,000,000 Indian Mohammedans live under rulers of their own faith. The revenues of the Mohammedan States are estimated at about 5,000,000*l.*, of which more than 4,000,000*l.* belong to Hyderabad.

The principal remnants of the Marátha power are the three States of Gwalior, Indore, and Baroda, and of these Gwalior is the most important. They all came into existence about the middle of the last century. Their chiefs are entirely foreign to the people. In the words of Sir Lepel Griffin, they are 'the representatives of the predatory hordes which, until crushed by British arms, turned the fertile plains of Central India into a wilderness. These Maratha dynasties have nothing in common with the people they govern. Their race is different and their language is not understood.' The population of the three Maratha States is about 6,250,000; but, except the rulers and their followers, there are no Marathas. Their aggregate revenues are about 3,500,000*l.* Of their governments I shall have something to say presently.

Among the Native States of which I have been speaking, there is not one the Government of which can be said to have a more legitimate or national origin than that of the British Government itself in its Indian dominions.

I come now to the second of the classes into which the Native States of India may be divided. Judged by their area and population and political importance, these States are inferior to those of the former class, but they are more numerous and far more interesting. They are the only parts of India where ancient political institutions and ancient dynasties still survive, and their preservation is entirely due to the British Government. The principal States of this class are those of Rájputána; and there are many others in Central India, in Bundelkhand, Baghelkhand, and in the Bombay Presidency. You will find in Sir Alfred Lyall's book a description of the States of Rájputána, the most interesting of the whole. They were saved by the British Government from destruction by the Maráthas. They are twenty in number, with an area of 150,000 square miles and a population of more than 10,000,000. The constitution of these States is very different from that of the Mohammedan and Marátha States. In the latter, the ruler, in theory at least, and subject to his responsibilities to the British Government, exercises absolute personal power. For instance (I am quoting from Sir Alfred Lyall), Sindhia, the head of the Maratha State of Gwalior, 'is the representative of the single family of a successful captain of armies who annexed in the last century all the territory he could lay hands on, and whose son finally encamped so long in one place that his camp grew into his capital some sixty years ago. . . . He is a despot of the ordinary Asiatic species, ruling absolutely the lands which his ancestor seized by the power of a mercenary army.'[1]

In States like those of Rájputána, on the other hand, where ancient institutions have been preserved, the constitution of the governing authority is very different. The chief is the hereditary head of a military clan the members of which have been for centuries lords of the soil. He and the minor chiefs and nobles are supposed to be descended from a common ancestor; he is *primus inter pares*, and while all the branches of the original stock are ready to join their chief in time

[1] *Asiatic Studies*, p. 196.

of danger, his actual power over them is, under ordinary circumstances, very greatly limited.

Owing to the custom of adoption, through which no Hindu family need become extinct from failure of heirs, some of the ruling families of Rájputána go back to an unknown antiquity. In the States of Oodepur, Jodhpur, and Jaipur, there seems no reason to doubt that the families to which the present chiefs belong have ruled in the same territories for more than a thousand years. In States of this kind there is often a strong feeling of attachment on the part of the people towards their chief.

There are other States of a different character, which, however, have this in common with those of which I have last spoken, that they owe their present existence to the British Government. The chief of these, inferior to Hyderabad alone, is Mysore. It has an area of 24,700 square miles, a population of more than 4,000,000, and a revenue of about 1,000,000*l*. Its Hindu rájas contrived to maintain more or less independence until the middle of the last century, when Hyder Ali took possession of their country. It remained in his hands and in those of his successor, Tippoo Sultan, until the capture of Seringapatam by the English in 1799. Mysore was then restored by Lord Wellesley to the old Hindu dynasty. In consequence of gross oppression and misgovernment, it became necessary in 1830 to place British officers in charge of the administration. The Rájá died in 1867, leaving an adopted son, and the British Government announced its intention of restoring the Government to the heir when he reached his majority. This promise was carried out in 1881 in a manner which I shall presently notice.

The ancient Hindu State of Travancore, at the

southern extremity of India, was rescued from Tippoo by the British, and still remains in the possession of its rájas.

The principal Native States of the Punjab also owe their continued existence to English protection. Without it they would have been utterly swept away by Ranjit Singh. There are altogether thirty-six of these States, with a population of nearly 4,000,000. They have always been conspicuously loyal, and their administration is good.

The important frontier State of Kashmir was created by the British Government in 1846, after the first Sikh war.

The supreme authority of the British Government has become a fact which no Native State in India thinks for a moment of disputing. These States are often called 'feudatory,' but there is no real analogy between their relations with the British Government and the incidents of ancient feudal tenure. The expression has come into use, as Sir Charles Aitchison says, 'merely from want of a better or more convenient term to denote the subordination of territorial sovereignties to a common superior, combined with the obligation to discharge certain duties and render certain services to that superior.'

In the case of the more important States, our supremacy was long ago recognised, more or less completely, by treaty; in the case of the smaller States, whether expressed and formally recorded or not, it has become one of the obvious conditions of their existence. Some of the States, so far as their internal administration is concerned, are substantially independent, unless their government becomes so scandalously bad and oppressive that intervention is forced upon us; in other

States the authority of the chiefs is more strictly limited; in many of the smaller States it hardly exists in any independent form. But, whether the State be great or small, there are certain rights which the paramount power always asserts. No Native State can have any political communication with any other Native State, or with any Foreign power, without the consent of the British Government; no Native State can maintain more troops or military establishments than are required for the purposes of internal administration, for the support of the reasonable dignity of the chief, or except in accordance with its recognised obligations towards the British Government; there is no Native State in which civil war would be permitted, or in which, in case of gross and systematic injustice and tyranny, the British Government would not interfere for the protection of the people. This last right is the necessary consequence of our absolute power, and it has been repeatedly exercised. There is no Native chief in India who might not be tried and punished for a crime of special atrocity by a tribunal constituted by the British Government.

There is no dynasty in India which would not, without the custom of adoption, long ago have become extinct. It may almost be said that it is the rule, as much as the exception, that a Native prince has no direct heirs. Since the time of Lord Canning, our Government, being anxious to maintain the existence of every Native State, has always recognised adoptions made in accordance with Hindu law, or with local custom, and in default of regular adoption it exercises the undisputed right of selecting the successor whom it may think most fit. In case of a minority, it invariably asserts a right of interference, limited only by its own sense of what is proper.

The supremacy of the British Government over all the Native States in India was declared in 1877, in a more emphatic form than it had received before, by the assumption by the Queen of the title of Kaisar-i-Hind, Empress of India. No such gathering of chiefs and princes has taken place in historical times as that seen at Delhi in January 1877, when the rulers of all the principal States of India formally acknowledged their dependence on the British Crown. The political effect of the assertion of the supremacy of the paramount power, thus formally made for the first time in India, has been marked and extremely important.

More than thirty years ago, Sir Henry Lawrence, speaking from long personal experience, declared that if ever there was a device for ensuring maladministration, it was that of a Native ruler backed up by British bayonets, and directed by an English Resident, and I am afraid this is sometimes not far from the truth at the present time. I have always thought that no part of our Indian administration has been less successful than the management of our relations with the Native States.

If a Native chief be vicious or incompetent, no advice or warning will make his government good. It may save him from the fate he deserves, but it will not give adequate protection to his subjects. In former times, there was always hanging over the chief the fear that the British Government might not be slow in seizing opportunities of extending its dominions, and that any grave misconduct might be followed by the summary annexation of his State. That fear has passed away. He knows that, unless his administration arrives at a point of insufferable badness, he runs no risk of deposition, and that he will have ample notice before active measures of interference are taken. Thus our anxiety to preserve the Native States has sometimes tended to diminish the checks on their misgovernment.

The character and capacity of the chief are accidents. It not unfrequently happens, especially in the smaller States, that Native princes or their ministers make great and successful efforts to improve their administration and to govern on the principles, although not necessarily by the methods, which we ourselves approve.

There are not many positions in which a man has larger powers for good than that of the enlightened ruler of a Native State. He is protected by the British Government from all anxiety outside his own territory. He requires no armed force except for the maintenance of order among his own people. He has at his disposal considerable resources. His State shares as a rule, without any charges being imposed on it, the benefits derived from the railways and other public works constructed by our Government. He has no difficulties such as those that beset on all sides our own administration. Wise and upright chiefs, followed by worthy successors, could, we may fancy, bring their States into a condition of almost utopian prosperity and happiness. But, if the opportunities of success are great, so are the temptations which lead an Indian prince to failure and dishonour, and unrestricted personal power is doomed in India to the same ultimate fate which has attended it elsewhere. Not unfrequently you find Native chiefs who deserve and obtain the respect and affection of their people, but it is seldom possible to be hopeful of the future. The chances are that the progress made by worthy rulers will be swept away by the vice and caprice of their successors. If we examine the history of the principal Native States during the last twenty or thirty years, we hardly find a single case in which the record is one of uninterrupted tranquillity and fairly good administration. From time to time, there is a just and benevolent chief, but sooner or later comes almost always the same story. There is a point at which our interference becomes unavoidable, and there is scarcely a single Native State in which we have not been forced to interfere or remonstrate for the protection of the people against their ruler. It has often been necessary to assume temporarily the government of the State; in more than one case, the ruler has been deposed because he has been guilty of atrocious crimes.

I have said that interference becomes unavoidable. I will give one or two instances to show the condition into which a Native State may fall before the British Government actively intervenes. I will take as one instance the circumstances which led to the annexation of Oudh. It is now an old story, for the Native Government ceased to exist there thirty years ago, but it is by no means out of date. There are at the present time States in India in which, but for the certainty of our interference, matters might soon be little better than they were in Oudh in 1856. I wish to refer to this story for another reason. We still sometimes hear the annexation of Oudh quoted as one of the iniquitous proceedings of the British Government, and as an illustration of its lust of dominion.

General Sleeman, the representative of our Government in Oudh, gave from personal observation a description of the country at that time, and its accuracy has never been called in question. I will give you some account, often in his own words, of his report.

Oudh is naturally one of the richest countries in India, as large as Holland and Belgium together, with a population at the present time of 11,000,000. Government in Oudh, deserving the name, there was none. The King did not pretend to concern himself with any public business. His ambition was limited to that of being reputed the best drum-beater, dancer, and poet of the day. Sometimes he might be seen going in procession through the streets of Lucknow, beating the drum tied round his neck. Singers, fiddlers, poets, eunuchs, and women were his only associates. The Prime Minister, 'a consummate knave,' after keeping an enormous share for himself and his creatures, distributed the revenues and patronage of the country. The fiddlers controlled the administration of civil justice; that of criminal justice was made over to the eunuchs; each of the King's favourites had authority over some court or office through which he might make a fortune for himself. The minister kept the land revenue, and 'employed none but knaves of the very worst kind in all branches of the administration.' Every office was sold; commands in the army were put up to auction every season, or oftener, and the purchase money was divided among the minister, the singers, the fiddlers, and the eunuchs. The principal singer had two regiments at his disposal. The minister was as inaccessible as the King himself. Petitions and reports were usually made over by him, if he gave any orders at all, to the commander-in-chief, who was an infant, to the King's chamberlain, or footman, or coachman, chief fiddler, eunuch, barber, or any person uppermost in his thoughts at the time. Courts of justice were unknown, except as affording means of extortion to the judges. The charge of the so-called police throughout the country was sold to the highest bidders. There was only one road that deserved the name in Oudh, made for the benefit of English travellers from Lucknow to Cawnpore, a distance of about 40 miles.

The atrocities that went on throughout the country would pass belief, if the evidence of the truth were less complete. I will give a few illustrations, taken from General Sleeman's narrative.

The districts of Bahraich and Gonda have an area of more than 5,000 square miles, and they now contain about 2,000,000 inhabitants. Shortly before General Sleeman's visit, a man called Raghubar Singh was their local Governor, with large bodies of the King's troops and of his own armed retainers at his disposal. In two years his extortions and crimes had reached such a point, that these districts, which had once been in a flourishing condition, and noted for their fertility, had become for the most part uncultivated. The English officer deputed by the Resident to inquire into the facts reported that 'villages completely deserted in the midst of lands devoid of all tillage everywhere meet the eye; and from Fyzabad to Bahraich he passed through these districts, a distance of eighty miles, over plains which had been fertile and well cultivated till Raghubar Singh got charge, but now lay entirely waste, a scene for two years of great misery, ending in desolation.'

The Rája of Bondi was one of the principal landholders in this part of Oudh; his estates contained some three hundred villages. He objected to the extortionate demands of Raghubar Singh, and this was the consequence. Parties of soldiers were sent out to plunder and seize all the respectable residents they could find. They sacked the town of Bondi, pulled down the houses of the Rája, and those of his relations and dependents; and, after looting all the towns and villages in the neighbourhood, they brought in 1,000 captives of both sexes and all ages, who were subjected to every sort of outrage till they paid the ransom demanded. The Rája escaped, but his agents and tenants were horribly tortured. Soon afterwards, detachments of soldiers were again sent out to plunder; 1,500 men and 500 women and children were brought in as prisoners, with 80,000 animals. All were driven off pell-mell through the rain for three days. The women were driven on by the troops with the butt-ends of their muskets; many of the children were trodden to death. The prisoners were tied up and flogged and tortured, red-hot ramrods thrust into their flesh, their tongues pulled out with hot pincers. Many perished from torture and starvation. The women and children were all stripped of their clothing. For two months these atrocities continued. Similar horrors went on in other parts of Bahraich, and a few years ago the English officer in charge of that district reported that its present comparatively small population was in a great measure due to the atrocities of Raghubar Singh. General Sleeman tells us that no single person concerned in these crimes was ever punished.

There were then in Oudh 250 forts in the possession of the great landholders, with 100,000 men, maintained to fight among themselves, or against the Government. General Sleeman's two volumes are filled with descriptions of the enormities that were going on, almost under his own eyes, of open war, of villages attacked and plundered, of horrible murders and outrages. 'Every day,' he writes, 'I have scores of petitions delivered to me by persons who have been plundered of all they possessed, had their dearest relations murdered or tortured to death, and their habitations burnt to the ground by gangs of ruffians, under landlords of high birth and pretensions, whom they had never wronged or offended. In these attacks neither age, nor sex, nor condition are spared.'

In General Sleeman's narrative I have found hardly anything to relieve the uniformity of his terrible story except this:—

> 'In the most crowded streets of Lucknow, Europeans are received with deference, courtesy, and kindness. The people of the country respect the British Government, its officers, and Europeans generally. Though the Resident has not been able to secure any very substantial or permanent reform in the administration, still he has often interposed with effect, in individual cases, to relieve suffering and secure redress for grievous wrongs. The people of the country see that he never interposes except for such purposes, and their only regret is that he interposes so seldom, and that his efforts when he does so should be so often frustrated or disregarded. In the remotest village or jungle in Oudh, as in the most crowded streets of the capital, a European gentleman is sure to be treated with affectionate respect, and the humblest European is as sure to receive protection and kindness, unless he forfeits all claim to it by his misconduct.'

For many years, one Governor-General after another had gone on protesting against the atrocities of which I have given you some illustrations. At last came 'the great Proconsul' Dalhousie. He knew that since the British Government, without moving a soldier or spending a rupee, had absolute power to put an immediate end to these abominations, it was on the British Government that the responsibility really rested for suffering them to continue. There was only one complete remedy, and Lord Dalhousie applied it by declaring the whole of Oudh to be British territory. I find one defect only in his most wise and righteous action; he was too merciful to the miserable King and to the demons who had been destroying one of the most populous and fertile countries of India. As I have told you, in our own administration of Oudh we have made some serious mistakes, not the less to be lamented because they were committed with excellent intentions. But with all our shortcomings, think of Oudh under its Native Government, and of what it has now become; it is now as peaceful as Cambridgeshire; life and property are as safe, and justice is as honestly administered.

This Oudh story is now an old one, but, unhappily, stories not much better can be told of a much later date.

Baroda is the principal Native State of Western India. It covers 8,600 square miles, and has a population of nearly 2,250,000. Its ruler, the Gaikwár, claims precedence over all the Native chiefs of India. In 1863, Malhár Ráo was imprisoned on a charge of having attempted the life of the Gaikwár, his brother; at the end of 1870, on his brother's death, he was released, and he assumed the government of the State. Before long his proceedings had become so scandalous that the British Government was compelled to make a formal inquiry into his administration. It was shown that general discontent prevailed through his dominions; in one district there was open rebellion; public offices were sold to the highest bidder; extortionate payment of demands of revenue was compelled by torture; respectable women were seized in open day in the streets of Baroda by the Gaikwár's servants, and taken to the palace to be converted into household slaves or worse; the condition of the agricultural classes was desperate; and the whole administration was infamous. The Prime Minister was forcibly poisoned in prison, and it was hardly possible to doubt that this was done under the direct orders of the Gaikwár. It was proved that, for an act by which he had been personally offended, the Gaikwár had caused one of his servants, without any trial, to be tortured to death.

In 1874 he was informed by the Government of India, Lord Northbrook being Viceroy at the time, that, if immediate and satisfactory reforms were not carried out in the administration of the State, his deposition would follow. He showed no inclination to alter his conduct. Soon afterwards an attempt was made to poison the British Resident at his court, and there was every reason to believe that the Gaikwár had personally instigated the crime. A commission, of which the Chief Justice of Bengal was president, and of which the rulers of two of the principal Native States were members, was appointed for his trial. The Native chiefs pronounced that the charges were not proved, but the Chief Justice and the English members found that he was guilty, and there was not the least doubt that they were right. As the judgment was not unanimous, the Gaikwár escaped the extreme penalty that he deserved, and which, if he had been formally convicted, he would probably have suffered. He was deposed, and a member of another branch of the Gaikwár's house was selected by the British Government as his successor. When the rule of Malhár Ráo ended, it was found that out of an expenditure in his last year of 1,700,000*l.*, which was enormously in excess of the revenue, he had squandered 700,000*l.* in gifts to favourites and on his personal pleasures, and 200*l.* remained in the public treasury.

I am far from wishing you to suppose that the misgovernment of Native States often reaches such an extreme as in the instances that I have given, but they show what may happen in India when power falls into the hands of worthless rulers; and if these cases are exceptional, it is unfortunately true that really good administration is exceptional also. I will give a few illustrations of a not uncommon state of affairs in quiet times.

The two important Maráthа States of Gwalior and Indore, ruled respectively by Sindhia and Holkar, have together an area of 37,000 square miles, and a population of more than 4,000,000. I make the following quotations from an official report for 1885 by Sir Lepel Griffin, Agent to the Governor-General in Central India:—

'The largest states in this agency, Gwalior and Indore, are those in which the rulers spend the least on administration and most neglect all those requirements which we specially associate with progress and civilisation. . . . Those districts that are under the direct control of Sindhia's officials give little cause for trouble or complaint to the Government, although the administration is lax and apathetic. Those, however, which are given in jagír to his great courtiers are constant sources of anxiety. Neglected by the grantees, who reside at the capital, they are made over to rack-renting agents, who support their authority by Afghán and Mekráni mercenaries, who are the scourge of the country-side. Damodar Panth, the agent of one of the principal nobles of the Maharája, has long been notorious for his open encouragement and support of crime in his master's jagír.

Having sufficient proof of his complicity in numerous cases of dacoity and robbery, I have, with the full consent of the Mahárája, caused his arrest, and he is now being tried on these serious charges, while the bands of dacoits, which had been allowed with impunity to plunder that part of Málwa, are being broken up. . . . During 1883–84 the oppression exercised in Indore city called for the severest condemnation on the part of the Government of India, and the senior Prince Shivaji Ráo Holkar was specially censured and removed from all concern with public business. I have had during the past year to remonstrate with the Durbár on many occasions and in strong terms against action which appeared to me to have been taken against individuals unjustly, and in defiance of the commonest principles of justice and equity. . . . The judicial administration of Indore must be held to be deteriorating and not improving. The reforms instituted by Sir Mádhava Ráo are being gradually abandoned from motives of false economy. . . . If I am unable to say much that is good of the two great Mahratta States included in Central India, this is no matter for surprise. In the Rájput States which abound in Central India, and which are rather oligarchical than autocratic, there is on the part of the chiefs a far more kindly and unselfish attitude towards the brotherhood and the people generally than in a Mahratta State, the despotic egoism of which is fatal to all progress and civilisation. The ruler considers the soil of the State as his own; the people are his slaves; the entire revenue is his private pocket-money, to hoard, lavish, or waste, without any right of remonstrance or complaint on the part of his subjects. The disease of such governments is chronic and intolerable. It is impossible that they can be other than evil, and it is a false and foolish policy to use towards them the language of false compliment and to pretend that they are other than irretrievably bad, until a higher civilisation and the example of the British Government shall have demonstrated that the rights of princes have no existence apart from the rights of the people.'

In 1884, the condition of Bhopál, a State with nearly 1,000,000 inhabitants, became such that it was necessary for the Government of India to remove the husband of the reigning princess from power, and to appoint an English minister to carry on the administration. The land revenue had been arbitrarily raised from 170,000*l.* to 410,000*l.*; the payment of more than 1,000,000*l.* was demanded in a lump sum from the people; justice became a mere engine of corruption and oppression; districts were ruined and depopulated; the police were no better than dacoits who shared their plunder with men in high places. Although, through the efforts of the English minister, all this has been reformed, we are told that many years must elapse before the people of Bhopál can recover from the ruin which they suffered. As lately as 1887, the Chief of a small Native State was removed from power under circumstances too abominable to be described.[1]

There is no one who can speak with greater experience of Native States than Sir Lepel Griffin. This is his account of the way in which the principal States of Central India are governed:—

'The peasants are little better than serfs. The importation of foreign slaves is prevented by the vigilance of the British

[1] The following passage is taken from the official report of 1884 that I have already quoted. It refers to a great gathering of pilgrims at Ujain, one of the sacred places of India, in the Gwalior State:—'The fakirs who attended in great numbers were absolutely defiant of all control, and resisted all restrictions on their movements. It is but a few years ago that the Durbar troops, with loaded cannons and muskets, were unable to preserve peace between the rival bands of worshippers seeking to bathe at the propitious moment in the most sacred portions of the stream, and numbers have been killed in these fierce contests. Even to-day the ascetics are very unmanageable, and the State officials are afraid of them. One instance of this may be recorded as showing the barbarism which still exists in the country. A band of that loathsome sect known as the Agori Panth came to Ujain at the beginning of the fair, and demanding some goats from the authorities were refused. On this they proceeded to the burning ghát, and, taking a corpse from the pile, began to devour it. The horrified spectators summoned the police, but these naked fanatics only desisted on being promised the goats which had before been refused them.'

authorities alone. Torture is a recognised part of judicial and police procedure. . . . Only a few months ago I was compelled to refuse to return the visit of a ruling chief who was openly accused of squeezing the juice of chillies into the eyes of recusant witnesses. He was an old gentleman of the most soft and courteous manners, and the idea that chillies could be objected to as a means of judicial investigation did not appear to have occurred to him. . . . Administration of justice has virtually no existence; a bribe procures the acquittal, or escape, or release of a criminal. Every offence can usually be compounded for money. Numerous boundary disputes between Native States come before me, and the consideration which governs every case is that both States have, as a matter of course, supported a wilfully exaggerated claim by perjured witnesses and forged documents. One of the first chiefs in India punishes and ruins the headman or cultivator of a village who may give truthful evidence contrary to any boundary claim the State has chosen unjustly to advance. . . . The actual demand of the Government per head of the population is double, treble, or quadruple what it is in British India.'[1]

Speaking of Kashmir with personal knowledge, Sir Lepel Griffin tells us that 'nothing escapes taxation, and bare life is all that the State leaves to the cultivator, whose position is harder and as hopeless as that of a slave;'[2] and his general conclusion is that, although there are many honourable exceptions, the Native States of India are 'a wilderness of oppression and misrule.' I asked an officer who is intimately acquainted with almost every important State in India to give me his opinion on this subject. He told me in reply that he thought Sir Lepel Griffin's remarks very accurate, and his language moderate and fair. For several years I was myself a member of the Govern-

[1] *Fortnightly Review*, October 1883.

[2] Since this was written there has been a change of rulers in Kashmir.

ment of India; I wish I could say that my own conclusions were different.

The British Government has for many years past ceased to desire further extensions of territory in India, and it is difficult to imagine circumstances under which the annexation of a Native State would now be considered expedient. The complete recognition of the right of adoption and the experience of the last quarter of a century have in this respect removed from the minds of the Native Princes all suspicion of the policy of our Government, and I have no doubt that with rare exceptions they are sincerely loyal. The mutinies of 1857 showed conclusively that the Native States are a source to us not of weakness but of strength. In the words of Lord Canning, 'these patches of Native Government served as a breakwater to the storm which would otherwise have swept over us in one great wave.' With hardly an exception they remained faithful under circumstances of the severest trial and difficulty. I believe that we may confidently rely on the loyalty of the Native Chiefs of India, but it is well not to deceive ourselves. Many of them are loyal, not because they love us, but because they know that we are strong, and that loyalty is the only policy which in their own interests is wise. We cannot reasonably expect more. If a time should come when they cease to believe in the permanence of our power, then they will inevitably cease to be loyal.

There is only one apparent cause by which the long-continued political existence of the Native States of India can now be imperilled. We need not desire their government to be like ours, but as our own administration improves, and everything in India becomes increasingly open to public criticism and inquiry, the more impossible will it be for us to tolerate gross oppression and misgovernment in Native States.

The problems to be solved are difficult, especially in those States, the most interesting in India, and the most worthy of preservation, where old political institutions still survive. Where the ruler is a petty despot, with few or no checks on his power, the principles on which we ought to act are easier to define. No real progress in such States is possible while their governments remain purely personal, and while the authority of the paramount power is exercised on no fixed system, but spasmodically, by special acts of intervention as necessity arises.

The first serious attempt to regulate in a definite and permanent shape the relations of the Imperial Government towards some at least of the Native States of India was made by Lord Lytton when he was Viceroy. In 1830 the administration of Mysore had fallen into a miserable condition. Offices were sold to the highest bidder, the people were oppressed and impoverished, and at last broke into revolt. Lord William Bentinck, who was then Governor-General, ordered, as the only sufficient remedy, the transfer of the entire administration into the hands of British officers. Mysore was fortunate in finding in Sir Mark Cubbon an admirable Governor. 'The history of the province under his rule (I quote from an official report) is the history of a people made happy by release from serfdom, and of a ruined state restored to financial prosperity.'

In 1868 the deposed Rája died, and the British Government resolved that when his adopted son, who was then only six years old, attained his majority, the Government of the State should be entrusted to him.

In 1879 it became necessary to settle the manner in which this resolution should be carried out; it was clear that more than 4,000,000 people, who had been under our Government for fifty years, could not be made over like sheep, and the following conditions were laid down:—

1st. A clear distinction must be drawn and permanently maintained between the private fortune of the Chief and the public revenues of the State; a civil list of fixed amount must be assigned to the Chief, and the rest of the revenues must remain available for public purposes only, through appropriation by constituted authorities.

2nd. There must be permanent security for the observance of established laws, rights, and usages, and the laws must only be altered by suitable legislative machinery.

3rd. Provision must be made for the judicial independence of the civil and criminal courts, and justice must be dispensed by regularly constituted tribunals.

4th. The assessment and collection of the revenues must be made under fixed rules; all rights in the land must be defined and maintained, and no fresh taxation imposed except in accordance with law.

Under the principles thus laid down, the administration was made over, in 1881, to the Native Chief. His civil list was fixed at 130,000*l.* a year, and he cannot appropriate more than that sum for his personal expenditure. The revenue of the State is about 1,000,000*l.* The administration is carried on by the Máháràja with the assistance of a Council. It consists of three members, with a Diwán, or chief minister; he is the head of all departments, and he conducts the executive administration. The Diwán and the Councillors are all Natives.

When the Government was transferred it was provided that all laws then in force should be maintained until altered by competent authority; new laws can only be made under a regular system of procedure, and they require the sanction of the Governor-General in Council.

The objects with which this system was initiated were summed up as follows by the Government of India :—

'The experiment of placing the Máhárája of Mysore at the head of a constitutional government—that is, a government conducted upon fixed and fundamental principles—makes a new departure in the policy of the Imperial Government towards the Native States of India. To determine the proper method of dealing with these States, and of discharging the responsibilities which they entail upon the paramount power, has always been, and still is, a problem of great difficulty; for the improvement of their condition, and their gradual assimilation to the general system and standard of the Imperial Government, is almost essential to their preservation . . . The Supreme Government has been obliged of late years to interpose frequently in the affairs of Native States. The incapacity or grave misconduct of a ruler has produced complications which have demanded immediate and stringent remedies, or the interval of a long minority has made it necessary to superintend more closely a State's management. . . . . The policy now framed proceeds upon the broad principle that in order to guard against chronic misrule in a Native State, and to obviate the necessity for frequent and arbitrary interposition by the Supreme Government to remedy the consequences of such misrule, it is expedient to avail ourselves of every opportunity of placing some reasonable limitations upon the personal power of the ruler, or of the minister to whom the administration may be entrusted. The limitations thus imposed must be brought on public record, in order to place them beyond question or controversy, and in certain cases the general power of supervision to be exercised by the Supreme Government may need to be strengthened and extended. These principles may form the groundwork of a settled policy which will guide the Government of India in the general discharge of its responsibilities towards Feudatory States. A new and valuable precedent will have been established, and this, with the experience which will have been gained in Mysore, may enable us in future to deal systematically with similar questions of reorganisation or reform. The contrast presented by the steady growth of orderly civilisation in British India, and the increased publicity that is now given to the internal condition of our Feudatory States, are likely to render more and more imperative the duty of interference in restraint of serious mismanagement. We may thus hope gradually to raise the general standard of administration in Native States, and to make some progress toward the important political object of consolidating their institutions upon an improved and stable foundation.'[1]

The system thus introduced into Mysore appears to be working in a highly efficient manner. More or less similar plans, but of a less elaborate kind, have been adopted with success in some other cases, and I hope that the time is not distant when the principles on which these measures have been based may be generally applied in the Native States of India, and the abuses and maladministration may cease that are now so frequent.

I have not yet referred to the armies of the Native States. They look formidable on paper, for they are said to number altogether about 380,000 men, of whom 69,000 are cavalry and 11,000 artillery, with some 4,000 guns. These figures are very deceptive. A small portion only of these so-called armies has any military organisation. They consist for the most part of men who can hardly be called soldiers. The majority of them are maintained for purposes of display, without the least idea that they can ever be

[1] Despatch from Government of India to Secretary of State, May 22, 1879. Parliamentary Return, Mysore, 1881.

used for fighting. The so-called army includes multitudes of the armed retainers of the chiefs and nobles, and nearly the whole of the men whom we should class as police. There are only two cases in which it seems, at the present time, possible that the armies of the Native States might become causes of anxiety to our Government.

The first is the army of Gwalior. Among all the armies of the Native States this is the most completely organised. It consists of about 11,000 men, of whom about 6,000 are cavalry, all fairly drilled and disciplined, with several fully equipped batteries of artillery. It has often been said that Sindhia's force is really stronger than it appears to be, because a system, similar to that adopted in Europe, has been introduced, by which a strong reserve is formed by passing rapidly a large proportion of the population through the army. There is no foundation for such statements. A very small part of Sindhia's troops consists of men recruited in his own country. The great majority of them come from our territories, and chiefly from the classes which before the mutinies of 1857 supplied the bulk of our Bengal army. The Government of Sindhia is, as I have shown, that of a foreign dynasty; the people are unwarlike and disinclined for military service. The strength of the forces which Sindhia may maintain is regulated by treaty with the British Government.

The largest of the armies of the Native States is that of the Nizam of Hyderabad, also a foreigner in the country belonging to him. It is so heterogeneous a body that it is difficult to state its numbers, but that part of it which may with some reason be called an army consists of about 45,000 men. 'Many of these (I am quoting from the Report of the Indian Army Commission) are foreign mercenaries from remote parts of India, and from the Afghan highlands beyond our northern frontier, who take service under the Nizam and his chiefs; they engage in faction fights and raids within his territory, and have recently shown themselves ready to join any discontented men who may be willing to pay them for raiding into British districts.' A considerable part of the Nizam's army has been reorganised and improved. The Indian Army Commission has pointed out in strong language the evils arising from the maintenance of these riotous mercenaries. While they perform no useful service to the Nizam, it is necessary to watch and overawe them, and the necessity is imposed on our treasury of always keeping a large force of British and Native troops at Hyderabad. A Native force, called the Hyderabad Contingent, consisting of more than 7,000 men of all arms, under the command of British officers, is also maintained by our Government at Hyderabad. The charges for the Contingent are met from the revenues of the Berár districts, which were assigned to us for the purpose in 1853 by treaty with the Nizam.

The armies of Sindhia and the Nizam, and especially the latter, might undoubtedly, under circumstances not difficult to conceive, become sources of anxiety. Being mainly composed of foreign mercenaries, their fidelity to their chiefs, themselves of foreign origin, cannot always be trusted. This was shown in 1857, when the troops of Sindhia, who was himself loyal, mutinied and joined in the revolt of the Bengal army. This is a difficult subject, and it has not hitherto been dealt with satisfactorily.

The troops of the Rájputána States consist, on paper, of more than 100,000 men, with 1,400 guns, but these figures have no military significance. The men are not, for the most part, soldiers in the service of the State, but the members of a military class. None of the guns are equipped for service. There is no doubt of the loyalty of the Rájput chiefs or of their followers.

The troops of the Sikh States deserve mention. 'They are composed (the Indian Army Commission tells us) of good material; they are well officered, and have on occasions done excellent service for the British Crown. They are devoted to their chiefs, who are conspicuously loyal, and bound to the British Government by mutual goodwill and good offices, which have extended over many years.'

The troops of no Native State possess arms of precision; they have no breech-loading rifles, no rifled ordnance, and very little organised artillery. They are, for the most part, as Sir Lepel Griffin says, 'an undrilled, wretchedly armed rabble, and two or three of our regiments, with a battery of horse artillery, would disperse 50,000 of them.' With the exceptions that I have named, they cannot cause us anxiety. They are not armies in the ordinary sense of the term.

LECTURE XII.

BENGAL—CONCLUSION

EXCEPTIONAL CHARACTER OF BENGAL AND ITS PEOPLE—THE BENGAL LIEUTENANT-GOVERNORSHIP—NATURAL FEATURES, AREA, AND POPULATION—PRODUCTS — SCENERY — CLIMATE — CITIES—ART—HINDUS AND MOHAMMEDANS—LORD MACAULAY'S DESCRIPTION OF THE BENGÁLIS—THEIR EXTRAORDINARY EFFEMINACY—THE PERMANENT SETTLEMENT—ZEMINDARS AND RYOTS—THE CONSEQUENCES OF THE PERMANENT SETTLEMENT—LOSS OF PUBLIC REVENUE—CONFISCATION OF THE RIGHTS OF THE PEASANTRY—WEAKNESS OF THE GOVERNMENT—ABSENCE OF RECORDS OF AGRICULTURAL RIGHTS—FORMER CONSTITUTION OF THE BENGAL GOVERNMENT—ITS INEFFICIENCY—A SEPARATE GOVERNMENT CONSTITUTED—IMPROVEMENTS IN THE ADMINISTRATION—DIFFICULTY OF PROBLEMS TO BE SOLVED—GREAT INCREASE IN RENTALS OF THE ZEMINDARS AND LOSS BY THE RYOTS—CONSEQUENT INJUSTICE TO OTHER PROVINCES—MAINTENANCE OF CONDITIONS OF THE PERMANENT SETTLEMENT—CLAIMS OF THE ZEMINDARS FOR EXEMPTION FROM TAXATION—THE PROPER REMEDIES FOR EXISTING EVILS—RATES ON THE LAND—CHANGES IN THE BENGAL RENT-LAW—CONDITION OF THE PEOPLE IN BEHÁR—THE TENANCY ACT—EFFECTS OF ENGLISH EDUCATION—ATTITUDE OF THE ENGLISH-SPEAKING BENGÁLIS—POLITICAL AGITATION—NEGLECT OF SOCIAL QUESTIONS—REASONS FOR AVOIDING DISCUSSION—THE EMPLOYMENT OF NATIVES IN THE PUBLIC SERVICE—THE PRINCIPLES TO BE OBSERVED AND AVOIDED—POLITICAL HYPOCRISY—THE DUTY OF MAINTAINING OUR DOMINION—OFFICES TO BE RETAINED BY ENGLISHMEN—THE SO-CALLED NATIVES OF INDIA OFTEN AS MUCH FOREIGNERS AS ENGLISHMEN—THE MANLIER RACES OF INDIA CANNOT BE RULED THROUGH BENGÁLIS—CONCLUSION—THE RESULTS OF BRITISH GOVERNMENT—THE POPULARITY OF OUR GOVERNMENT—LORD LAWRENCE'S OPINION—REASONS WHY OUR GOVERNMENT CANNOT BE POPULAR—THE PRINCIPLES ON WHICH OUR GOVERNMENT MUST BE CARRIED ON.

I HAVE endeavoured to give you some general idea of what India is, and to illustrate the manner in which the administration of a British province is carried on, and I have told you something of the government of the Native Princes who still rule a third part of India and a fifth of its population. Before concluding these lectures I propose to give some sketches of another great British Province, Bengal. I am the more desirous of doing this because Englishmen are frequently under the impression that Bengal and Bengális are types of India and its people, the truth being that there is no province which is in all respects so exceptional, and no people so curiously distinct.

I have explained the various significations which the name Bengal has had at different times. It now usually means the country included within the Bengal Lieutenant-Governorship, but this again includes four provinces—Bengal Proper, comprising the tracts between the Ganges and Bráhmaputra, and the deltas of those rivers; Behár, on the north-west of Bengal Proper, adjoining the North-Western Provinces, to which in its physical character it is very similar; Chota Nagpur, a wild and hilly country between Bengal Proper and Central India; and Orissa, south-west from Calcutta, the country of the river Máhánadi, with the sea on its eastern side.

A description of any one of these provinces would be wholly inapplicable to the rest. Their physical conditions, the character of the population, and their languages are all different. The Lieutenant-Governorship of Bengal covers an area as large as that of France, and contains 67,000,000 people. As Sir William Hunter has observed, 'its elements exhibit every stage of human enlightenment and superstition, from the sceptical educated classes, represented by the Hindu gentleman who distinguishes himself at a London Inn of Court, to the hill chieftain, who a few years ago sacrificed an idiot on the top of a mountain to obtain a favourable decision in a Privy Council appeal.'[1] Although I shall have to

[1] *Imperial Gazetteer of India*, Art. 'India.'

make some references to Behár, it is almost solely of Bengal Proper that I now propose to speak. It is the largest and most populous and richest of the provinces that make up the Lieutenant-Governorship. It has an area of more than 70,000 square miles, and contains a population of 35,500,000.

Bengal Proper is everywhere intersected by the channels and tributaries of the Ganges and Bráhmaputra. Some two hundred miles from the sea the two rivers begin to throw out branches, and lower down they join their waters. Sir William Hunter has given, in the 'Imperial Gazetteer of India,' a graphic description of this part of the province:—

'The delta of the Ganges,' he says, 'where it borders on the sea, becomes a labyrinth of creeks and rivers, running through the dense forests of the Sundarbans, and exhibiting during the annual inundations the appearance of an immense sea. Higher up, the rice-fields, to the extent of thousands of square miles, are submerged. The scene presents to a European eye a panorama of singular novelty and interest—the crops covered with water; the ears of grain floating on the surface; the stupendous embankments, which restrain, without altogether preventing, the excesses of the inundations; and peasants in all quarters going out to their daily work with their cattle in canoes or on rafts. The navigable streams which fall into or diverge from the Ganges intersect the country in every direction, and afford abundant facilities for internal communication. In many parts, boats can approach, by means of lakes, rivulets, and water-courses, to the door of almost every cottage. The lower region of the Ganges is the richest and most productive portion of Bengal, and abounds in valuable produce.'

The inundation of the Bráhmaputra produces similar conditions. The rivers in Lower Bengal render, to a great extent, the services which are rendered in other countries by the roads. In many parts of the province a well-to-do man keeps his boat as elsewhere he would keep his cart. Railways have penetrated into some of the districts, but they will not diminish the usefulness of the rivers or the traffic which they carry. Marts are held every year, on a great scale, at convenient places on the chief rivers, and the agricultural produce of the country is carried off in all directions by the navigable channels. The list of the useful products of Bengal would be a long one. Almost everything is provided in abundance that a people in a tropical climate requires. Rice, jute, indigo, opium, oilseeds, and tea are the principal articles which come into the export trade from Calcutta, but tea is only cultivated on the mountainous borders of the province, and not in Bengal Proper, and the opium comes from Behár and the North-Western Provinces. The great agricultural staple, more important than any other, is rice which constitutes the chief food of the people.

Although the endless stretches of the rice-fields are monotonous, few flat countries can be more beautiful than parts of Bengal. A constant succession of admirable pictures is afforded by the reaches of the rivers, busy with traffic; the boats with their great sails; the cocoanuts, and other palms, huge figs, tamarinds and mangoes, bamboos and plantains; the villages, with tanks green with slime and water-lilies; neat cottages covered with creeping gourds and cucumbers and melons; the delicate forms of the men and women, in scanty but graceful costume—these, and a thousand picturesque details, and the colouring of its hot and steamy atmosphere, make Bengal one of the most beautiful countries of India. Nor is it so disagreeable for Englishmen to live in, as might be supposed. Although it has not the advantage of the pleasantly cold winter of Northern India, the heat of the summer is tempered by the greater moisture and by the nearness of the sea. Heat like that of June at Agra or Lahore is unknown, and for three or four months in the winter the climate is very agreeable.

Although there is hardly any part of India where trade is so active, there are few cities and important towns. With the exception of Calcutta, which with its suburbs contains 870,000 people, and is in population the second city in the British Empire, there is hardly a town in Bengal Proper which, according to a European standard, can be called large. Dacca, with 79,000 people, is the largest. Almost the whole population is rural. There are scarcely any manufactures, except of common cloth and other articles which can be made by the ordinary village artisans. Bengal has never, within historical times, been distinguished, as other Indian countries have been, for excellence in art. The native portion of Calcutta, although full of wealth, can hardly be surpassed in mean ugliness; people who are comparatively rich are often content to live in hovels; and among the zemindars and rájas of Bengal, with incomes which even in England would be thought immense, there is hardly one who lives in a house which in its architecture and decoration is not detestable. In this respect the modern native city of Bombay is a striking contrast to that of Calcutta. The western and eastern capitals of India have grown up under not very dissimilar circumstances; but while the latter, in its native quarter, is everywhere contemptible, the former can show streets which in picturesqueness and decoration are inferior to those of few modern cities in Europe. The admirable Indian styles of architecture which are living arts in other provinces are practically unrepresented in Bengal.

Throughout nearly the whole of Bengal Proper the

people speak the same language, Bengáli. About one-half of them are classified as Hindu, and half as Mohammedan. In some of the Eastern districts the Mohammedans constitute three-fourths of the whole population. But, as I have already observed, in speaking of the religions of Northern India, they are often Mohammedans in name only, and the religion of multitudes of them might not unfitly be classed among the varieties of Hinduism. Changes, however, have been in progress in this respect during the last half century, and there has been a tendency among the Mohammedans of Bengal towards the purification of their faith from Hindu superstitions and from Brahmanical influence. The great mass of the Mussulman population is agricultural, but, even where it is most numerous, wealth and property in land are chiefly in the hands of the Hindus. If we look merely to numbers, the Lieutenant-Governor of Bengal is, as Sir William Hunter says, 'as great a Mussulman power as the Sultan of Turkey himself,' but in our political speculations we need not alarm ourselves about the millions of Mohammedans in Bengal.

The educated Mohammedans deserve to be named with respect. They are not very numerous or wealthy, but they often present, by their loyalty and good sense, a happy contrast to the English-speaking Hindus, of whom I shall have again to speak.

I shall not attempt to give any detailed account of the people or of the administration. I can only point out a few of the more remarkable facts.

Many years ago Lord Macaulay gave a description of the Natives of Bengal. There is good reason, as I have already said, for calling in question the accuracy of some of his historical pictures, based on fallacious records, which have taught to thousands of Englishmen almost all that they know about India, but when Lord Macaulay wrote his character of the Bengális he was describing, from personal knowledge and observation, a people among whom he had himself lived. Its accuracy has hardly been denied by the Bengális themselves, and will be disputed by no Englishman.

'The men,' he writes, 'by whom this rich tract was peopled, enervated by a soft climate and accustomed to peaceful employments, bore the same relation to other Asiatics which the Asiatics generally bear to the bold and energetic children of Europe. The Castilians have a proverb that in Valencia the earth is water and the men women; and this description is at least equally applicable to the vast plain of the Lower Ganges. Whatever the Bengalee does he does languidly. His favourite pursuits are sedentary. He shrinks from bodily exertion; and, though voluble in dispute, and singularly pertinacious in the war of chicane, he seldom engages in a personal conflict, and scarcely ever enlists as a soldier. There never, perhaps, existed a people so thoroughly fitted by habit for a foreign yoke.'[1]

In another passage Lord Macaulay has passed upon the Bengális a similar judgment. I will quote a portion of it:—

'The physical organisation of the Bengalee is feeble even to effeminacy. He lives in a constant vapour-bath. His pursuits are sedentary, his limbs delicate, his movements languid. During many ages he has been trampled upon by men of bolder and more hardy breeds. . . . His mind bears a singular analogy to his body. It is weak even to helplessness for purposes of manly resistance; but its suppleness and tact move the children of sterner climates to admiration not unmingled with contempt. . . . Nor does he lack a certain kind of courage which is often wanting to his masters. To inevitable evils he is sometimes found to oppose a passive fortitude, such as the Stoics attributed to their ideal sage. An European warrior who rushes

[1] *Macaulay's Essays.* 'Lord Clive.'

on a battery of cannon with a loud hurrah will sometimes shriek under the surgeon's knife, and fall into an agony of despair at the sentence of death. But the Bengalee, who would see his country overrun, his house laid in ashes, his children murdered or dishonoured, without having the spirit to strike one blow, has yet been known to endure torture with the firmness of Mucius, and to mount the scaffold with the steady step and even pulse of Algernon Sidney.'[1]

Lord Macaulay would have been the first to declare that you might find Bengális of a different stamp. Courage is no more an invariable virtue among the hardiest races of Europe than cowardice an invariable infirmity among the population of Bengal. There have been many changes since Lord Macaulay wrote, but the general character of the people throughout a great part of the province remains as he represented it. His description may be applied without exaggeration to the majority of the people of Western Bengal, and especially to those with whom Englishmen come most into communication in Calcutta and the neighbouring districts. The Mohammedan peasantry of the eastern portion of the province are men of robuster character. It has often been said, and it is probably true, that Bengal is the only country in the world where you can find a great population among whom personal cowardice is looked upon as in no way disgraceful. This is no invention of their enemies; the Bengális have themselves no shame or scruple in declaring it to be a fact.

Although it cannot, I am afraid, be said that English education, which has taken so deep a root, has hitherto made any class of Bengális more manly, it is, we may hope, encouraging the growth of this among other virtues. For a Bengáli it is something to have begun to talk in grandiloquent English about patriotism

[1] *Macaulay's Essays.* 'Warren Hastings.'

and manliness and courage. Even the academic admiration of such things is perhaps a mark of progress. The people generally are acute and intelligent, patient and industrious, and when they get more knowledge they may become more self-reliant, less timid, and less helpless against wrong.

Leaving speculations on possible changes that may come to pass if our dominion should last sufficiently long, and looking to present facts, it is difficult to conceive for Bengal any independent political future. What expectations can be formed for a people that no necessity would induce to fight? In all the Native armies of India there is not, and I suppose there never has been, a Bengáli soldier. We may think of troopers from the Punjab riding with Englishmen in a Balaclava charge, of Sikhs and Gúrkhas fighting as French and Germans fought at Gravelotte, but is it possible by the wildest stretch of the imagination to suppose such things of Bengális? But for the presence of our power, Bengal would inevitably and immediately become the prey of the hardier races of other Indian countries. It is for such reasons that Englishmen who know Bengal, and the extraordinary effeminacy of its people, find it difficult to treat seriously many of the political declamations in which the English-speaking Bengális are often fond of indulging.

The condition of the people of Bengal has been profoundly affected by action taken nearly a century ago by the British Government. In 1793 the so-called Permanent Settlement of the Land Revenue was introduced.

We found in Bengal, when we succeeded to the Government, a class of middle-men, called Zemindars, who collected the land revenue and the taxes, and we continued to employ them. As a matter of convenience and expediency, but not of right, the office of zemindar was often hereditary. The zemindars had never been in any sense the owners of the land, but it was supposed by Lord Cornwallis and the English rulers of the time that it would be an excellent thing for Bengal to have a class of landlords something like those of England; the zemindars were the only people that seemed available for the purpose, and they were declared to be the proprietors of the land. It was by no means intended that injustice should thus be done to others.

Excepting the State, there was only one great class, that of the ryots or actual cultivators, which, according to immemorial custom, could be held to possess permanent rights in the land. The existence of those rights was recognised, and, as it was supposed, guarded by the law. It was provided that 'the Governor-General in Council will, whenever he may deem it proper, enact such regulations as he may think necessary for the protection of the dependent talookdars, ryots, and other cultivators of the soil.' There has been much dispute as to the exact nature of the rights given to the zemindars, but every one agrees that it was not the intention of the authors of the Permanent Settlement to confiscate anything which, according to the customs of the country, had belonged to the cultivators. The right of property given to the zemindars was a portion of those rights which had always been exercised by the State, and of which the State was at liberty to dispose; it was not intended that they should receive anything else. The land revenue, representing the share of the produce or rental to which the State was entitled, was fixed in perpetuity. The ryots were to continue to hold their lands permanently at the 'rates established in the purgunnah;' when the amount of these rates was disputed it was to be settled by the courts; so long as rents at those rates were paid, the ryot could not be evicted. The intention was to secure to the ryot fixity of tenure and fixity of rent. Unfortunately, these rights were only secured upon paper.

If the intentions with which the Permanent Settlement was made had been carried out, the result would, at any rate, have been beneficial to the ryots of Bengal, whatever might have been the effect on the interests of the State. I described in a former lecture[1] the nature of the right which the ruling power has always exercised in India, of reserving for its own purposes a portion of the rent of the land. It was a right which had been exercised in Bengal from time immemorial. This resource, which would have gone on growing with the increasing prosperity of the country, has been thrown away in Bengal. The consequences at the present time are these:—Even if it be assumed that the share of the rent which the State can wisely take is smaller than the share which any Government, Native or English, has ever taken or proposed to take in India, the amount now received by the State from the land in Bengal must be held to fall short of what it might be by a sum that can hardly be less than 5,000,000*l.* a year; this is a moderate computation; probably the loss is much more. This is given away in return for no service to the State or to the public; the zemindars are merely the receivers of rent; with exceptions so rare as to deserve no consideration, they take no part in the improvement of the land, and, until a very few years ago they bore virtually no share of the public burdens. The result of these proceedings of the last century, to

[1] Lecture III., p. 75.

the maintenance of which for ever the faith of the British Government is said to have been pledged, is that the poorer classes in poorer provinces have to make good to the State the millions which have been thrown away in Bengal.

If this were all, it would be bad enough, but worse remains to be told. More serious evils have followed in the train of the Permanent Settlement. The crowning misfortune has been the destruction or non-recognition of those rights of the masses of the agricultural population which the authors of the Settlement undoubtedly intended to preserve.

'The original intention of the framers of the Permanent Settlement [I am quoting from Sir George Campbell] was to record all rights. The Canoongoes (District Registrars) and Putwarees (Village Accountants) were to register all holdings, all transfers, all rent-rolls, and all receipts and payments; and every five years there was to be filed in the public offices a complete register of all land tenures. But the task was a difficult one; there was delay in carrying it out. English ideas of the rights of a landlord, and of the advantage of non-interference, began more and more to prevail in Bengal. The executive more and more abrogated the functions of recording rights and protecting the inferior holders, and left everything to the judicial tribunals. The putwarees fell into disuse or became the mere servants of the zemindars; the canoongoes were abolished. No record of the rights of the ryots and inferior holders was ever made, and even the quinquennial register of superior rights, which was maintained for a time, fell into disuse. When a regular police was established, the zemindars were in practice freed from any effective responsibility for the suppression of crime, or other administrative functions. They became in every sense mere rent-receivers.'[1]

The consequences of the Permanent Settlement did not become immediately prominent. At the beginning

[1] *System of Land Tenures in Various Countries*, published by the Cobden Club, p. 176.

of this century the population was far smaller, there was much waste land to be occupied, and there was little disposition or power on the part of the zemindars to disregard the old customary terms on which the land was held. But, as time went on, and population and wealth increased, as cultivators were more readily found, and custom began to give way to competition, the position of the ryots became worse and that of the zemindars became stronger. Other circumstances helped the process of confiscation of the rights of the peasantry. For more than half a century after the Permanent Settlement was made, the executive Government in Bengal was extremely weak. The English principle that in the ordinary affairs of life the less the State interferes with individual action the better, and that for the protection of private rights little more is required than the maintenance of order, with good courts of justice accessible to all, is admirable when applied to the government of Englishmen, but there could be no people to which it was less applicable than the people of Bengal. This principle of non-interference was carried out to an extent unkown in any other part of India. Nothing would have so much helped the timid people of Bengal in social and political progress as the just and active and masterful administration of Englishmen, resolute that the rights should be respected of those who had not the courage or the knowledge to protect themselves. To talk of self-reliance and self-government among such a people as that of Bengal was, and is, little better than childish. You cannot govern an infant school on a system appropriate for grown men.

I showed in a former lecture[1] that in other provinces of India an elaborate machinery has been spread over

[1] Lecture IX., pp. 243-249.

the whole country, extending its ramifications into every village, for the purpose of maintaining an accurate record of the rights and liabilities of all classes of the agricultural population. In Bengal nothing of the sort exists. There has been no cadastral survey and no record of agricultural rights. Under the arrangements of the Permanent Settlement, the Government has no anxiety about the collection of its land revenue. The whole responsibility for punctual payment falls upon the zemindar. If he does not pay at the district treasury on the appointed date, no questions are asked; there may or may not have been causes which make immediate payment difficult; these are matters with which the Government does not concern itself; it is enough that the revenue is due; the estate is put up to public auction, and the demand of the State is the first claim on the proceeds of the sale. In consequence of this system, the executive Government, so far as the collection of the land revenue is concerned, has little to do in the interior of a Bengal district, and financially there is no direct reason for interference with any interests in the land.

There were other causes for the weakness of government in Bengal. This being the province in which British authority was first established on that side of India, and from which our chief conquests were gradually made, the Government of Bengal was for a long time the Supreme Government in British India. Until 1833, the Governor-General was called the Governor-General of Fort William in Bengal, not the Governor-General of India, and it was not until 1853 that he was relieved from the duty of governing Bengal. While the empire was being constantly extended, he could spend comparatively little time in Calcutta. When he was there, he was by law Governor, but it was impossible for him to attend personally to the details of Bengal administration. When he was absent from Calcutta, the senior member of Council for the time being became Deputy Governor. Thus there was a frequent change of rulers, and no one man was long responsible for the good government of the province. At last, the contrast between the condition of Bengal and that of other parts of India became too obvious to be neglected. This was especially seen when Bengal was compared with the neighbouring province on the north, which in 1835 had been placed under a separate Government. When the North-Western Provinces, under their admirable Lieutenant-Governor, Mr. Thomason, were becoming a model of good and vigorous administration, Bengal was the most backward of the great provinces of the empire. There were almost no roads or bridges or schools, and there was no proper protection to life and property. The police was worthless, and robberies and violent crimes by gangs of armed men, which were unheard of in other provinces, were common not far from Calcutta.

By the Act of 1853 a separate provincial Government was constituted for Bengal, and a Lieutenant-Governor was appointed. From that time a great change began, and constant improvement has been going on ever since. The courts have been purified, the police has been organised, crimes of violence have almost ceased, public works have been constructed, education has made great progress, and, although still weak when judged by the standard of other provinces, the executive administration has become stronger. Not the least beneficial of these changes were the measures which soon began to be adopted, but of which we have not nearly seen the end, for the protection of the rights of the agricultural population.

The difficulty of the problems to be solved in Bengal has been and still is great. The confiscation of the rights of the ryots has reached vast proportions. In 1793 the rental left to the zemindars under the Permanent Settlement, after payment of the land revenue, is supposed not to have exceeded 400,000*l.*; according to some estimates it was less. If the intentions of the Government had been carried out, it was to the ryots that the greater portion of any future increase in the annual value of the land would have belonged, in those parts at least of the province which were at that time well cultivated. It is not possible to state with confidence the present gross annual rental of the landlords of Bengal. An imperfect valuation made some years ago showed it to be 13,000,000*l.* It is now called 17,000,000*l.*, but there can be little doubt that it is much more. Thus, after deducting the land revenue, which is about 3,800,000*l.*,[1] the net rental has risen from 400,000*l.* in the last century to more than 13,000,000*l.* at the present time. No portion of this increase has been due to the action of the zemindars. It has been due to the industry of the ryots, to whom the greater part of it rightfully belonged, to the peaceful progress of the country, and to the expenditure of the State, an expenditure mainly defrayed from the taxation of poorer provinces. If ever there was an 'unearned increment,' it is this.

We cannot now restore to the ryots the vast property of which they have been deprived, but they may

[1] The demand on account of land revenue from the permanently settled estates, which constitute 93 per cent. of the whole number of estates in Bengal, is 3,230,000*l.* The remaining 7 per cent. of estates have been temporarily assessed since the Permanent Settlement, and the revenue paid by them is about 580,000*l.* The total land revenue of Bengal is about 3,810,000*l.*

at least be saved from further spoliation, and the people of other provinces may be protected against the necessity of bearing burdens on behalf of the landlords of Bengal. When other Indian countries understand that, in consequence of an unwise arrangement entered into in Bengal a century ago, they are compelled to pay every year several millions of taxation which would otherwise have been unnecessary, their demands for justice will be too strong to be disregarded. They do not yet know the truth. In the words of Mr. H. S. Cunningham, 'the richest province of India has been, to a large extent, defended, administered, educated, supplied with roads, barracks, hospitals, railways and canals, and relieved in famine,[1] at the expense of the rest of the community. Ryots have been toiling in Madras, and toiling in the Deccan, in order that gentlemen like the Rajas of Durbunga and Burdwan may enjoy incomes of several hundred thousand pounds a year, free from the rude contact of the tax collector's hand.'[2] It must not, however, be supposed that the land of Bengal now belongs to a very small and wealthy class of proprietors. Although some of the estates of the zemindars are great tracts of country, yielding immense incomes to their owners, a constant process of subdivision has been going on. In 1883 there were 110,456 estates on the revenue-roll of Bengal and Behár, and about 88 per cent. of these had an area of less than 500 acres.

I am not suggesting that pledges given at the time of the Permanent Settlement should be set aside, nor that the zemindars should be deprived of privileges

[1] In 1874, nearly 7,000,000*l.* was expended by the Government from the general revenues of India on the relief of famine in Bengal.

[2] *British India and its Rulers*, p. 169.

which, although wrongfully acquired, have been enjoyed through a long course of years. The evils that I have been describing can, I believe, be sufficiently if not completely remedied by measures which are open to no reasonable objection.

The zemindars have repeatedly put forward the claim that in consequence of the stipulations of the Permanent Settlement they are entitled to exemption for ever from all taxation upon profits derived from the land. In 1859, when an income tax was first imposed on every kind of property throughout India, they loudly protested that the conditions of the Settlement were violated, and that the Government had been guilty of a gross breach of faith. In 1871, and again in 1877, they demanded, on similar grounds, exemption from liability to rates imposed on land and other immoveable property for local and provincial roads and other public works. These claims have always been rejected, and the time has passed in which there was danger that any British Government would listen to the preposterous pretension that it was the design of the framers of the Permanent Settlement that no taxation should ever fall upon profits drawn from the land. The intention of the Settlement was simply to fix permanently the share of the produce or rental to which the State, in its capacity of superior landlord, intended to limit its demand. No questions of taxation were touched or involved. In the words of Sir James Stephen, the Permanent Settlement 'reduced to a certainty one particular charge on the land, which had previously been of variable amount, and so freed the landholders from uncertainty which had previously hung over them in respect of it. . . . Since the Permanent Settlement the proprietory right of the zemindars has been undoubted, and the line between their property and that of the State has been clearly defined, and is no longer subject to increase "in consequence [to use the words of the Permanent Settlement itself] of the improvement of their respective estates."'[1] As Sir James Stephen goes on to say, to affirm, that because this has been done the land has been freed from that liability to taxation which is the common liability of all property in all countries, is a confusion of thought against which it is difficult to argue. The rates levied under the Acts passed in 1871 and 1877, and consolidated by Bengal Act IX. of 1880, yielded in 1886–87 about 757,000*l.* By these rates, and by the previous imposition of the income tax, the principle that profits derived from the land are liable to taxation both for local and imperial purposes was affirmed, and if these examples be wisely followed, no questions of interference with the pledges of the Permanent Settlement need arise when the zemindars are compelled, as they some day will be, to contribute their proper share towards meeting the liabilities of the State.

The first serious effort for the improvement of the rent-law of Bengal was made in 1859, when an Act dealing with the subject was passed. It was described by Lord Canning as 'a real and earnest attempt to improve the position of the ryots of Bengal, and to open to them a prospect of freedom and independence which they have not hitherto enjoyed, by clearly defining their rights, and by placing restrictions on the power of the zemindars such as ought long ago to have been provided.' The intentions of the Legislature were excellent, but the Act proved imperfect and insufficient, and in some respects made matters worse than they were before. As time went on the difficulties increased.

[1] Speech in the Legislative Council, April 6, 1871.

In Eastern Bengal the state of affairs became highly unsatisfactory; combinations of ryots occurred, and violent collisions took place between them and the zemindars, aggravated by the fact that the former were mostly Mohammedans and the latter Hindus. In 1876 it became necessary to legislate for the prevention of agrarian disputes.

In Behár the case was more serious. This great province of Bengal has an area of 44,000 square miles, and a population of 23,000,000. There is hardly any part of British India possessing greater natural advantages of soil and climate, and no part where the condition of the agricultural population is so wretched. This was a cause of much anxiety to Lord Lawrence, and he stated his belief that legislation would become necessary for the protection of the ryot, 'and make him what he is now only in name, a free man.' In 1878, Sir Ashley Eden, then Lieutenant-Governor of Bengal, described the ryots of Behár as 'poor, helpless, discontented men, bound down to a state of extreme depression and misery, tenants of the richest province in Bengal, yet the poorest and most wretched class we find in the country. . . . The loose system of zemindari accounts, the entire absence of leases and counterparts, the universal prevalence of illegal distraint, the practice of amalgamating holdings so as to destroy evidence of continuous occupation, are evils which necessarily prevent any possible development of agricultural prosperity among the tenant class, and place them entirely at the mercy of their landlords.' The Indian Famine Commissioners, not long afterwards, pressed the same subject on the attention of the Government.

'Where,' they said, 'as in Behár, the relations of landlord and tenant are those of a high-handed proprietary body on the one hand, habitually disregarding the law, and on the other a tenantry, ignorant, very helpless, and sunk in the most abject poverty, the onus of bringing complaints ought not to be laid on the tenants, and the first and most important duty of the Bengal Government and of the officials would seem to be to guard zealously against infringements of the law by the rich, and to put them down as if they were offences against the public peace.' 'It was proved,' writes Mr. Finucane, the head of the Agricultural Department in Bengal, 'by indisputable evidence that the rents of ryots in Behár have during the past fifty years been illegally and arbitrarily enhanced out of all proportion to what the landlords were under the law entitled to demand, and to what the tenants were legally liable to pay. Though the rent law gave the ryot certain rights, he was so helpless or so ignorant that he was unable to assert these rights out of court, or to go into court to enforce them.'

I will make a few more extracts from official reports regarding the condition of the people in parts of Behár.

'The gross rental of permanently settled estates being at the lowest estimate five times the amount payable by landholders as Government revenue, there can, as a matter of course, be no difficulty in realising that revenue under the sunset law. But there are certain tracts in which, though the permanently settled land revenue may be realised, yet the sums realised by the Government have had again to be expended, many fold increased, on charitable relief which became necessary in order to prevent mortality by starvation. Such pre-eminently is the province of Behár, and specially the three northern districts of Darbhanga, Mozaffarpur, and Sáran. Within a period of seventeen years there have been five in which a portion of the people of this part of the province have died of starvation. The whole conditions of agricultural industry are such as to render it precarious. It is impossible for the people to fall back in one year of partial failure of crops on the accumulated reserves of a previous year, whether of grain, property, money, or credit. Thus, in the one district of Darbhanga, which is taken as being the worst of all in these respects—a district which is one of the most fertile, best cultivated, and highly favoured by nature in all India—it was necessary for the Government to expend in one year, on one famine in 1874, by way of charitable relief, no less than 370,000*l.* in cash, and 118,000 tons of grain, valued in Burma at 9*l.* per ton. If to this be added the cost of transport, and cost of famine establishment, it will not be too much to put down the net cost of famine to Government in this single district at 1,500,000*l.*, the Government revenue being less than 50,000*l.* per annum. The famine expenditure in this district, in one year, was more than thirty times the amount of the Government revenue, and far more than its capitalised value. . . . Yet the rental of the district was no less than twelve times the amount of the Government revenue. It is not alone on famine relief that enormous sums have been expended in this part of the country. There has been also a great outlay on State railways, which, though they may facilitate the importation of gràin in times of distress, can in ordinary times be of little benefit to the mass of the peasantry; for it is evident that so long as landlords are permitted to take advantage of the local competition for land in order to enhance rents illegally, it is they, and they only, who appropriate the profits resulting from that rise in prices which attends the opening up of means of communication. Besides 200,000*l.* expended on a temporary famine railway to Darbhanga in 1874, there has been an expenditure on the Tirhut State railway of 1,300,000*l.* within the past ten years.'[1]

Some of the zemindars of Behár are among the richest men in India. The estates of the Raja of Darbhanga, in the district just mentioned, have an area of 2,400 square miles, a population of 750,000, and a rental exceeding 200,000*l.* a year.

Happily, the condition of the peasantry in the greater part of Bengal Proper is much better than in Behár. The confiscation of their rights has been lamentable, and the necessity for their future protection has been, and still is urgent, but they have not been reduced to a condition such as that common in Behár, and they live, as a rule, in reasonable comfort.

[1] Report of the Agricultural Department in Bengal for 1886.

The discussion of the measures required for placing the law of landlord and tenant throughout Bengal on a better footing has continued for many years. The opposition on the part of the zemindars and their advocates to every proposal which had for its object the diminution of the arbitrary powers of landlords, and the protection of ryots against oppression and the further destruction of their rights, was unceasing and powerful, but at last, in 1885, the 'Bengal Tenancy Act' was passed by the Governor-General in Council. I will not attempt to describe all its provisions, but its value cannot be doubted. It is an attempt to give protection to the ryots without interfering with the rights of landlords. It defines the position of the various classes of landlords and tenants, the incidents of the various tenures, the conditions under which rights of occupancy in the land are acquired and maintained, the manner in which rents are to be regulated, enhanced, and reduced, the circumstances under which evictions may take place; it imposes penalties for illegal exactions, lays down rules regarding compensation for improvements, gives power to the Government to order surveys and the preparation of records of rights, and deals with a multitude of other matters of importance.

The passing of this Act has been an excellent measure, but more is required. I have shown that in other parts of British India there has been a survey of every field, and that a permanent and continuous record is maintained of all rights and interests in the land. This, in other provinces, is the basis of our system of administration. Without such basis, in a country where nearly the whole population is agricultural, neither the executive authorities nor the courts of justice have the means of obtaining the knowledge essential to the protection of the most important interests of the people. In Bengal there are virtually no surveys, no maps, no records of rights; there is universal ignorance of almost all facts connected with the greatest industry of the country and which it is the most necessary to know. Until this want has been supplied there will be no really efficient government in Bengal, and no adequate relief for sufferings such as those of the ryots of Behár. I cannot doubt that Mr. Finucane is right when he says of those unfortunate people that a mere declaration of their rights, recorded in the statute-book and published in the Gazette, will afford to them little or no relief. I look forward, however, with much hope to the future of the peasantry of Bengal, because I see that the rising generation of Englishmen in India has, in respect to these matters, different ideas from those of the generation that is passing away.

English education has unfortunately hardly begun to penetrate to the cultivating classes in Bengal, and until lately they have found few champions among their own countrymen. The sympathies and the support of that section of the English-speaking Bengális which has been able or desirous to make its voice heard have been for the most part enlisted on the side of the zemindars, and to the detriment of the ryots. The time will come when this will cease to be true—already, I hope, things are better than they were—but hitherto the ryots have had mainly to look to their English rulers for the defence of their interests.

Every measure of political importance is discussed by the organs of the educated classes in Bengal. Not long ago there could be no doubt as to what would be the reception of any measure that seemed to threaten the interests of the zemindars. No taxation affecting them could be imposed without the cry being raised that the solemn pledges of the Permanent Settlement were being violated by an unscrupulous Government. Every measure which has had for its object the more just distribution of the public burdens has, as a rule, met with nothing but opposition. We were told that to reduce the salt tax was folly; let it be increased if the Government wants more money. The abolition of customs duties on cotton goods was solely prompted by the desire to benefit the manufacturers of Manchester, and by the base political purpose of gaining votes in Lancashire. Educated Bengális were not to be deceived by the profession that we desired to give to the people of India cheaper salt and cheaper clothing.

Thus, through the influence of the associations and the newspapers of Bengális taught in our schools and colleges, English education in Bengal has given frequent aid to the perpetuation of past injustice and to the prevention of reform. I am happy to believe that this is now less true than it was, for I am told that the ryots of Bengal are beginning to find earnest and capable friends among their own people. Still, I fear, there can be no doubt that, for a long time to come, it will be only to their English rulers that they will be able to look for protection and justice. I said in a former lecture[1] that an unfortunate result of our system of higher education in India has been the want of sympathy which many of the English-speaking Natives, especially in Bengal, show towards the poorer and less instructed classes of their countrymen. The shallow and imperfect education, which is all that they usually obtain, is derived entirely from English sources. They learn enough of English habits of thought to enable

[1] Lecture VII., p. 196.

them to imitate us, sometimes in things that are good, but sometimes in things that it would have been better to avoid. They learn almost nothing about their own country, and seem frequently to care little for their own people. I need hardly say that there are very many honourable exceptions to be made to general statements of this kind. Some of the most benevolent and most enlightened men that I have known in India have been educated natives of Bengal.

It is a serious misfortune that discredit should so often be thrown on the results of English education by the foolish talk and disloyal writing of a section of the English-speaking Bengális. Many of them are gifted with a very remarkable faculty of fluent speech and writing. I have heard of no men in any country enamoured of their own verbosity in so extraordinary a degree. Although to our taste their English is often ridiculously magniloquent, few foreigners master so completely the difficulties of our language. Their newspapers, published in English, are sometimes, so far as their style is concerned, extremely well written, but, with honourable exceptions, they are disloyal, foolish, and sometimes shamefully scurrilous.

There is no province in India without customs which we think must be repugnant to all civilised men, but which are almost universally respected because they are believed to have been divinely ordained, or to have come down from a remote antiquity. There is hardly a province in which horrid and cruel practices would not instantly spring into vigorous life if our watchfulness were relaxed. The prohibition of the burning of widows was, and is still, utterly disapproved by all but a small minority of Hindus. I do not believe that the majority even of the most highly educated classes approve it. I gave you, in a previous lecture, an account of the wholesale murder of female children, which has gone on for centuries, a custom against which no Hindu, however enlightened, raises his voice, and which, with all our efforts, we have not yet succeeded in eradicating. But for us, even in the provinces where education has made its greatest progress, Káli would still claim her human victims. Not many years ago, in a time of drought, near a railway station twenty-five miles from Calcutta, a human head was found before her idol, decked with flowers; and in another temple in Bengal a boy was savagely murdered and offered to the goddess.[1] While this book was passing through the press, a ghastly story came from the Central Provinces of the sacrifice of a young man to the local gods, in obedience to a widely prevalent belief and ancient practice that this is a sure means of obtaining a plentiful harvest. Horrors such as these receive no general condemnation in India, nor does the determination of our Government that they shall be suppressed gain for us any approval even from the educated classes.

There are in India many questions of another order which it is far more difficult to solve, because we cannot deal with them by the strong hand of the law. I will mention one only as an illustration, the custom of child marriage. It would be difficult to imagine anything more abominable than its frequent consequences, by which multitudes of girls of ten or twelve or less are given over to outrage, or are doomed to lives of miserable and degraded widowhood. Some of the most holy Brahmans of Bengal make a living by being husbands. A child of twelve is given as perhaps the fortieth or fiftieth wife of some old man; sometimes

[1] *Imperial Gazetteer of India*, Art. 'India.'

two sisters are given to the same man, and sometimes to one who has not long to live. Though it may be certain that the girl must soon be a widow, even this is considered preferable to allowing her to remain unmarried. Everyone has heard of the wretched fate which widowhood in India involves.[1]

What could be more valuable and interesting than to learn the opinions and receive the advice of highly educated Natives of India on such subjects as these, and to know that they were striving, by the example of their own lives, to teach their less instructed countrymen to abandon these abominations? What greater encouragement could be given to those who desire to see educated Natives admitted to a larger share in the administration than the certainty that they were anxious to help us towards ampler knowledge of the wants and feelings of the people, and to make us better able to deal with problems that now seem too hard to solve?

You would be much mistaken if you supposed that in regard to any of these great social questions the Government has ever received advice or assistance from the much talking section of the Bengális. I must class with them a considerable number of the Marátha Brahmans of Bombay, and of the English-speaking Hindus of Madras. You might search the proceedings of their societies, you might examine the files of their newspapers and the reports of their speeches at their public meetings, and you would not find one word of reprobation of the atrocious practices which, under the cover of immemorial custom, are followed throughout India, or one word of a desire to help our Government to suppress them.

[1] *Modern Hinduism*, by W. J. Wilkins p. 347.

It is not difficult to understand why these terrible questions are avoided. Some of these Native gentlemen are silent because they dare not, by speaking of them, bring themselves into collision with the cherished beliefs and prejudices of their countrymen; others, and I have no doubt the majority, are silent because in regard to these matters they are at heart as intensely conservative as the mass of the population, and have no desire for changes in social and religious usages which have come down from a venerable antiquity. It is much safer to talk about 'political enfranchisement,' and it is easy in this way to obtain the applause of Englishmen who know nothing of the facts and the difficulties with which the true friends of Indian progress have to deal, but who have an undoubting faith that so-called popular institutions are good for all men under all circumstances.

I have now before me the report of a great political gathering, the so-called 'Indian National Congress.' This, we are informed by the report, 'was a political body met together to represent to our rulers our political aspirations,' and we are expressly told that it had nothing to do with social questions. The object aimed at was 'the political enfranchisement of the country' by the introduction of representative institutions.

I do not propose to refer at any length to the declared objects of these political agitators who have lately been making themselves more and more prominent in India. If you look at their voluminous speeches and proceedings, you will not discern the smallest recognition of the terrible problems of which I have given some illustrations, but you will find no lack of sedition and hatred of the British Government thinly veiled under frequent and fulsome expressions of devotion and loyalty.[1] I am far from believing that the majority of these gentlemen are really disloyal. They are, for the most part, well meaning men of small education, but with a good knowledge of our language, who have learnt to pour forth the commonplaces of English politics, and who listen with delight to their own eloquence, which they half believe to be inspired by feelings akin to those which they have read about in Burke and Macaulay. They easily obtain a hearing from sentimental philanthropists and from those Englishmen who see nothing good in any political institutions except those of their own peculiar type, and assume that certain abstract principles are always applicable to the government of all sorts and conditions of men. Many Englishmen who read these harangues honestly believe that they are listening to the genuine expression of the just expectations of the great 'People of India,' which has no existence, but the non-existence of which I am afraid they are not likely to learn.

Men of a very different stamp, who well deserve the respect of their countrymen and of their rulers, have not unfrequently been drawn into apparent and partial agreement with these political agitators by the legitimate feeling that Natives of India do not obtain their just share in the public administration. This is a feeling which has my sympathy. There are political aspirations which loyal Natives may with complete propriety express, and which it is right that we should endeavour to satisfy; but let us take care that we satisfy them wisely.

I said, in a previous lecture,[2] that I should return to the subject of the admission of the Natives of India

[1] See Appendix.

[2] Lecture X., pp. 261, 262.

to the more important public offices. I showed that the greater part of the civil administration is already in their hands, that the Native Civil Service performs its duties, as a whole, with high efficiency, but at the same time I stated my opinion that much remains to be done in throwing open to Natives posts now reserved for Englishmen.

Subject to certain conditions, the true principle on which we ought to treat this question of the wider employment of Natives in posts of importance was laid down in the Act of Parliament passed in 1870 to which I have already referred, but I cannot think that it has hitherto been properly applied. That principle is that almost all offices in India shall be open to Natives, but to those only 'of proved merit and ability.'

In the case of Englishmen, whether in India or at home, it is safe to say that appointments to offices in the higher branches of the public service shall ordinarily be filled by those who, in competitive examinations in their boyhood, are successful in satisfying certain literary and other tests; but to think of applying such a system to the Natives of India is nothing less than absurd. Not the least important part of the competitive examination of the young Englishman was passed for him by his forefathers, who, as we have a right to assume, have transmitted to him not only their physical courage, but the powers of independent judgment, the decision of character, the habits of thought, and generally those qualities that are necessary for the government of men, and the discharge of the various duties of civilised life, and which have given us our empire. The stock-in-trade with which Englishmen start in life is not that of Bengális; but I must not say this of Englishmen only, for it is equally true of the nobler races of India, although their time has not come for competitive examinations.

Few would go further than I would go in opening the public service in India to Natives 'of proved merit and ability,' but it is well to avoid 'political hypocrisy.' 'Is there,' Lord Salisbury asked, 'any man who will have the hardihood to tell me that it is within the range of possibility that a man in India should be appointed Lieutenant-Governor of a province, or Chief Commissioner, or Commander-in-Chief of the Army, or Viceroy, without any regard whatever to his race?' Some will answer even this question in the affirmative. There will always be people ready to accept with composure any political folly, provided that it involves some triumph of sentiment over sense, and some appearance of national humiliation. When we say that we cannot always, in our government of India, ignore differences of race, this is only another way of saying that the English in India are a handful of foreigners governing 250 millions of people. I have said that we are not foreigners in India in the sense in which we are foreigners in Paris, and that the people of one Indian province are often as much foreigners to the people of another province as we are ourselves; still, we are foreigners, and although I suppose that no foreign government was ever accepted with less repugnance than that with which the British Government is accepted in India, the fact remains that there never was a country, and never will be, in which the government of foreigners is really popular. It will be the beginning of the end of our empire when we forget this elementary fact, and entrust the greater executive powers to the hands of Natives, on the assumption that they will always be faithful and strong supporters of our government. In this there is nothing offensive or disparaging to the Natives of India. It simply means that we are foreigners, and that, not only in our own interests, but because it is our highest duty towards India itself, we intend to maintain our dominion. We cannot foresee the time in which the cessation of our rule would not be the signal for universal anarchy and ruin, and it is clear that the only hope for India is the long continuance of the benevolent but strong government of Englishmen. Let us give to the Natives the largest possible share in the administration. In some branches of the service there is almost no limit to the share of public employment which they may properly receive. This is especially true of the judicial service, for which Natives have shown themselves eminently qualified, and in which the higher offices are equal in importance and dignity and emolument to almost any of the great offices of the State. I would grudge them no such offices. But let there be no hypocrisy about our intention to keep in the hands of our own people those executive posts—and there are not very many of them—on which, and on our political and military power, our actual hold of the country depends. Our Governors of provinces, the chief officers of our army, our magistrates of districts and their principal executive subordinates ought to be Englishmen under all circumstances that we can now foresee.

It is not only in regard to the employment in India of our own countrymen that we ought never to forget differences of race. It is quite as essential to remember them in connection with the employment of Natives. I have, in these lectures, repeatedly insisted on the fact that there is really no such country as India; that such terms as 'People of India' and 'Natives of

India' are meaningless in the sense in which they are frequently used; that no countries and no peoples in Europe differ from each other so profoundly as countries and peoples differ in India; that it would be as reasonable to suppose that English, French, Spaniards, Greeks, and Germans will ultimately become one nation as to suppose such a thing of Bengális, Sikhs, Maráthas, Rájputs, and Patháns. No good administration or permanent political security is possible unless facts of this kind are remembered. It ought never to be forgotten that you can never assume that because a man is a 'Native of India' he has any natural claim, different in kind from that of an Englishman, to be employed in the public service in every part of India. Often, indeed, you may go much further. I used no terms of exaggeration when I said that a Native of Calcutta is more of a foreigner to the hardy races on the frontiers of Northern India than an Englishman can be. To suppose that the manlier races of India could ever be governed through feeble and effeminate foreigners of another Indian country, however intellectually acute those foreigners may be—that Sikhs and Patháns, for instance, should submit to be ruled by Bengális—is to suppose an absurdity. The Mohammedan gentleman, who remembers the position which his ancestors once held, accepts with natural regret, but with no humiliation, the government of Englishmen. Although he may not love them, he admits that they must be respected. But the thought of being subject to the orders of a Bengáli fills him with indignation and contempt. The educated Bengáli, although his reasons might be very different, would feel equal disgust at the thought of having his affairs administered by Sikhs and by Patháns. To allow Natives 'of proved merit and ability' to take a larger part in the administration of their own country is right and politic; to affirm that they have any similar claims in countries where they are foreigners is foolish.

I remember a conversation which I once had with a Native of Northern India, a man of great sagacity, whose position, wealth, and influence made him one of the most important personages in his province. Discussions were going on respecting the propriety of making it easier for Natives of India to enter the Covenanted Civil Service, and on the suggestion that with that object competitive examinations should be held in India as well as in England. I asked him what he thought about this proposal, and his first answer, given in a manner which showed that he took little interest in the subject, was to the effect that he supposed it was a good one. 'I am afraid,' I said, 'that for a long time to come there would be no candidates from this part of India; it is only in Bengal that young men could be found who would have any chance of success in such an examination as that required. The result would be that you would some day have a Bengáli as your chief district officer.' I shall not forget the scorn with which he drew himself up and replied to me, 'And does anyone think that we, the men of this country, would stand that? Do you suppose that you could govern us with Bengális? Never!'

This book was almost ready for the press when the reports reached England of some remarkable speeches made by Sir Syad Ahmad Khan at two great meetings of Mohammedans in Northern India. I referred in a previous lecture to Sir Syad Ahmad Khan, and to the work to which his life has been devoted.[1] I mention these speeches because they illustrate, with greater

[1] Lecture VII., pp. 175–179.

authority than that of any Englishman, the practical importance of the fact on which I have repeatedly insisted, with which I began these lectures, and with which I wish to end them, that the most essential of all things to be learnt about India is that India is a continent filled with the most diverse elements. The special aim of Sir Syad Ahmad Khan was to protest on behalf of his Mohammedan fellow-countrymen against the notion that they—'men of the blood of those who made not only Arabia but Asia and Europe to tremble, who for seven hundred years in India had imperial sway'—could be treated as belonging to the same nation as Bengális, and to express his contempt for the political nostrums which the so-called 'National Congresses' propose to apply throughout India. If these were adopted, the result, he says, would be that 'there would be no part of the country in which we should see at the tables of justice and authority any faces except those of Bengális. I am delighted to see the Bengális making progress, but what would be the result on the public administration? Do you think that the Rájput and the fiery Pathán would remain in peace under Bengális?' These are illustrations of the opinions of a man universally honoured, who is entitled to speak on behalf of all that is best and most enlightened among the Mohammedans of Northern India.

'It is better,' says Machiavelli, 'to follow the real truth of things than an imaginary view of them. For many republics and princedoms have been imagined which were never seen or known to exist in reality.' If intelligent people in England would make themselves acquainted with 'the real truth of things,' they would appreciate at their true value the utterances of those agitators who, with some success in this country, pose as the representatives of an imaginary Indian nation, 'never seen or known to exist in reality.'

I must now bring these lectures to a close. I have endeavoured to give to you some general idea of what India is and of the results which she has obtained from the establishment of our power. No reasonable man can doubt the answer that we must give to the question whether the 200 millions of our Indian subjects have benefited by our government.

The first great and obvious fact, overshadowing all other facts in significance, is this, that in place of a condition of society given up, as it was immediately before our time, to anarchy and to the liability to every conceivable form of violence and oppression, you have now absolute peace. Let not this unspeakable blessing of the Pax Britannica be forgotten. There are not many European countries where protection to life and property is so complete. Excepting England and her colonies and the United States of America, there is hardly a country in the world where there is so little needless interference on the part of the Government with personal liberty, or such freedom in the public expression of opinion in matters of politics and religion. Except when sometimes for a moment the fanaticism and intolerance of rival sects of Mohammedans and Hindus burst into violent conflict, and show what would instantly follow if the strong hand of our Government were withdrawn, unbroken tranquillity prevails. Justice is administered under laws of unequalled excellence and simplicity. There is no country possessing a civilised administration where taxation is so light or commerce is more free. Mr. J. S. Mill declared his belief that the British Government in India was 'not only one of the purest in intention, but one of the most beneficent in act, ever known among mankind.' I do not doubt that this is still truer now.

Whether all this makes our Government really popular is another question.

When Lord Lawrence was Viceroy, in 1867, many of the most experienced officers in India were invited to give their opinion whether our Government was more generally popular than that in the Native States. As might have been anticipated, nearly all the answers were affirmative, but I shall only refer to that of Lord Lawrence himself. His conclusion was given in these words: 'The masses of the people are incontestably more prosperous, and—*sua si bona nôrint*—far more happy in British territory than they are under Native rulers.' No Englishman knew India better than Lord Lawrence. That the people had been made more prosperous by our administration was, in his opinion, beyond controversy, but when it came to the question of their happiness and of our popularity, well—yes; at any rate they *ought* to be more happy. The proviso is significant, *sua si bona nôrint*.

The truth is that, in a country in the condition of India, the more actively enlightened our Government becomes, the less likely it is to be popular. Our Government is highly respected; the confidence of the people in our justice is unlimited. That accomplished traveller, Baron von Hübner, says in his excellent book, 'Through the British Empire,' that if proof were needed to show how deeply rooted among the people is this trust in English justice, he would quote the fact that throughout India the Native prefers, in civil and still more in criminal cases, to go before an English judge. 'I think,' he says, 'it would be impossible to render a more flattering testimony to British rule.'

The duty was once imposed upon me of transferring a number of villages which had long been included in a British district to one of the best governed of the Native States. I shall not forget the loud and universal protests of the people against the cruel injustice with which they considered they were being treated. Everyone who has had experience of similar cases tells the same story. Nevertheless, I cannot say that our Government is loved; it is too good for that.

The sympathies between the people and their English rulers can hardly be anything but imperfect. The system of caste and the differences in all our habits make social intimacy difficult. The stories that are sometimes told about the frequent insolence and brutality of Englishmen are false, but it cannot be denied that the ordinary Englishman is too rough and vigorous and straightforward to be a very agreeable person to the majority of the Natives of India. These, however, are not reasons which seriously affect the popularity of our Government. I repeat that because it is good it can hardly be popular.

I never heard of a great measure of improvement that was popular in India, even among the classes that have received the largest share of education. The people are intensely conservative and intensely ignorant, wedded, to an extent difficult for Europeans to understand, to every ancient custom, and between their customs and religion no line of distinction can be drawn. We often deceive ourselves in regard to the changes that are taking place. We believe that our Western knowledge, our railways, and our telegraphs must be breaking up the whole fabric of Hinduism, but these things have touched in reality only the merest fringe of the ideas and beliefs of the population of India. The vast masses of the people remain in a different world from ours. They hate everything new, and they especially hate almost everything that we look upon as progress.

It would thus be an error to suppose that the British Government is administered in a manner that altogether commends itself to the majority of the Indian population. This we cannot help. Considerations of political prudence compel us to tolerate much that we should wish to alter, but, subject to this condition, our duty is plain. It is to use the power which we possess for no other purpose than to govern India on the principles which our superior knowledge tells us are right, although they may often be unpopular, and may offend the prejudices and superstitions of the people. I will quote to you Sir James Stephen's summary of the principles which would be really popular in India, and of those which we enforce, and with it I may fitly close these lectures :—

'The English in India are the representatives of a belligerent civilisation. The phrase is epigrammatic, but it is strictly true. The English in India are the representatives of peace compelled by force. The Mohammedans would like to tyrannise over Hindus in particular, and in general to propose to everyone the alternative between the Koran, the tribute, and the sword. The Hindus would like to rule—over Hindus at least—according to the principles of the Brahmanical religion. They would like to be able to condemn to social infamy everyone who, being born a Hindu, did not observe their rites. They would like to see suttee practised, to prevent the remarriage of widows who were not burnt, to do away with the laws which prevent a change of religion from producing civil disabilities, to prevent a low-caste man from trying or even testifying against a Brahman; and Mohammedans, and Hindus, and Sikhs would all alike wish to settle their old accounts and see who is master. The belligerent civilisation of which I spoke consists in the suppression by force of all these pretensions, and in compelling by force all sorts and conditions of men in British India to tolerate each other. Should the British Government abdicate its functions, it would soon turn order into chaos. No country in the world is more orderly, more quiet, or more peaceful than British India as it is; but if the vigour of the Government should ever be relaxed, if it should lose its essential unity of purpose, and fall into hands either weak or unfaithful, chaos would come again like a flood.'

APPENDIX.

In the last of these lectures, referring to the speeches and writings of the political agitators who have lately been making themselves prominent in India, I said that 'You will find in them no lack of sedition and hatred of the British Government thinly veiled under frequent and fulsome expressions of devotion and loyalty.'

It would be easy, by extracts from newspapers and other publications, to justify language far stronger than any that I have used on this subject, but it has been said that these are not the sources from which we can learn the truth regarding the views of the acknowledged leaders of native political thought, and that for this we must go to the authorised reports of the proceedings of the great gatherings of the 'Indian National Congress,' held at Bombay, Calcutta, and Madras, in 1885, 1886, and 1887. I will give, therefore, from those proceedings, some illustrations of the manner in which these gentlemen are carrying on their work.

In the Report of the Congress for 1887 we are told that 'The National Party have undertaken through the Congress the political regeneration of two hundred millions of men.' Among the methods by which 'the awakening of the masses' is to be accomplished, much importance is assigned to 'the missionary labours' of the members of the Congress. It is stated that 'throughout the year, in and near their homes, as standing congress committees and sub-committees, by lectures, public meetings, and the distribution of tens of thousands of single tracts in the local vernaculars, they were expected to spread from mind to mind an elementary knowledge of the burning political questions of the day, and, generally, of the rights and duties of all good citizens of a civilised state. It is to the eternal honour alike of England, the beneficent teacher, and India, the docile pupil, that at the close of this the Third Congress, we are in a position to assert that there is not one of these objects that has not been already partially achieved, and not one single one of them of which the perfect accomplishment, in a not distant future, does not appear to be, humanly speaking, certain.'

Translations of two of the tracts thus referred to are appended to the Report of the Congress; we are told that 30,000 copies of one of them had been circulated in Tamil in Southern India, and that 25,000 copies of the other had been circulated in Northern India, in Urdu and Hindi. It was subsequently stated in April, 1888, that these tracts 'are to be met with in every one of the twelve languages of India, and perhaps half a million copies will be circulated during the present year.'

The tract circulated in Northern India, in the Punjab, in the North-Western Provinces, and in Oudh, is in the form of a conversation between a native barrister of the High Court and a villager called Rambaksh. The latter begins by relating how a Bengali gentleman had come to his village. 'We told him how bad the times were, and how the police bullied us, and how hard the zemindar and the money-lender were, and how everything seemed going wrong. Then he said it was all our own fault, that if we chose to undergo all this and all the trouble that pervaded the country, that was our look-out; no one could help us if we did not help ourselves. . . . He said, by yourselves you are very weak and can do nothing; you are very ignorant, and can hardly see beyond the ends of your own fields; but for all that, if all you ryots all over the country would join those of your countrymen who are better off and better educated, in calling upon the Government to concede to us "Representative Institutions," then the good people in England would insist on these being given to us, and then soon many things would be altered for the better, and many of your causes of complaint would be removed.' Rambaksh says that he thinks this is all nonsense, but still he would like to know what 'Representation' and 'Representative Institutions' mean, and this the Barrister proceeds to explain. There are two kinds of government, he says, one of which is good and the other bad, and to enable Rambaksh to understand the difference his attention is directed to the extraordinary contrast between his own village called Kambakhtpur and another village called Shamshpur in the same neighbourhood. The latter is described as a model of contentment and prosperity. There are never any law suits, there are no liquor shops, and it is managed on behalf of the proprietors of the village, of whom there are 200, by their own good old Lumberdar or Head-man. 'Though he is ten times as rich and as clever as any of the rest he never does anything without consulting them. There is not a farthing of village expenses but what every shareholder has his say about it.'

Rambaksh's village, on the other hand, belongs to an absentee Rája, and is managed by his servants who are strangers to the place. Not a day passes without litigation in the courts, the people are growing poorer and poorer, the land is going out of cultivation, there are scarcely oxen enough for ploughing, half of the houses are in ruins, and the liquor shops that the Government has set up are always full.

'The Rája,' says Rambaksh, 'never comes near us, and never reads any of our petitions and never consults any of us; indeed he won't see us, but sends out an order for us to speak to the Naib (agent) or the Gomashtah (factor), who lives in the Rája's house here; and as for the Gomashtah, he never knows anything about us or the village, for one comes for six months and then goes, and then another comes for a couple of years, and then he goes, and then another comes and so on. . . . I don't say that the Rája is a bad man, but we never see him. So far as any good is concerned, he might be dead, but for all that he must have his money, and almost every year, more money and more money, till we poor people are almost skin and bone. Ah! if we were only cattle, as the Sahib said, we might perhaps make a rupee or two out of our skins; it is about all we have left. . . . The Rája's agents order this and order that, press us for money in season and out of season; they know nothing of village matters themselves, and they won't hear a word from us because they think they are all wise and we utter fools—and under such a system how can a village be otherwise than ruined? What does it matter that the Rája is not a bad man, or that his agents don't purposely injure us; nay, at times some of them, after their own fashion, try to help us. It is the bad system that is ruining us.'

'Ah, Rambaksh,' says the Barrister, 'this evil system that is ruining you and your neighbours and village is the "Despotic" system; and when rulers govern their subjects in this same way we call theirs a "Despotic" Government, and "Despotic" governments always ruin the countries in which they are carried on for long. They may be necessary in the infancy of a nation; they become crimes when it grows up. Now you have a practical knowledge of both systems; you see how Shamshpur is prospering under a "Constitutional" system, and you know only too thoroughly what Kambakhtpur is coming to under the "Despotic" system. . . . Well, now, you are only a villager, but you are a thoughtful man, and how would you call our present government: may its shadow never be less? Do you think our government is a constitutional one, or do you think it is a despotic one? . . . Take the trouble to think it out; compare the management of this country under our present rulers with the management of Shamshpur and with that of Kambakhtpur by the Rája and his agents, and say which does it most resemble.'

'Well,' answers Rambaksh, 'there is our good Queen-Empress. She never comes here certainly, and we never see her, and I hear the people sent her a petition last year, but she never took any notice of it. But they say she is so busy there, over in England, and has so many countries elsewhere belonging to her that she has no time to attend to us Indians. And when I come to think of it, may God long preserve her, but I don't know that it does signify much to us who sits upon the throne over there in England. I must say that all this is rather like our Rája's system. Certainly I never heard that she consulted any of us Indians on any point, and as to village expenses, well—I have heard what millions and millions of money are every year spent by the European gentlemen and without consulting any one! No! This is not at all like the Shamshpur system.'

'And then look,' says the Barrister, 'at the agents she sends. Are they not like your Rája? Very respectable men, no doubt; they don't take bribes, they don't certainly try to injure us, but what do they know of us and our real wants?

Don't they pooh-pooh our old customs, and each who comes insists on introducing some newfangled device for improving the condition of the country, which not infrequently does it harm.'

'Ah,' says Rambaksh, 'I see now what you mean, and I suppose our government is what you call a despotic one, and that perhaps is why the whole country is discontented, and everything seems, from all I hear, to be going wrong.'

The Barrister then goes on to explain how all this is to be remedied by transforming the present despotic government into a constitutional one, and a graphic description follows of a former English magistrate and collector of the district, Mr. Zabardast or Bully. He rides into Rambaksh's village, and is told there is no grass for his horses. Rambaksh is said to be responsible for this, and he relates what followed:—'Oh, said the sahib, striking me with his whip, you are the son of a pig, the misbegotten. I'll teach you how to attend to orders. Here, tent-pitcher, tie him up and give him thirty blows with a cane, and lay it well in. . . . I tried to explain, but the sahib hit me over the mouth and face with his whip, shouting out, "Hold your tongue, I'll teach you, tie him up, flog his life out." And I was dragged away and flogged till I became insensible. It was a month before I could walk. Yes, he was a bad one; many collectors have I known, some good, some indifferent, but this was the only real devil.' This, we are told, was twenty years ago, and there are no men quite so bad in the service now, but there are still many who grossly abuse their powers, and the remedy is to be found in 'Representative Institutions.' 'That is a huge bundle of stalks that you have here tied up,' says the Barrister. 'It must be very heavy and strong. Do you think you could break it over your knee?' 'Break it over my knee,' replies Rambaksh; 'no, nor could the Rája's elephant, let him try ever so! But what do you mean?' 'See,' said the Barrister, 'I pull out one stem and I break it easily over my knee, and now another and now a third and a fourth. See! in about ten minutes I could break the whole. Let that teach you that weak and feeble as you and your fellows are, if once you all unite in good earnest in a good cause you will be so powerful that no Rája's elephant can break you.' 'But surely,' rejoins

Rambaksh, 'you don't want us to join together and fight with the Government. If we killed all the Europeans how should we get along? All would be anarchy. You cannot mean this.' 'God forbid,' says the Barrister, 'this would be a sin. Why should we kill the poor Europeans? Many of them are really good men, most of them mean at any rate to do right. They are ignorant no doubt of the rights of most matters concerning us; they blunder, they cause us misery, but they do it from ignorance—from an ignorance unavoidable under the system which they work on, and which, even did they wish it, they could not change without our help. Besides, though we of the new generation are growing up able to assist them, and to do much for the country, the whole of us put together have not yet sufficient experience and self-reliance to manage the administration entirely without their help. Kill the Europeans! No, Rambaksh, let us say rather God bless all of them (and there are many such) who feel kindly towards us in their hearts, and according to their lights mean well towards us, and God forgive those amongst them (and let us hope they are not many) who dislike and despise us, and care nothing what becomes of us.'

The English at home, the Barrister goes on to explain, have none of the prejudices of those in India on these matters, and 'if once they saw us all, high and low, banded together and determined to obtain these "Representative Institutions," then they have too much common sense not to allow us to have them. Now, perhaps, you understand what I meant by the bundle of stalks, that union is strength. . . . You want some one to write a little book about these matters? Well, if such a book be written, we should want at least five thousand copies for this district only, for there must be at least one copy for every village and hamlet, and in the larger places there should be two, three, five, ten, twenty copies according to the size of the place. . . . If the truths I have been trying to impress upon your mind are to be imprinted within any reasonable period on the minds of the entire population, merely distributing the books will not do. We must have earnest and clever men to go round from village to village and expound them, and though some of us, whenever we have leisure, do this, such work is intermittent, and we want men who will do nothing else but keep at it every day and all day; and though such men may do it for the love of their country, still they must live; and it is not among the rich and happy that we can usually look for such, but rather amongst those who are poor and have suffered, and can therefore feel for all the suffering so rife amongst us.'

The tract circulated in Southern India is called a 'Catechism of the Indian National Congress.' Although less offensively disloyal than that of which I have given some account, its tendency is the same. India, the people are told, is a vast country with a population of 250 millions; the English are natives of a small island and number only 35 millions. The English at home have an excellent government, but they are not aware of the grievances of India. The English officials in India never report the truth, and they know that their salaries or their powers would certainly be reduced if the English public were to learn it. Representative Councils, similar to the Parliament of Great Britain, must be elected by the people of India. No law must be passed or tax imposed except by these councils, and 'we should then have arrived at the commencement of the political regeneration of India. We should constantly press on the British people the paramount necessity of carrying into effect these reforms, through the telegraph, associations, newspapers, and delegates. It is only by persisting in the agitation that we can make our grievances heard in England. If the English nation begin to evince interest in the affairs of this country, the opposition of the Anglo-Indian officials, who wish to keep matters as they are, will soon cease to be effective.' The whole object of the tract is to convince the people to whom it is addressed that the British Government in India is oppressive and ignorant, that until it is reconstructed on a representative basis no improvement is possible, and that the necessary changes can certainly be gained if all classes throughout the country join in demanding them. 'The Congress will gradually, when India is fit for this, be converted into an Indian Parliament, which will take the place of the sham councils of the present day. . . . If the Congress goes on meeting regularly once a year, and working throughout the year, and the whole nation join in electing their delegates to it, and in making plain that they approve and ratify its resolutions, the Government will very soon be obliged by public opinion in England to consider carefully the decisions the Congress arrives at. The present English Parliament in its infant stage resembled in many respects our present Congress, and just as a grand tree grows out of a small seed, so the small temporary gatherings of a former day have now attained the dimensions of the glorious English Parliament.'

One of the leaders of the Congress movement—an Englishman—has described these foolish productions as 'loyal and kindly alike in spirit and word.' It is unnecessary to quote from them further, or to comment at length upon their character. None can know better than their authors that the accusations and insinuations in which they abound are absolutely false; that the Government of India does not impoverish the country, or spread intemperance among the people, or refuse to consult native opinion in matters connected with the administration; and that English magistrates do not strike and ill-use defenceless cultivators. It is impossible to attribute the circulation of such falsehoods to any other motive than a desire to excite hatred of the British Government and its representatives in the minds of the ignorant masses of India, while concealing from people in England the true character of the movement by exaggerated professions of loyalty. I do not wish to overrate the present extent or importance of this agitation, or to countenance in any way the absurd pretence that its leaders 'represent' the Indian 'people.' But it would not be wise to treat it as merely contemptible, and to assume that it is as powerless for evil as for good. The danger is not that the natives of India in general are likely to adopt any directly seditious scheme, or to form any wide-spread desire for objects incompatible with the maintenance of British rule. The danger lies in the method adopted by those who are agitating for such objects, and in the falsehoods and misrepresentations which they are not ashamed to use. The 'Catechism' and the 'Conversation' from which I have quoted, are not addressed to people trained in the ways of European political controversy, and able to distinguish between constitutional criticism of the measures of Government and a desire to overthrow its authority. In England assertions that the Government is the cause of all the poverty and other misfortunes of the people would be harmless, and the most virulent attacks on the Government could hardly have any worse effect than the unpopularity and defeat of a ministry. In India their effect, so far as they are believed, is likely to be a conviction that the country will never be prosperous until the British administration has been destroyed.

When the extreme ignorance and the extreme credulity of the natives are taken into account, it is easy to conceive that false and absurd reports regarding the intentions of the Government might create a panic, with results as terrible as those of the panic of 1857. The danger is not an imaginary one. There have been lately in Northern India signs of a religious agitation which might at any moment be connected with the Congress, if its leaders considered such a course likely to advance their objects.

Political agitation might safely be disregarded so long as it did not spread beyond Bengal and Southern India. But matters would be very different if agitators succeeded in teaching any considerable number among the manly races of Northern India to hate their rulers. Sir Syad Ahmad has warned the Government in emphatic language that a Mohammedan agitation 'is not the same as a Bengali agitation,' and that Rajputs or Pathans if once excited into hostility, are not likely to stop at speeches and newspaper articles. So far there is nothing to show that the Congress has made any real impression upon the people of Northern India, but its leaders are making every effort to extend their influence in the North-Western Provinces and the Punjab, and the next of their great annual meetings is to be held at Allahabad. The possible effect of the agitation upon the native army, the most efficient part of which is recruited in Northern India, must not be left out of account. One of the Englishmen who have taken a prominent part in the proceedings of the Congress boasted not long ago that he and his colleagues 'hold the keys of a good many magazines of physical force, though they are not going to put those keys in the locks,' and that 'as for the native army, every Sepoy and native officer has a home, and often visits it on leave and furlough, and every one of them could be got at without the slightest difficulty and (the facts of the case are so plain, simple, and irrefutable) converted to the views held by the great mass of his educated and half-educated countrymen. In two years the great bulk of the native army could be converted into sound politicians, and strong supporters of the reform movement.' It would be rash to assert that these statements are mere empty threats.

Whether an agitation conducted in the manner I have described should be allowed to develop further, or what should be done to check it, are serious questions, but this is not the proper occasion to discuss them.

There are happily among the educated natives of India, many men who are capable of exercising a sound and useful political influence upon their fellow-countrymen, and who properly appreciate the tendency of this Bengali agitation. I will give as an illustration of this fact the following passages translated from a speech made by Sir Syad Ahmad at Meerut, in March, 1888.

'I wish to explain what method my nation, nay rather the whole people of this country, ought to pursue in political matters. I will treat in regular sequence the political questions of India, in order that you may have full opportunity of giving your attention to them. The first of all is this—in whose hands shall the administration and the Empire of India rest? Now, suppose that all the English and the whole English army were to leave India, taking with them all their cannon and their splendid weapons and everything—then who would be rulers of India? Is it possible that under these circumstances two nations—the Mahomedans and the Hindus—could sit on the same throne and remain equal in power? Most certainly not. It is necessary that one of them should conquer the other and thrust it down. To hope that both could remain equal is to desire the impossible and the inconceivable. At the same time, you must remember that although the number of Mahomedans is less than that of the Hindus, and although they contain far fewer people who have received a high English education, yet they must not be thought insignificant or weak. Probably they would be by themselves enough to maintain their own position. But suppose they were not. Then our Musalman brothers, the Pathans, would come out as a swarm of locusts from their mountain valleys—like a swarm of locusts would they come—and make rivers of blood to flow from their frontier on the north to the extreme end of Bengal. This thing—who after the departure of the English would be conquerors, would rest on the will of God. But until one nation had conquered the other and made it obedient, peace could not reign in the land. This conclusion is based on proofs so absolute that no one can deny it. . . .

'When it is granted that the maintenance of the British Government, and of no other, is necessary for the progress of our country, then I ask whether there is any example in the world of one nation having conquered and ruled over another nation, and that conquered nation claiming it as a right that they should have representative government. The principle of representative Government is that it is government by a nation, and that the nation in question rules over its own people and its own land. Can you tell me of any case in the world's history in which any foreign nation after conquering another and establishing its empire over it has given representative government to the conquered people? Such a thing has never taken place. It is necessary for those who have conquered us to maintain their empire on a strong basis. When rulers and ruled are one nation, representative government is possible. For example in Afghanistan, of which Amir Abdur Rahman Khan is the ruler, where all the people are brother-Afghans, it might be possible. If they want, they can have representative government. But to think that representative government can be established in a country over which a foreign race rules, is utterly vain, nor can a trace of such a state of things be discovered in the history of the world. Therefore to ask that we should be appointed by election to the Legislative Council is opposed to the true principles of government, and no government whatever, whether English or German, or French or Russian, or Musalman, could accept this principle. The meaning of it is this:—"Abandon the rule of the country and put it in our hands." Hence it is in no way expedient that our nation should join in and echo these monstrous proposals. . . .

'The aspirations of our friends the Bengalis have made such progress that they want to scale a height to which it is beyond their powers to attain. But if I am not in error, I believe that the Bengalis have never at any period held sway over a particle of land. They are altogether ignorant of the method by which a foreign race can maintain its rule over other races. Therefore reflect on the doings of your ancestors, and be not unjust to the British Government, to whom God has given the rule of India. And look honestly, and see what is necessary for it to do to maintain its empire and its hold on the country. You can appreciate these matters; but they cannot who have never held a country in their hands nor won a victory. Oh! my brother Musalmans! I again remind you that you have ruled nations, and have for centuries held different countries in your grasp. For seven hundred years in India you have had Imperial sway. You know what it is to rule. Be not unjust to that nation which is ruling over you. And think also on this, how upright is her rule. Of such benevolence as the English Government shows to the foreign nations under her there is no example in the history of the world. See what freedom she has given in her laws, and how careful she is to protect the rights of her subjects. She has not been backward in promoting the progress of the natives of India, and in throwing open to them high appointments. At the commencement of her rule, except clerkships and kaziships, there was nothing. The kazis of the pergunah, who were called commissioners, decided small civil suits, and received very small pay. Up to 1832 or 1833 this state of things lasted. If my memory is not wrong, it was in the time of Lord William Bentinck that natives of India began to get honourable posts. The positions of Munsiff, Subordinate Judge, and Deputy Collector on respectable pay were given to natives, and progress has been steadily going on ever since. In the Calcutta High Court, a Kashmiri Pandit was first appointed equal to the English judges. After him Bengalis have been appointed as High Court Judges. At this time there are, perhaps, three Bengalis in the Calcutta High Court, and in the same way some Hindus in Bombay and Madras. It was your bad fortune that there was for a long time no Mahomedan High Court Judge, but now there is one in the Allahabad High Court. Native High Court Judges can cancel the decision of English judges and collectors. They can ask them for explanations. The subordinate native officers also have full authority in their posts. A deputy collector, a sub-judge, or a munsiff decides cases according to his opinion, and is independent of the opinion of the judge or collector. None of these things have been acquired by fighting or opposition. As far as you have made yourselves worthy of the confidence of Government, to that extent you have received high positions. Make yourselves her friends, and prove to her that your friendship with her is like that of the English and the Scotch. After this what you have to claim, claim—on condition that you are qualified for it.

. . . .

'If we also have some complaints against the English Government, it is no wonderful thing. People are not even grateful to God for His Government. I do not tell you to ask nothing from Government. I will myself fight on your behalf for legitimate objects. But ask for such things as they can give you, or such things to which, having due regard to the administration of the country, you can claim a right. If you ask for such things as Government cannot give you, then it is not the fault of Government, but the folly of the askers. But what you ask, do it not in this fashion; that you accuse Government in every action of oppression, abuse the highest officials, use the hardest and harshest words you can find for Lord Lytton and Lord Dufferin, call all Englishmen tyrants, and blacken columns on columns of newspapers with these subjects. You can gain nothing this way. God has made them your rulers. This is the will of God. We should be content with the will of God. And, in obedience to the will of God, you should remain friendly and faithful to them. Do not do this: bring false accusations against them and give birth to enmity. This is neither wisdom nor in accordance with our holy religion.'

INDEX.

A LIST OF

KEGAN PAUL, TRENCH, & CO.'S PUBLICATIONS.

10.82

1 Paternoster Square,
London.

A LIST OF
KEGAN PAUL, TRENCH, & CO.'S
PUBLICATIONS.

CONTENTS.

A. K. H. B.—From a Quiet Place. A New Volume of Sermons. Crown 8vo. 5*s.*

AINSWORTH (F. W.)—Personal Narrative of the Euphrates Expedition. 2 vols. 8vo. 30*s.*

ALEXANDER (William, D.D., Bishop of Derry)—The Great Question, and other Sermons. Crown 8vo. 6*s.*

ALLIES (T. W.) M.A.—Per Crucem ad Lucem. The Result of a Life. 2 vols. Demy 8vo. 25*s.*

A Life's Decision. Crown 8vo. 7*s.* 6*d.*

AMHERST (Rev. W. J.)—The History of Catholic Emancipation and the Progress of the Catholic Church in the British Isles (chiefy in England) from 1771–1820. 2 vols. Demy 8vo. 24*s.*

AMOS (Prof. Sheldon)—The History and Principles of the Civil Law of Rome. Demy 8vo. 16*s.*

ARISTOTLE—The Nicomachean Ethics of Aristotle. Translated by F. H. Peters, M.A. Third Edition. Crown 8vo. 6*s.*

AUBERTIN (J. J.)—A Flight to Mexico. With 7 full-page Illustrations and a Railway Map of Mexico. Crown 8vo. 7*s.* 6*d.*

Six Months in Cape Colony and Natal. With Illustrations and Map. Crown 8vo. 6*s.*

A Fight with Distances. With 8 Illustrations and 2 Maps. Crown 8vo. 7*s.* 6*d.*

Aucassin and Nicolette. Edited in Old French and rendered in Modern English by F. W. Bourdillon. Fcap. 8vo. 7*s.* 6*d.*

AUCHMUTY (A. C.)—Dives and Pauper, and other Sermons. Crown 8vo. 3*s.* 6*d.*

AZARIAS (Brother)—Aristotle and the Christian Church. Small crown 8vo. 3*s.* 6*d.*

BADGER (George Percy) D.C.L.—An English-Arabic Lexicon. In which the equivalents for English Words and Idiomatic Sentences are rendered into literary and colloquial Arabic. Royal 4to. 80*s.*

BAGEHOT (Walter)—THE ENGLISH CONSTITUTION. Fifth Edition. Crown 8vo. 7*s*. 6*d*.

LOMBARD STREET. A Description of the Money Market. Ninth Edition. Crown 8vo. 7*s*. 6*d*.

ESSAYS ON PARLIAMENTARY REFORM. Crown 8vo. 5*s*.

SOME ARTICLES ON THE DEPRECIATION OF SILVER, AND TOPICS CONNECTED WITH IT. Demy 8vo. 5*s*.

BAGOT (Alan) C.E.—ACCIDENTS IN MINES: Their Causes and Prevention. Crown 8vo. 6*s*.

THE PRINCIPLES OF COLLIERY VENTILATION. Second Edition, greatly enlarged, crown 8vo. 5*s*.

THE PRINCIPLES OF CIVIL ENGINEERING IN ESTATE MANAGEMENT. Crown 8vo. 7*s*. 6*d*.

BAIRD (Henry M.)—THE HUGUENOTS AND HENRY OF NAVARRE. 2 vols. 8vo. With Maps. 24*s*.

BALDWIN (Capt. J. H.)—THE LARGE AND SMALL GAME OF BENGAL AND THE NORTH-WESTERN PROVINCES OF INDIA. With 20 Illustrations. New and Cheaper Edition. Small 4to. 10*s*. 6*d*.

BALLIN (Ada S. and F. L.)—A HEBREW GRAMMAR. With Exercises selected from the Bible. Crown 8vo. 7*s*. 6*d*.

BALL (John, F.R.S.)—NOTES OF A NATURALIST IN SOUTH AMERICA. Crown 8vo. 8*s*. 6*d*.

BARCLAY (Edgar)—MOUNTAIN LIFE IN ALGERIA. Crown 4to. With numerous Illustrations by Photogravure. 16*s*.

BASU (K. P.) M.A.—STUDENTS' MATHEMATICAL COMPANION. Containing problems in Arithmetic, Algebra, Geometry, and Mensuration, for Students of the Indian Universities. Crown 8vo. 6*s*.

BAUR (Ferdinand) Dr. Ph., Professor in Maulbronn.—A PHILOLOGICAL INTRODUCTION TO GREEK AND LATIN FOR STUDENTS. Translated and adapted from the German by C. KEGAN PAUL, M.A., and the Rev. E. D. STONE, M.A. Third Edition. Crown 8vo. 6*s*.

BENN (Alfred W.)—THE GREEK PHILOSOPHERS. 2 vols. Demy 8vo. 28*s*.

BENSON (A. C.)—WILLIAM LAUD, SOMETIME ARCHBISHOP OF CANTERBURY. A Study. With Portrait. Crown 8vo. 6*s*.

BIBLE FOLK-LORE.—A STUDY IN COMPARATIVE MYTHOLOGY. Large crown 8vo. 10*s*. 6*d*.

BIRD (Charles) F.G.S.—HIGHER EDUCATION IN GERMANY AND ENGLAND: Being a Brief Practical Account of the Organisation and Curriculum of the German Higher Schools. With Critical Remarks and Suggestions with reference to those of England. Small crown 8vo. 2*s*. 6*d*.

BIRTH AND GROWTH OF RELIGION. A Book for Workers. Crown 8vo. cloth, 2*s*.; paper covers, 1*s*.

BLACKBURN (Mrs. Hugh)—BIBLE BEASTS AND BIRDS. A New Edition of 'Illustrations of Scripture by an Animal Painter.' With Twenty-two Plates, Photographed from the Originals, and Printed in Platinotype. 4to. cloth extra, gilt edges, 42*s*.

BLOOMFIELD (*The Lady*)—REMINISCENCES OF COURT AND DIPLOMATIC LIFE. New and Cheaper Edition. With Frontispiece. Crown 8vo. 6*s.*

BLUNT (*The Ven. Archdeacon*)—THE DIVINE PATRIOT, AND OTHER SERMONS, Preached in Scarborough and in Cannes. Crown 8vo. 4*s.* 6*d.*

BLUNT (*Wilfrid S.*)—THE FUTURE OF ISLAM. Crown 8vo. 6*s.*

IDEAS ABOUT INDIA. Crown 8vo. cloth, 6*s.*

BOSANQUET (*Bernard*)—KNOWLEDGE AND REALITY. A Criticism of Mr. F. H. Bradley's 'Principles of Logic.' Crown 8vo. 9*s.*

BOUVERIE-PUSEY (*S. E. B.*)—PERMANENCE AND EVOLUTION. An Inquiry into the supposed Mutability of Animal Types. Crown 8vo. 5*s.*

BOWEN (*H. C.*) *M.A.*—STUDIES IN ENGLISH, for the use of Modern Schools. 7th Thousand. Small crown 8vo. 1*s.* 6*d.*

ENGLISH GRAMMAR FOR BEGINNERS. Fcp. 8vo. 1*s.*

SIMPLE ENGLISH POEMS. English Literature for Junior Classes. In Four Parts. Parts I., II., and III. 6*d.* each; Part IV. 1*s.*; complete, 3*s.*

BRADLEY (*F. H.*)—THE PRINCIPLES OF LOGIC. Demy 8vo. 16*s.*

BRADSHAW (*Henry*)—MEMOIR. By G. W. PROTHERO. 8vo. 16*s.*

BRIDGETT (*Rev. T. E.*)—HISTORY OF THE HOLY EUCHARIST IN GREAT BRITAIN. 2 vols. Demy 8vo. 18*s.*

BROOKE (*Rev. S. A.*)—LIFE AND LETTERS OF THE LATE REV. F. W. ROBERTSON, M.A. Edited by.

I. Uniform with Robertson's Sermons. 2 vols. With Steel Portrait, 7*s.* 6*d.*
II. Library Edition. 8vo. With Portrait, 12*s.*
III. A Popular Edition. In 1 vol. 8vo. 6*s.*

THE FIGHT OF FAITH. Sermons preached on various occasions. Fifth Edition. Crown 8vo. 7*s.* 6*d.*

THE SPIRIT OF THE CHRISTIAN LIFE. Third Edition. Crown 8vo. 5*s.*

THEOLOGY IN THE ENGLISH POETS.—Cowper, Coleridge, Wordsworth, and Burns. Sixth Edition. Post 8vo. 5*s.*

CHRIST IN MODERN LIFE. Sixteenth Edition. Crown 8vo. 5*s.*

SERMONS. First Series. Thirteenth Edition. Crown 8vo. 5*s.*

SERMONS. Second Series. Sixth Edition. Crown 8vo. 5*s.*

BROWN (*Horatio F.*)—LIFE ON THE LAGOONS. With two Illustrations and a Map. Crown 8vo. 6*s.*

VENETIAN STUDIES. Crown 8vo. 7*s.* 6*d.*

BROWN (*Rev. J. Baldwin*) *B.A.*—THE HIGHER LIFE: its Reality, Experience, and Destiny. Seventh Edition. Crown 8vo. 5*s.*

DOCTRINE OF ANNIHILATION IN THE LIGHT OF THE GOSPEL OF LOVE. Five Discourses. Fourth Edition. Crown 8vo. 2*s.* 6*d.*

THE CHRISTIAN POLICY OF LIFE. A Book for Young Men of Business. Third Edition. Crown 8vo. 3*s.* 6*d.*

BURDETT (*Henry C.*)—HELP IN SICKNESS: Where to Go and What to Do. Crown 8vo. 1*s.* 6*d.*

HELPS TO HEALTH: The Habitation, The Nursery, The Schoolroom, and The Person. With a Chapter on Pleasure and Health Resorts. Crown 8vo. 1*s.* 6*d.*

BURKE (*Oliver J.*)—SOUTH ISLES OF ARAN (COUNTY GALWAY). Crown 8vo. 2*s*. 6*d*.

BURKE (*The late Very Rev. T. N.*)—HIS LIFE. By W. J. FITZPATRICK. 2 vols. With Portrait. Demy 8vo. 30*s*.

BURTON (*Mrs. Richard*)—THE INNER LIFE OF SYRIA, PALESTINE, AND THE HOLY LAND. Post 8vo. 6*s*.

CANDLER (*C.*)—THE PREVENTION OF CONSUMPTION. A Mode of Prevention founded on a New Theory of the Nature of the Tubercle-Bacillus. Demy 8vo. 10*s*. 6*d*.

CARLYLE AND THE OPEN SECRET OF HIS LIFE. By HENRY LARKIN. Demy 8vo. 14*s*.

CARPENTER (*W. B.*) *LL.D., M.D., F.R.S., &c.*—THE PRINCIPLES OF MENTAL PHYSIOLOGY. With their Applications to the Training and Discipline of the Mind, and the Study of its Morbid Conditions. Illustrated. Sixth Edition. 8vo. 12*s*.

NATURE AND MAN: Essays, Scientific and Philosophical. With Memoir of the Author and Portrait. Large crown 8vo. 8*s*. 6*d*.

CATHOLIC DICTIONARY—Containing some account of the Doctrine, Discipline, Rites, Ceremonies, Councils, and Religious Orders of the Catholic Church. By WILLIAM E. ADDIS and THOMAS ARNOLD, M.A. Third Edition, demy 8vo. 21*s*.

CHEYNE (*Rev. Canon, M.A., D.D., Edin.*)—JOB AND SOLOMON; or, the Wisdom of the Old Testament. Demy 8vo. 12*s*. 6*d*.

THE PROPHECIES OF ISAIAH. Translated with Critical Notes and Dissertations. 2 vols. Fourth Edition. Demy 8vo. 25*s*.

THE BOOK OF PSALMS; or, THE PRAISES OF ISRAEL. A New Translation, with Commentary. Demy 8vo. 16*s*.

CHURGRESS, THE. By The Prig. Fcp. 8vo. 3*s*. 6*d*.

CLAIRAUT—ELEMENTS OF GEOMETRY. Translated by Dr. KAINES. With 145 Figures. Crown 8vo. 4*s*. 6*d*.

CLAPPERTON (*Jane Hume*)—SCIENTIFIC MELIORISM AND THE EVOLUTION OF HAPPINESS. Large crown 8vo. 8*s*. 6*d*.

CLODD (*Edward*) *F.R.A.S.*—THE CHILDHOOD OF THE WORLD: a Simple Account of Man in Early Times. Eighth Edition. Crown 8vo. 3*s*.
A Special Edition for Schools, 1*s*.

THE CHILDHOOD OF RELIGIONS. Including a Simple Account of the Birth and Growth of Myths and Legends. Eighth Thousand. Crown 8vo. 5*s*.
A Special Edition for Schools. 1*s*. 6*d*.

JESUS OF NAZARETH. With a brief sketch of Jewish History to the Time of His Birth. Second Edition. Small crown 8vo. 6*s*.

COGHLAN (*J. Cole*) *D.D.*—THE MODERN PHARISEE, AND OTHER SERMONS. Edited by the Very Rev. H. H. DICKINSON, D.D., Dean of Chapel Royal, Dublin. New and Cheaper Edition. Crown 8vo. 7*s*. 6*d*.

COLERIDGE (*Sara*)—MEMOIR AND LETTERS OF SARA COLERIDGE. Edited by her Daughter. With Index. Cheap Edition. With one Portrait. 7*s*. 6*d*.

COLERIDGE (*The Hon. Stephen*)—DEMETRIUS. Crown 8vo. 5*s*.

COOPER (*James Fenimore*)—LIFE. By. T. R. LOUNDSBURY. With Portrait. Crown 8vo. 5*s.*

CORY (*William*)—A GUIDE TO MODERN ENGLISH HISTORY. Part I.—MDCCCXV.–MDCCCXXX. Demy 8vo. 9*s.* Part II.—MDCCCXXX.–MDCCCXXXV. 15*s.*

COTTERILL (*H. B.*)—AN INTRODUCTION TO THE STUDY OF POETRY. Crown 8vo. 7*s.* 6*d.*

COTTON (*H. J. S.*)—NEW INDIA, OR INDIA IN TRANSITION. Third Edition. Crown 8vo. 4*s.* 6*d.* Popular Edition, paper covers, 1*s.*

COWIE (*Right Rev. W. G.*)—OUR LAST YEAR IN NEW ZEALAND. 1887. Crown 8vo. 7*s.* 6*d.*

COX (*Rev. Sir George W.*) *M.A., Bart.*—THE MYTHOLOGY OF THE ARYAN NATIONS. New Edition. Demy 8vo. 16*s.*

TALES OF ANCIENT GREECE. New Edition. Small crown 8vo. 6*s.*

A MANUAL OF MYTHOLOGY IN THE FORM OF QUESTION AND ANSWER. New Edition. Fcp. 8vo. 3*s.*

AN INTRODUCTION TO THE SCIENCE OF COMPARATIVE MYTHOLOGY AND FOLK-LORE. Second Edition. Crown 8vo. 7*s.* 6*d.*

COX (*Rev. Sir G. W.*) *M.A., Bart., and JONES* (*Eustace Hinton*)—POPULAR ROMANCES OF THE MIDDLE AGES. Third Edition, in 1 vol. Crown 8vo. 6*s.*

COX (*Rev. Samuel*) *D.D.*—A COMMENTARY ON THE BOOK OF JOB. With a Translation. Second Edition. Demy 8vo. 15*s.*

SALVATOR MUNDI; or, Is Christ the Saviour of all Men? Eleventh Edition. Crown 8vo. 2*s.* 6*d.*

THE LARGER HOPE: a Sequel to 'SALVATOR MUNDI.' Second Edition. 16mo. 1*s.*

THE GENESIS OF EVIL, AND OTHER SERMONS, mainly expository. Third Edition. Crown 8vo. 6*s.*

BALAAM: An Exposition and a Study. Crown 8vo. 5*s.*

MIRACLES. An Argument and a Challenge. Crown 8vo. 2*s.* 6*d.*

CRAVEN (*Mrs.*)—A YEAR'S MEDITATIONS. Crown 8vo. 6*s.*

CRAWFURD (*Oswald*)—PORTUGAL, OLD AND NEW. With Illustrations and Maps. New and Cheaper Edition. Crown 8vo. 6*s.*

CRUISE (*F. R.*) *M.D.*—THOMAS À KEMPIS. Notes of a Visit to the Scenes in which his Life was spent, with some Account of the Examination of his Relics. Demy 8vo. Illustrated. 12*s.*

CUNNINGHAM (*W., B.D.*)—POLITICS AND ECONOMICS: An Essay on the Nature of the Principles of Political Economy, together with a Survey of Recent Legislation. Crown 8vo. 5*s.*

DARMESTETER (*Arsène*)—THE LIFE OF WORDS AS THE SYMBOLS OF IDEAS. Crown 8vo. 4*s.* 6*d.*

DAVIDSON (*Rev. Samuel*) *D.D., LL.D.*—CANON OF THE BIBLE: Its Formation, History, and Fluctuations. Third and revised Edition. Small crown 8vo. 5*s.*

THE DOCTRINE OF LAST THINGS, contained in the New Testament, compared with the Notions of the Jews and the Statements of Church Creeds. Small crown 8vo. 3*s.* 6*d.*

DAWSON (Geo.) M.A.—PRAYERS, WITH A DISCOURSE ON PRAYER. Edited by his Wife. First Series. New and Cheaper Edition. Crown 8vo. 3*s.* 6*d.*

PRAYERS, WITH A DISCOURSE ON PRAYER. Edited by GEORGE ST. CLAIR. Second Series. Crown 8vo. 6*s.*

SERMONS ON DISPUTED POINTS AND SPECIAL OCCASIONS. Edited by his Wife. Fourth Edition. Crown 8vo. 6*s.*

SERMONS ON DAILY LIFE AND DUTY. Edited by his Wife. Fifth Edition. Crown 8vo. 3*s.* 6*d.*

THE AUTHENTIC GOSPEL, and other Sermons. Edited by GEORGE ST. CLAIR. Third Edition. Crown 8vo. 6*s.*

EVERY-DAY COUNSELS. Edited by GEORGE ST. CLAIR, F.G.S. Crown 8vo. 6*s.*

BIOGRAPHICAL LECTURES. Edited by GEORGE ST. CLAIR, F.G.S. Second Edition. Large crown 8vo. 7*s.* 6*d.*

HAKESPEARE, and other Lectures. Edited by GEORGE ST. CLAIR, F.G.S. Large crown 8vo. 7*s.* 6*d.*

DE BURY (Richard)—THE PHILOBIBLON. Translated and Edited by ERNEST C. THOMAS.

DE JONCOURT (Madame Marie)—WHOLESOME COOKERY. Fourth Edition. Crown 8vo. cloth, 1*s.* 6*d.*; paper covers, 1*s.*

DENT (H. C.)—A YEAR IN BRAZIL. With Notes on Religion, Meteorology, Natural History, &c. Maps and Illustrations. Demy 8vo. 18*s.*

DOCTOR FAUST. The Old German Puppet Play, turned into English, with Introduction, etc., by T. C. H. HEDDERWICK. Large post 8vo. 7*s.* 6*d.*

DOWDEN (Edward) LL.D.—SHAKSPERE: a Critical Study of his Mind and Art. Eighth Edition. Post 8vo. 12*s.*

STUDIES IN LITERATURE, 1789–1877. Fourth Edition. Post 8vo. 6*s.*

TRANSCRIPTS AND STUDIES. Post 8vo. 12*s.*

DRUMMOND (Thomas)—LIFE. By R. BARRY O'BRIEN. 8vo. 14*s.*

DULCE DOMUM. Fcp. 8vo. 5*s.*

DU MONCEL (Count)—THE TELEPHONE, THE MICROPHONE, AND THE PHONOGRAPH. With 74 Illustrations. Third Edition. Small crown 8vo. 5*s.*

DUNN (H. Percy) F.R.C.S.—INFANT HEALTH. The Physiology and Hygiene of Early Life. Crown 8vo. 3*s.* 6*d.*

DURUY (Victor)—HISTORY OF ROME AND THE ROMAN PEOPLE. Edited by Professor MAHAFFY, with nearly 3,000 Illustrations. 4to. 6 Vols. in 12 Parts, 30*s.* each volume.

EDUCATION LIBRARY. Edited by Sir PHILIP MAGNUS:—

INDUSTRIAL EDUCATION. By Sir PHILIP MAGNUS.

AN INTRODUCTION TO THE HISTORY OF EDUCATIONAL THEORIES. By OSCAR BROWNING, M.A. Second Edition. 3*s.* 6*d.*

OLD GREEK EDUCATION. By the Rev. Prof. MAHAFFY, M.A. Second Edition. 3*s.* 6*d.*

SCHOOL MANAGEMENT; including a General View of the Work of Education. By JOSEPH LANDON. Sixth Edition. 6*s.*

EDWARDES (Major-General Sir Herbert B.)—MEMORIALS OF HIS LIFE. By his WIFE. With Portrait and Illustrations. 2 vols. 8vo. 36*s.*

EIGHTEENTH CENTURY ESSAYS. Selected and Edited by AUSTIN DOBSON. Fcp. 8vo. 1*s*. 6*d*.

ELSDALE (*Henry*)—STUDIES IN TENNYSON'S IDYLLS. Crown 8vo. 5*s*.

EMERSON'S (*Ralph Waldo*) LIFE. By OLIVER WENDELL HOLMES. [English Copyright Edition.] With Portrait. Crown 8vo. 6*s*.

ERANUS. A COLLECTION OF EXERCISES IN THE ALCAIC AND SAPPHIC METRES. Edited by F. W. CORNISH, Assistant Master at Eton. Second Edition. Crown 8vo. 2*s*.

FIVE O'CLOCK TEA. Containing Receipts for Cakes of every description, Savoury Sandwiches, Cooling Drinks, &c. Fcp. 8vo. 1*s*. 6*d*., or 1*s*. sewed.

FLINN (*D. Edgar*)—IRELAND: its Health Resorts and Watering-Places. With Frontispiece and Maps. Demy 8vo. 5s.

FORBES (*Bishop*)—A MEMOIR, by the Rev. DONALD J. MACKEY. Portrait and Map. Crown 8vo. 7*s*. 6*d*.

FORDYCE (*John*)—THE NEW SOCIAL ORDER. Crown 8vo. 3*s*. 6*d*.

FOTHERINGHAM (*James*)—STUDIES IN THE POETRY OF ROBERT BROWNING. Crown 8vo. 6*s*.

FRANKLIN (*Benjamin*)—AS A MAN OF LETTERS. By J. B. MCMASTER. Crown 8vo. 5*s*.

FROM WORLD TO CLOISTER; or, My Novitiate. By BERNARD. Crown 8vo. 5*s*.

GARDINER (*Samuel R.*) *and J. BASS MULLINGER, M.A.*—INTRODUCTION TO THE STUDY OF ENGLISH HISTORY Second Edition. Large crown 8vo. 9*s*.

GEORGE (*Henry*)—PROGRESS AND POVERTY: an Inquiry into the Causes of Industrial Depressions, and of Increase of Want with Increase of Wealth. The Remedy. Library Edition. Post 8vo. 7*s*. 6*d*. Cabinet Edition, crown 8vo. 2*s*. 6*d*.

SOCIAL PROBLEMS. Crown 8vo. 5*s*.

PROTECTION, OR FREE TRADE. An Examination of the Tariff Question, with especial regard to the Interests of Labour. Second Edition. Crown 8vo. 5*s*.

*** Also Cheap Editions of each of the above, limp cloth, 1*s*. 6*d*.; paper covers, 1*s*.

GILBERT (*Mrs.*)—AUTOBIOGRAPHY, and other Memorials. Edited by JOSIAH GILBERT. Fifth Edition. Crown 8vo. 7*s*. 6*d*.

GILLMORE (*Col. Parker*)—DAYS AND NIGHTS BY THE DESERT. With numerous Illustrations. Demy 8vo. 10*s*. 6*d*.

GLANVILL (*Joseph*)—SCEPSIS SCIENTIFICA; or, Confest Ignorance, th Way to Science; in an Essay of the Vanity of Dogmatising and Confiden Opinion. Edited, with Introductory Essay, by JOHN OWEN. Elzevir 8vo. printed on hand-made paper, 6*s*.

GLASS (*Henry Alex.*)—THE STORY OF THE PSALTERS. Crown 8vo. 5*s*.

GLOSSARY OF TERMS AND PHRASES. Edited by the Rev. H. PERCY SMITH and others. Medium 8vo. 7*s*. 6*d*.

GLOVER (*F.*) *M.A.*—EXEMPLA LATINA. A First Construing Book, with Short Notes, Lexicon, and an Introduction to the Analysis of Sentences. Second Edition. Fcp. 8vo. 2*s*.

GOODENOUGH (*Commodore J. G.*)—MEMOIR OF, with Extracts from his Letters and Journals. Edited by his Widow. With Steel Engraved Portrait. Third Edition. Crown 8vo. 5*s*.

GORDON (Major-Gen. C. G.)—HIS JOURNALS AT KARTOUM. Printed from the Original MS. With Introduction and Notes by A. EGMONT HAKE. Portrait, 2 Maps, and 30 Illustrations. 2 vols. Demy 8vo. 21*s*. Also a Cheap Edition in 1 vol., 6*s*.

GORDON'S (GENERAL) LAST JOURNAL. A Facsimile of the last Journal received in England from General Gordon. Reproduced by Photo-lithography. Imperial 4to. £3. 3*s*.

EVENTS IN HIS LIFE. From the Day of his Birth to the Day of his Death. By Sir H. W. GORDON. With Maps and Illustrations. Demy 8vo. 7*s*. 6*d*.

GOSSE (Edmund)—SEVENTEENTH CENTURY STUDIES. A Contribution to the History of English Poetry. Demy 8vo. 10*s*. 6*d*.

GOULD (Rev. S. Baring) M.A.—GERMANY, PRESENT AND PAST. New and Cheaper Edition. Large crown 8vo. 7*s*. 6*d*.

THE VICAR OF MORWENSTOW: a Life of Robert Stephen Hawker, M.A. New and Cheaper Edition. Crown 8vo. 5*s*.

GOWAN (Major Walter E.)—A. IVANOFF'S RUSSIAN GRAMMAR. (16th Edition). Translated, enlarged, and arranged for use of Students of the Russian Language. Demy 8vo. 6*s*.

GOWER (Lord Ronald)—MY REMINISCENCES. Limp Parchment, Antique, with Etched Portrait, 10*s*. 6*d*.

BRIC-À-BRAC. Being some Photoprints illustrating Art objects at Gower Lodge, Windsor. Super royal 8vo. 15*s*.; Persian leather, 21*s*.

LAST DAYS OF MARY ANTOINETTE. An Historical Sketch. With Portrait and Facsimiles. Fcp. 4to. 10*s*. 6*d*.

NOTES OF A TOUR FROM BRINDISI TO YOKOHAMA, 1883–1884. Fcp. 8vo. 2*s*. 6*d*.

GRAHAM (William) M.A.—THE CREED OF SCIENCE, Religious, Moral, and Social. Second Edition, revised. Crown 8vo. 6*s*.

THE SOCIAL PROBLEM IN ITS ECONOMIC, MORAL, AND POLITICAL ASPECTS. Demy 8vo. 14*s*.

GRIMLEY (Rev. H. N.) M.A.—TREMADOC SERMONS, CHIEFLY ON THE SPIRITUAL BODY, THE UNSEEN WORLD, AND THE DIVINE HUMANITY. Fourth Edition. Crown 8vo. 6*s*.

THE TEMPLE OF HUMANITY, and other Sermons. Crown 8vo. 6*s*.

GURNEY (Edmund)—TERTIUM QUID: Chapters on various Disputed Questions. 2 vols. Crown 8vo. 12*s*.

HADDON (Caroline)—THE LARGER LIFE, STUDIES IN HINTON'S ETHICS. Crown 8vo. 5*s*.

HAECKEL (Prof. Ernst)—THE HISTORY OF CREATION. Translation revised by Professor E. RAY LANKESTER, M.A., F.R.S. With Coloured Plates and Genealogical Trees of the various groups of both plants and animals. 2 vols. Third Edition. Post 8vo. 32*s*.

THE HISTORY OF THE EVOLUTION OF MAN. With numerous Illustrations. 2 vols. Post 8vo. 32*s*.

A VISIT TO CEYLON. Post 8vo. 7*s*. 6*d*.

FREEDOM IN SCIENCE AND TEACHING. With a Prefatory Note by T. H. HUXLEY, F.R.S. Crown 8vo. 5*s*.

HALCOMBE (*J. J.*)—GOSPEL DIFFICULTIES DUE TO A DISPLACED SECTION OF ST. LUKE. Second Edition. Crown 8vo. 6*s*.

HAMILTON, MEMOIRS OF ARTHUR, B.A., of Trinity College, Cambridge. Crown 8vo. 6*s*.

HANDBOOK OF HOME RULE, being Articles on the Irish Question by Various Writers. Edited by JAMES BRYCE, M.P. Second Edition. Crown 8vo. 1*s*. sewed, or 1*s*. 6*d*. cloth.

HART (*Rev. J. W. T.*)—AUTOBIOGRAPHY OF JUDAS ISCARIOT. A Character-Study. Crown 8vo. 3*s*. 6*d*.

HAWEIS (*Rev. H. R.*) *M.A.*—CURRENT COIN. Materialism—The Devil—Crime—Drunkenness—Pauperism—Emotion—Recreation—The Sabbath. Fifth Edition. Crown 8vo. 5*s*.

ARROWS IN THE AIR. Fifth Edition. Crown 8vo. 5*s*.

SPEECH IN SEASON. Fifth Edition. Crown 8vo. 5*s*.

THOUGHTS FOR THE TIMES. Fourteenth Edition. Crown 8vo. 5*s*.

UNSECTARIAN FAMILY PRAYERS. New Edition. Fcp. 8vo. 1*s*. 6*d*.

HAWTHORNE (*Nathaniel*)—WORKS. Complete in 12 vols. Large post 8vo. each vol. 7*s*. 6*d*.

VOL. I. TWICE-TOLD TALES.
II. MOSSES FROM AN OLD MANSE.
III. THE HOUSE OF THE SEVEN GABLES, and THE SNOW IMAGE.
IV. THE WONDER BOOK, TANGLEWOOD TALES, and GRANDFATHER'S CHAIR.
V. THE SCARLET LETTER, and THE BLITHEDALE ROMANCE.
VI. THE MARBLE FAUN. (Transformation.)
VII. & VIII. OUR OLD HOME, and ENGLISH NOTE-BOOKS.
IX. AMERICAN NOTE-BOOKS.
X. FRENCH AND ITALIAN NOTE-BOOKS.
XI. SEPTIMIUS FELTON, THE DOLLIVER ROMANCE, FANSHAWE, and, in an appendix, THE ANCESTRAL FOOTSTEP.
XII. TALES AND ESSAYS, AND OTHER PAPERS, WITH A BIOGRAPHICAL SKETCH OF HAWTHORNE.

HEATH (*Francis George*)—AUTUMNAL LEAVES. Third and Cheaper Edition. Large crown 8vo. 6*s*.

SYLVAN WINTER. With 70 Illustrations. Large crown 8vo. 14*s*.

HEGEL—THE INTRODUCTION TO HEGEL'S PHILOSOPHY OF FINE ART. Translated from the German, with Notes and Prefatory Essay, by BERNARD BOSANQUET, M.A. Crown 8vo. 5*s*.

HEIDENHAIN (*Rudolph*) *M.D.*—HYPNOTISM; or Animal Magnetism. With Preface by G. J. ROMANES, F.R.S. Second Edition. Small crown 8vo. 2*s*. 6*d*.

HENNESSY (*Sir John Pope*)—RALEGH IN IRELAND, WITH HIS LETTERS ON IRISH AFFAIRS AND SOME CONTEMPORARY DOCUMENTS. Large crown 8vo. printed on hand-made paper, parchment, 10*s*. 6*d*.

HENRY (*Philip*)—DIARIES AND LETTERS. Edited by MATTHEW HENRY LEE, M.A. Large crown 8vo. 7*s*. 6*d*.

HINTON (*J.*)—THE MYSTERY OF PAIN. New Edition. Fcp. 8vo. 1*s*.

LIFE AND LETTERS. With an Introduction by Sir W. W. GULL, Bart., and Portrait engraved on Steel by C. H. JEENS. Fifth Edition. Crown 8vo. 8*s*. 6*d*.

HINTON (J.)—continued.

PHILOSOPHY AND RELIGION. Selections from the MSS. of the late JAMES HINTON. Edited by CAROLINE HADDON. Second Edition. Crown 8vo. 5*s.*

THE LAW BREAKER AND THE COMING OF THE LAW. Edited by MARGARET HINTON. Crown 8vo. 6*s.*

HOOPER (Mary)—LITTLE DINNERS: HOW TO SERVE THEM WITH ELEGANCE AND ECONOMY. Twentieth Edition. Crown 8vo. 2*s.* 6*d.*

COOKERY FOR INVALIDS, PERSONS OF DELICATE DIGESTION, AND CHILDREN. Fifth Edition. Crown 8vo. 2*s.* 6*d.*

EVERY-DAY MEALS. Being Economical and Wholesome Recipes for Breakfast, Luncheon, and Supper. Seventh Edition. Crown 8vo. 2*s.* 6*d.*

HOPKINS (Ellice)—WORK AMONGST WORKING MEN. Fifth Edition. Crown 8vo. 3*s.* 6*d.*

HORNADAY (W. T.)—TWO YEARS IN A JUNGLE. With Illustrations. Demy 8vo. 21*s.*

HOSPITALIER (E.)—THE MODERN APPLICATIONS OF ELECTRICITY. Translated and Enlarged by JULIUS MAIER, Ph.D. 2 vols. Second Edition, revised, with many additions and numerous Illustrations. Demy 8vo. 12*s.* 6*d.* each volume.

VOL. I.—Electric Generators, Electric Light.
II.—Telephone: Various Applications: Electrical Transmission of Energy.

HOWARD (Robert) M.A.—THE CHURCH OF ENGLAND AND OTHER RELIGIOUS COMMUNIONS. A Course of Lectures delivered in the Parish Church of Clapham. Crown 8vo. 7*s.* 6*d.*

HOW TO MAKE A SAINT; or, The Process of Canonisation in the Church of England. By The Prig. Fcp. 8vo. 3*s.* 6*d.*

HYNDMAN (H. M.)—THE HISTORICAL BASIS OF SOCIALISM IN ENGLAND. Large crown 8vo. 8*s.* 6*d.*

IM THURN (Everard F.)—AMONG THE INDIANS OF GUIANA. Being Sketches, chiefly Anthropologic, from the Interior of British Guiana. With 53 Illustrations and a Map. Demy 8vo. 18*s.*

IXORA: A Mystery. Crown 8vo. 6*s.*

JACCOUD (Prof. S.)—THE CURABILITY AND TREATMENT OF PULMONARY PHTHISIS. Translated and Edited by M. LUBBOCK, M.D. 8vo. 15*s.*

JAUNT IN A JUNK: A Ten Days' Cruise in Indian Seas. Large crown 8vo. 7*s.* 6*d.*

JENKINS (E.) and RAYMOND (J.)—THE ARCHITECT'S LEGAL HANDBOOK. Third Edition, Revised. Crown 8vo. 6*s.*

JENKINS (Rev. Canon R. C.)—HERALDRY: English and Foreign. With a Dictionary of Heraldic Terms and 156 Illustrations. Small crown 8vo. 3*s.* 6*d.*

STORY OF THE CARAFFA. Small crown 8vo. 3*s.* 6*d.*

JEROME (Saint)—LIFE, by Mrs. CHARLES MARTIN. Large cr. 8vo. 6*s.*

JOEL (L.)—A CONSUL'S MANUAL AND SHIPOWNER'S AND SHIPMASTER'S PRACTICAL GUIDE IN THEIR TRANSACTIONS ABROAD. With Definitions of Nautical, Mercantile, and Legal Terms; a Glossary of Mercantile Terms in English, French, German, Italian, and Spanish; Tables of the Money, Weights, and Measures of the Principal Commercial Nations and their Equivalents in British Standards; and Forms of Consular and Notarial Acts. Demy 8vo. 12*s.*

JORDAN (Furneaux) F.R.C.S.—ANATOMY AND PHYSIOLOGY IN CHARACTER. Crown 8vo. 5*s.*

KAUFMANN (*Rev. M.*) *M.A.*—SOCIALISM: its Nature, its Dangers, and its Remedies considered. Crown 8vo. 7*s.* 6*d.*

UTOPIAS; or, Schemes of Social Improvement, from Sir Thomas More to Karl Marx. Crown 8vo. 5*s.*

CHRISTIAN SOCIALISM. Crown 8vo. 4*s.* 6*d.*

KAY (*David*)—EDUCATION AND EDUCATORS. Crown 8vo. 7*s.* 6*d.*

MEMORY: What it is, and how to improve it. Crown 8vo. 6*s.*

KAY (*Joseph*)—FREE TRADE IN LAND. Edited by his Widow. With Preface by the Right Hon. JOHN BRIGHT, M.P. Seventh Edition. Crown 8vo. 5*s.*

*** Also a cheaper edition, without the Appendix, but with a Review of Recent Changes in the Land Laws of England, by the Right Hon. G. OSBORNE MORGAN, Q.C., M.P. Cloth, 1*s.* 6*d.*; Paper covers, 1*s.*

KELKE (*W. H. H.*)—AN EPITOME OF ENGLISH GRAMMAR FOR THE USE OF STUDENTS. Adapted to the London Matriculation Course and Similar Examinations. Crown 8vo. 4*s.* 6*d.*

KEMPIS (*Thomas à*)—OF THE IMITATION OF CHRIST. Parchment Library Edition, parchment or cloth, 6*s.*; vellum, 7*s.* 6*d.* The Red Line Edition, fcp. 8vo. cloth extra, 2*s.* 6*d.* The Cabinet Edition, small 8vo. cloth limp, 1*s.*; or cloth boards, red edges, 1*s.* 6*d.* The Miniature Edition, 32mo. cloth limp, 1*s.*; or with red lines, 1*s.* 6*d.*

*** All the above Editions may be had in various extra bindings.

KENNARD (*Rev. H. B.*)—MANUAL OF CONFIRMATION. 16mo. cloth, 1*s.* Sewed, 3*d.*

KENDALL (*Henry*)—THE KINSHIP OF MEN: Genealogy viewed as a Science. Crown 8vo. 5*s.*

KETTLEWELL (*Rev. S.*) *M.A.*—THOMAS À KEMPIS AND THE BROTHERS OF COMMON LIFE. 2 vols. With Frontispieces. Demy 8vo. 30*s.*

*** Also an Abridged Edition in 1 vol. With Portrait. Crown 8vo. 7*s.* 6*d.*

KIDD (*Joseph*) *M.D.*—THE LAWS OF THERAPEUTICS; or, the Science and Art of Medicine. Second Edition. Crown 8vo. 6*s.*

KINGSFORD (*Anna*) *M.D.*—THE PERFECT WAY IN DIET. A Treatise advocating a Return to the Natural and Ancient Food of Race. Small crown 8vo. 2*s.*

KINGSLEY (*Charles*) *M.A.*—LETTERS AND MEMORIES OF HIS LIFE. Edited by his WIFE. With Two Steel Engraved Portraits and Vignettes. Sixteenth Cabinet Edition, in 2 vols. Crown 8vo. 12*s.*

*** Also a People's Edition in 1 vol. With Portrait. Crown 8vo. 6*s.*

ALL SAINTS' DAY, and other Sermons. Edited by the Rev. W. HARRISON. Third Edition. Crown 8vo. 7*s.* 6*d.*

TRUE WORDS FOR BRAVE MEN. A Book for Soldiers' and Sailors' Libraries. Fourteenth Edition. Crown 8vo. 2*s.* 6*d.*

KNOX (*Alexander A.*)—THE NEW PLAYGROUND; or, Wanderings in Algeria. New and Cheaper Edition. Large crown 8vo. 6*s.*

LAMARTINE (*Alphonse de*). By Lady MARGARET DOMVILE. Large crown 8vo., with Portrait, 7*s.* 6*d.*

LAND CONCENTRATION AND IRRESPONSIBILITY OF POLITICAL POWER, as causing the Anomaly of a Widespread State of Want by the Side of the Vast Supplies of Nature. Crown 8vo. 5*s*.

LANDON (*Joseph*)—SCHOOL MANAGEMENT; including a General View of the Work of Education, Organisation, and Discipline. Sixth Edition. Crown 8vo. 6*s*.

LAURIE (*S. S.*)—LECTURES ON THE RISE AND EARLY CONSTITUTION OF UNIVERSITIES. With a Survey of Mediæval Education. Crown 8vo. 6*s*.

LEE (*Rev. F. G.*) *D.C.L.*—THE OTHER WORLD; or, Glimpses of the Supernatural. 2 vols. A New Edition. Crown 8vo. 15*s*.

LEFEVRE (*Right Hon. G. Shaw*)—PEEL AND O'CONNELL. Demy 8vo. 10*s*. 6*d*.

INCIDENTS OF COERCION. A Journal of Visits to Ireland. Crown 8vo. 1*s*.

LETTERS FROM AN UNKNOWN FRIEND. By the Author of 'Charles Lowder.' With a Preface by the Rev. W. H. Cleaver. Fcp. 8vo. 1*s*.

LEWARD (*Frank*)—Edited by CHAS. BAMPTON. Crown 8vo. 7*s*. 6*d*.

LIFE OF A PRIG. By ONE. Third Edition. Fcp. 8vo. 3*s*. 6*d*.

LILLIE (*Arthur*) *M.R.A.S.*—THE POPULAR LIFE OF BUDDHA. Containing an Answer to the Hibbert Lectures of 1881. With Illustrations. Crown 8vo. 6*s*.

BUDDHISM IN CHRISTENDOM; or, Jesus, the Essene. Demy 8vo. with Illustrations. 15*s*.

LOCHER (*Carl*)—EXPLANATION OF THE ORGAN STOPS, with Hints for Effective Combinations. Illustrated. Demy 8vo. 5*s*.

LONGFELLOW (*H. Wadsworth*)—LIFE. By his Brother, SAMUEL LONGFELLOW. With Portraits and Illustrations. 3 vols. Demy 8vo. 42*s*.

LONSDALE (*Margaret*)—SISTER DORA: a Biography. With Portrait. Cheap Edition. Crown 8vo. 2*s*. 6*d*.

GEORGE ELIOT: Thoughts upon her Life, her Books, and Herself. Second Edition. Small crown 8vo. 1*s*. 6*d*.

LOWDER (*Charles*)—A BIOGRAPHY. By the Author of 'St. Teresa.' New and Cheaper Edition. Crown 8vo. With Portrait. 3*s*. 6*d*.

LÜCKES (*Eva C. E.*)—LECTURES ON GENERAL NURSING, delivered to the Probationers of the London Hospital Training School for Nurses. Second Edition. Crown 8vo. 2*s*. 6*d*.

LYTTON (*Edward Bulwer, Lord*)—LIFE, LETTERS, AND LITERARY REMAINS. By his Son the EARL OF LYTTON. With Portraits, Illustrations, and Facsimiles. Demy 8vo. cloth. Vols. I. and II. 32*s*.

MACHIAVELLI (*Niccolò*)—HIS LIFE AND TIMES. By Prof. VILLARI. Translated by LINDA VILLARI. 4 vols. Large post 8vo. 48*s*.

DISCOURSES ON THE FIRST DECADE OF TITUS LIVIUS. Translated from the Italian by NINIAN HILL THOMSON, M.A. Large crown 8vo. 12*s*.

THE PRINCE. Translated from the Italian by N. H. T. Small crown 8vo. printed on hand-made paper, bevelled boards, 6*s*.

MACNEILL (*J. G. Swift*)—HOW THE UNION WAS CARRIED. Crown 8vo. cloth, 1*s*. 6*d*.; paper covers, 1*s*.

MAGNUS (*Lady*)—ABOUT THE JEWS SINCE BIBLE TIMES. From the Babylonian Exile till the English Exodus. Small crown 8vo. 6*s*.

MAGUIRE (*Thomas*)—LECTURES ON PHILOSOPHY. Demy 8vo. 9*s*.

MAINTENON (*Madame de*). By EMILY BOWLES. With Portrait. Large crown 8vo. 7*s*. 6*d*.

MANY VOICES.—Extracts from Religious Writers, from the First to the Sixteenth Century. With Biographical Sketches. Crown 8vo. cloth extra, 6*s*.

MARKHAM (*Capt. Albert Hastings*) *R.N.*—THE GREAT FROZEN SEA: a Personal Narrative of the Voyage of the *Alert* during the Arctic Expedition of 1875–6. With 33 Illustrations and Two Maps. Sixth Edition. Crown 8vo. 6*s*.

MARTINEAU (*Gertrude*)—OUTLINE LESSONS ON MORALS. Small crown 8vo. 3*s*. 6*d*.

MASON (*Charlotte M.*)—HOME EDUCATION. A Course of Lectures to Ladies, delivered in Bradford in the winter of 1885–1886. Crown 8vo. 3*s*. 6*d*.

MATTER AND ENERGY: An Examination of the Fundamental Conceptions of Physical Force. By B. L. L. Small crown 8vo. 2*s*.

MATUCE (*H. Ogram*)—A WANDERER. Crown 8vo. 5*s*.

MAUDSLEY (*H.*) *M.D.*—BODY AND WILL. Being an Essay Concerning Will, in its Metaphysical, Physiological, and Pathological Aspects. 8vo. 12*s*.

NATURAL CAUSES AND SUPERNATURAL SEEMINGS. Second Edition. Crown 8vo. 6*s*.

McGRATH (*Terence*)—PICTURES FROM IRELAND. New and Cheaper Edition. Crown 8vo. 2*s*.

McKINNEY (*S. B. G.*)—THE SCIENCE AND ART OF RELIGION. Crown 8vo. 8*s*. 6*d*.

MILLER (*Edward*)—THE HISTORY AND DOCTRINES OF IRVINGISM; or, the so-called Catholic and Apostolic Church. 2 vols. Large post 8vo. 15*s*.

THE CHURCH IN RELATION TO THE STATE. Large crown 8vo. 4*s*.

MILLS (*Herbert*)—POVERTY AND THE STATE; or, Work for the Unemployed. An Enquiry into the Causes and Extent of Enforced Idleness. Cr. 8vo. 6*s*.

MINTON (*Rev. Francis*)—CAPITAL AND WAGES. 8vo. 15*s*.

MITCHELL (*John*)—LIFE. By WILLIAM DILLON. With Portrait. Demy 8vo.

MITCHELL (*Lucy M.*)—A HISTORY OF ANCIENT SCULPTURE. With numerous Illustrations, including six Plates in Phototype. Super royal, 42*s*.

SELECTIONS FROM ANCIENT SCULPTURE. Being a Portfolio containing Reproductions in Phototype of 36 Masterpieces of Ancient Art, to illustrate Mrs. MITCHELL'S 'History of Ancient Sculpture.' 18*s*.

MIVART (*St. George*)—ON TRUTH. 8vo. 16*s*.

MOCKLER (*E.*)—A GRAMMAR OF THE BALOOCHEE LANGUAGE, as it is spoken in Makran (Ancient Gedrosia), in the Persia-Arabic and Roman characters. Fcp. 8vo. 5*s*.

MOHL (*Julius and Mary*)—LETTERS AND RECOLLECTIONS OF. By M. C. M. SIMPSON. With Portraits and Two Illustrations. Demy 8vo. 15*s*.

MOLESWORTH (*W. Nassau*)—HISTORY OF THE CHURCH OF ENGLAND FROM 1660. Large crown 8vo. 7*s*. 6*d*.

MORELL (J. R.)—EUCLID SIMPLIFIED IN METHOD AND LANGUAGE. Being a Manual of Geometry. Compiled from the most important French Works, approved by the University of Paris and the Minister of Public Instruction. Fcp. 8vo. 2*s*. 6*d*.

MORISON (James Cotter)—THE SERVICE OF MAN. An Essay towards the Religion of the Future. Demy 8vo. 10*s*. 6*d*.; Cheap Edition, crown 8vo. 5*s*.

MORSE (E. S.) Ph.D.—FIRST BOOK OF ZOOLOGY. With numerous Illustrations. New and Cheaper Edition. Crown 8vo. 2*s*. 6*d*.

MY LAWYER : A Concise Abridgment of the Laws of England. By a Barrister-at-Law. Crown 8vo. 6*s*. 6*d*.

NELSON (J. H.) M.A.—A PROSPECTUS OF THE SCIENTIFIC STUDY OF THE HINDÛ LAW. Demy 8vo. 9*s*.

INDIAN USAGE AND JUDGE-MADE LAW IN MADRAS. Demy 8vo. 12*s*.

NEW SOCIAL TEACHINGS. By POLITICUS. Small crown 8vo. 5*s*.

NEWMAN (Cardinal)—CHARACTERISTICS FROM THE WRITINGS OF. Being Selections from his various Works. Arranged with the Author's personal Approval. Seventh Edition. With Portrait. Crown 8vo. 6*s*.

*** A Portrait of Cardinal Newman, mounted for framing, can be had, 2*s*. 6*d*.

NEWMAN (Francis William)—ESSAYS ON DIET. Small crown 8vo. 2*s*.

MISCELLANIES. Vol. II. : Essays, Tracts, and Addresses, Moral and Religious. Demy 8vo. 12*s*.

REMINISCENCES OF TWO EXILES AND TWO WARS. Crown 8vo. 3*s*. 6*d*.

NICOLS (Arthur) F.G.S., F.R.G.S.—CHAPTERS FROM THE PHYSICAL HISTORY OF THE EARTH: an Introduction to Geology and Palæontology. With numerous Illustrations. Crown 8vo. 5*s*.

NIHILL (Rev. H. D.)—THE SISTERS OF ST. MARY AT THE CROSS: SISTERS OF THE POOR AND THEIR WORK. Crown 8vo. 2*s*. 6*d*.

NOEL (The Hon. Roden)—ESSAYS ON POETRY AND POETS. Demy 8vo. 12*s*.

NOPS (Marianne)—CLASS LESSONS ON EUCLID. Part I. containing the First Two Books of the Elements. Crown 8vo. 2*s*. 6*d*.

NUCES: EXERCISES ON THE SYNTAX OF THE PUBLIC SCHOOL LATIN PRIMER. New Edition in Three Parts. Crown 8vo. each 1*s*.

*** The Three Parts can also be had bound together in cloth, 3*s*.

OATES (Frank) F.R.G.S.—MATABELE LAND AND THE VICTORIA FALLS. A Naturalist's Wanderings in the Interior of South Africa. Edited by C. G. OATES, B.A. With numerous Illustrations and 4 Maps. Demy 8vo. 21*s*.

O'BRIEN (R. Barry)—IRISH WRONGS AND ENGLISH REMEDIES, with other Essays. Crown 8vo. 5*s*.

OGLE (W.) M.D., F.R.C.P.—ARISTOTLE ON THE PARTS OF ANIMALS. Translated, with Introduction and Notes. Royal 8vo. 12*s*. 6*d*.

OLIVER (Robert)—UNNOTICED ANALOGIES. A Talk on the Irish Question. Crown 8vo. 3*s*. 6*d*.

O'MEARA (Kathleen)—HENRI PERREYVE AND HIS COUNSELS TO THE SICK. Small crown 8vo. 5*s*.

ONE AND A HALF IN NORWAY. A Chronicle of Small Beer. By Either and Both. Small crown 8vo. 3*s*. 6*d*.

O'NEIL (The late Rev. Lord).—SERMONS. With Memoir and Portrait. Crown 8vo. 6*s*.

ESSAYS AND ADDRESSES. Crown 8vo. 5*s*.

OTTLEY (*Henry Bickersteth*)—THE GREAT DILEMMA: Christ His own Witness or His own Accuser. Six Lectures. Second Edition. Crown 8vo. 3*s*. 6*d*.

OUR PRIESTS AND THEIR TITHES. By a Priest of the Province of Canterbury. Crown 8vo. 5*s*.

OUR PUBLIC SCHOOLS—ETON, HARROW, WINCHESTER, RUGBY, WESTMINSTER, MARLBOROUGH, THE CHARTERHOUSE. Crown 8vo. 6*s*.

OWEN (*F. M.*)—JOHN KEATS: a Study. Crown 8vo. 6*s*.

PADGHAM (*Richard*)—IN THE MIDST OF LIFE WE ARE IN DEATH. Crown 8vo. 5*s*.

PALMER (*the late William*)—NOTES OF A VISIT TO RUSSIA IN 1840–41. Selected and arranged by JOHN H. CARDINAL NEWMAN. With Portrait. Crown 8vo. 8*s*. 6*d*.

EARLY CHRISTIAN SYMBOLISM. A series of Compositions from Fresco-Paintings, Glasses, and Sculptured Sarcophagi. Edited by the Rev. PROVOST NORTHCOTE, D.D., and the Rev. CANON BROWNLOW, M.A. With Coloured Plates, folio, 42*s*.; or with plain plates, folio, 25*s*.

PARCHMENT LIBRARY. Choicely printed on hand-made paper, limp parchment antique or cloth, 6*s*.; vellum, 7*s*. 6*d*. each volume.

CARLYLE'S SARTOR RESARTUS.

MILTON'S POETICAL WORKS. 2 vols.

CHAUCER'S CANTERBURY TALES. 2 vols. Edited by ALFRED W. POLLARD.

SELECTIONS FROM THE PROSE WRITINGS OF JONATHAN SWIFT. With a Preface and Notes by STANLEY LANE-POOLE, and Portrait.

ENGLISH SACRED LYRICS.

SIR JOSHUA REYNOLDS' DISCOURSES. Edited by EDMUND GOSSE.

SELECTIONS FROM MILTON'S PROSE WRITINGS. Edited by ERNEST MYERS.

THE BOOK OF PSALMS. Translated by the Rev. Canon CHEYNE, D.D.

THE VICAR OF WAKEFIELD. With Preface and Notes by AUSTIN DOBSON.

ENGLISH COMIC DRAMATISTS. Edited by OSWALD CRAWFURD.

ENGLISH LYRICS.

THE SONNETS OF JOHN MILTON. Edited by MARK PATTISON. With Portrait after Vertue.

FRENCH LYRICS. Selected and Annotated by GEORGE SAINTSBURY. With miniature Frontispiece, designed and etched by H. G. Glindoni.

FABLES by MR. JOHN GAY. With Memoir by AUSTIN DOBSON, and an etched Portrait from an unfinished Oil-sketch by Sir Godfrey Kneller.

SELECT LETTERS OF PERCY BYSSHE SHELLEY. Edited, with an Introtion, by RICHARD GARNETT.

THE CHRISTIAN YEAR; Thoughts in Verse for the Sundays and Holy Days throughout the Year. With etched Portrait of the Rev. J. Keble, after the Drawing by G. Richmond, R.A.

SHAKSPERE'S WORKS. Complete in Twelve Volumes.

EIGHTEENTH CENTURY ESSAYS. Selected and Edited by AUSTIN DOBSON. With a Miniature Frontispiece by R. Caldecott.

PARCHMENT LIBRARY—continued.

Q. HORATI FLACCI OPERA. Edited by F. A. CORNISH, Assistant Master at Eton. With a Frontispiece after a design by L. ALMA TADEMA. Etched by LEOPOLD LOWENSTAM.

EDGAR ALLAN POE'S POEMS. With an Essay on his Poetry by ANDREW LANG, and a Frontispiece by Linley Sambourne.

SHAKSPERE'S SONNETS. Edited by EDWARD DOWDEN. With a Frontispiece etched by Leopold Lowenstam, after the Death Mask.

ENGLISH ODES. Selected by EDMUND GOSSE. With Frontispiece on India paper by Hamo Thornycroft, A.R.A.

OF THE IMITATION OF CHRIST. By THOMAS À KEMPIS. A revised Translation. With Frontispiece on India paper, from a Design by W. B. Richmond.

POEMS: Selected from PERCY BYSSHE SHELLEY. Dedicated to Lady Shelley. With Preface by RICHARD GARNETT and a Miniature Frontispiece.

LETTERS AND JOURNALS OF JONATHAN SWIFT. Selected and edited, with a Commentary and Notes, by STANLEY LANE POOLE.

DE QUINCEY'S CONFESSIONS OF AN ENGLISH OPIUM EATER. Reprinted from the First Edition. Edited by RICHARD GARNETT.

THE GOSPEL ACCORDING TO MATTHEW, MARK, AND LUKE.

PARSLOE (*Joseph*)—OUR RAILWAYS. Sketches, Historical and Descriptive. With Practical Information as to Fares and Rates, &c., and a Chapter on Railway Reform. Crown 8vo. 6*s*.

PASCAL (*Blaise*)—THE THOUGHTS OF. Translated from the Text of AUGUSTE MOLINIER by C. KEGAN PAUL. Large crown 8vo. with Frontispiece, printed on hand-made paper, parchment antique, or cloth, 12*s*.; vellum, 15*s*. New Edition, crown 8vo. 6*s*.

PATON (*W. A.*)—DOWN THE ISLANDS; a Voyage to the Caribbees. Illustrations. Demy 8vo. 16*s*.

PAUL (*C. Kegan*)—BIOGRAPHICAL SKETCHES. Printed on hand-made paper, bound in buckram. Second Edition. Crown 8vo. 7*s*. 6*d*.

PEARSON (*Rev. S.*)—WEEK-DAY LIVING. A Book for Young Men and Women. Second Edition. Crown 8vo. 5*s*.

PENRICE (*Major J.*)—ARABIC AND ENGLISH DICTIONARY OF THE KORAN. 4to. 21*s*.

PESCHEL (*Dr. Oscar*)—THE RACES OF MAN AND THEIR GEOGRAPHICAL DISTRIBUTION. Second Edition, large crown 8vo. 9*s*.

PETERS (*F. H.*)—THE NICOMACHEAN ETHICS OF ARISTOTLE. Translated by. Crown 8vo. 6*s*.

PIDGEON (*D.*)—AN ENGINEER'S HOLIDAY; or, Notes of a Round Trip from Long. 0° to 0°. New and Cheaper Edition. Large crown 8vo. 7*s*. 6*d*.

OLD WORLD QUESTIONS AND NEW WORLD ANSWERS. Large crown 8vo. 7*s*. 6*d*.

PLAIN THOUGHTS FOR MEN. Eight Lectures delivered at the Foresters' Hall, Clerkenwell, during the London Mission, 1884. Crown 8vo. 1*s*. 6*d*.; paper covers, 1*s*.

PLOWRIGHT (*C. B.*)—THE BRITISH UREDINEÆ AND USTILAGINEÆ. With Illustrations. Demy 8vo. 10*s*. 6*d*.

POE (*Edgar Allan*)—Works of. With an Introduction and a Memoir by Richard Henry Stoddard. In 6 vols. with Frontispieces and Vignettes. Large crown 8vo. 6*s*. each vol.

PRICE (*Prof. Bonamy*)—Chapters on Practical Political Economy. Being the Substance of Lectures delivered before the University of Oxford. New and Cheaper Edition. Large post 8vo. 5*s*.

Prig's Bede: The Venerable Bede Expurgated, Expounded, and Exposed. By the Prig, Author of 'The Life of a Prig.' Fcp. 8vo. 3*s*. 6*d*.

Prigment (The). A Collection of 'The Prig' Books. Crown 8vo. 6*s*.

Pulpit Commentary (The). Old Testament Series. Edited by the Rev. J. S. Exell and the Very Rev. Dean H. D. M. Spence.

Genesis. By Rev. T. Whitelaw, M.A. With Homilies by the Very Rev. J. F. Montgomery, D.D., Rev. Prof. R. A. Redford, M.A., LL.B., Rev. F. Hastings, Rev. W. Roberts, M.A.; an Introduction to the Study of the Old Testament by the Venerable Archdeacon Farrar, D.D., F.R.S.; and Introductions to the Pentateuch by the Right Rev. H. Cotterill, D.D., and Rev. T. Whitelaw, M.A. Eighth Edition. One vol. 15*s*.

Exodus. By the Rev. Canon Rawlinson. With Homilies by Rev. J. Orr, Rev. D. Young, Rev. C. A. Goodhart, Rev. J. Urquhart, and Rev. H. T. Robjohns. Fourth Edition. Two vols. each 9*s*.

Leviticus. By the Rev. Prebendary Meyrick, M.A. With Introductions by Rev. R. Collins, Rev. Professor A. Cave, and Homilies by Rev. Prof. Redford, LL.B., Rev. J. A. Macdonald, Rev. W. Clarkson, Rev. S. R. Aldridge, LL.B., and Rev. McCheyne Edgar. Fourth Edition. 15*s*.

Numbers. By the Rev R. Winterbotham, LL.B. With Homilies by the Rev. Professor W. Binnie, D.D., Rev. E. S. Prout, M.A., Rev. D. Young, Rev. J. Waite; and an Introduction by the Rev. Thomas Whitelaw, M.A. Fifth Edition. 15*s*.

Deuteronomy. By Rev. W. L. Alexander, D.D. With Homilies by Rev. D. Davies, M.A., Rev. C. Clemance, D.D., Rev. J. Orr, B.D., and Rev. R. M. Edgar, M.A. Fourth Edition. 15*s*.

Joshua. By Rev. J. J. Lias, M.A. With Homilies by Rev. S. R. Aldridge, LL.B., Rev. R. Glover, Rev. E. De Pressensé, D.D., Rev. J. Waite, B.A. Rev. W. F. Adeney, M.A.; and an Introduction by the Rev. A. Plummer, M.A. Fifth Edition. 12*s*. 6*d*.

Judges and Ruth. By the Bishop of Bath and Wells and Rev. J. Morison, D.D. With Homilies by Rev. A. F. Muir, M.A., Rev. W. F. Adeney, M.A., Rev. W. M. Statham, and Rev. Professor J. Thomson, M.A. Fifth Edition. 10*s*. 6*d*.

1 and 2 Samuel. By the Very Rev. R. P. Smith, D.D. With Homilies by Rev. Donald Fraser, D.D., Rev. Prof. Chapman, Rev. B. Dale, and Rev G. Wood. Vol. I. Sixth Edition, 15*s*. Vol. II. 15*s*.

1 Kings. By the Rev. Joseph Hammond, LL.B. With Homilies by the Rev. E De Pressensé, D.D., Rev. J. Waite, B.A., Rev. A. Rowland, LL.B., Rev. J. A. Macdonald, and Rev. J. Urquhart. Fifth Edition. 15*s*.

1 Chronicles. By the Rev. Prof. P. C. Barker, M.A., LL.B. With Homilies by Rev. Prof. J. R. Thomson, M.A., Rev. R. Tuck, B.A., Rev. W. Clarkson, B.A., Rev. F. Whitfield, M A., and Rev. Richard Glover. 15*s*.

PULPIT COMMENTARY (THE). Old Testament Series—continued.

EZRA, NEHEMIAH, AND ESTHER. By Rev. Canon G. RAWLINSON, M.A. With Homilies by Rev. Prof. J. R. THOMSON, M.A., Rev. Prof. R. A. REDFORD, LL.B., M.A., Rev. W. S. LEWIS, M.A., Rev. J. A. MACDONALD, Rev. A. MACKENNAL, B.A., Rev. W. CLARKSON, B.A., Rev. F. HASTINGS, Rev. W. DINWIDDIE, LL.B., Rev. Prof. ROWLANDS, B.A., Rev. G. WOOD, B.A., Rev. Prof. P. C. BARKER, LL.B., M.A., and Rev. J. S. EXELL, M.A. Sixth Edition. One vol. 12*s.* 6*d.*

ISAIAH. By the Rev. Canon G. RAWLINSON, M.A. With Homilies by Rev. Prof. E. JOHNSON, M.A., Rev. W. CLARKSON, B.A., Rev. W. M. STATHAM, and Rev. R. TUCK, B.A. Second Edition. 2 vols. each 15*s.*

JEREMIAH (Vol. I.). By the Rev. Canon CHEYNE, D.D. With Homilies by the Rev W. F. ADENEY, M.A., Rev. A. F. MUIR, M.A., Rev. S. CONWAY, B.A., Rev. J. WAITE, B.A., and Rev. D. YOUNG, B.A. Third Edition. 15*s.*

JEREMIAH (Vol. II.), AND LAMENTATIONS. By the Rev. Canon CHEYNE, D.D. With Homilies by Rev. Prof. J. R. THOMSON, M.A., Rev. W. F. ADENEY, M.A., Rev. A. F. MUIR, M.A., Rev. S. CONWAY, B.A., Rev. D. YOUNG, B.A. 15*s.*

HOSEA AND JOEL. By the Rev. Prof. J. J. GIVEN, Ph.D., D.D. With Homilies by the Rev. Prof. J. R. THOMSON, M.A., Rev. A. ROWLAND, B.A., LL.B., Rev. C. JERDAN, M.A., LL.B., Rev. J. ORR, M.A., B.D., and Rev. D. THOMAS, D.D. 15*s.*

PULPIT COMMENTARY (THE). New Testament Series.

ST. MARK. By the Very Rev. E. BICKERSTETH, D.D., Dean of Lichfield. With Homilies by the Rev. Prof. THOMSON, M.A., Rev. Prof. GIVEN, M.A., Rev. Prof. JOHNSON, M.A., Rev. A. ROWLAND, LL.B., Rev. A. MUIR, M.A., and Rev. R. GREEN. Fifth Edition. 2 vols. each 10*s.* 6*d.*

ST. JOHN. By the Rev. Prof. H. R. REYNOLDS, D.D. With Homilies by Rev. Prof. T. CROSKERY, D.D., Rev. Prof. J. R. THOMSON, Rev. D. YOUNG, Rev. B. THOMAS, and Rev. G. BROWN. 2 vols. each 15*s.*

THE ACTS OF THE APOSTLES. By the Bishop of BATH AND WELLS. With Homilies by Rev. Prof. P. C. BARKER, M.A., Rev. Prof. E. JOHNSON, M.A., Rev. Prof. R. A. REDFORD, M.A., Rev. R. TUCK, B.A., Rev. W. CLARKSON, B.A. Fourth Edition. Two vols. each 10*s.* 6*d.*

I CORINTHIANS. By the Ven. Archdeacon FARRAR, D.D. With Homilies by Rev. Ex-Chancellor LIPSCOMB, LL.D., Rev. DAVID THOMAS, D.D., Rev. DONALD FRASER, D.D., Rev. Prof. J. R. THOMSON, M.A., Rev. R. TUCK, B.A., Rev. E. HURNDALL, M.A., Rev. J. WAITE, B.A., Rev. H. BREMNER, B.D. Third Edition. 15*s.*

II CORINTHIANS AND GALATIANS. By the Ven. Archdeacon FARRAR, D.D., and Rev. Preb. E. HUXTABLE. With Homilies by Rev. Ex-Chancellor LIPSCOMB, LL.D., Rev. DAVID THOMAS, D.D., Rev. DONALD FRASER, D.D., Rev. R. TUCK, B.A., Rev. E. HURNDALL, M.A., Rev. Prof. J. R. THOMSON, M.A., Rev. R. FINLAYSON, B.A., Rev. W. F. ADENEY, M.A., Rev. R. M. EDGAR, M.A., and Rev. T. CROSKERY, D.D. 21*s.*

EPHESIANS, PHILIPPIANS, AND COLOSSIANS. By the Rev. Prof. W. G. BLAIKIE, D.D., Rev. B. C. CAFFIN, M.A., and Rev. G. G. FINDLAY, B.A. With Homilies by Rev. D. THOMAS, D.D., Rev. R. M. EDGAR, M.A., Rev. R. FINLAYSON, B.A., Rev. W. F. ADENEY, M.A., Rev. Prof. T. CROSKERY, D.D., Rev. E. S. PROUT, M.A., Rev. Canon VERNON HUTTON, and Rev. U. R. THOMAS, D.D. Second Edition. 21*s.*

PULPIT COMMENTARY (THE). New Testament Series—continued.

THESSALONIANS, TIMOTHY, TITUS, AND PHILEMON. By the BISHOP OF BATH AND WELLS, Rev. Dr. GLOAG, and Rev. Dr. EALES. With Homilies by the Rev. B. C. CAFFIN, M.A., Rev. R. FINLAYSON, B.A., Rev. Prof. T. CROSKERY, D.D., Rev. W. F. ADENEY, M.A., Rev. W. M. STATHAM, and Rev. D. THOMAS, D.D. 15*s.*

HEBREWS AND JAMES. By the Rev. J. BARMBY, D.D., and Rev. Prebendary E. C. S. GIBSON, M.A. With Homiletics by the Rev. C. JERDAN, M.A., LL.B., and Rev. Prebendary E. C. S. GIBSON. And Homilies by the Rev. W. JONES, Rev. C. NEW, Rev. D. YOUNG, B.A., Rev. J. S. BRIGHT, Rev. T. F. LOCKYER, B.A., and Rev. C. JERDAN, M.A., LL.B. Second Edition. Price 15*s.*

***PUSEY* (*Dr.*)**—SERMONS FOR THE CHURCH'S SEASONS FROM ADVENT TO TRINITY. Selected from the published Sermons of the late EDWARD BOUVERIE PUSEY, D.D. Crown 8vo. 5*s.*

***QUEKETT* (*Rev. William*)**—MY SAYINGS AND DOINGS, WITH REMINISCENCES OF MY LIFE. Demy 8vo. 18*s.*

***RANKE* (*Leopold von*)**—UNIVERSAL HISTORY. The Oldest Historical Group of Nations and the Greeks. Edited by G. W. PROTHERO. Demy 8vo. 16*s.*

***RENDELL* (*J. M.*)**—CONCISE HANDBOOK OF THE ISLAND OF MADEIRA. With Plan of Funchal and Map of the Island. Fcp. 8vo. 1*s.* 6*d.*

***REYNOLDS* (*Rev. J. W.*)**—THE SUPERNATURAL IN NATURE. A Verification by Free Use of Science. Third Edition, revised and enlarged. Demy 8vo. 14*s.*

THE MYSTERY OF MIRACLES. Third and Enlarged Edition. Crown 8vo. 6*s.*

THE MYSTERY OF THE UNIVERSE: Our Common Faith. Demy 8vo. 14*s.*

THE WORLD TO COME: Immortality a Physical Fact. Crown 8vo. 6*s.*

***RIBOT* (*Prof. Th.*)**—HEREDITY: a Psychological Study on its Phenomena, its Laws, its Causes, and its Consequences. Second Edition. Large crown 8vo. 9*s.*

***RIVINGTON* (*Luke*)**—AUTHORITY, OR A PLAIN REASON FOR JOINING THE CHURCH OF ROME. Crown 8vo. 3*s.* 6*d.*

ROBERTSON* (*The late Rev. F. W.*) *M.A.—LIFE AND LETTERS OF. Edited by the Rev. Stopford Brooke, M.A.

I. Two vols., uniform with the Sermons. With Steel Portrait. Crown 8vo. 7*s.* 6*d.*

II. Library Edition, in demy 8vo. with Portrait. 12*s.*

III. A Popular Edition, in 1 vol. Crown 8vo. 6*s.*

SERMONS. Four Series. Small crown 8vo. 3*s.* 6*d.* each.

THE HUMAN RACE, and other Sermons. Preached at Cheltenham, Oxford, and Brighton. New and Cheaper Edition. Small crown 8vo. 3*s.* 6*d.*

NOTES ON GENESIS. New and Cheaper Edition. Small crown 8vo. 3*s.* 6*d.*

EXPOSITORY LECTURES ON ST. PAUL'S EPISTLES TO THE CORINTHIANS. A New Edition. Small crown 8vo. 5*s.*

LECTURES AND ADDRESSES, with other Literary Remains. A New Edition. Small crown 8vo. 5*s.*

AN ANALYSIS OF TENNYSON'S 'IN MEMORIAM.' (Dedicated by Permission to the Poet-Laureate.) Fcp. 8vo. 2*s.*

THE EDUCATION OF THE HUMAN RACE. Translated from the German of Gotthold Ephraim Lessing. Fcp. 8vo. 2*s.* 6*d.*

*** A Portrait of the late Rev. F. W. Robertson, mounted for framing, can be had, 2*s.* 6*d.*

ROGERS (*William*)—REMINISCENCES. Compiled by R. H. HADDEN. With Portrait. Third Edition. Crown 8vo. 6*s*.

ROMANCE OF THE RECUSANTS. By the Author of 'Life of a Prig.' Cr. 8vo. 5*s*.

ROMANES (*G. J.*)—MENTAL EVOLUTION IN ANIMALS. With a Posthumous Essay on Instinct, by CHARLES DARWIN, F.R.S. Demy 8vo. 12*s*.

. MENTAL EVOLUTION IN MAN. Vol. I. 8vo. 14*s*.

ROSMINI SERBATI (*A.*) *Founder of the Institute of Charity*—LIFE. By FATHER LOCKHART. 2 vols. Crown 8vo. 12*s*.

ROSMINI'S ORIGIN OF IDEAS. Translated from the Fifth Italian Edition of the Nuovo Saggio. *Sull' origine delle idee.* 3 vols. Demy 8vo. 10*s*. 6*d*. each.

ROSMINI'S PSYCHOLOGY. 3 vols. Demy 8vo. [Vols. I. & II. now ready, 10*s*. 6*d*. each.

ROSS (*Janet*)—ITALIAN SKETCHES. With 14 full-page Illustrations. Crown 8vo. 7*s*. 6*d*.

RULE (*Martin*) *M.A.*—THE LIFE AND TIMES OF ST. ANSELM, ARCHBISHOP OF CANTERBURY AND PRIMATE OF THE BRITAINS. 2 vols. Demy 8vo. 32*s*.

SAMUEL (*Sydney M.*)—JEWISH LIFE IN THE EAST. Small crown 8vo. 3*s*. 6*d*.

SAYCE (*Rev. Archibald Henry*)—INTRODUCTION TO THE SCIENCE OF LANGUAGE. 2 vols. Second Edition. Large post 8vo. 21*s*.

SCOONES (*W. Baptiste*)—FOUR CENTURIES OF ENGLISH LETTERS: A Selection of 350 Letters by 150 Writers, from the Period of the Paston Letters to the Present Time. Third Edition. Large crown 8vo. 6*s*.

SÉE (*Prof. Germain*)—BACILLARY PHTHISIS OF THE LUNGS. Translated and Edited for English Practitioners, by WILLIAM HENRY WEDDELL, M.R.C.S. Demy 8vo. 10*s*. 6*d*.

SELWYN (*Augustus*) *D.D.*—LIFE. By Canon G. H. CURTEIS. Crown 8vo. 6*s*.

SEYMOUR (*W. Digby*)—HOME RULE AND STATE SUPREMACY. Crown 8vo. 3*s*. 6*d*.

SHAKSPERE—WORKS. The Avon Edition, 12 vols. fcp. 8vo. cloth, 18*s*.; in cloth box, 21*s*.; bound in 6 vols., cloth, 15*s*.

SHAKSPERE—WORKS (An Index to). By EVANGELINE O'CONNOR. Crown 8vo. 5*s*.

SHELLEY (*Percy Bysshe*).—LIFE. By EDWARD DOWDEN, LL.D. With Portraits and Illustrations, 2 vols., demy 8vo. 36*s*.

SHILLITO (*Rev. Joseph*)—WOMANHOOD: its Duties, Temptations, and Privileges. A Book for Young Women. Third Edition. Crown 8vo. 3*s*. 6*d*.

SHOOTING, PRACTICAL HINTS ON. Being a Treatise on the Shot Gun and its Management. By '20-Bore.' With 55 Illustrations. Demy 8vo. 12*s*.

SISTER AUGUSTINE, Superior of the Sisters of Charity at the St. Johannis Hospital at Bonn. Cheap Edition. Large crown 8vo. 4*s*. 6*d*.

SKINNER (JAMES). A Memoir. By the Author of 'Charles Lowder.' With a Preface by Canon CARTER, and Portrait. Large crown 8vo. 7*s*. 6*d*.

*** Also a Cheap Edition, with Portrait. Crown 8vo. 3*s*. 6*d*.

SMEATON (*Donald*).—THE LOYAL KARENS OF BURMAH. Crown 8vo. 4*s*. 6*d*.

SMITH (*Edward*) *M.D., LL.B., F.R.S.*—TUBERCULAR CONSUMPTION IN ITS EARLY AND REMEDIABLE STAGES. Second Edition. Crown 8vo. 6*s*.

SMITH (*L. A.*)—Music of the Waters: Sailors' Chanties, or Working Songs of the Sea of all Maritime Nations. Demy 8vo. 12*s.*

SMITH (*Sir W. Cusack, Bart.*)—Our War Ships. A Naval Essay. Crown 8vo. 5*s.*

Spanish Mystics. By the Editor of 'Many Voices.' Crown 8vo. 5*s.*

Specimens of English Prose Style from Malory to Macaulay. Selected and Annotated, with an Introductory Essay, by George Saintsbury. Large crown 8vo., printed on hand-made paper, parchment antique, or cloth, 12*s.*; vellum, 15*s.*

SPEDDING (*James*)—Reviews and Discussions, Literary, Political, and Historical not relating to Bacon. Demy 8vo. 12*s.* 6*d.*

Evenings with a Reviewer; or, Bacon and Macaulay. With a Prefatory Notice by G. S. Venables, Q.C. 2 vols. Demy 8vo. 18*s.*

STRACHEY (*Sir John*)—Lectures on India. 8vo. 15*s.*

Stray Papers on Education and Scenes from School Life. By B. H. Second Edition. Small crown 8vo. 3*s.* 6*d.*

STREATFEILD (*Rev. G. S.*) *M.A.*—Lincolnshire and the Danes. Large crown 8vo. 7*s.* 6*d.*

STRECKER-WISLICENUS—Organic Chemistry. Translated and Edited, with Extensive Additions, by W. R. Hodgkinson, Ph.D., and A. J. Greenaway, F.I.C. Demy 8vo. 12*s.* 6*d.*

Suakin, 1885; being a Sketch of the Campaign of this Year. By an Officer who was there. Second Edition. Crown 8vo. 2*s.* 6*d.*

SULLY (*James*) *M.A.*—Pessimism: a History and a Criticism. Second Edition. Demy 8vo. 14*s.*

TARRING (*Charles James*) *M.A.*—A Practical Elementary Turkish Grammar. Crown 8vo. 6*s.*

TAYLOR (*Hugh*)—The Morality of Nations. A Study in the Evolution of Ethics. Crown 8vo. 6*s.*

TAYLOR (*Rev. Isaac*)—The Alphabet. An Account of the Origin and Development of Letters. Numerous Tables and Facsimiles. 2 vols. 8vo. 36*s.*

Leaves from an Egyptian Note-book. Crown 8vo. 5*s.*

TAYLOR (*Reynell*) *C.B.*, *C.S.I.*—A Biography. By E. Gambier Parry. With Portrait and Map. Demy 8vo. 14*s.*

THOM (*John Hamilton*)—Laws of Life after the Mind of Christ. Two Series. Crown 8vo. 7*s.* 6*d.* each.

THOMPSON (*Sir H.*)—Diet in Relation to Age and Activity. Fcp. 8vo. cloth, 1*s.* 6*d.*; Paper covers, 1*s.*

TIDMAN (*Paul F.*)—Gold and Silver Money. Part I.—A Plain Statement. Part II.—Objections Answered. Third Edition. Crown 8vo. 1*s.*

Money and Labour. 1*s.* 6*d.*

TODHUNTER (*Dr. J.*)—A Study of Shelley. Crown 8vo. 7*s.*

TOLSTOI (*Count Leo*)—Christ's Christianity. Translated from the Russian. Large crown 8vo. 7*s.* 6*d.*

TRANT (*William*)—Trade Unions; Their Origin and Objects, Influence and Efficacy. Small crown 8vo. 1*s.* 6*d.*; paper covers, 1*s.*

TRENCH (*The late R. C., Archbishop*)—LETTERS AND MEMORIALS. Edited by the Author of 'Charles Lowder, a Biography,' &c. With two Portraits. 2 vols. demy 8vo. 21*s.*

SERMONS NEW AND OLD. Crown 8vo. 6*s.*

WESTMINSTER AND DUBLIN SERMONS. Crown 8vo. 6*s.*

NOTES ON THE PARABLES OF OUR LORD. Fourteenth Edition. 8vo. 12*s.*; Popular Edition, crown 8vo. 7*s.* 6*d.*

NOTES ON THE MIRACLES OF OUR LORD. Twelfth Edition. 8vo. 12*s.*; Popular Edition, crown 8vo. 7*s.* 6*d.*

STUDIES IN THE GOSPELS. Fifth Edition, Revised. 8vo. 10*s.* 6*d.*

BRIEF THOUGHTS AND MEDITATIONS ON SOME PASSAGES IN HOLY Scripture. Third Edition. Crown 8vo. 3*s.* 6*d.*

SYNONYMS OF THE NEW TESTAMENT. Tenth Edition, Enlarged. 8vo. 12*s.*

ON THE AUTHORISED VERSION OF THE NEW TESTAMENT. Second Edition. 8vo. 7*s.*

COMMENTARY ON THE EPISTLE TO THE SEVEN CHURCHES IN ASIA. Fourth Edition, Revised. 8vo. 8*s.* 6*d.*

THE SERMON ON THE MOUNT. An Exposition drawn from the Writings of St. Augustine, with an Essay on his Merits as an Interpreter of Holy Scripture. Fourth Edition, Enlarged. 8vo. 10*s.* 6*d.*

SHIPWRECKS OF FAITH. Three Sermons preached before the University of Cambridge in May 1867. Fcp. 8vo. 2*s.* 6*d.*

LECTURES ON MEDIÆVAL CHURCH HISTORY. Being the Substance of Lectures delivered at Queen's College, London. Second Edition. 8vo. 12*s.*

ENGLISH, PAST AND PRESENT. Thirteenth Edition, Revised and Improved. Fcp. 8vo. 5*s.*

ON THE STUDY OF WORDS. Nineteenth Edition, Revised. Fcp. 8vo. 5*s.*

SELECT GLOSSARY OF ENGLISH WORDS USED FORMERLY IN SENSES DIFFERENT FROM THE PRESENT. Sixth Edition, Revised and Enlarged. Fcp. 8vo. 5*s.*

PROVERBS AND THEIR LESSONS. Seventh Edition, Enlarged. Fcp. 8vo. 4*s.*

POEMS. Collected and Arranged Anew. Ninth Edition. Fcp. 8vo. 7*s.* 6*d.*

POEMS. Library Edition. 2 vols. Small crown 8vo. 10*s.*

SACRED LATIN POETRY. Chiefly Lyrical, Selected and Arranged for Use. Third Edition, Corrected and Improved. Fcp. 8vo. 7*s.*

A HOUSEHOLD BOOK OF ENGLISH POETRY. Selected and Arranged, with Notes. Fourth Edition, Revised. Extra fcp. 8vo. 5*s.* 6*d.*

AN ESSAY ON THE LIFE AND GENIUS OF CALDERON. With Translations from his 'Life's a Dream' and 'Great Theatre of the World.' Second Edition, Revised and Improved. Extra fcp. 8vo. 5*s.* 6*d.*

GUSTAVUS ADOLPHUS IN GERMANY, AND OTHER LECTURES ON THE THIRTY YEARS' WAR. Third Edition, Enlarged. Fcp. 8vo. 4*s.*

PLUTARCH: HIS LIFE, HIS LIVES, AND HIS MORALS. Second Edition, Enlarged. Fcap. 8vo. 3*s.* 6*d.*

REMAINS OF THE LATE MRS. RICHARD TRENCH. Being Selections from her Journals, Letters, and other Papers. New and Cheaper Issue. With Portrait. 8vo. 6*s.*

TUTHILL (*C. A. H.*)—ORIGIN AND DEVELOPMENT OF CHRISTIAN DOGMA. Crown 8vo. 3*s*. 6*d*.

TWINING (*Louisa*)—WORKHOUSE VISITING AND MANAGEMENT DURING TWENTY-FIVE YEARS. Small crown 8vo. 2*s*.

TWO CENTURIES OF IRISH HISTORY. Edited by JAMES BRYCE, M.P. 8vo. 16*s*.

UMLAUFT (*F.*)—THE ALPS. Illustrated. 8vo.

VAL D'EREMAO (*J. P.*) *D.D.*—THE SERPENT OF EDEN. Crown 8vo. 4*s*. 6*d*.

VAUGHAN (*H. Halford*)—NEW READINGS AND RENDERINGS OF SHAKESPEARE'S TRAGEDIES. 3 vols. Demy 8vo. 12*s*. 6*d*. each.

VICARY (*J. Fulford*)—SAGA TIME. With Illustrations. Cr. 8vo. 7*s*. 6*d*.

VOLCKXSOM (*E. W. v.*)—CATECHISM OF ELEMENTARY MODERN CHEMISTRY. Small crown 8vo. 3*s*.

WALPOLE (*Chas. George*)—A SHORT HISTORY OF IRELAND FROM THE EARLIEST TIMES TO THE UNION WITH GREAT BRITAIN. With 5 Maps and Appendices. Third Edition. Crown 8vo. 6*s*.

WARD (*William George*) *Ph.D.*—ESSAYS ON THE PHILOSOPHY OF THEISM. Edited, with an Introduction, by WILFRID WARD. 2 vols. demy 8vo. 21*s*.

WARD (*Wilfrid*)—THE WISH TO BELIEVE: A Discussion concerning the Temper of Mind in which a reasonable Man should undertake Religious Inquiry. Small crown 8vo. 5*s*.

WARNER (*Francis*) *M.D.*—LECTURES ON THE ANATOMY OF MOVEMENT. Crown 8vo. 4*s*. 6*d*.

WARTER (*J. W.*)—AN OLD SHROPSHIRE OAK. 2 vols. demy 8vo. 28*s*.

WEDMORE (*Frederick*)—THE MASTERS OF GENRE PAINTING. With Sixteen Illustrations. Post 8vo. 7*s*. 6*d*.

WHIBLEY (*Charles*)—CAMBRIDGE ANECDOTES. Crown 8vo. 7*s*. 6*d*.

WHITMAN (*Sidney*)—CONVENTIONAL CANT: Its Results and Remedy. Crown 8vo. 6*s*.

WHITNEY (*Prof. William Dwight*)—ESSENTIALS OF ENGLISH GRAMMAR, for the Use of Schools. Second Edition, crown 8vo. 3*s*. 6*d*.

WHITWORTH (*George Clifford*)—AN ANGLO-INDIAN DICTIONARY: a Glossary of Indian Terms used in English. Demy 8vo. cloth, 12*s*.

WILBERFORCE (*Samuel*) *D.D.*—LIFE. By R. G. WILBERFORCE. Crown 8vo. 6*s*.

WILSON (*Mrs. R. F.*)—THE CHRISTIAN BROTHERS: THEIR ORIGIN AND WORK. Crown 8vo. 6*s*.

WOLTMANN (*Dr. Alfred*), *and* *WOERMANN* (*Dr. Karl*)—HISTORY OF PAINTING. Vol. I. Ancient, Early, Christian, and Mediæval Painting. With numerous Illustrations. Super-royal 8vo. 28*s*.; bevelled boards, gilt leaves, 30*s*. Vol. II. The Painting of the Renascence. Cloth, 42*s*.; cloth extra, bevelled boards, 45*s*.

WORDS OF JESUS CHRIST TAKEN FROM THE GOSPELS. Small crown 8vo. 2*s*. 6*d*.

YOUMANS (*Eliza A.*)—FIRST BOOK OF BOTANY. Designed to cultivate the Observing Powers of Children. With 300 Engravings. New and Cheaper Edition. Crown 8vo. 2*s*. 6*d*.

YOUMANS (*Edward L.*) *M.D.*—A CLASS BOOK OF CHEMISTRY, on the Basis of the New System. With 200 Illustrations. Crown 8vo. 5*s*.

YOUNG (*Arthur*).—AXIAL POLARITY OF MAN'S WORD-EMBODIED IDEAS, AND ITS TEACHING. Demy 4to. 15*s*.

THE INTERNATIONAL SCIENTIFIC SERIES.

I. Forms of Water: a Familiar Exposition of the Origin and Phenomena of Glaciers. By J. Tyndall, LL.D., F.R.S. With 25 Illustrations. Ninth Edition. Crown 8vo. 5*s*.

II. Physics and Politics; or, Thoughts on the Application of the Principles of 'Natural Selection' and 'Inheritance' to Political Society. By Walter Bagehot. Eighth Edition. Crown 8vo. 5*s*.

III. Foods. By Edward Smith, M.D., LL.B., F.R.S. With numerous Illustrations. Ninth Edition. Crown 8vo. 5*s*.

IV. Mind and Body: the Theories and their Relation. By Alexander Bain, LL.D. With Four Illustrations. Eighth Edition. Crown 8vo. 5*s*.

V. The Study of Sociology. By Herbert Spencer. Thirteenth Edition. Crown 8vo. 5*s*.

VI. On the Conservation of Energy. By Balfour Stewart, M.A., LL.D., F.R.S. With 14 Illustrations. Seventh Edition. Crown 8vo. 5*s*.

VII. Animal Locomotion; or, Walking, Swimming, and Flying. By J. B. Pettigrew, M.D., F.R.S., &c. With 130 Illustrations. Third Edition. Crown 8vo. 5*s*.

VIII. Responsibility in Mental Disease. By Henry Maudsley, M.D. Fourth Edition. Crown 8vo. 5*s*.

IX. The New Chemistry. By Professor J. P. Cooke. With 31 Illustrations. Ninth Edition, remodelled and enlarged. Crown 8vo. 5*s*.

X. The Science of Law. By Professor Sheldon Amos. Sixth Edition. Crown 8vo. 5*s*.

XI. Animal Mechanism: a Treatise on Terrestrial and Aërial Locomotion. By Professor E. J. Marey. With 117 Illustrations. Third Edition. Crown 8vo. 5*s*.

XII. The Doctrine of Descent and Darwinism. By Professor Oscar Schmidt. With 26 Illustrations. Seventh Edition. Crown 8vo. 5*s*.

XIII. The History of the Conflict between Religion and Science. By J. W. Draper, M.D., LL.D. Twentieth Edition. Crown 8vo. 5*s*.

XIV. Fungi: their Nature, Influences, Uses, &c. By M. C. Cooke, M.D., LL.D. Edited by the Rev. M. J. Berkeley, M.A., F.L.S. With numerous Illustrations. Fourth Edition. Crown 8vo. 5*s*.

XV. The Chemical Effects of Light and Photography. By Dr. Hermann Vogel. Translation thoroughly revised. With 100 Illustrations. Fifth Edition. Crown 8vo. 5*s*.

XVI. The Life and Growth of Language. By Professor William Dwight Whitney. Fifth Edition. Crown 8vo. 5*s*.

XVII. Money and the Mechanism of Exchange. By W. Stanley Jevons, M.A., F.R.S. Eighth Edition. Crown 8vo. 5*s*.

XVIII. The Nature of Light. With a General Account of Physical Optics. By Dr. Eugene Lommel. With 188 Illustrations and a Table of Spectra in Chromo-lithography. Fourth Edit. Crown 8vo. 5*s*.

XIX. Animal Parasites and Messmates. By P. J. Van Beneden. With 83 Illustrations. Third Edition. Crown 8vo. 5*s*.

XX. Fermentation. By Professor Schützenberger. With 28 Illustrations. Fourth Edition. Crown 8vo. 5*s*.

XXI. The Five Senses of Man. By Professor Bernstein. With 91 Illustrations. Fifth Edition. Crown 8vo. 5*s*.

XXII. The Theory of Sound in its Relation to Music. By Professor Pietro Blaserna. With numerous Illustrations. Third Edition. Crown 8vo. 5*s*.

XXIII. Studies in Spectrum Analysis. By J. Norman Lockyer, F.R.S. Fourth Edition. With six Photographic Illustrations of Spectra, and numerous Engravings on Wood. Crown 8vo. 6*s*. 6*d*.

XXIV. A HISTORY OF THE GROWTH OF THE STEAM ENGINE. By Professor R. H. Thurston. With numerous Illustrations. Fourth Edition. Crown 8vo. 5*s*.

XXV. EDUCATION AS A SCIENCE. By Alexander Bain, LL.D. Sixth Edition. Crown 8vo. 5*s*.

XXVI. THE HUMAN SPECIES. By Prof. A. De Quatrefages. Fourth Edition. Crown 8vo. 5*s*.

XXVII. MODERN CHROMATICS. With Applications to Art and Industry. By Ogden N. Rood. With 130 original Illustrations. Second Edition. Crown 8vo. 5*s*.

XXVIII. THE CRAYFISH: an Introduction to the Study of Zoology. By Professor T. H. Huxley. With 82 Illustrations. Fourth Edition. Crown 8vo. 5*s*.

XXIX. THE BRAIN AS AN ORGAN OF MIND. By H. Charlton Bastian, M.D. With numerous Illustrations. Third Edition. Crown 8vo. 5*s*.

XXX. THE ATOMIC THEORY. By Prof. Wurtz. Translated by G. Cleminshaw, F.C.S. Fifth Edition. Crown 8vo. 5*s*.

XXXI. THE NATURAL CONDITIONS OF EXISTENCE AS THEY AFFECT ANIMAL LIFE. By Karl Semper. With 2 Maps and 106 Woodcuts. Third Edition. Crown 8vo. 5*s*.

XXXII. GENERAL PHYSIOLOGY OF MUSCLES AND NERVES. By Prof. J. Rosenthal. Third Edition. With Illustrations. Crown 8vo. 5*s*.

XXXIII. SIGHT: an Exposition of the Principles of Monocular and Binocular Vision. By Joseph Le Conte, LL.D. Second Edition. With 132 Illustrations. Crown 8vo. 5*s*.

XXXIV. ILLUSIONS: a Psychological Study. By James Sully. Third Edition. Crown 8vo. 5*s*.

XXXV. VOLCANOES: WHAT THEY ARE AND WHAT THEY TEACH. By Professor J. W. Judd, F.R.S. With 92 Illustrations on Wood. Fourth Edition. Crown 8vo. 5*s*.

XXXVI. SUICIDE: an Essay on Comparative Moral Statistics. By Prof. H. Morselli. Second Edition. With Diagrams. Crown 8vo. 5*s*.

XXXVII. THE BRAIN AND ITS FUNCTIONS. By J. Luys. Second Edition. With Illustrations. Crown 8vo. 5*s*.

XXXVIII. MYTH AND SCIENCE: an Essay. By Tito Vignoli. Third Edition. Crown 8vo. 5*s*.

XXXIX. THE SUN. By Professor Young. With Illustrations. Third Edition. Crown 8vo. 5*s*.

XL. ANTS, BEES, AND WASPS: a Record of Observations on the Habits of the Social Hymenoptera. By Sir John Lubbock, Bart., M.P. With 5 Chromolithographic Illustrations. Ninth Edition. Crown 8vo 5*s*.

XLI. ANIMAL INTELLIGENCE. By G. J. Romanes, LL.D., F.R.S. Fourth Edition. Crown 8vo. 5*s*.

XLII. THE CONCEPTS AND THEORIES OF MODERN PHYSICS. By J. B. Stallo. Third Edition. Crown 8vo. 5*s*.

XLIII. DISEASES OF MEMORY: an Essay in the Positive Pyschology. By Prof. Th. Ribot. Third Edition. Crown 8vo. 5*s*.

XLIV. MAN BEFORE METALS. By N. Joly. Fourth Edition. Crown 8vo. 5*s*.

XLV. THE SCIENCE OF POLITICS. By Prof. Sheldon Amos. Third Edit. Crown. 8vo. 5*s*.

XLVI. ELEMENTARY METEOROLOGY. By Robert H. Scott. Fourth Edition. With numerous Illustrations. Crown 8vo. 5*s*.

XLVII. THE ORGANS OF SPEECH AND THEIR APPLICATION IN THE FORMATION OF ARTICULATE SOUNDS By Georg Hermann von Meyer. With 47 Woodcuts. Crown 8vo. 5*s*.

XLVIII. FALLACIES: a View of Logic from the Practical Side. By Alfred Sidgwick. Second Edition. Crown 8vo. 5*s*.

XLIX. ORIGIN OF CULTIVATED PLANTS. By Alphonse de Candolle. Second Edition. Crown 8vo. 5*s*.

L. JELLY FISH, STAR FISH, AND SEA URCHINS. Being a Research on Primitive Nervous Systems. By G. J. Romanes. Crown 8vo. 5*s*.

LI. THE COMMON SENSE OF THE EXACT SCIENCES. By the late William Kingdon Clifford. Second Edition. With 100 Figures. 5*s*.

LII. PHYSICAL EXPRESSION: ITS MODES AND PRINCIPLES. By Francis Warner, M.D., F.R.C.P. With 50 Illustrations. 5*s*.

LIII. ANTHROPOID APES. By Robert Hartmann. With 63 Illustrations. 5*s*.

LIV. THE MAMMALIA IN THEIR RELATION TO PRIMEVAL TIMES. By Oscar Schmidt. With 51 Woodcuts. 5*s*.

LV. COMPARATIVE LITERATURE. By H. Macaulay Posnett, LL.D. 5*s*.

LVI. EARTHQUAKES AND OTHER EARTH MOVEMENTS. By Prof. JOHN MILNE. With 38 Figures. Second Edition. 5*s*.

LVII. MICROBES, FERMENTS, AND MOULDS. By E. L. TROUESSART. With 107 Illustrations. 5*s*.

LVIII. GEOGRAPHICAL AND GEOLOGICAL DISTRIBUTION OF ANIMALS. By Professor A. Heilprin. With Frontispiece. 5*s*.

LIX. WEATHER. A Popular Exposition of the Nature of Weather Changes from Day to Day. By the Hon. Ralph Abercromby. With 96 Illustrations. Second Edition. 5*s*.

LX. ANIMAL MAGNETISM. By Alfred Binet and Charles Féré. 5*s*.

LXI. MANUAL OF BRITISH DISCOMYCETES, with descriptions of all the Species of Fungi hitherto found in Britain included in the Family, and Illustrations of the Genera. By William Phillips, F.L.S. 5*s*.

LXII. INTERNATIONAL LAW. With Materials for a Code of International Law. By Professor Leone Levi. 5*s*.

LXIII. THE GEOLOGICAL HISTORY OF PLANTS. By Sir J. William Dawson. With 80 Illustrations. 5*s*.

LXIV. THE ORIGIN OF FLORAL STRUCTURES THROUGH INSECT AND OTHER AGENCIES. By Professor G. Henslow.

LXV. ON THE SENSES, INSTINCTS, AND INTELLIGENCE OF ANIMALS. With special Reference to Insects. By Sir John Lubbock, Bart., M.P. 100 Illustrations. 5*s*.

MILITARY WORKS.

BARRINGTON (Capt. J. T.)—ENGLAND ON THE DEFENSIVE; or, the Problem of Invasion Critically Examined. Large crown 8vo. with Map, 7*s*. 6*d*.

BRACKENBURY (Col. C. B.) R.A.—MILITARY HANDBOOKS FOR REGIMENTAL OFFICERS:

I. MILITARY SKETCHING AND RECONNAISSANCE. By Colonel F. J. Hutchison and Major H. G. MacGregor. Fifth Edition. With 15 Plates. Small crown 8vo. 4*s*.

II. THE ELEMENTS OF MODERN TACTICS PRACTICALLY APPLIED TO ENGLISH FORMATIONS. By Lieut.-Col. Wilkinson Shaw. Sixth Edit. With 25 Plates and Maps. Small crown 8vo. 9*s*.

III. FIELD ARTILLERY: its Equipment, Organisation, and Tactics. By Major Sisson C. Pratt, R.A. With 12 Plates. Third Edition. Small crown 8vo. 6*s*.

IV. THE ELEMENTS OF MILITARY ADMINISTRATION. First Part: Permanent System of Administration. By Major J. W. Buxton. Small crown 8vo. 7*s*. 6*d*.

BRACKENBURY (Col. C. B.) R.A.—continued.

V. MILITARY LAW: its Procedure and Practice. By Major Sisson C. Pratt, R.A. Third Edition. Small crown 8vo. 4*s*. 6d.

VI. CAVALRY IN MODERN WAR. By Major-General F. Chenevix Trench. Small crown 8vo. 6*s*.

VII. FIELD WORKS. Their Technical Construction and Tactical Application. By the Editor, Col. C. B. Brackenbury, R.A. Small crown 8vo.

BROOKE (Major C. K.)—A SYSTEM OF FIELD TRAINING. Small crown 8vo. 2*s*.

CLERY (Col. C. Francis) C.B.—MINOR TACTICS. With 26 Maps and Plans. Eighth Edition. Crown 8vo. 9*s*.

COLVILE (Lieut.-Col. C. F.)—MILITARY TRIBUNALS. Sewed, 2*s*. 6*d*.

CRAUFURD (Capt. H. J.)—SUGGESTIONS FOR THE MILITARY TRAINING OF A COMPANY OF INFANTRY. Crown 8vo. 1*s*. 6*d*.

HAMILTON (*Capt. Ian*) *A.D.C.*—THE FIGHTING OF THE FUTURE. 1*s.*

HARRISON (*Lieut.-Col. R.*) — THE OFFICER'S MEMORANDUM BOOK FOR PEACE AND WAR. Fourth Edition. Oblong 32mo. roan, with pencil, 3*s.* 6*d.*

NOTES ON CAVALRY TACTICS, ORGANISATION, &c. By a Cavalry Officer. With Diagrams. Demy 8vo. 12*s.*

PARR (*Col. H. Hallam*) *C.M.G.*—THE DRESS, HORSES, AND EQUIPMENT OF INFANTRY AND STAFF OFFICERS. Crown 8vo. 1*s.*

FURTHER TRAINING AND EQUIPMENT OF MOUNTED INFANTRY. Crown 8vo. 1*s.*

SCHAW (*Col. H.*)—THE DEFENCE AND ATTACK OF POSITIONS AND LOCALITIES. Third Edition, revised and corrected. Crown 8vo. 3*s.* 6*d.*

STONE (*Capt. F. Gleadowe*) *R.A.*—TACTICAL STUDIES FROM THE FRANCO-GERMAN WAR OF 1870-71. With 22 Lithographic Sketches and Maps. Demy 8vo. 10*s.* 6*d.*

THE CAMPAIGN OF FREDERICKSBURG, November-December, 1862: a Study for Officers of Volunteers. By a Line Officer. Second Edition. Crown 8vo. With Five Maps and Plans. 5*s.*

WILKINSON (*H. Spenser*) *Capt. 20th Lancashire R.V.*—CITIZEN SOLDIERS. Essays towards the Improvement of the Volunteer Force. Cr. 8vo. 2*s.* 6*d.*

POETRY.

ADAM OF ST. VICTOR—THE LITURGICAL POETRY OF ADAM OF ST. VICTOR. From the text of Gautier. With Translations into English in the Original Metres, and Short Explanatory Notes. By Digby S. Wrangham, M.A. 3 vols. Crown 8vo. printed on hand-made paper, boards, 21*s.*

ALEXANDER (*William*) *D.D., Bishop of Derry*—ST. AUGUSTINE'S HOLIDAY, and other Poems. Crown 8vo. 6*s.*

AUCHMUTY (*A. C.*)—POEMS OF ENGLISH HEROISM: From Brunanburgh to Lucknow; from Athelstan to Albert. Small crown 8vo. 1*s.* 6*d.*

BARNES (*William*)—POEMS OF RURAL LIFE, IN THE DORSET DIALECT. New Edition, complete in one vol. Crown 8vo. 6*s.*

BAYNES (*Rev. Canon H. R.*)—HOME SONGS FOR QUIET HOURS. Fourth and cheaper Edition. Fcp. 8vo. 2*s.* 6*d.*

BEVINGTON (*L. S.*)—KEY NOTES. Small crown 8vo. 5*s.*

BLUNT (*Wilfrid Scawen*)—THE WIND AND THE WHIRLWIND. Demy 8vo. 1*s.* 6*d.*

THE LOVE SONNETS OF PROTEUS. Fifth Edition. 18mo. cloth extra, gilt top, 5*s.*

BOWEN (*H. C.*) *M.A.*—SIMPLE ENGLISH POEMS. English Literature for Junior Classes. In Four Parts. Parts I. II. and III. 6*d.* each, and Part IV. 1*s.*, complete 3*s.*

BRYANT (*W. C.*) — POEMS. Cheap Edition, with Frontispiece. Small crown 8vo. 3*s.* 6*d.*

CALDERON'S DRAMAS: the Wonder-working Magician—Life is a Dream—the Purgatory of St. Patrick. Translated by Denis Florence MacCarthy. Post 8vo. 10*s.*

CAMPBELL (*Lewis*)—SOPHOCLES. The Seven Plays in English Verse. Crown 8vo. 7*s.* 6*d.*

CERVANTES. — JOURNEY TO PARNASSUS. Spanish Text, with Translation into English Tercets, Preface, and Illustrative Notes, by JAMES Y. GIBSON. Crown 8vo. 12*s.*

NUMANTIA; a Tragedy. Translated from the Spanish, with Introduction and Notes, by JAMES Y. GIBSON. Crown 8vo., printed on hand-made paper, 5*s.*

CID BALLADS, and other Poems. Translated from Spanish and German by J. Y. Gibson. 2 vols. Crown 8vo. 12*s.*

CHRISTIE (*A. J.*)—THE END OF MAN. Fourth Edition. Fcp. 8vo. 2*s.* 6*d.*

COXHEAD (*Ethel*)—BIRDS AND BABIES. Imp. 16mo. With 33 Illustrations. 1*s.*

DANTE—THE DIVINA COMMEDIA OF DANTE ALIGHIERI. Translated, line for line, in the 'Terza Rima' of the original, with Notes, by FREDERICK K. H. HASELFOOT, M.A. Demy 8vo. 16*s.*

DE BERANGER.—A SELECTION FROM HIS SONGS. In English Verse. By WILLIAM TOYNBEE. Small crown 8vo. 2*s.* 6*d.*

DENNIS (*J.*) — ENGLISH SONNETS. Collected and Arranged by. Small crown 8vo. 2*s.* 6*d.*

DE VERE (*Aubrey*)—POETICAL WORKS:
I. THE SEARCH AFTER PROSERPINE, &c. 6*s.*
II. THE LEGENDS OF ST. PATRICK, &c. 6*s.*
III. ALEXANDER THE GREAT, &c. 6*s.*

THE FORAY OF QUEEN MEAVE, and other Legends of Ireland's Heroic Age. Small crown 8vo. 5*s.*

LEGENDS OF THE SAXON SAINTS. Small crown 8vo. 6*s.*

LEGENDS AND RECORDS OF THE CHURCH AND THE EMPIRE. Small crown 8vo. 6*s.*

DOBSON (*Austin*)—OLD WORLD IDYLLS, and other Verses. Eighth Edition. Elzevir 8vo. cloth extra, gilt tops, 6*s.*

AT THE SIGN OF THE LYRE. Fifth Edition. Elzevir 8vo., gilt top, 6*s.*

DOWDEN (*Edward*) *LL.D.*—SHAKSPERE'S SONNETS. With Introduction and Notes. Large post 8vo. 7*s.* 6*d.*

DUTT (*Toru*)—A SHEAF GLEANED IN FRENCH FIELDS. New Edition. Demy 8vo. 10*s.* 6*d.*

ANCIENT BALLADS AND LEGENDS OF HINDUSTAN. With an Introductory Memoir by EDMUND GOSSE. Second Edition. 18mo. Cloth extra, gilt top, 5*s.*

ELLIOTT (*Ebenezer*), *The Corn Law Rhymer*—POEMS. Edited by his Son, the Rev. Edwin Elliott, of St. John's, Antigua. 2 vols. crown 8vo. 18*s.*

ENGLISH VERSE. Edited by W. J. LINTON and R. H. STODDARD. In 5 vols. Crown 8vo. each 5*s.*

1. CHAUCER TO BURNS.
2. TRANSLATIONS.
3. LYRICS OF THE NINETEENTH CENTURY.
4. DRAMATIC SCENES AND CHARACTERS.
5. BALLADS AND ROMANCES.

EVANS (*Anne*)—POEMS AND MUSIC. With Memorial Preface by ANN THACKERAY RITCHIE. Large crown 8vo. 7*s.*

GOSSE (*Edmund W.*)—NEW POEMS. Crown 8vo. 7*s.* 6*d.*

FIRDAUSI IN EXILE, and other Poems. Elzevir 8vo. gilt top, 6*s.*

GURNEY (*Rev. Alfred*)—THE VISION OF THE EUCHARIST, and other Poems. Crown 8vo. 5*s.*

A CHRISTMAS FAGGOT. Small crown 8vo. 5*s.*

HARRISON (*Clifford*)—IN HOURS OF LEISURE. Second Edition. Crown 8vo. 5*s.*

KEATS (*John*) — POETICAL WORKS. Edited by W. T. ARNOLD. Large crown 8vo. choicely printed on hand-made paper, with Portrait in *eau forte*. Parchment, or cloth, 12*s.*; vellum, 15*s.*

Also, a smaller Edition. Crown 8vo. 3*s.* 6*d.*

KING (*Mrs. Hamilton*)—THE DISCIPLES. Eighth Edition, with Portrait and Notes. Crown 8vo. 5*s.* Elzevir Edition, 6*s.*

A BOOK OF DREAMS. Third Edition. Crown 8vo. 3*s.* 6*d.*

THE SERMON IN THE HOSPITAL. Reprinted from 'The Disciples.' Fcp. 8vo. 1*s.* Cheap Edition, 3*d.*, or 20*s.* per 100.

KNOX (*The Hon. Mrs. O. N.*)—FOUR PICTURES FROM A LIFE, and other Poems. Small crown 8vo. 3*s.* 6*d.*

LANG (*A.*)—XXXII BALLADES IN BLUE CHINA. Elzevir 8vo. parchment, or cloth, 5*s.*

RHYMES À LA MODE. With Frontispiece by E. A. Abbey. Elzevir 8vo. cloth extra, gilt top, 5*s.*

LAWSON (*Right Hon. Mr. Justice*)—HYMNI USITATI LATINE REDDITI, with other Verses. Small 8vo. parchment, 5*s.*

LIVING ENGLISH POETS. MDCCCLXXXII. With Frontispiece by Walter Crane. Second Edition. Large crown 8vo. printed on hand-made paper. Parchment, or cloth, 12*s.*; vellum, 15*s.*

LOCKER (*F.*)—LONDON LYRICS. New Edition, with Portrait. 18mo. cloth extra, gilt tops, 5*s.*

LOVE IN IDLENESS. A Volume of Poems. With an etching by W. B. Scott. Small crown 8vo. 5*s.*

LUMSDEN (Lieut.-Col. H. W.)—BEOWULF: an Old English Poem. Translated into Modern Rhymes. Second and revised Edition. Small crown 8vo. 5*s.*

MAGNUSSON (Eirikr) M.A., and PALMER (E. H.) M.A.—JOHAN LUDVIG RUNEBERG'S LYRICAL SONGS, IDYLLS, AND EPIGRAMS. Fcp. 8vo. 5*s.*

MEREDITH (Owen) [The Earl of Lytton]—LUCILE. New Edition. With 32 Illustrations. 16mo. 3*s.* 6*d.*; cloth extra, gilt edges, 4*s.* 6*d.*

MORRIS (Lewis)—POETICAL WORKS. New and Cheaper Editions, with Portrait, complete in 4 vols. 5*s.* each.

Vol. I. contains Songs of Two Worlds. Twelfth Edition.

Vol. II. contains The Epic of Hades. Twenty-second Edition.

Vol. III. contains Gwen and the Ode of Life. Seventh Edition.

Vol. IV. contains Songs Unsung and Gycia. Fifth Edition.

SONGS OF BRITAIN. Third Edition. Fcp. 8vo. 5*s.*

THE EPIC OF HADES. With 16 Autotype Illustrations after the drawings by the late George R. Chapman. 4to. cloth extra, gilt leaves, 21*s.*

THE EPIC OF HADES. Presentation Edit. 4to. cloth extra, gilt leaves, 10*s.* 6*d.*

THE LEWIS MORRIS BIRTHDAY BOOK. Edited by S. S. Copeman. With Frontispiece after a design by the late George R. Chapman. 32mo. cloth extra, gilt edges, 2*s.*; cloth limp, 1*s.* 6*d.*

MORSHEAD (E. D. A.)—THE HOUSE OF ATREUS. Being the Agamemnon, Libation-Bearers, and Furies of Æschylus. Translated into English Verse. Crown 8vo. 7*s.*

THE SUPPLIANT MAIDENS OF ÆSCHYLUS. Crown 8vo. 3*s.* 6*d.*

MULHOLLAND (Rosa). — VAGRANT VERSES. Small crown 8vo. 5*s.*

NADEN (Constance C. W.)—A MODERN APOSTLE, and other Poems. Small crown 8vo. 5*s.*

NOEL (The Hon. Roden)—A LITTLE CHILD'S MONUMENT. Third Edition. Small crown 8vo. 3*s.* 6*d.*

THE RED FLAG, and other Poems. New Edition. Small crown 8vo. 6*s.*

THE HOUSE OF RAVENSBURG. New Edition. Small crown 8vo. 6*s.*

NOEL (The Hon. Roden)—continued.

SONGS OF THE HEIGHTS AND DEEPS. Crown 8vo. 6*s.*

A MODERN FAUST. Small crown 8vo.

O'BRIEN (Charlotte Grace)—LYRICS. Small crown 8vo. 3*s.* 6*d.*

O'HAGAN (John)—THE SONG OF ROLAND. Translated into English Verse. New and Cheaper Edition. Crown 8vo. 5*s.*

PFEIFFER (Emily)—THE RHYME OF THE LADY OF THE ROCK AND HOW IT GREW. Small crown 8vo. 3*s.* 6*d.*

GERARD'S MONUMENT, and other Poems. Second Edition. Crown 8vo. 6*s.*

UNDER THE ASPENS: Lyrical and Dramatic. With Portrait. Crown 8vo. 6*s.*

PIATT (J. J.)—IDYLS AND LYRICS OF THE OHIO VALLEY. Crown 8vo. 5*s.*

PIATT (Sarah M. B.)—A VOYAGE TO THE FORTUNATE ISLES, and other Poems. 1 vol. Small crown 8vo. gilt top, 5*s.*

IN PRIMROSE TIME. A New Irish Garland. Small crown 8vo. 2*s.* 6*d.*

RARE POEMS OF THE 16TH AND 17TH CENTURIES. Edited by W. J. Linton. Crown 8vo. 5*s.*

RHOADES (James)—THE GEORGICS OF VIRGIL. Translated into English Verse. Small crown 8vo. 5*s.*

ROBINSON (A. Mary F.)—A HANDFUL OF HONEYSUCKLE. Fcp. 8vo. 3*s.* 6*d.*

THE CROWNED HIPPOLYTUS. Translated from Euripides. With New Poems. Small crown 8vo. cloth, 5*s.*

SHAKSPERE'S WORKS. The Avon Edition, 12 vols. fcp. 8vo. cloth, 18*s.*; and in box, 21*s.*; bound in 6 vols. cloth, 15*s.*

SOPHOCLES: The Seven Plays in English Verse. Translated by Lewis Campbell. Crown 8vo. 7*s.* 6*d.*

SYMONDS (John Addington)—VAGABUNDULI LIBELLUS. Crown 8vo. 6*s.*

TAYLOR (Sir H.)—Works Complete in Five Volumes. Crown 8vo. 30*s.*

PHILIP VAN ARTEVELDE. Fcp. 8vo. 3*s.* 6*d.*

THE VIRGIN WIDOW, &c. Fcp. 8vo. 3*s.* 6*d.*

THE STATESMAN. Fcp. 8vo. 3*s.* 6*d.*

TODHUNTER (*Dr. J.*) — LAURELLA, and other Poems. Crown 8vo. 6*s.* 6*d.*

FOREST SONGS. Small crown 8vo. 3*s.* 6*d.*

THE TRUE TRAGEDY OF RIENZI: a Drama. Crown 8vo. 3*s.* 6*d.*

ALCESTIS: a Dramatic Poem. Extra fcp. 8vo. 5*s.*

HELENA IN TROAS. Small crown 8vo. 2*s.* 6*d.*

TYNAN (*Katherine*)—LOUISE DE LA VALLIERE, and other Poems. Small crown 8vo. 3*s.* 6*d.*

SHAMROCKS. Small crown 8vo. 5*s.*

VICTORIAN HYMNS: English Sacred Songs of Fifty Years. Dedicated to the Queen. Large post 8vo. 10*s.* 6*d.*

WATTS (*Alaric Alfred and Emma Mary Howitt*) — AURORA: a Medley of Verse. Fcp. 8vo. 5*s.*

WORDSWORTH — SELECTIONS. By Members of the Wordsworth Society. Large crown 8vo parchment, 12*s.*; vellum, 15*s.* Also, cr. 8vo. cl. 4*s.* 6*d.*

WORDSWORTH BIRTHDAY BOOK, THE. Edited by ADELAIDE and VIOLET WORDSWORTH. 32mo. limp cloth, 1*s.* 6*d.*; cloth extra, 2*s.*

WORKS OF FICTION.

'ALL BUT:' a Chronicle of Laxenford Life. By PEN OLIVER, F.R.C.S. With 20 Illustrations. Second Edit. Crown 8vo. 6*s.*

BANKS (*Mrs. G. L.*)—GOD'S PROVIDENCE HOUSE. New Edition. Crown 8vo. 6*s.*

CHICHELE (*Mary*)—DOING AND UNDOING: a Story. Crown 8vo. 4*s.* 6*d.*

CRAWFURD (*Oswald*)—SYLVIA ARDEN. Crown 8vo. 6*s.*

GARDINER (*Linda*)—HIS HERITAGE. Crown 8vo. 6*s.*

GRAY (*Maxwell*)—THE SILENCE OF DEAN MAITLAND. Fourth Edition. Crown 8vo. 6*s.*

GREY (*Rowland*)—BY VIRTUE OF HIS OFFICE. Crown 8vo. 6*s.*

IN SUNNY SWITZERLAND. Small crown 8vo. 5*s.*

LINDENBLUMEN, and other Stories. Small crown 8vo. 5*s.*

HUNTER (*Hay*)—CRIME OF CHRISTMAS DAY. A Tale of the Latin Quarter. By the Author of 'My Ducats and My Daughter.' 1*s.*

HUNTER (*Hay*) *and WHYTE* (*Walter*) MY DUCATS AND MY DAUGHTER. New and Cheaper Edition. With Frontispiece. Crown 8vo. 6*s.*

INGELOW (*Jean*)—OFF THE SKELLIGS. A Novel. With Frontispiece. Second Edition. Crown 8vo. 6*s.*

INORA. A Mystery. Crown 8vo. 6*s.*

JENKINS (*Edward*)—A SECRET OF TWO LIVES. Crown 8vo. 2*s.* 6*d.*

KIELLAND (*Alexander L.*)—GARMAN AND WORSE. A Norwegian Novel. Authorised Translation by W. W. Kettlewell. Crown 8vo. 6*s.*

LANG (*Andrew*)—IN THE WRONG PARADISE, and other Stories. Crown 8vo. 6*s.*

MACDONALD (*G.*)—DONAL GRANT. Crown 8vo. 6*s.*

CASTLE WARLOCK. Crown 8vo. 6*s.*

MALCOLM. With Portrait of the Author engraved on Steel. Crown 8vo. 6*s.*

THE MARQUIS OF LOSSIE. Crown 8vo. 6*s.*

ST. GEORGE AND ST. MICHAEL. Crown 8vo. 6*s.*

PAUL FABER, SURGEON. Crown 8vo. 6*s.*

THOMAS WINGFOLD, CURATE. Crown 8vo. 6*s.*

WHAT'S MINE'S MINE. Second Edition. Crown 8vo. 6*s.*

ANNALS OF A QUIET NEIGHBOURHOOD. Crown 8vo. 6*s.*

THE SEABOARD PARISH: a Sequel to 'Annals of a Quiet Neighbourhood.' Crown 8vo. 6*s.*

WILFRED CUMBERMEDE. An Autobiographical Story. Crown 8vo. 6*s.*

THE ELECT LADY. Crown 8vo. 6*s.*

MALET (*Lucas*)—COLONEL ENDERBY'S WIFE. Crown 8vo. 6*s.*

A COUNSEL OF PERFECTION. Crown 8vo. 6*s.*

MULHOLLAND (*Rosa*) — MARCELLA GRACE. An Irish Novel. Crown 8vo. 6*s.*

A FAIR EMIGRANT. Crown 8vo. 6*s.*

OGLE (*A. C.*) ('*Ashford Owen.*') A LOST LOVE. Small crown 8vo. 2*s.* 6*d.*

PALGRAVE (*W. Gifford*)—HERMANN AGHA: an Eastern Narrative. Third Edition. Crown 8vo. 6*s.*

SEVERNE (*Mrs.*)—THE PILLAR HOUSE. With Frontispiece. Crown 8vo. 6*s.*

SHAW (*Flora L.*)—CASTLE BLAIR; a Story of Youthful Days. New and Cheaper Edition. Crown 8vo. 3*s.* 6*d.*

STRETTON (*Hesba*) — THROUGH A NEEDLE'S EYE. A Story. New and Cheaper Edition, with Frontispiece. Crown 8vo. 6*s.*

TAYLOR (*Col. Meadows*) *C.S.I., M.R.I.A.*
SEETA. A Novel. New and Cheaper Edition. With Frontispiece. Crown 8vo. 6*s.*

TAYLOR (*Col. Meadows*) *C.S.I., M.R.I.A.*—continued.

TIPPOO SULTAUN: a Tale of the Mysore War. New Edition, with Frontispiece. Crown 8vo. 6*s.*

RALPH DARNELL. New and Cheaper Edition. With Frontispiece. Crown 8vo. 6*s.*

A NOBLE QUEEN. New and Cheaper Edition. With Frontispiece. Crown 8vo. 6*s.*

THE CONFESSIONS OF A THUG. Crown 8vo. 6*s.*

TARA: a Mahratta Tale. Crown 8vo. 6*s.*

WITHIN SOUND OF THE SEA. New and Cheaper Edition, with Frontispiece. Crown 8vo. 6*s.*

BOOKS FOR THE YOUNG.

BRAVE MEN'S FOOTSTEPS. A Book of Example and Anecdote for Young People. By the Editor of 'Men who have Risen.' With Four Illustrations by C. Doyle. Eighth Edition. Crown 8vo. 2*s.* 6*d.*

COXHEAD (*Ethel*)—BIRDS AND BABIES. With 33 Illustrations. Imp. 16mo. cloth gilt, 1*s.*

DAVIES (*G. Christopher*) — RAMBLES AND ADVENTURES OF OUR SCHOOL FIELD CLUB. With Four Illustrations. New and Cheaper Edition. Crown 8vo. 3*s.* 6*d.*

EDMONDS (*Herbert*) — WELL-SPENT LIVES: a Series of Modern Biographies. New and Cheaper Edition. Crown 8vo. 3*s.* 6*d.*

EVANS (*Mark*)—THE STORY OF OUR FATHER'S LOVE, told to Children. Sixth and Cheaper Edition of Theology for Children. With Four Illustrations. Fcp. 8vo. 1*s.* 6*d.*

MAC KENNA (*S. J.*)—PLUCKY FELLOWS. A Book for Boys. With Six Illustrations. Fifth Edition. Crown 8vo. 3*s.* 6*d.*

MALET (*Lucas*)—LITTLE PETER. A Christmas Morality for Children of any Age. With numerous Illustrations. 5*s.*

REANEY (*Mrs. G. S.*)—WAKING AND WORKING; or, From Girlhood to Womanhood. New and Cheaper Edition. With a Frontispiece. Cr. 8vo. 3*s.* 6*d.*

BLESSING AND BLESSED: a Sketch of Girl Life. New and Cheaper Edition. Crown 8vo. 3*s.* 6*d.*

ROSE GURNEY'S DISCOVERY. A Book for Girls. Dedicated to their Mothers. Crown 8vo. 3*s.* 6*d.*

ENGLISH GIRLS: Their Place and Power. With Preface by the Rev. R. W. Dale. Fourth Edition. Fcp. 8vo. 2*s.* 6*d.*

JUST ANYONE, and other Stories. Three Illustrations. Royal 16mo. 1*s.* 6*d.*

SUNBEAM WILLIE, and other Stories. Three Illustrations. Royal 16mo. 1*s.* 6*d.*

SUNSHINE JENNY, and other Stories. Three Illustrations. Royal 16mo. 1*s.* 6*d.*

STORR (*Francis*) *and TURNER* (*Hawes*). CANTERBURY CHIMES; or, Chaucer Tales Re-told to Children. With Six Illustrations from the Ellesmere MS. Third Edition. Fcp. 8vo. 3*s.* 6*d.*

STRETTON (*Hesba*)—DAVID LLOYD'S LAST WILL. With Four Illustrations. New Edition. Royal 16mo. 2*s.* 6*d.*

WHITAKER (*Florence*)—CHRISTY'S INHERITANCE: A London Story. Illustrated. Royal 16mo. 1*s.* 6*d.*